NO LONGER PROPERTY OF
SEATTLE PUBLIC LIBRARY

THE// ACTIVITY ™

JUN 13 2013

IMAGE COMICS, INC.
Robert Kirkman - chief operating officer
Erik Larsen - chief financial officer
Todd McFarlane - president
Marc Silvestri - chief executive officer
Jim Valentino - vice-president

Eric Stephenson - publisher
Ron Richards - director of business development
Jennifer de Guzman - pr & marketing director
Branwyn Bigglestone - accounts manager
Emily Miller - accounting assistant
Jamie Parreno - marketing assistant
Jenna Savage - administrative assistant
Kevin Yuen - digital rights coordinator
Jonathan Chan - production manager
Drew Gill - art director
Monica Garcia - production artist
Vincent Kukua - production artist
Jana Cook - production artist
www.imagecomics.com

BOOK DESIGN// MITCH_GERADS
PRODUCTION// JEFF_POWELL AND MITCH_GERADS

THE ACTIVITY VOLUME 2
ISBN-13: 978-1-60706-719-1
First Printing

Published by Image Comics, Inc. Office of publication: 2001 Center Street, 6th Floor, Berkeley, CA 94704. Copyright © 2013 Nathan Edmondson & Mitch Gerads. Originally published in single magazine form as THE ACTIVITY #6-11. All rights reserved. THE ACTIVITY™ (including all prominent characters featured herein), its logo and all character likenesses are trademarks of Nathan Edmondson & Mitch Gerads, unless otherwise noted. Image Comics® and its logos are registered trademarks of Image Comics, Inc. No part of this publication may be reproduced or transmitted, in any form or by any means (except for short excerpts for review purposes) without the express written permission of Image Comics, Inc. All names, characters, events and locales in this publication are entirely fictional. Any resemblance to actual persons (living or dead), events or places, without satiric intent, is coincidental. For International Rights contact: foreignlicensing@imagecomics.com PRINTED IN THE USA

THE// ACTIVITY ™

STORY//
NATHAN_EDMONDSON

ART//
MITCH_GERADS
AND// **MARC_LAMING** (#6)

COLOR_ASSISTANTS//
JOSEPH FRAZZETTA
WITH//
CHRIS CANIBANO (#8)

LETTERS//
JEFF POWELL

//FOREWORD_

About a year ago, I was asked by a third party if it was ok to pass my contact information on to Nathan. I heard he was a graphic novel writer and that his recent work called "The Activity" was taking off and doing very well. He was looking for someone who could offer objective criticism of his work. Before giving the go ahead to pass on my info, I decided to take a look at THE ACTIVITY to see if it was a project I wanted to be involved with or not.

I was amazed with his work. The level of detail and authenticity was and is incredible. The completed work has a look, vibe, and feel that isn't like any other I had seen in the graphic novel field. It is as if Nathan and Mitch are capturing snapshots of situations and places I have myself fought and operated.

After reviewing his work and the graphic depictions by Mitch, I gave the third party the go ahead to pass on my information so that Nathan could contact me.

This is where my story with Nathan and Mitch begins.

I participated in the "global war on terror" in a capacity unique to the history of warfare on the planet. I dropped into "non-permissive environments" in a variety of ways, often in secret. I carried and wore customized weapons and outfits specifically tailored to my duties and skills.

I agreed to write this foreword though I most certainly cannot talk about specific missions I participated in. I can't give my real name or the name of my former organization.

This may seem to some like a dramatic thing to say, but it is a very real part of the life of someone in a Special Mission Unit. I pursued for a significant part of my life an enemy who, if he could, would seek me out and my family for my actions. Operational Security is imperative to the Special Operations community. It is one of the things that gives us our "power," which is to say, my team was effective because it could operate in the shadows, in the dark of night, out of the news, out of the public eye.

This book, while a work of fiction, depicts a very real world. A world I lived for many years.

One of the many aspects of THE ACTIVITY that appeals to me is the small team concept. Since the beginning of my military career, and even before, it was the aspect of Special Operations that appealed to me most. While serving in several SOF units, I sought to find the closeness of a small, tight knit group that would span the globe in search of terrorists and HVT's. It wasn't until I landed in a Special Mission Unit that I truly found what I was after... a group of us that would train and fight together for years before moving up the chain or on to bigger and better things.

When the shit hit the fan, we all knew how the others would react and knew beyond all, that we had each other's back.

My team became a well oiled machine that conducted hundreds of real world CT operations in a myriad of operational environments. None of them without flaw but what separates Special Mission Units from other SOF forces is the ability for one team to remain intact operating together for years at a time. Our ability to read and assess a target or target area and act/react accordingly all while reacting to each other's movements was like watching a well choreographed movie scene. It was fluid and graceful but very violent and fast.

My teammates and I operated like a machines, but we are of course, human. That's another aspect of this book that speaks to me. To see the way the characters engage and speak to one another--there is very little "drama" in the SOF community, but we are humans and we get mad and frustrated at ourselves or one another, especially when we fail or make costly mistakes.

THE ACTIVITY presents operators and their tactics realistically and in a way that does not compromise OPSEC or real world tactics, techniques, or procedures.

My team has parachuted from airplanes at 24,000 feet, we've taken on militant groups five times our size, and we've operated clandestinely worldwide. The US military will continue to need groups like those represented in THE ACTIVITY, because we don't fight large scale wars. We don't carpet-bomb cities and send in battalions of troops. The course of events in the world is directed now, often times, by special, covert warfare like the actions of TEAM OMAHA in the book. Soldiers and other government agents who do the seemingly impossible because they are trained beyond what most people think is possible and because they can trust one another and those supporting them. They don't care about politics, they care about completing their mission, at all cost.

Nathan is an extremely talented writer with an awesome sense of humor and knack for this type of work. He and I have talked through scenarios and his intent is always to get the most realistic effort possible, which is a testament to his attention to detail. He has never used real life situations, concepts, or TTP's that are sensitive in nature in hopes of selling more copies.

That's probably what I admire most about his work. His and Mitch's ability to present a fresh and realistic look at a seldom seen group of operators. I believe that any of the issues of THE ACTIVITY could easily have happened in real life, kept secret by those who live that life and serve this country free of accolades or public acknowledgement.

I've had the chance to develop a friendship with Nathan. He's a really personable guy and we kid with each other just as my teammates and I did back in the team room ergo dark humor and ruthlessly ranking on each other. None of it affecting us because there's mutual respect between us. I look forward to continuing to work with Nathan and Mitch to make THE ACTIVITY the best that it can be, the most realistic and honest graphic novel out there without giving up any secrets.

- NAME/RANK/UNIT/_UNDISCLOSED ∎

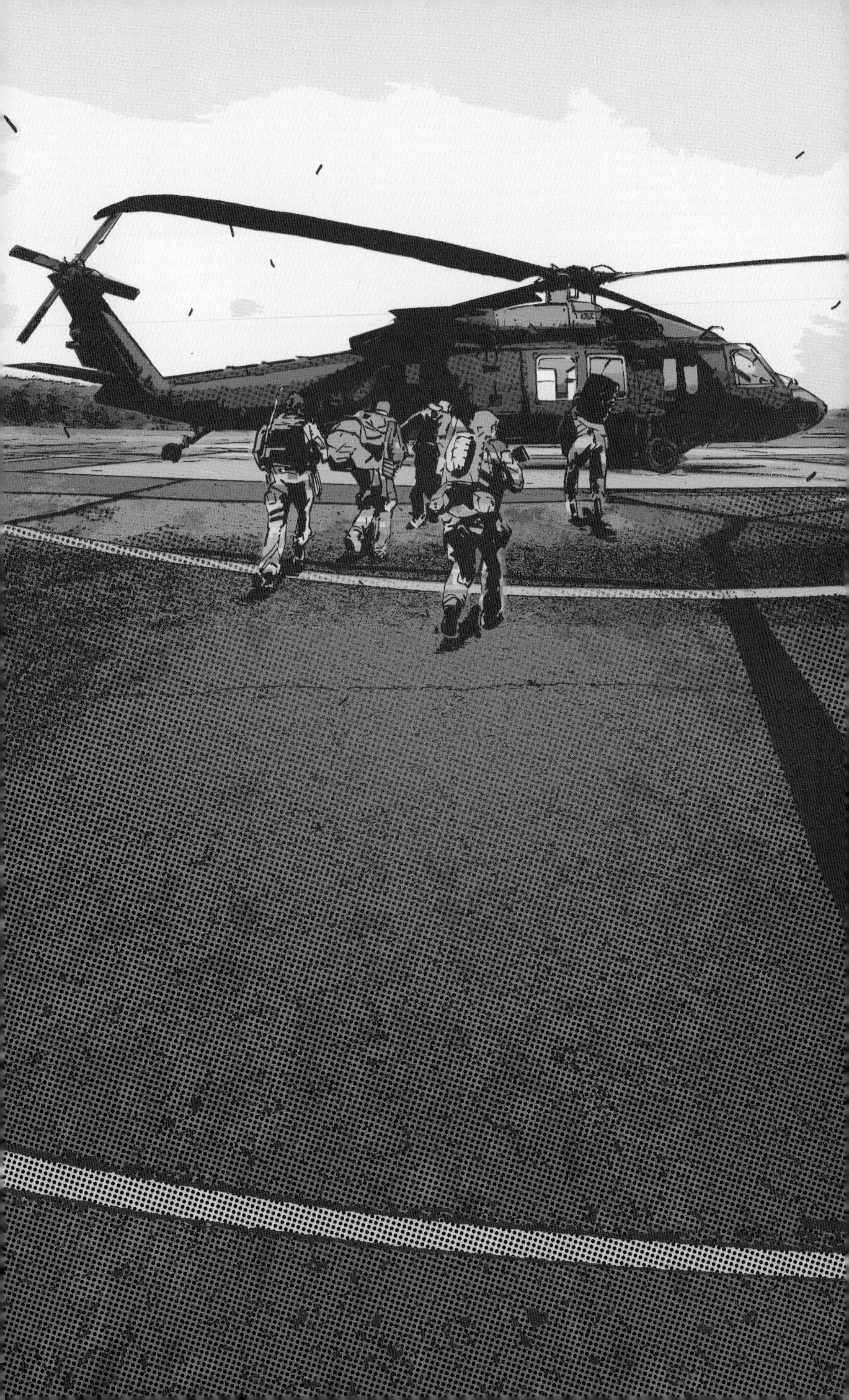

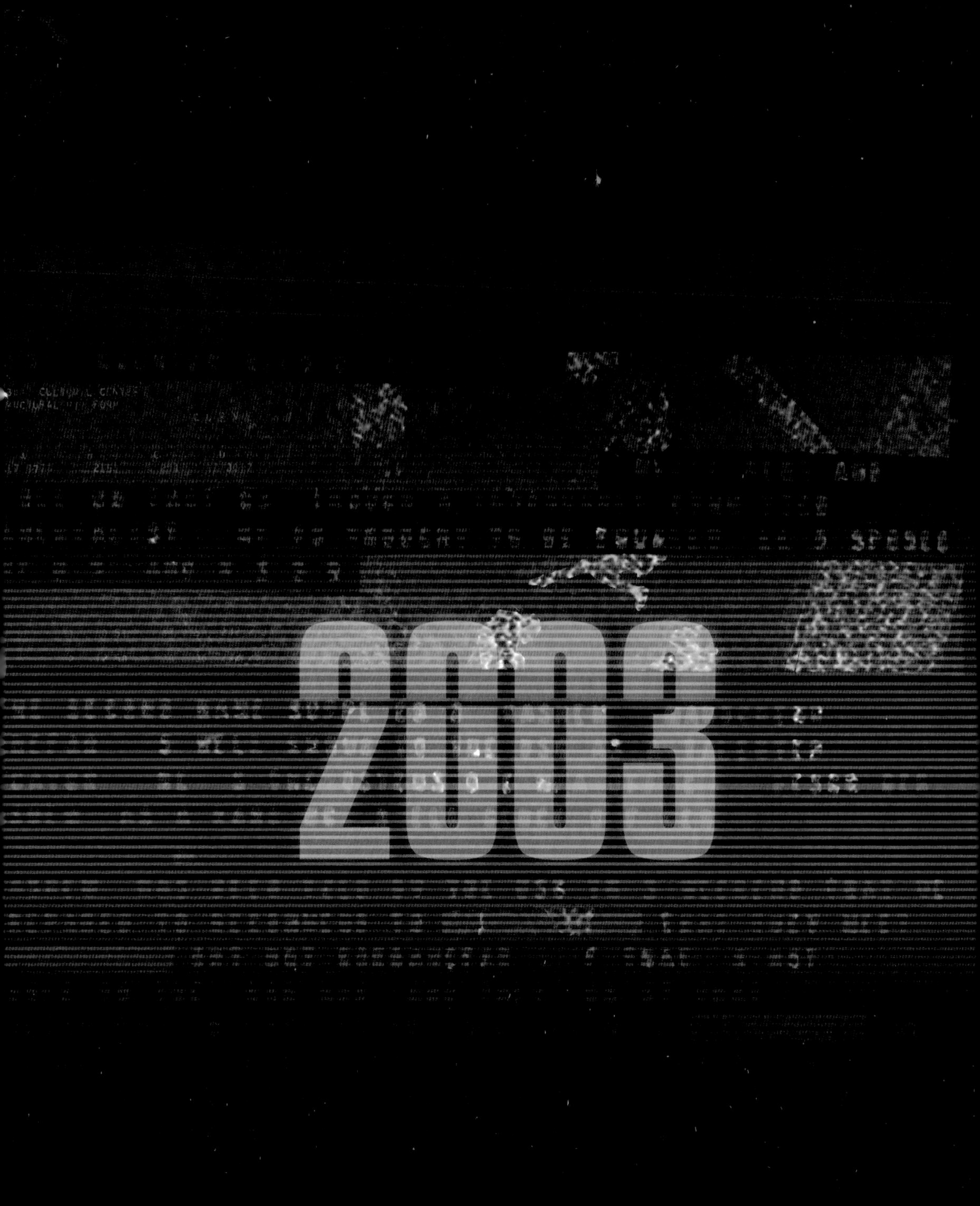
2003

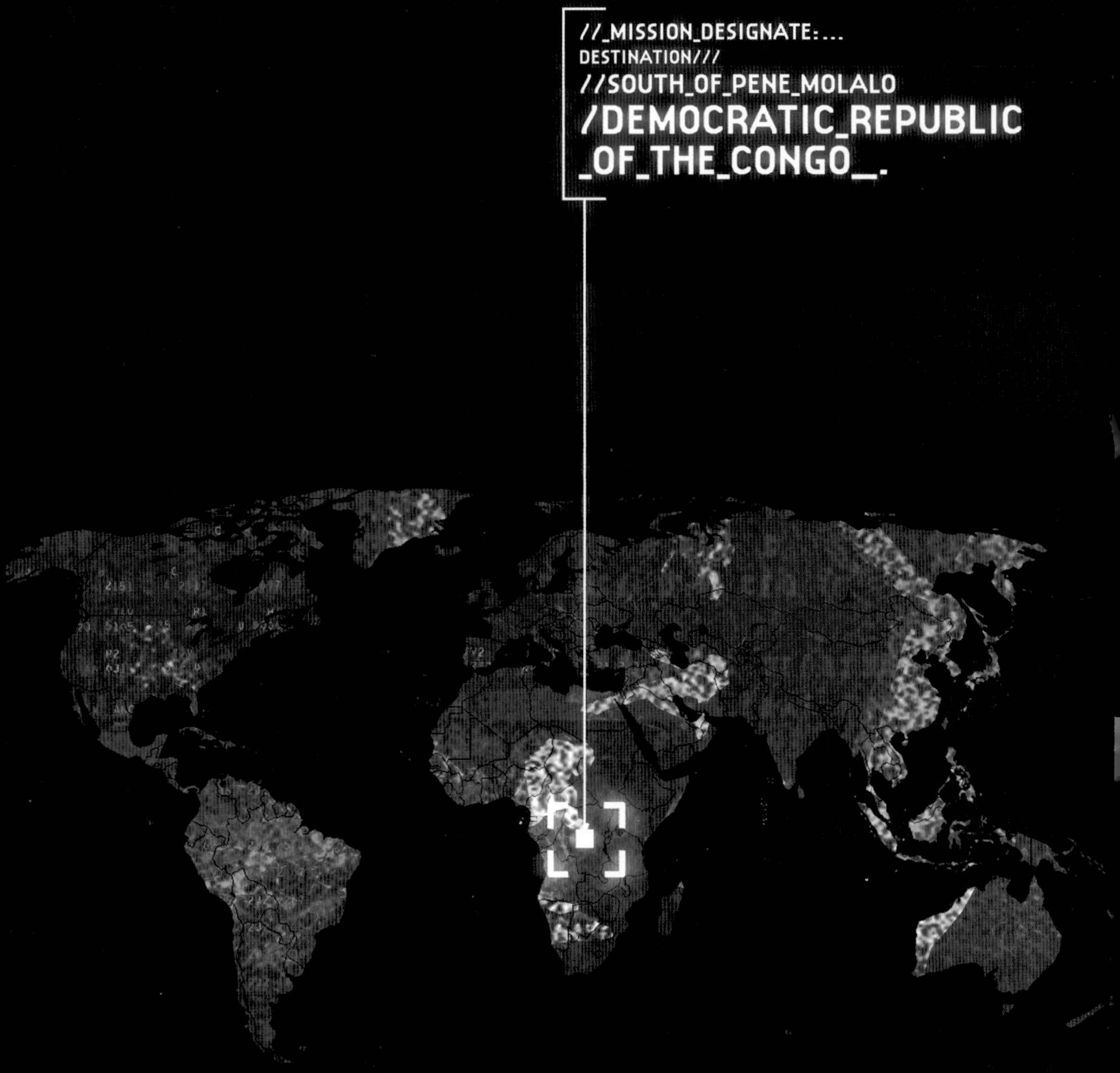
//_MISSION_DESIGNATE:...
DESTINATION///
//SOUTH_OF_PENE_MOLALO
/DEMOCRATIC_REPUBLIC
_OF_THE_CONGO_.

//MISSION_REPORT_
//INITIALIZING____

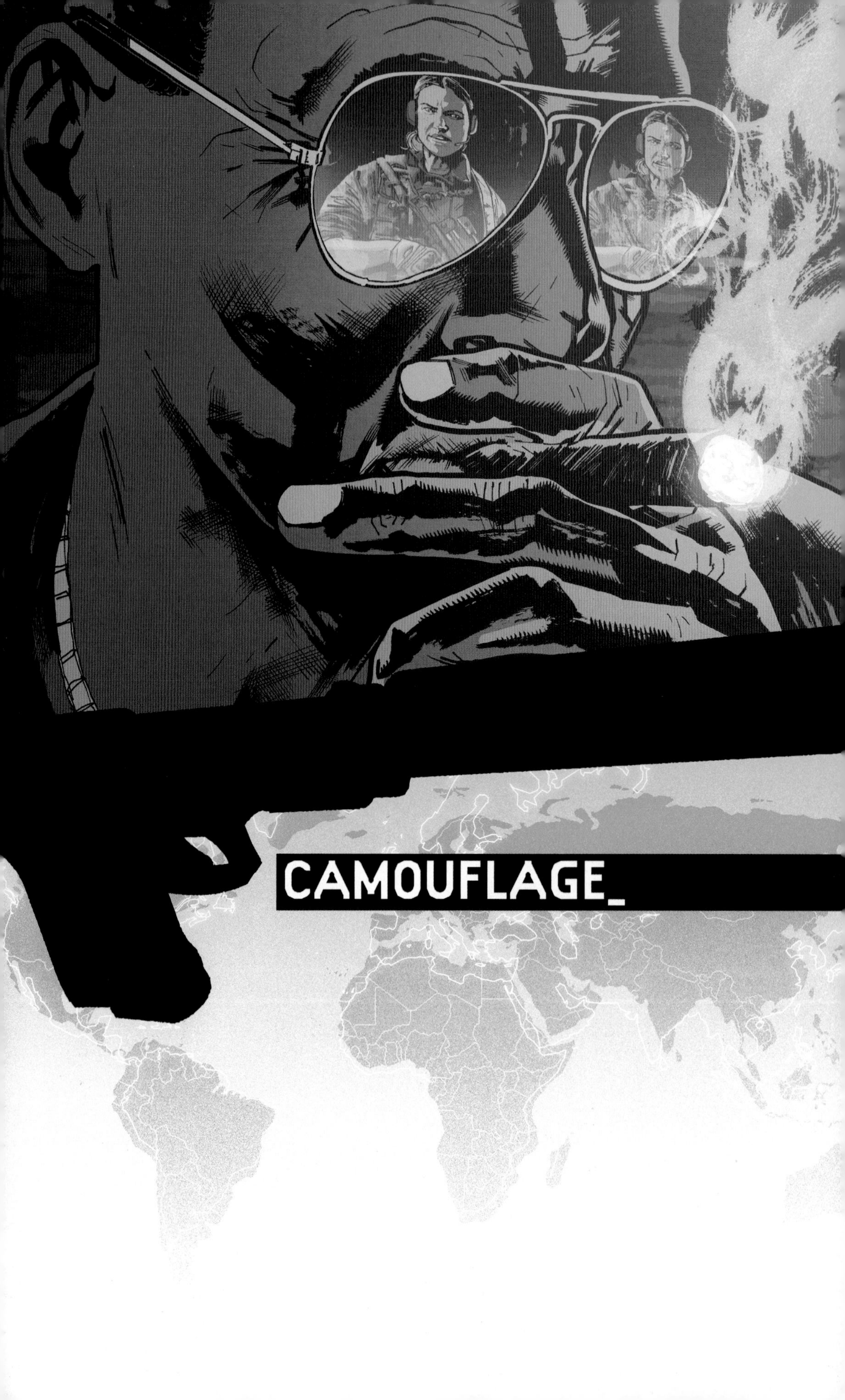
CAMOUFLAGE_

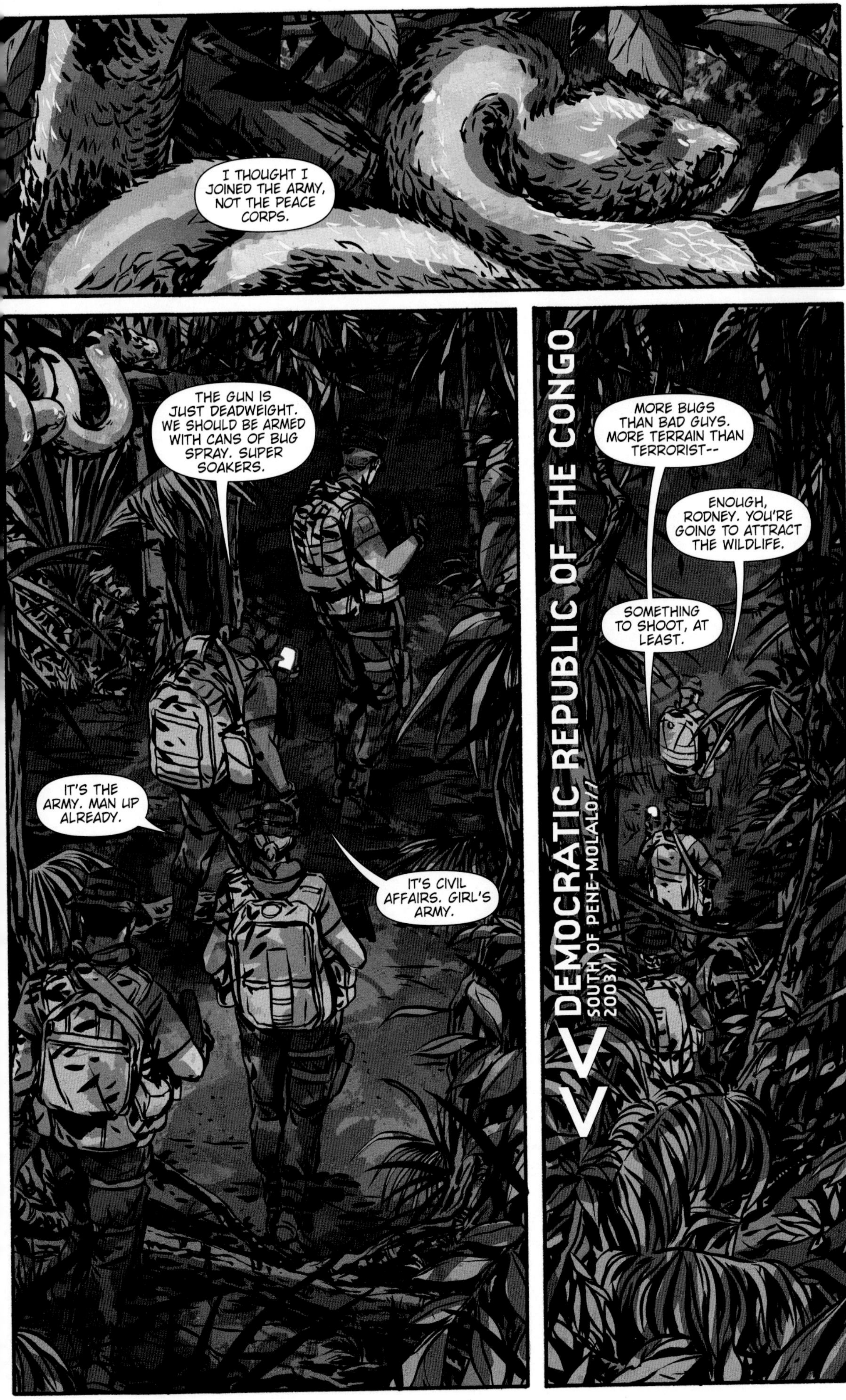
I THOUGHT I JOINED THE ARMY, NOT THE PEACE CORPS.
THE GUN IS JUST DEADWEIGHT. WE SHOULD BE ARMED WITH CANS OF BUG SPRAY. SUPER SOAKERS.
IT'S THE ARMY. MAN UP ALREADY.
IT'S CIVIL AFFAIRS. GIRL'S ARMY.
DEMOCRATIC REPUBLIC OF THE CONGO
SOUTH OF PENE-MOLALO//
2003//
MORE BUGS THAN BAD GUYS. MORE TERRAIN THAN TERRORIST--
SOMETHING TO SHOOT, AT LEAST.
ENOUGH, RODNEY. YOU'RE GOING TO ATTRACT THE WILDLIFE.

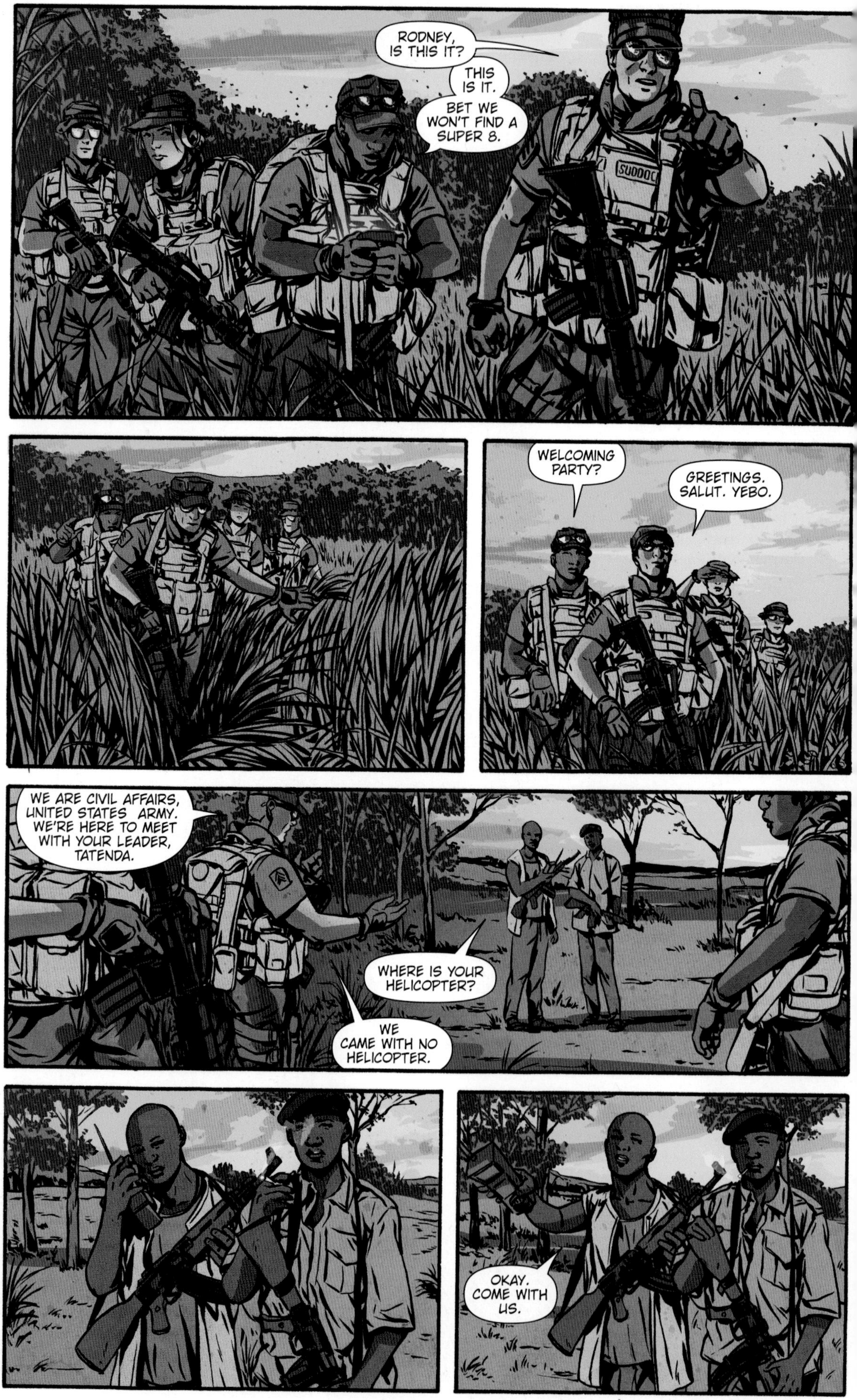
RODNEY, IS THIS IT?
THIS IS IT.
BET WE WON'T FIND A SUPER 8.
SUDDOC
WELCOMING PARTY?
GREETINGS. SALUT. YEBO.
WE ARE CIVIL AFFAIRS, UNITED STATES ARMY. WE'RE HERE TO MEET WITH YOUR LEADER, TATENDA.
WHERE IS YOUR HELICOPTER?
WE CAME WITH NO HELICOPTER.
OKAY. COME WITH US.

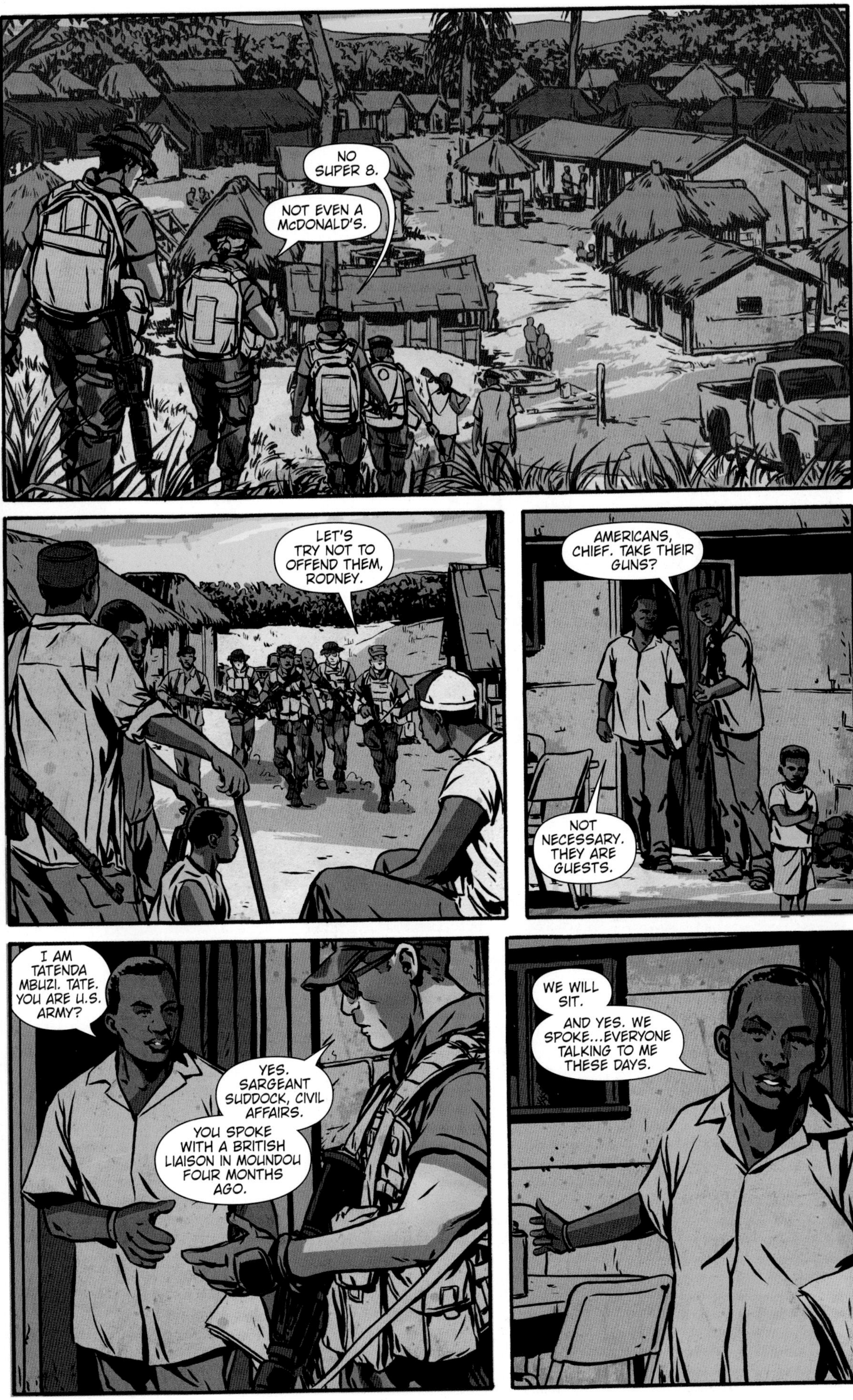
NO SUPER 8.
NOT EVEN A McDONALD'S.
LET'S TRY NOT TO OFFEND THEM, RODNEY.
AMERICANS, CHIEF. TAKE THEIR GUNS?
NOT NECESSARY. THEY ARE GUESTS.
I AM TATENDA MBUZI. TATE. YOU ARE U.S. ARMY?
YES. SARGEANT SUDDOCK, CIVIL AFFAIRS.
YOU SPOKE WITH A BRITISH LIAISON IN MOUNDOU FOUR MONTHS AGO.
WE WILL SIT.
AND YES. WE SPOKE...EVERYONE TALKING TO ME THESE DAYS.

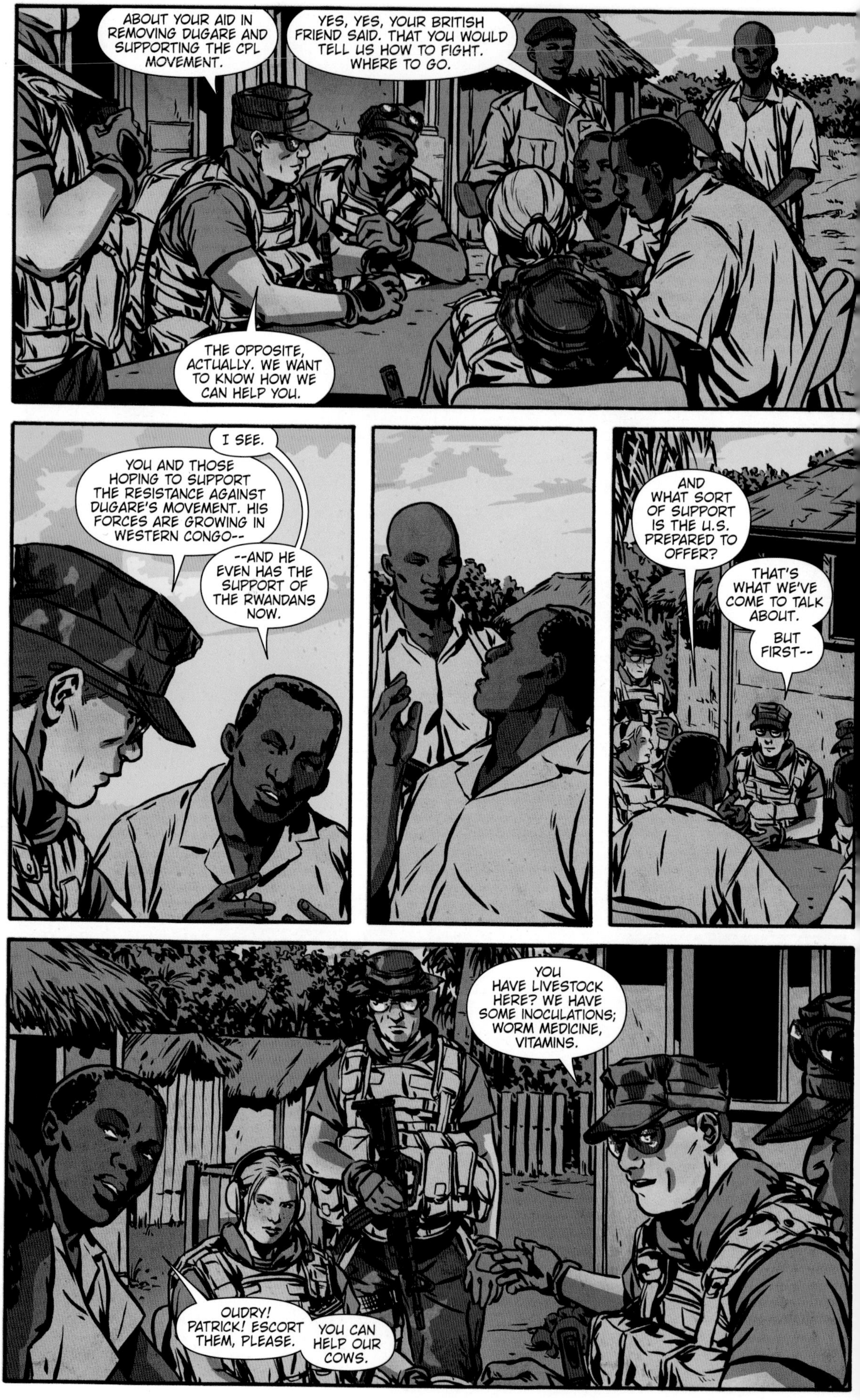
ABOUT YOUR AID IN REMOVING DUGARE AND SUPPORTING THE CPL MOVEMENT.
YES, YES, YOUR BRITISH FRIEND SAID. THAT YOU WOULD TELL US HOW TO FIGHT. WHERE TO GO.
THE OPPOSITE, ACTUALLY. WE WANT TO KNOW HOW WE CAN HELP YOU.
I SEE.
YOU AND THOSE HOPING TO SUPPORT THE RESISTANCE AGAINST DUGARE'S MOVEMENT. HIS FORCES ARE GROWING IN WESTERN CONGO--
--AND HE EVEN HAS THE SUPPORT OF THE RWANDANS NOW.
AND WHAT SORT OF SUPPORT IS THE U.S. PREPARED TO OFFER?
THAT'S WHAT WE'VE COME TO TALK ABOUT.
BUT FIRST--
YOU HAVE LIVESTOCK HERE? WE HAVE SOME INOCULATIONS; WORM MEDICINE, VITAMINS.
OUDRY! PATRICK! ESCORT THEM, PLEASE.
YOU CAN HELP OUR COWS.

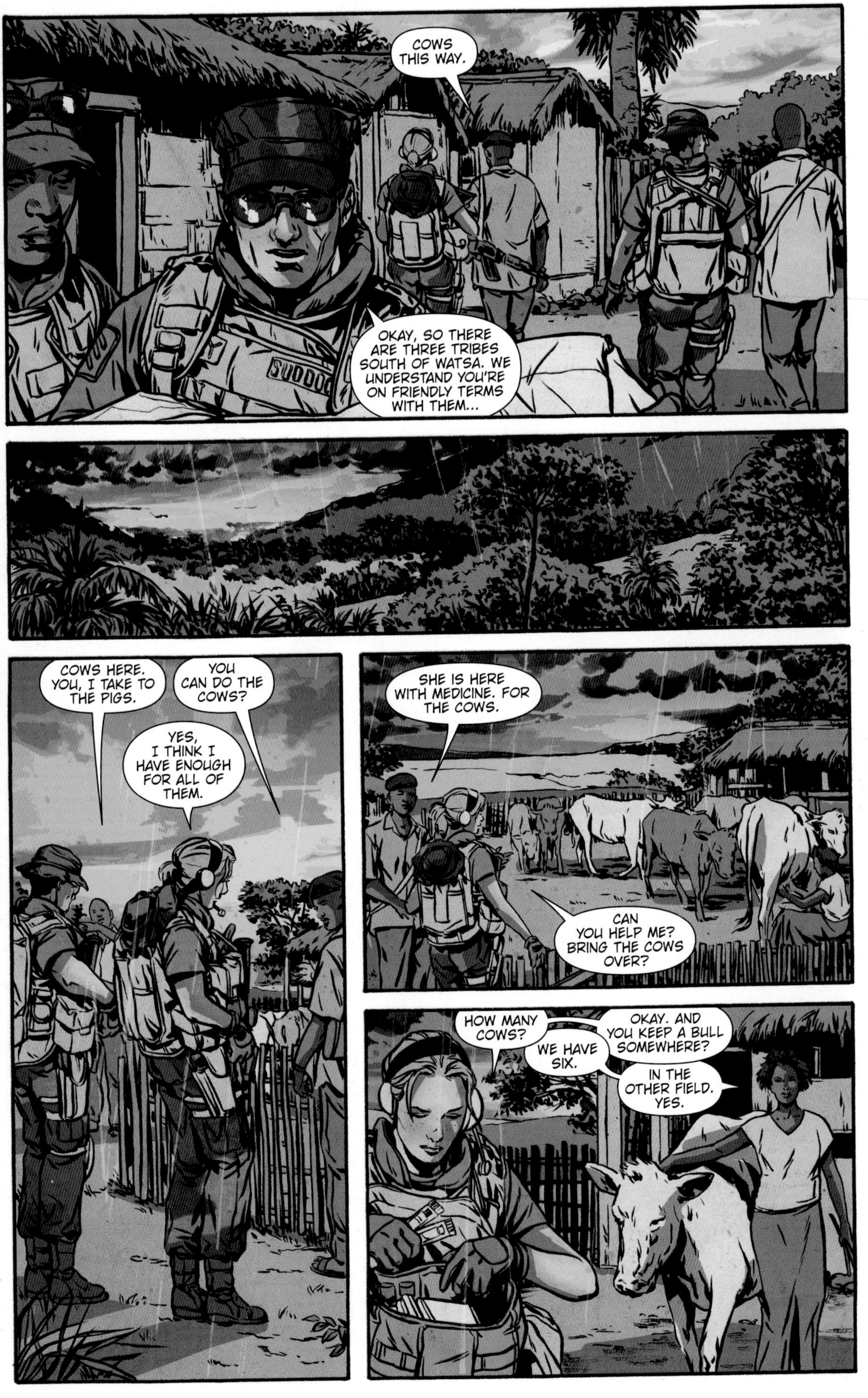
COWS THIS WAY.
OKAY, SO THERE ARE THREE TRIBES SOUTH OF WATSA. WE UNDERSTAND YOU'RE ON FRIENDLY TERMS WITH THEM...
COWS HERE. YOU, I TAKE TO THE PIGS.
YOU CAN DO THE COWS?
YES, I THINK I HAVE ENOUGH FOR ALL OF THEM.
SHE IS HERE WITH MEDICINE. FOR THE COWS.
CAN YOU HELP ME? BRING THE COWS OVER?
HOW MANY COWS?
WE HAVE SIX.
OKAY. AND YOU KEEP A BULL SOMEWHERE?
IN THE OTHER FIELD. YES.

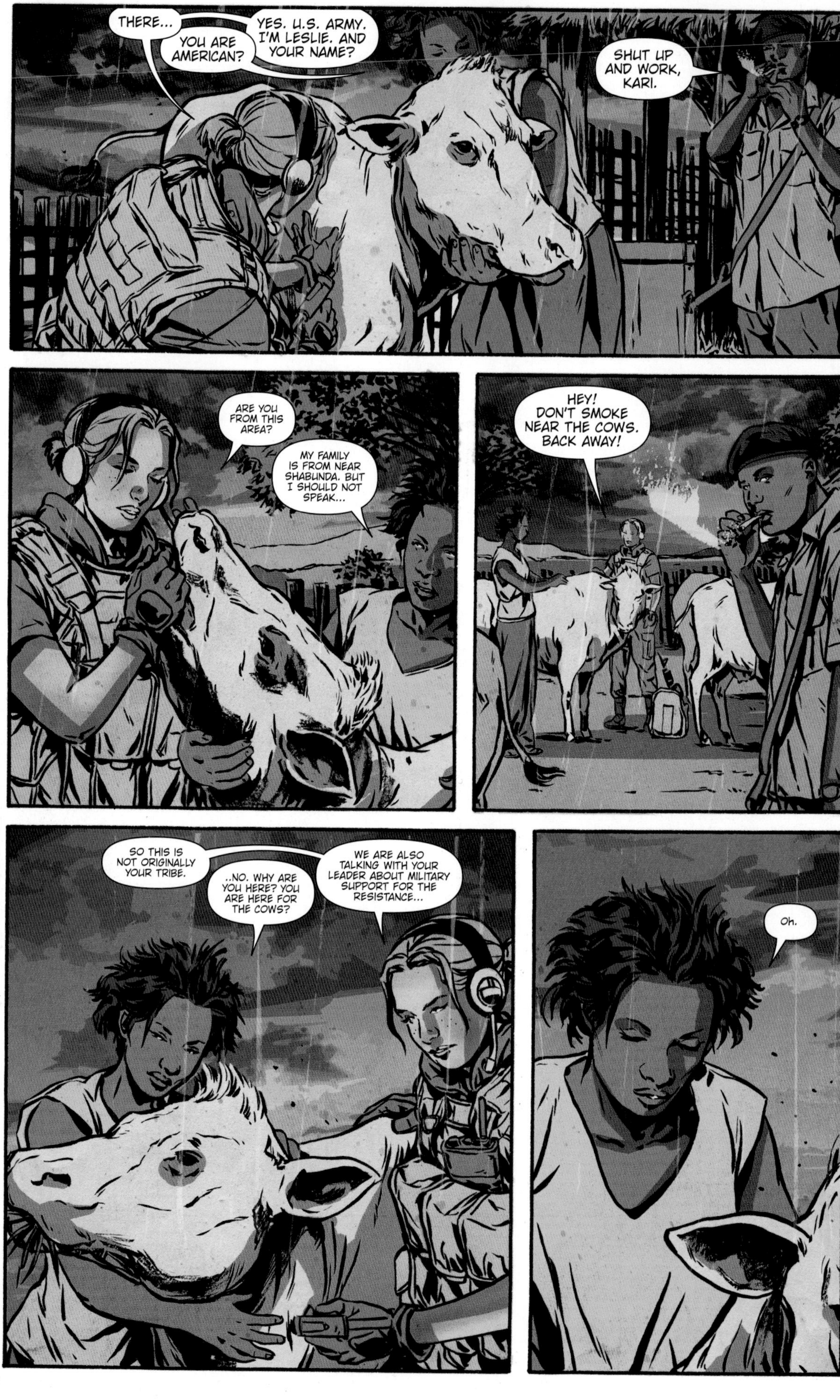

THERE...
YOU ARE AMERICAN?
YES. U.S. ARMY. I'M LESLIE. AND YOUR NAME?
SHUT UP AND WORK, KARI.
ARE YOU FROM THIS AREA?
MY FAMILY IS FROM NEAR SHABUNDA. BUT I SHOULD NOT SPEAK...
HEY! DON'T SMOKE NEAR THE COWS. BACK AWAY!
SO THIS IS NOT ORIGINALLY YOUR TRIBE.
..NO. WHY ARE YOU HERE? YOU ARE HERE FOR THE COWS?
WE ARE ALSO TALKING WITH YOUR LEADER ABOUT MILITARY SUPPORT FOR THE RESISTANCE...
Oh.

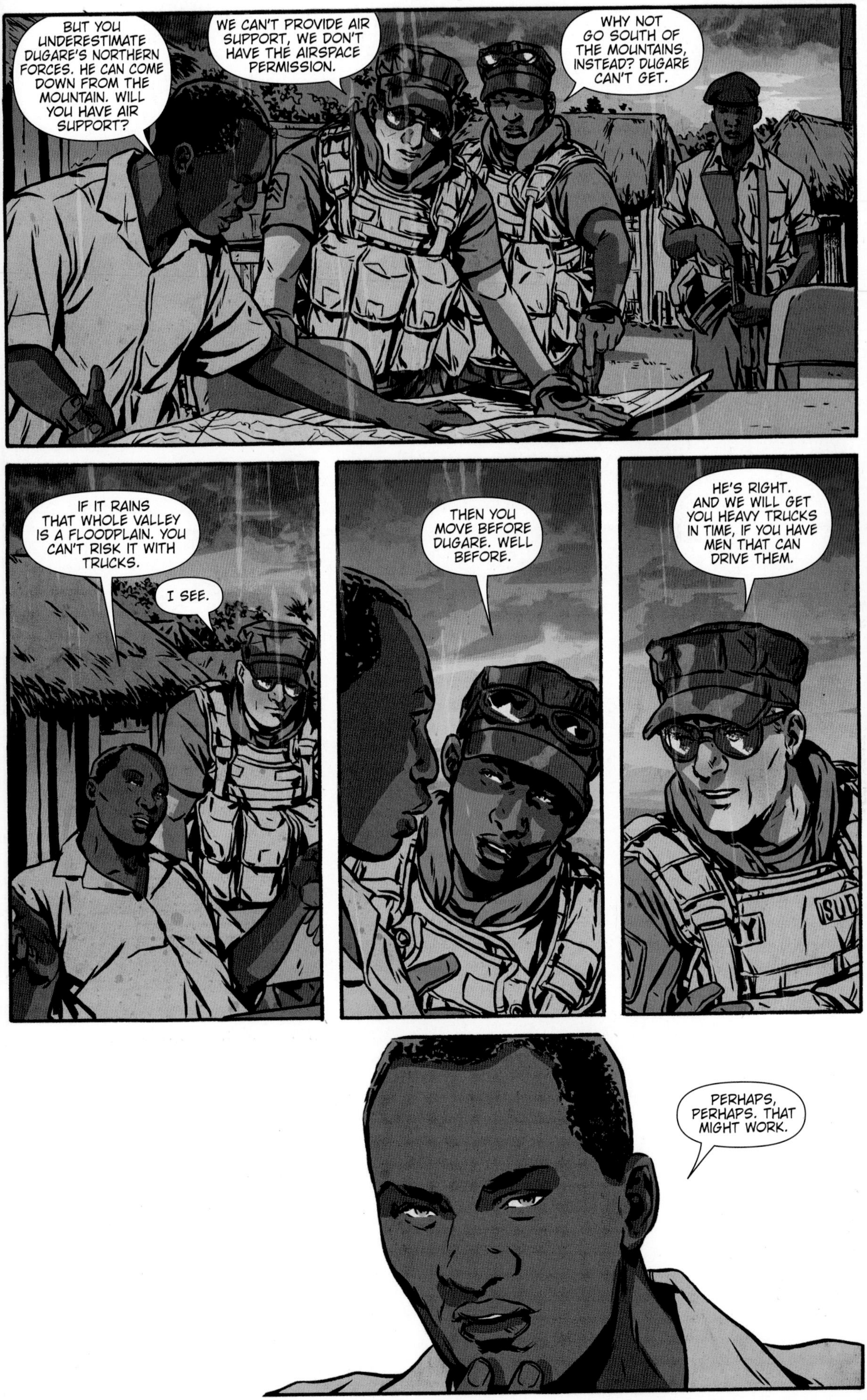
BUT YOU UNDERESTIMATE DUGARE'S NORTHERN FORCES. HE CAN COME DOWN FROM THE MOUNTAIN. WILL YOU HAVE AIR SUPPORT?
WE CAN'T PROVIDE AIR SUPPORT, WE DON'T HAVE THE AIRSPACE PERMISSION.
WHY NOT GO SOUTH OF THE MOUNTAINS, INSTEAD? DUGARE CAN'T GET.
IF IT RAINS THAT WHOLE VALLEY IS A FLOODPLAIN. YOU CAN'T RISK IT WITH TRUCKS.
I SEE.
THEN YOU MOVE BEFORE DUGARE. WELL BEFORE.
HE'S RIGHT. AND WE WILL GET YOU HEAVY TRUCKS IN TIME, IF YOU HAVE MEN THAT CAN DRIVE THEM.
PERHAPS, PERHAPS. THAT MIGHT WORK.

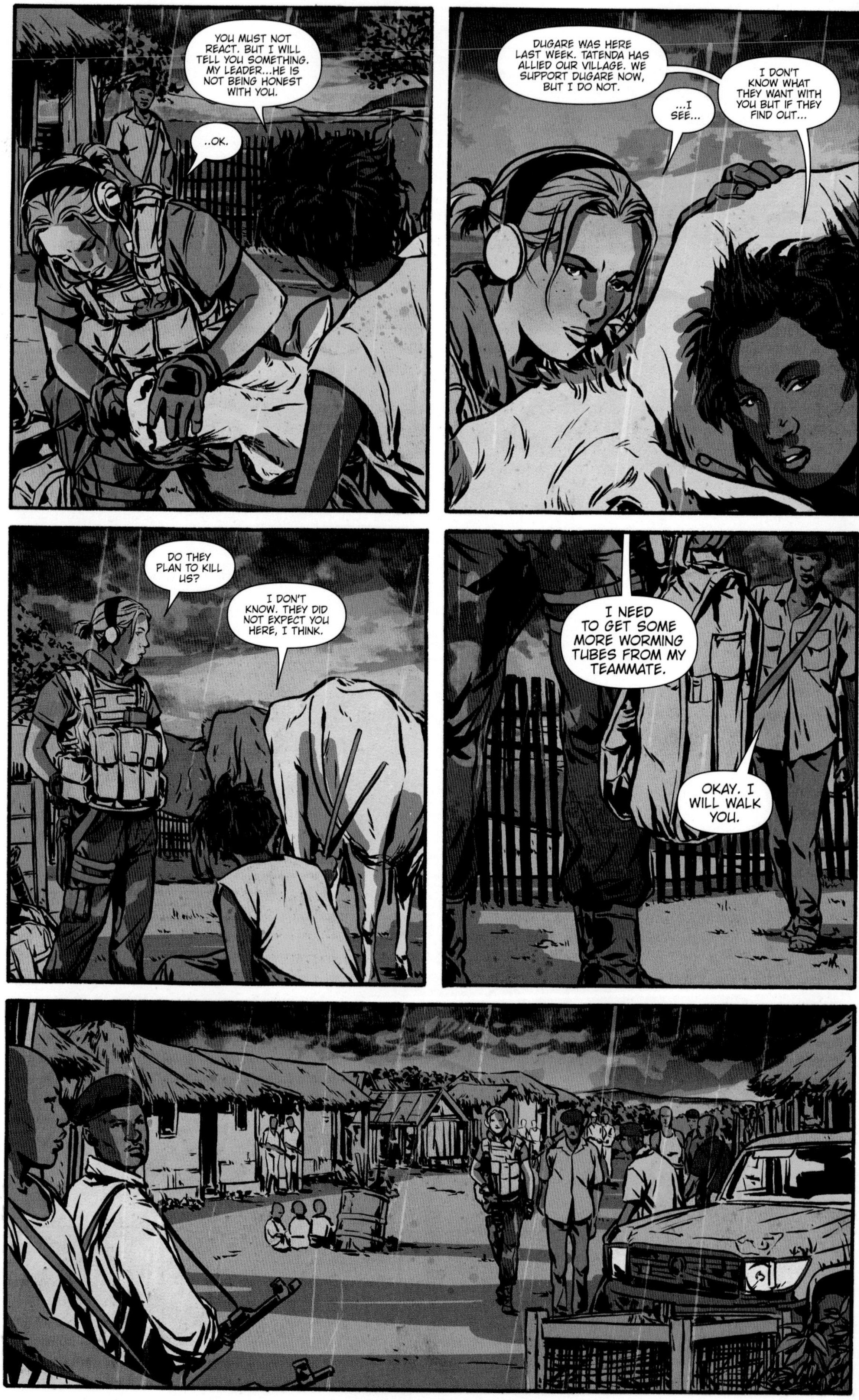
YOU MUST NOT REACT. BUT I WILL TELL YOU SOMETHING. MY LEADER...HE IS NOT BEING HONEST WITH YOU.
..OK.
DUGARE WAS HERE LAST WEEK. TATENDA HAS ALLIED OUR VILLAGE. WE SUPPORT DUGARE NOW, BUT I DO NOT.
...I SEE...
I DON'T KNOW WHAT THEY WANT WITH YOU BUT IF THEY FIND OUT...
DO THEY PLAN TO KILL US?
I DON'T KNOW. THEY DID NOT EXPECT YOU HERE, I THINK.
I NEED TO GET SOME MORE WORMING TUBES FROM MY TEAMMATE.
OKAY. I WILL WALK YOU.

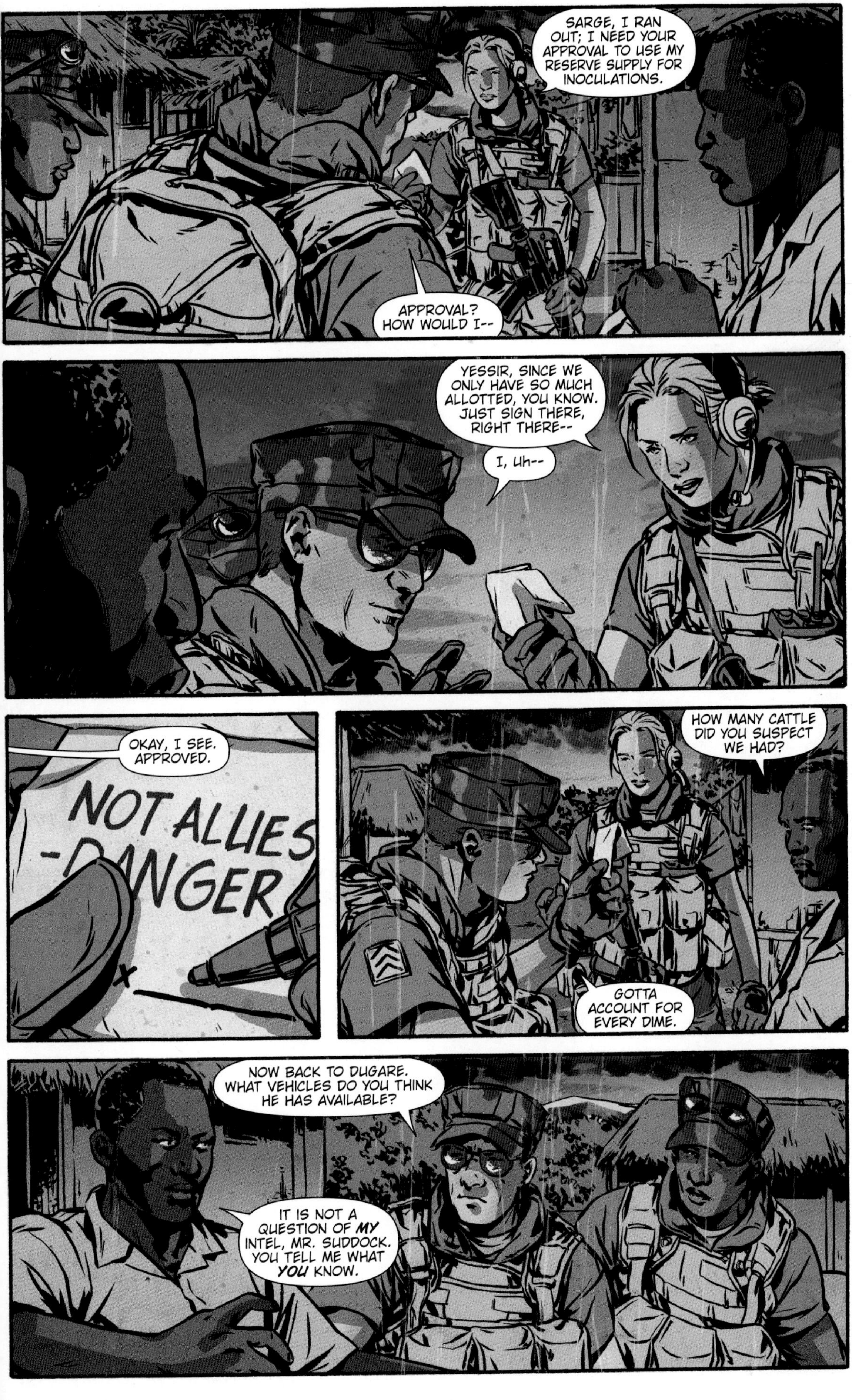
SARGE, I RAN OUT; I NEED YOUR APPROVAL TO USE MY RESERVE SUPPLY FOR INOCULATIONS.
APPROVAL? HOW WOULD I--
YESSIR, SINCE WE ONLY HAVE SO MUCH ALLOTTED, YOU KNOW. JUST SIGN THERE, RIGHT THERE--
I, UH--
OKAY, I SEE. APPROVED.
NOT ALLIES -DANGER
HOW MANY CATTLE DID YOU SUSPECT WE HAD?
GOTTA ACCOUNT FOR EVERY DIME.
NOW BACK TO DUGARE. WHAT VEHICLES DO YOU THINK HE HAS AVAILABLE?
IT IS NOT A QUESTION OF *MY* INTEL, MR. SUDDOCK. YOU TELL ME WHAT *YOU* KNOW.

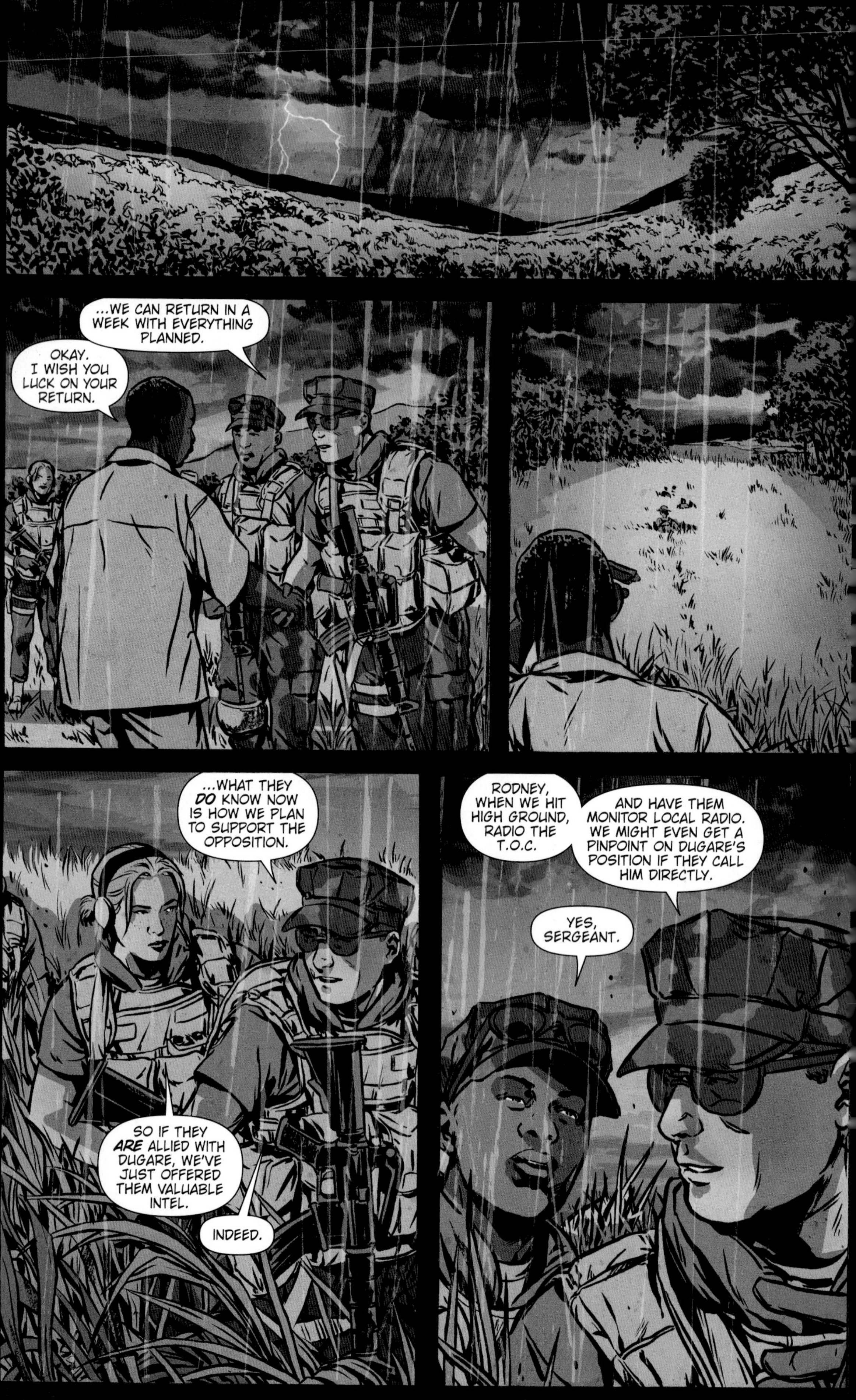

...WE CAN RETURN IN A WEEK WITH EVERYTHING PLANNED.
OKAY. I WISH YOU LUCK ON YOUR RETURN.
...WHAT THEY *DO* KNOW NOW IS HOW WE PLAN TO SUPPORT THE OPPOSITION.
SO IF THEY *ARE* ALLIED WITH DUGARE, WE'VE JUST OFFERED THEM VALUABLE INTEL.
INDEED.
RODNEY, WHEN WE HIT HIGH GROUND, RADIO THE T.O.C.
AND HAVE THEM MONITOR LOCAL RADIO. WE MIGHT EVEN GET A PINPOINT ON DUGARE'S POSITION IF THEY CALL HIM DIRECTLY.
YES, SERGEANT.

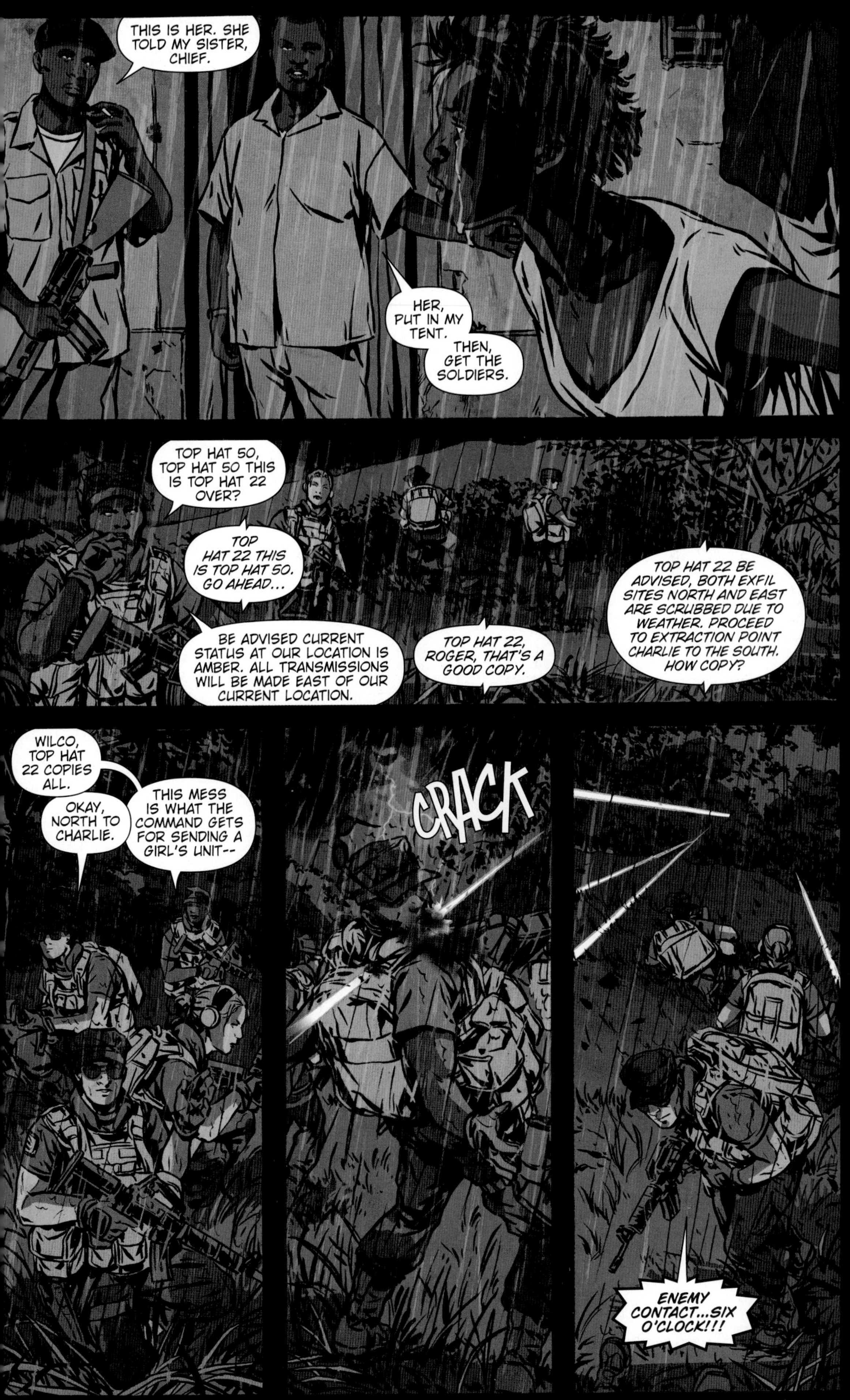
THIS IS HER. SHE TOLD MY SISTER, CHIEF.
HER, PUT IN MY TENT.
THEN, GET THE SOLDIERS.
TOP HAT 50, TOP HAT 50 THIS IS TOP HAT 22 OVER?
TOP HAT 22 THIS IS TOP HAT 50. GO AHEAD...
BE ADVISED CURRENT STATUS AT OUR LOCATION IS AMBER. ALL TRANSMISSIONS WILL BE MADE EAST OF OUR CURRENT LOCATION.
TOP HAT 22, ROGER, THAT'S A GOOD COPY.
TOP HAT 22 BE ADVISED, BOTH EXFIL SITES NORTH AND EAST ARE SCRUBBED DUE TO WEATHER. PROCEED TO EXTRACTION POINT CHARLIE TO THE SOUTH. HOW COPY?
WILCO, TOP HAT 22 COPIES ALL.
OKAY, NORTH TO CHARLIE.
THIS MESS IS WHAT THE COMMAND GETS FOR SENDING A GIRL'S UNIT--
CRACK
ENEMY CONTACT...SIX O'CLOCK!!!

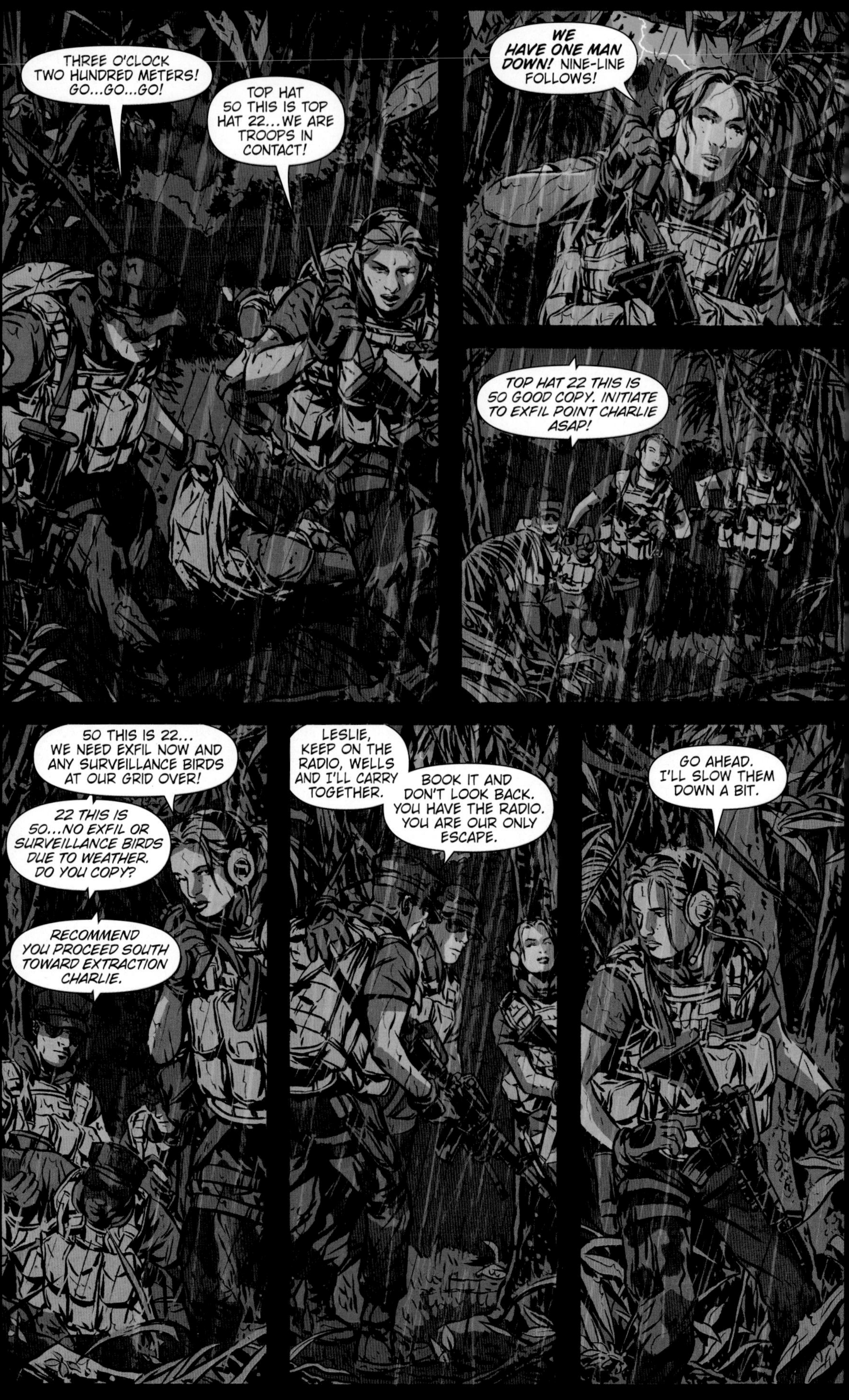

THREE O'CLOCK TWO HUNDRED METERS! GO...GO...GO!
TOP HAT 50 THIS IS TOP HAT 22...WE ARE TROOPS IN CONTACT!
WE HAVE ONE MAN DOWN! NINE-LINE FOLLOWS!
TOP HAT 22 THIS IS 50 GOOD COPY. INITIATE TO EXFIL POINT CHARLIE ASAP!
50 THIS IS 22... WE NEED EXFIL NOW AND ANY SURVEILLANCE BIRDS AT OUR GRID OVER!
22 THIS IS 50...NO EXFIL OR SURVEILLANCE BIRDS DUE TO WEATHER. DO YOU COPY?
RECOMMEND YOU PROCEED SOUTH TOWARD EXTRACTION CHARLIE.
LESLIE, KEEP ON THE RADIO, WELLS AND I'LL CARRY TOGETHER.
BOOK IT AND DON'T LOOK BACK. YOU HAVE THE RADIO. YOU ARE OUR ONLY ESCAPE.
GO AHEAD. I'LL SLOW THEM DOWN A BIT.

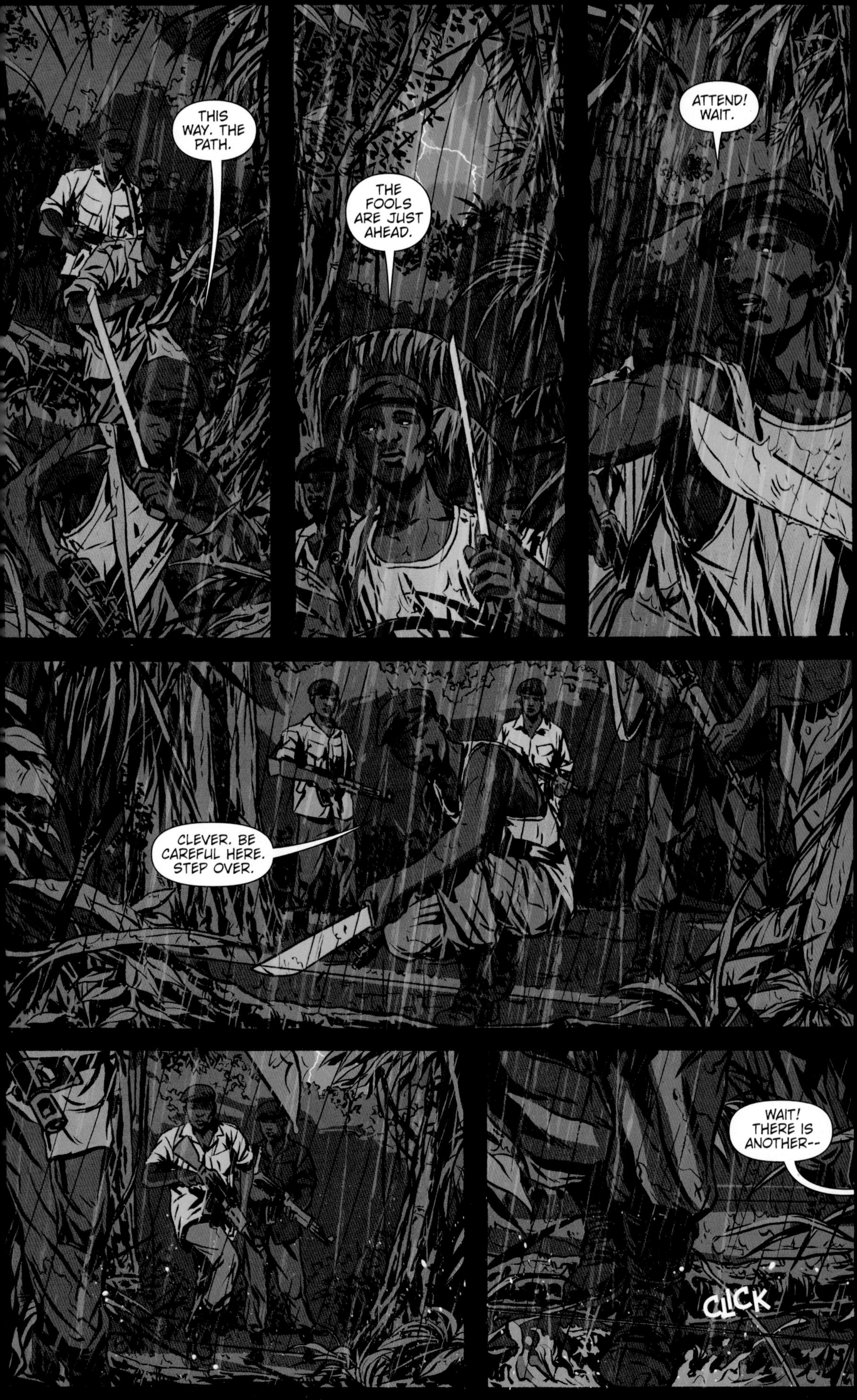
THIS WAY. THE PATH.
THE FOOLS ARE JUST AHEAD.
ATTEND! WAIT.
CLEVER. BE CAREFUL HERE. STEP OVER.
WAIT! THERE IS ANOTHER--
CLICK

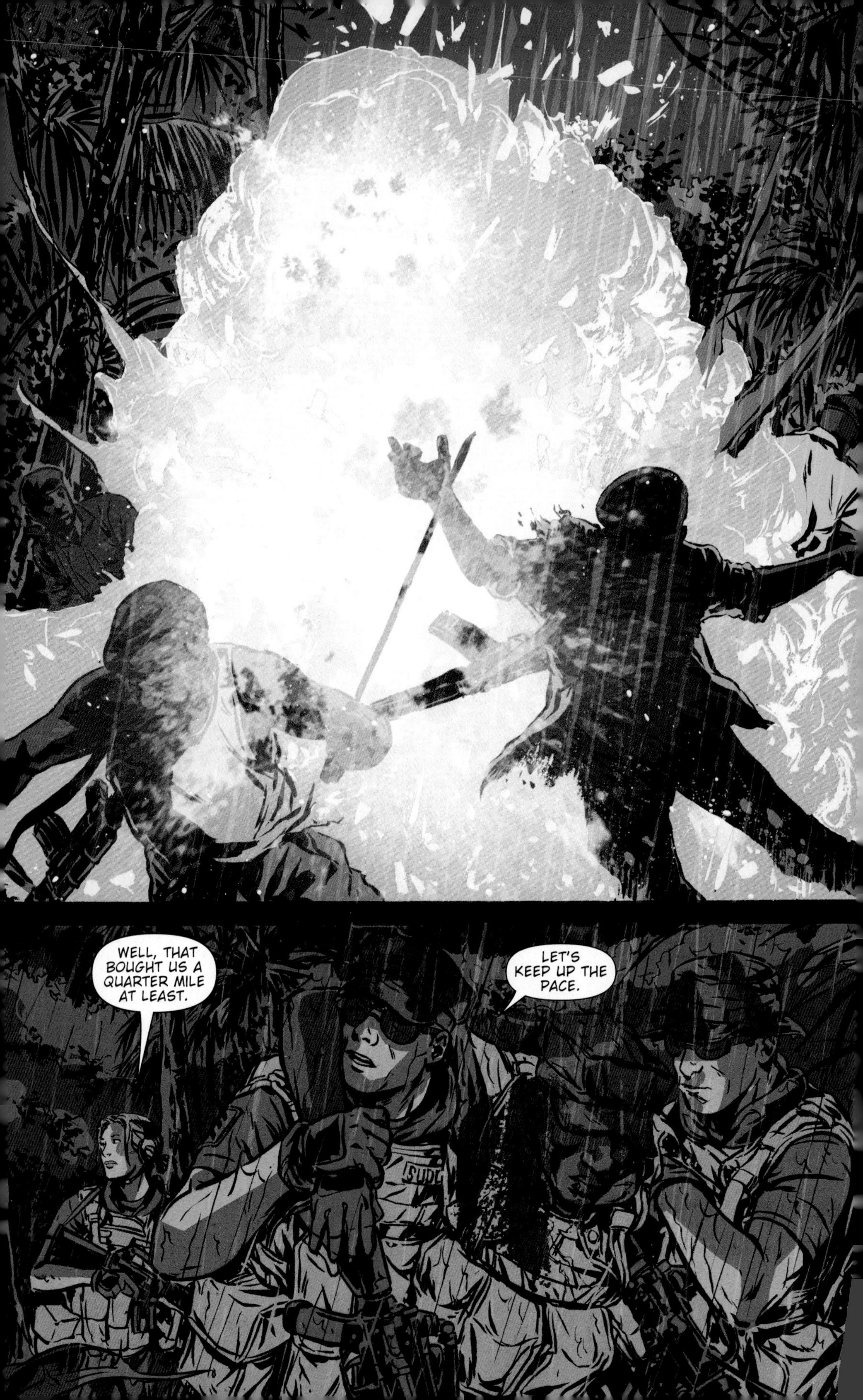
WELL, THAT BOUGHT US A QUARTER MILE AT LEAST.
LET'S KEEP UP THE PACE.

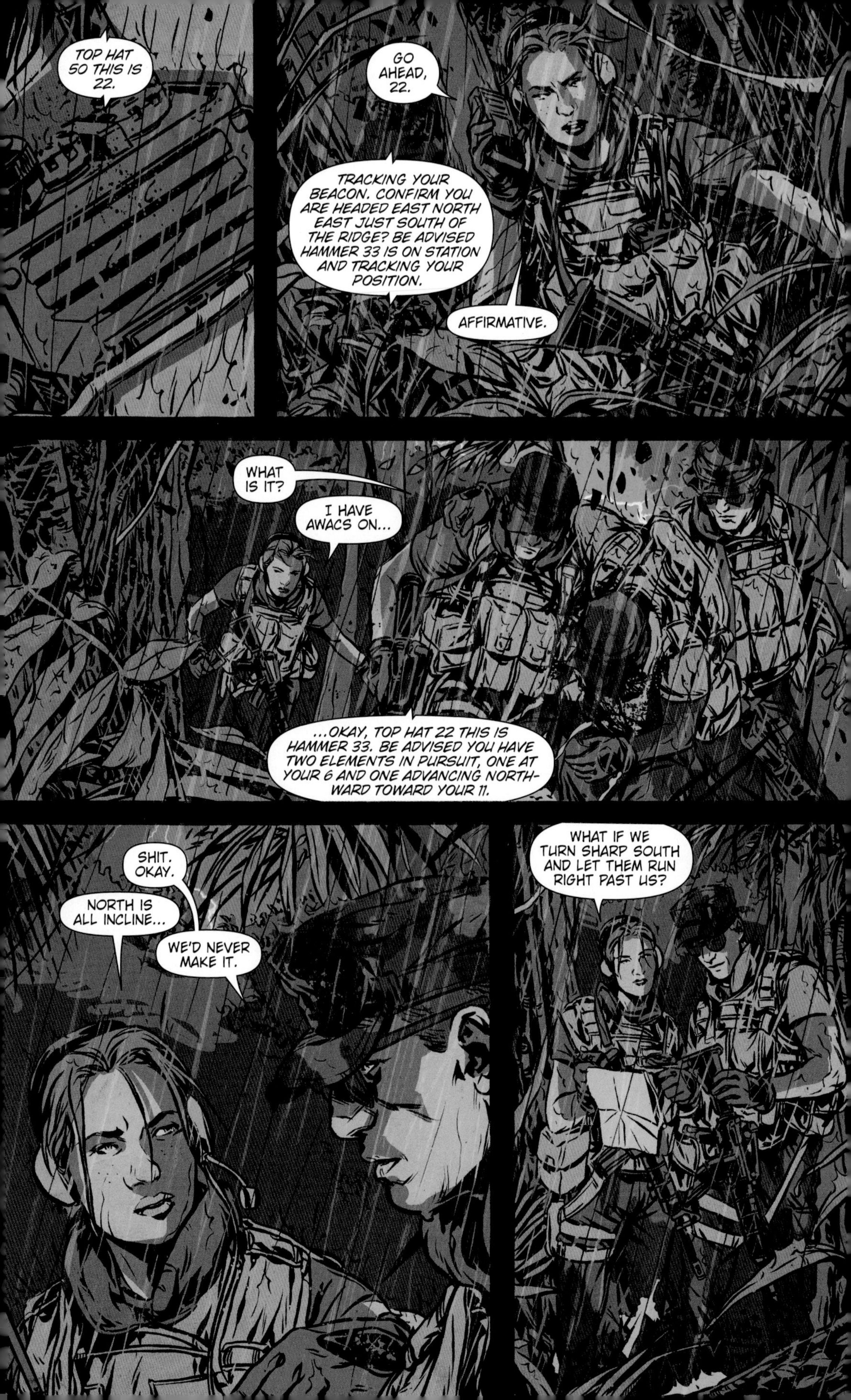
TOP HAT 50 THIS IS 22.
GO AHEAD, 22.
TRACKING YOUR BEACON. CONFIRM YOU ARE HEADED EAST NORTH EAST JUST SOUTH OF THE RIDGE? BE ADVISED HAMMER 33 IS ON STATION AND TRACKING YOUR POSITION.
AFFIRMATIVE.
WHAT IS IT?
I HAVE AWACS ON...
...OKAY, TOP HAT 22 THIS IS HAMMER 33. BE ADVISED YOU HAVE TWO ELEMENTS IN PURSUIT, ONE AT YOUR 6 AND ONE ADVANCING NORTH-WARD TOWARD YOUR 11.
SHIT. OKAY.
NORTH IS ALL INCLINE...
WE'D NEVER MAKE IT.
WHAT IF WE TURN SHARP SOUTH AND LET THEM RUN RIGHT PAST US?

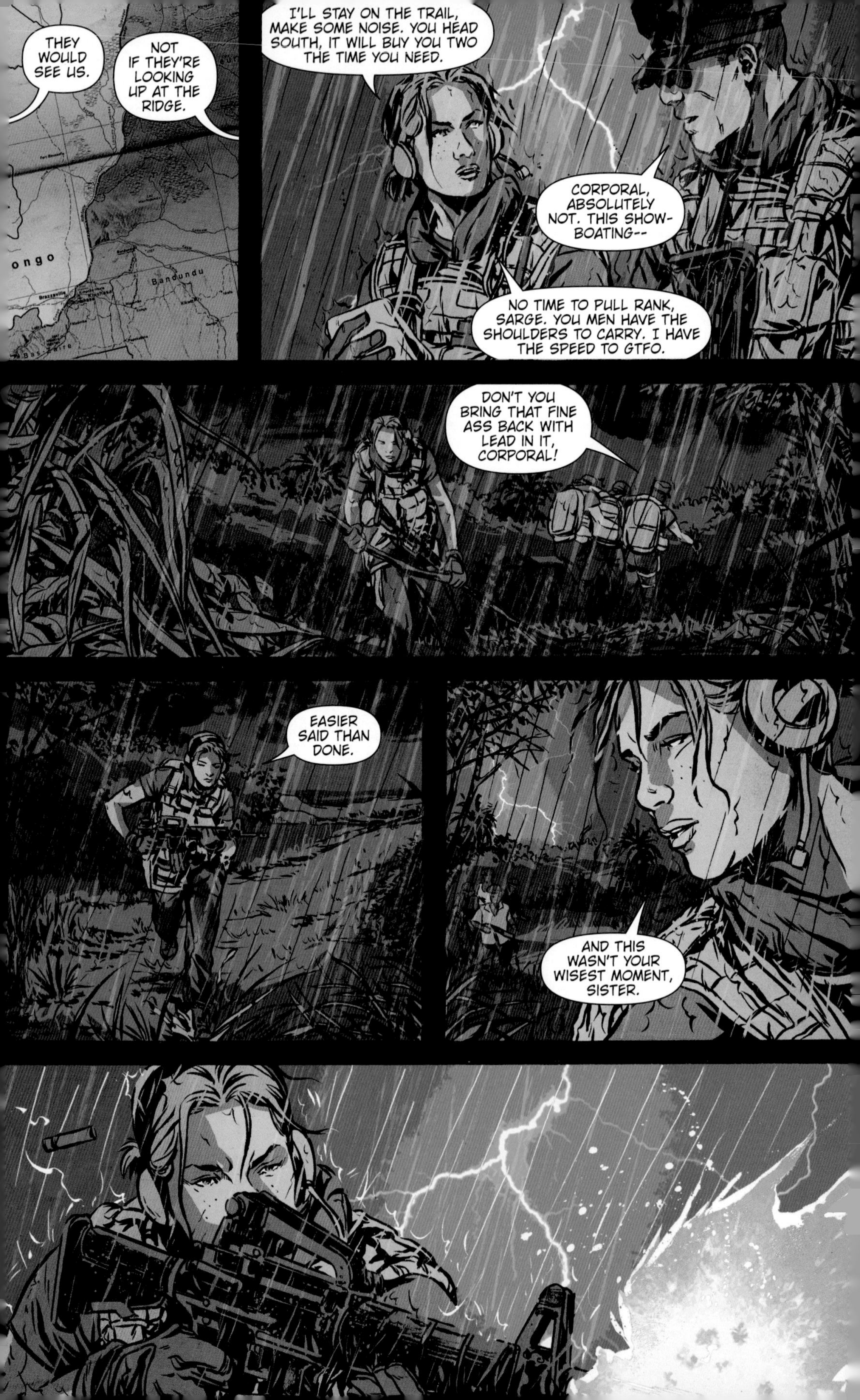

THEY WOULD SEE US.
NOT IF THEY'RE LOOKING UP AT THE RIDGE.
ongo
Bandundu
I'LL STAY ON THE TRAIL, MAKE SOME NOISE. YOU HEAD SOUTH, IT WILL BUY YOU TWO THE TIME YOU NEED.
CORPORAL, ABSOLUTELY NOT. THIS SHOW-BOATING--
NO TIME TO PULL RANK, SARGE. YOU MEN HAVE THE SHOULDERS TO CARRY. I HAVE THE SPEED TO GTFO.
DON'T YOU BRING THAT FINE ASS BACK WITH LEAD IN IT, CORPORAL!
EASIER SAID THAN DONE.
AND THIS WASN'T YOUR WISEST MOMENT, SISTER.

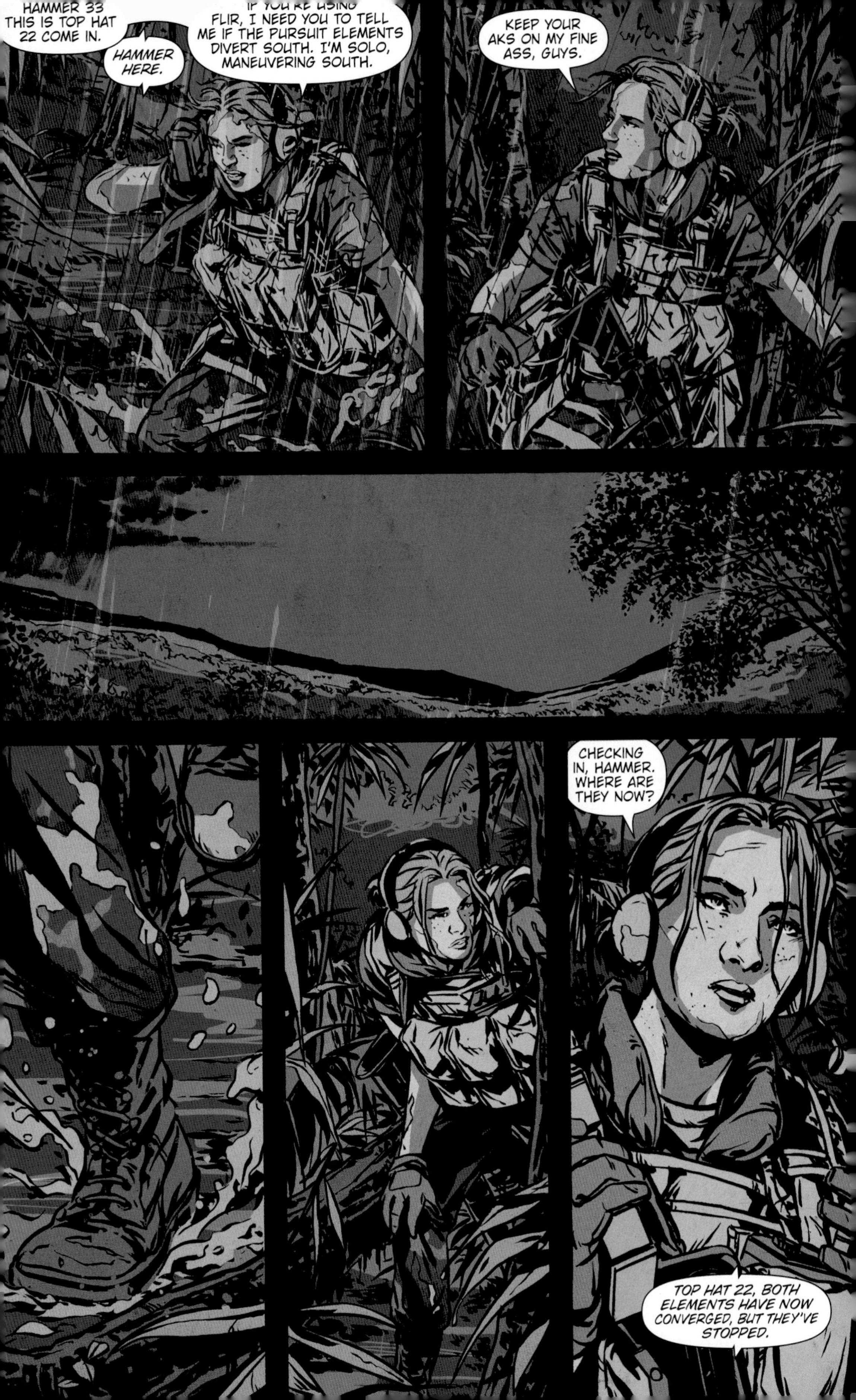
HAMMER 33 THIS IS TOP HAT 22 COME IN.
HAMMER HERE.
IF YOU'RE USING FLIR, I NEED YOU TO TELL ME IF THE PURSUIT ELEMENTS DIVERT SOUTH. I'M SOLO, MANEUVERING SOUTH.
KEEP YOUR AKS ON MY FINE ASS, GUYS.
CHECKING IN, HAMMER. WHERE ARE THEY NOW?
TOP HAT 22, BOTH ELEMENTS HAVE NOW CONVERGED, BUT THEY'VE STOPPED.

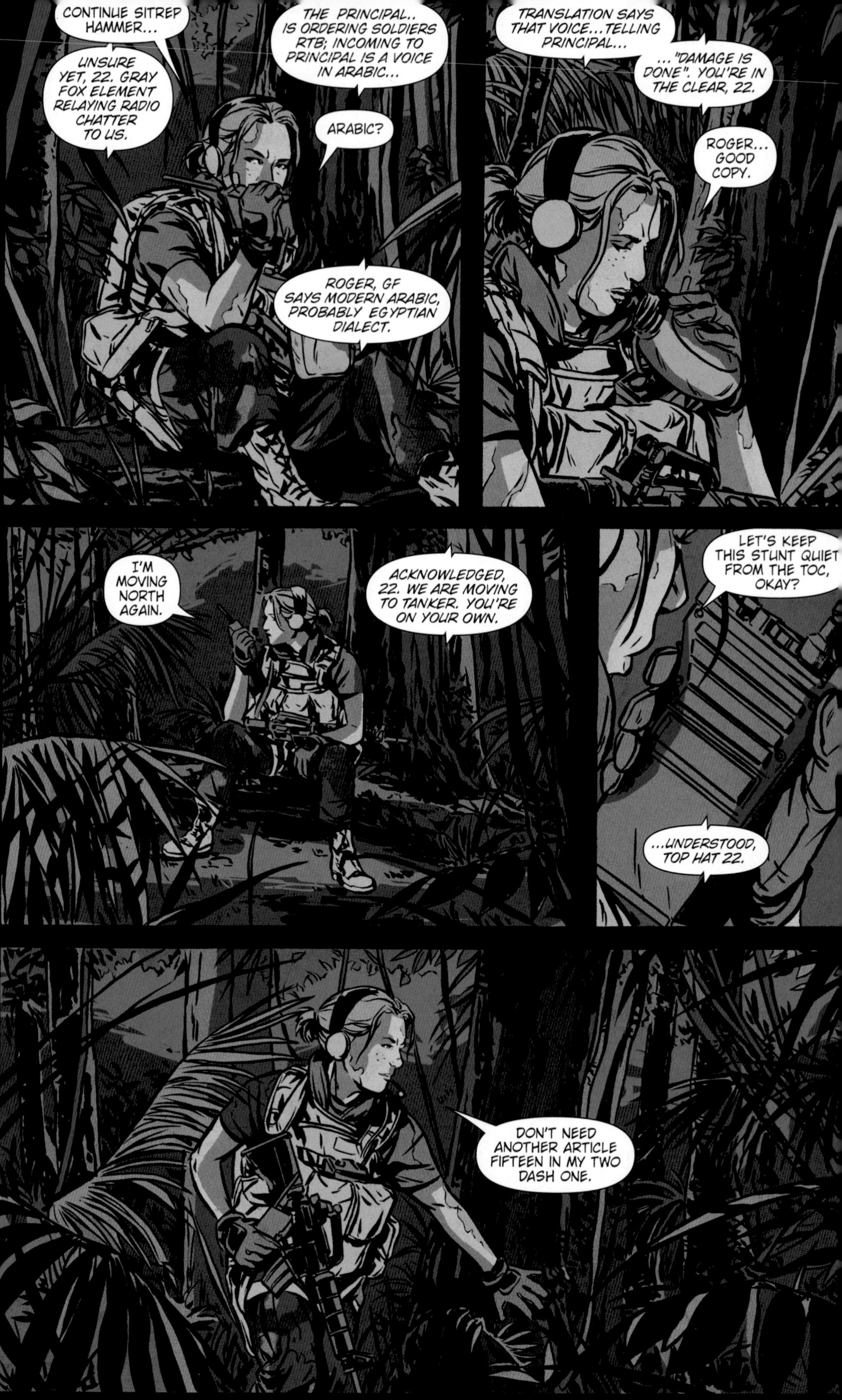
CONTINUE SITREP HAMMER...
UNSURE YET, 22. GRAY FOX ELEMENT RELAYING RADIO CHATTER TO US.
THE PRINCIPAL.. IS ORDERING SOLDIERS RTB; INCOMING TO PRINCIPAL IS A VOICE IN ARABIC...
ARABIC?
ROGER, GF SAYS MODERN ARABIC, PROBABLY EGYPTIAN DIALECT.
TRANSLATION SAYS THAT VOICE...TELLING PRINCIPAL...
..."DAMAGE IS DONE". YOU'RE IN THE CLEAR, 22.
ROGER... GOOD COPY.
I'M MOVING NORTH AGAIN.
ACKNOWLEDGED, 22. WE ARE MOVING TO TANKER. YOU'RE ON YOUR OWN.
LET'S KEEP THIS STUNT QUIET FROM THE TOC, OKAY?
...UNDERSTOOD, TOP HAT 22.
DON'T NEED ANOTHER ARTICLE FIFTEEN IN MY TWO DASH ONE.

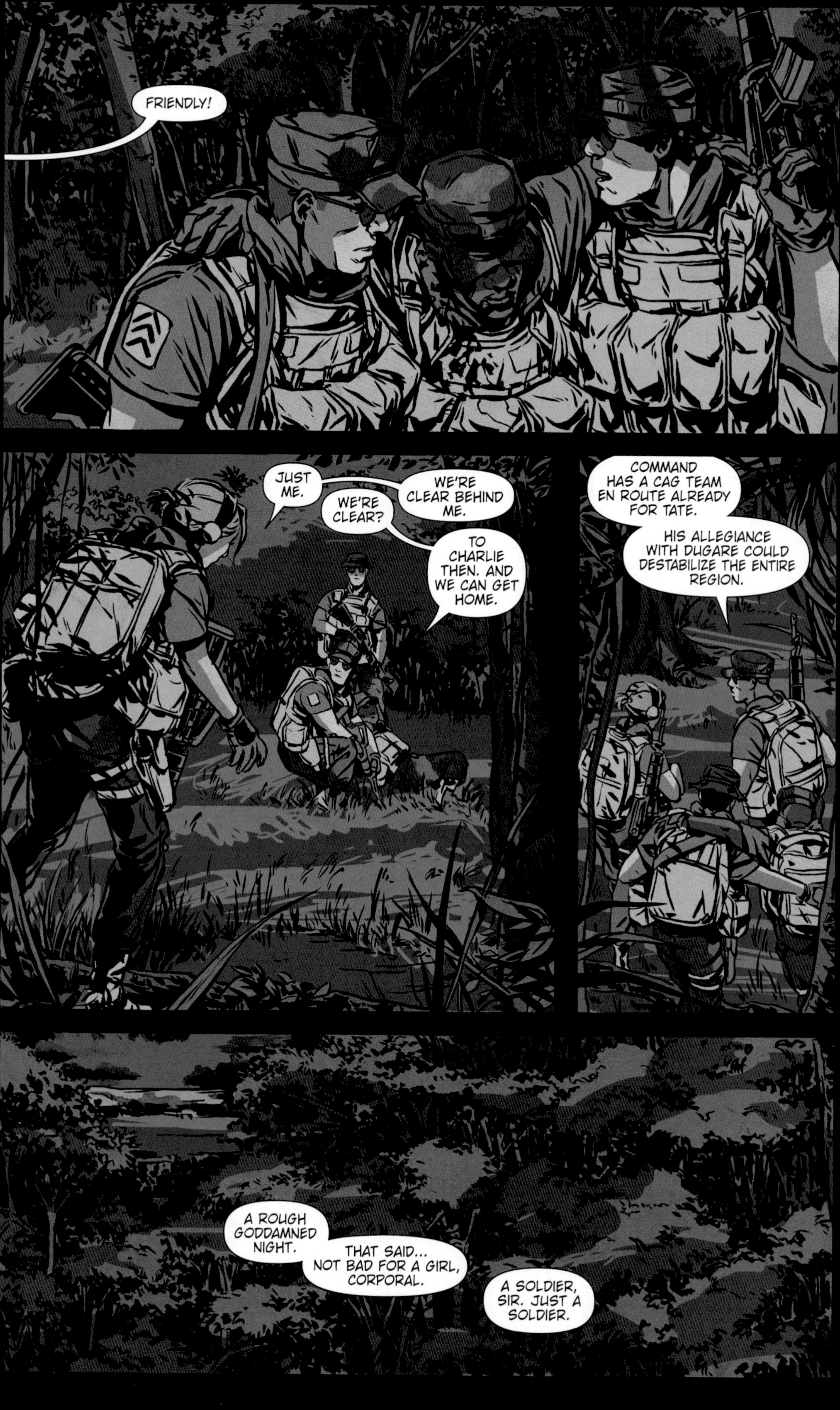
FRIENDLY!
JUST ME.
WE'RE CLEAR BEHIND ME.
WE'RE CLEAR?
TO CHARLIE THEN. AND WE CAN GET HOME.
COMMAND HAS A CAG TEAM EN ROUTE ALREADY FOR TATE.
HIS ALLEGIANCE WITH DUGARE COULD DESTABILIZE THE ENTIRE REGION.
A ROUGH GODDAMNED NIGHT.
THAT SAID... NOT BAD FOR A GIRL, CORPORAL.
A SOLDIER, SIR. JUST A SOLDIER.

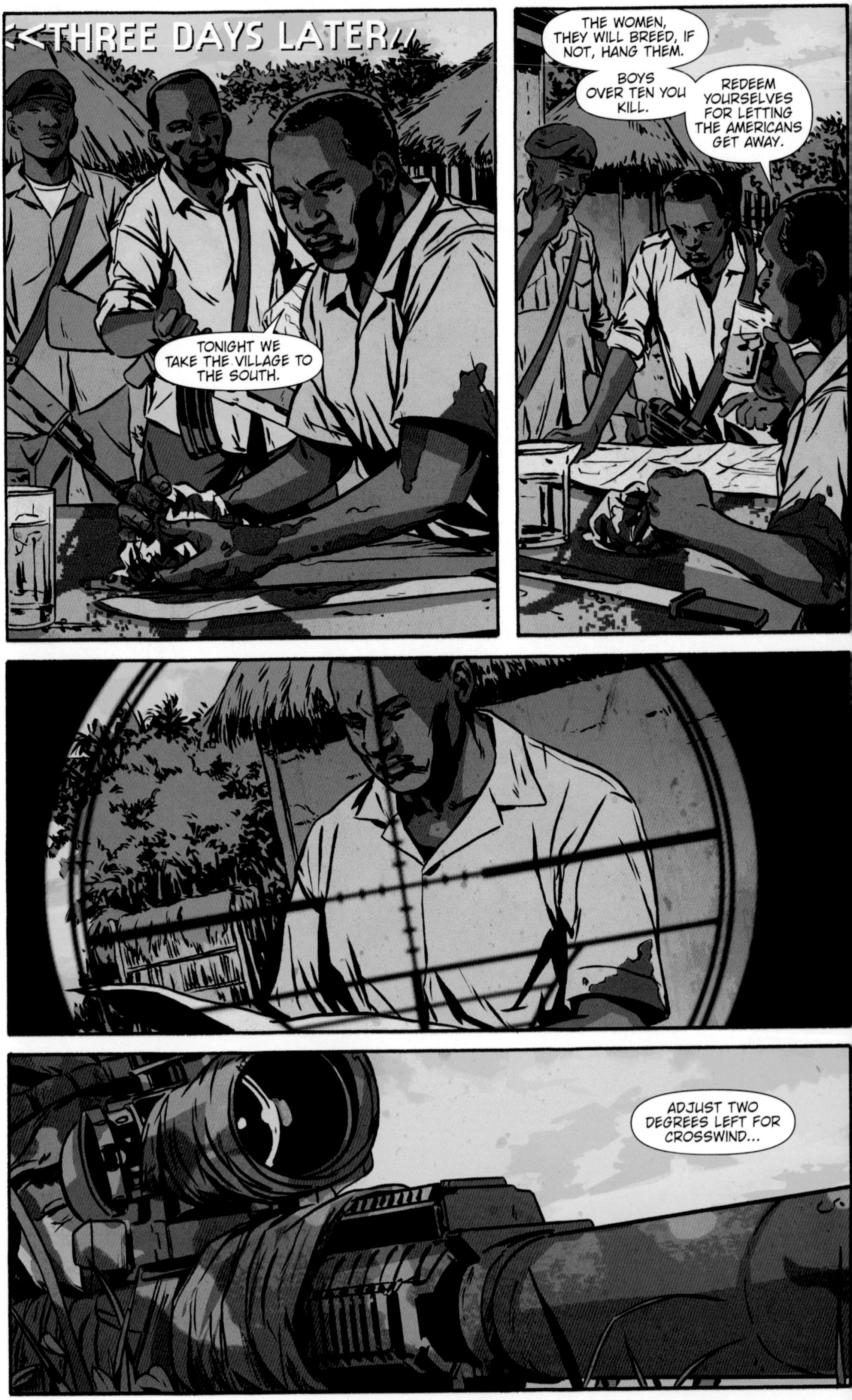

<<THREE DAYS LATER//
TONIGHT WE TAKE THE VILLAGE TO THE SOUTH.
THE WOMEN, THEY WILL BREED, IF NOT, HANG THEM.
BOYS OVER TEN YOU KILL.
REDEEM YOURSELVES FOR LETTING THE AMERICANS GET AWAY.
ADJUST TWO DEGREES LEFT FOR CROSSWIND...

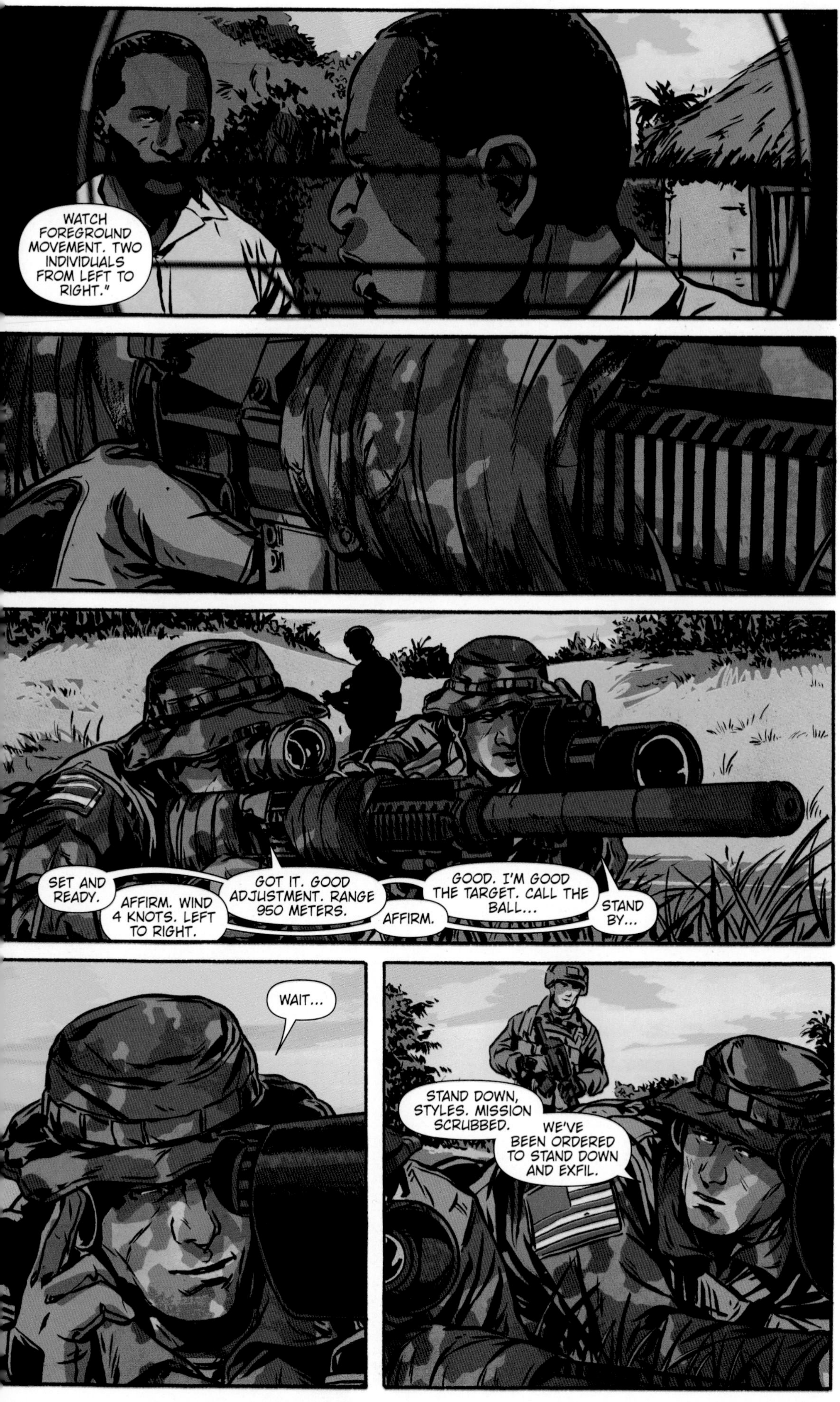
WATCH FOREGROUND MOVEMENT. TWO INDIVIDUALS FROM LEFT TO RIGHT."
SET AND READY.
AFFIRM. WIND 4 KNOTS. LEFT TO RIGHT.
GOT IT. GOOD ADJUSTMENT. RANGE 950 METERS.
AFFIRM.
GOOD. I'M GOOD THE TARGET. CALL THE BALL...
STAND BY...
WAIT...
STAND DOWN, STYLES. MISSION SCRUBBED.
WE'VE BEEN ORDERED TO STAND DOWN AND EXFIL.

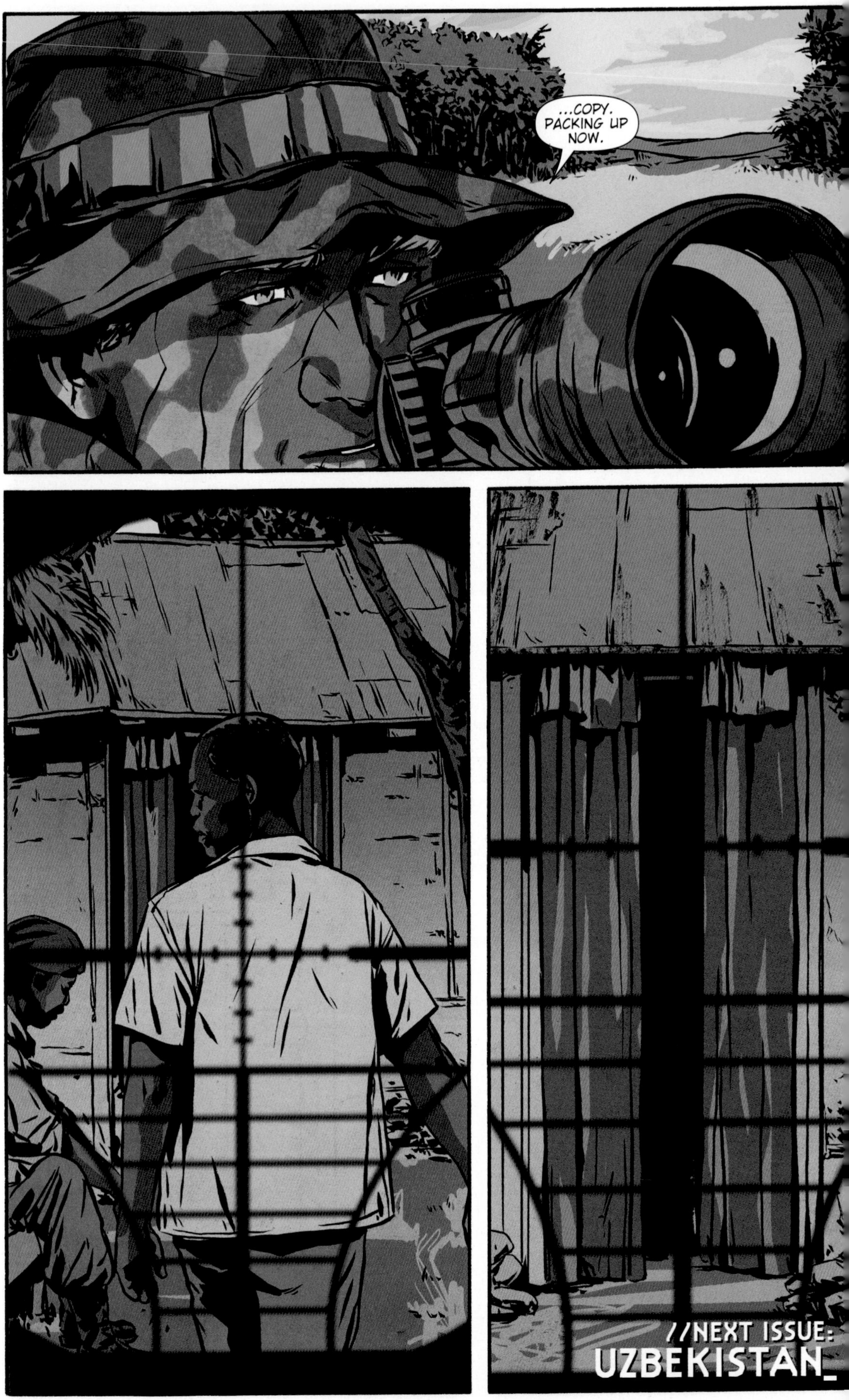
...COPY. PACKING UP NOW.
//NEXT ISSUE:
UZBEKISTAN_

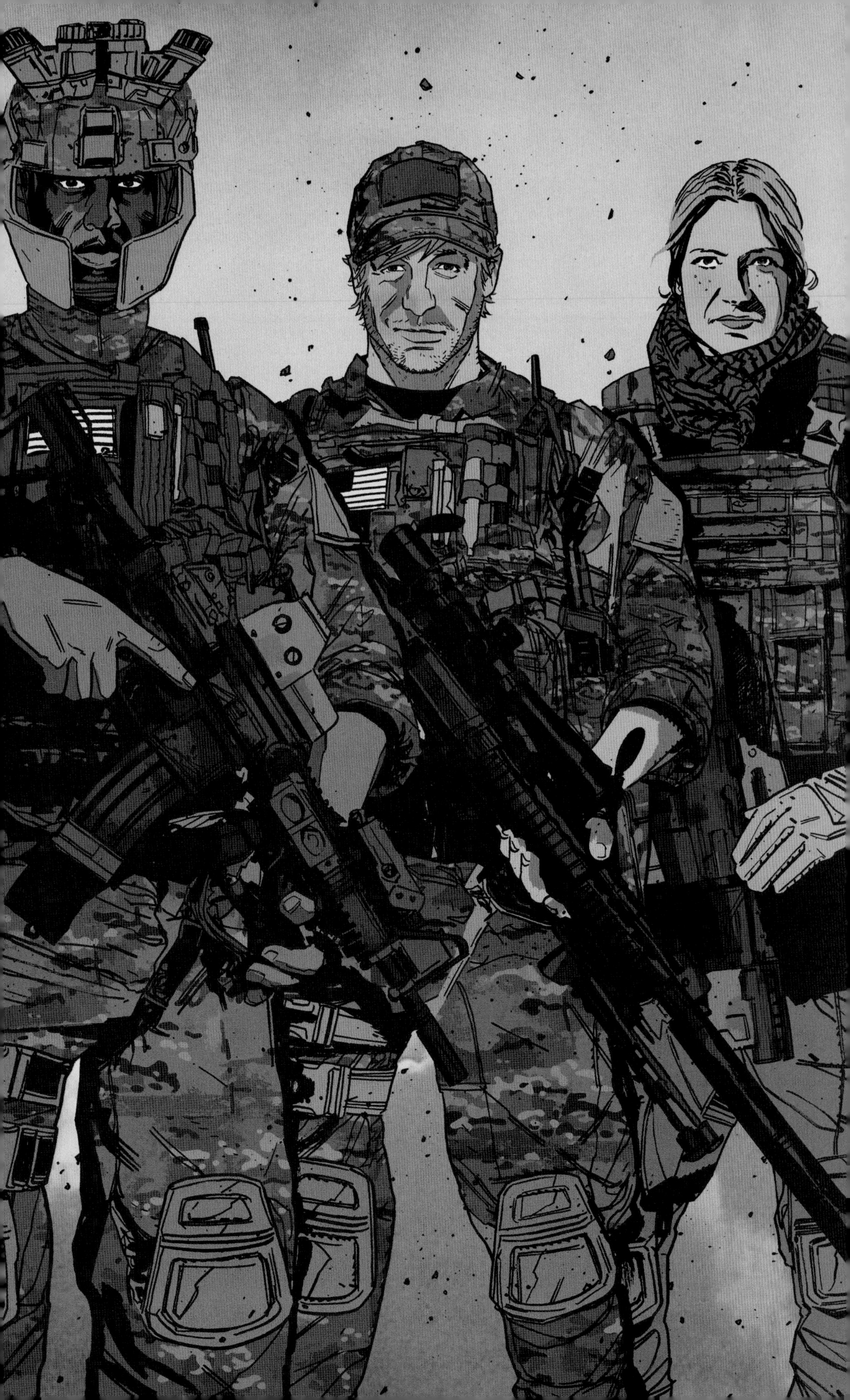

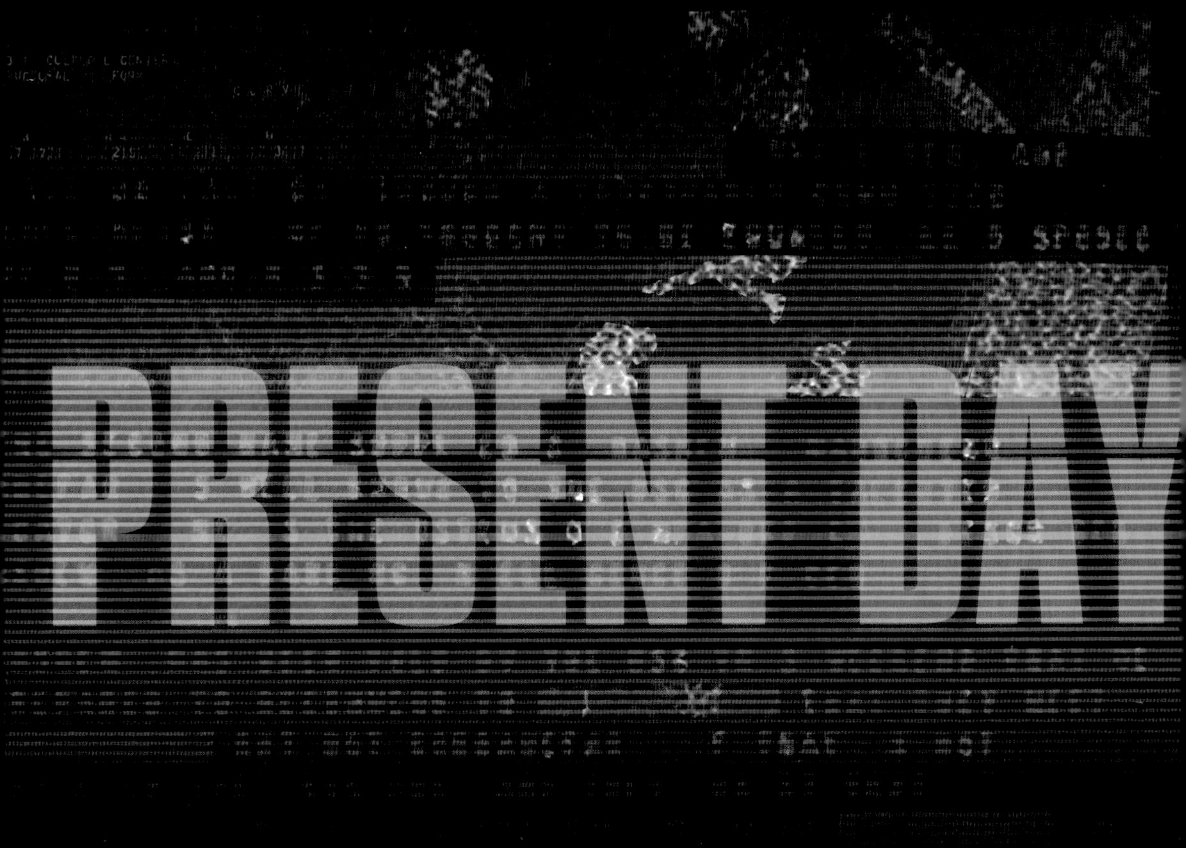
PRESENT DAY

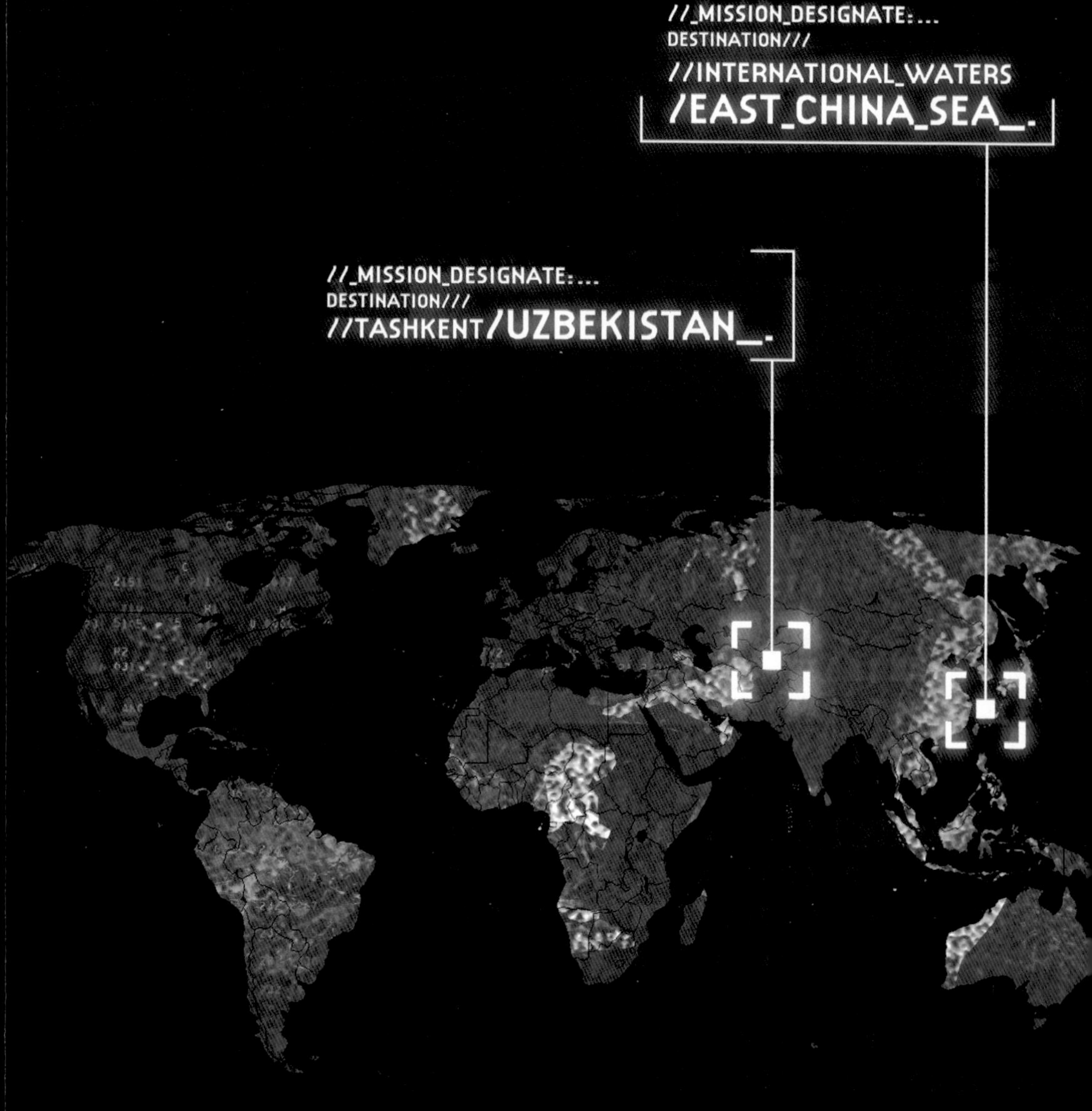
//_MISSION_DESIGNATE:...
DESTINATION///
//INTERNATIONAL_WATERS
/EAST_CHINA_SEA_.
//_MISSION_DESIGNATE:...
DESTINATION///
//TASHKENT/UZBEKISTAN_.

//MISSION_REPORT_
//INITIALIZING____

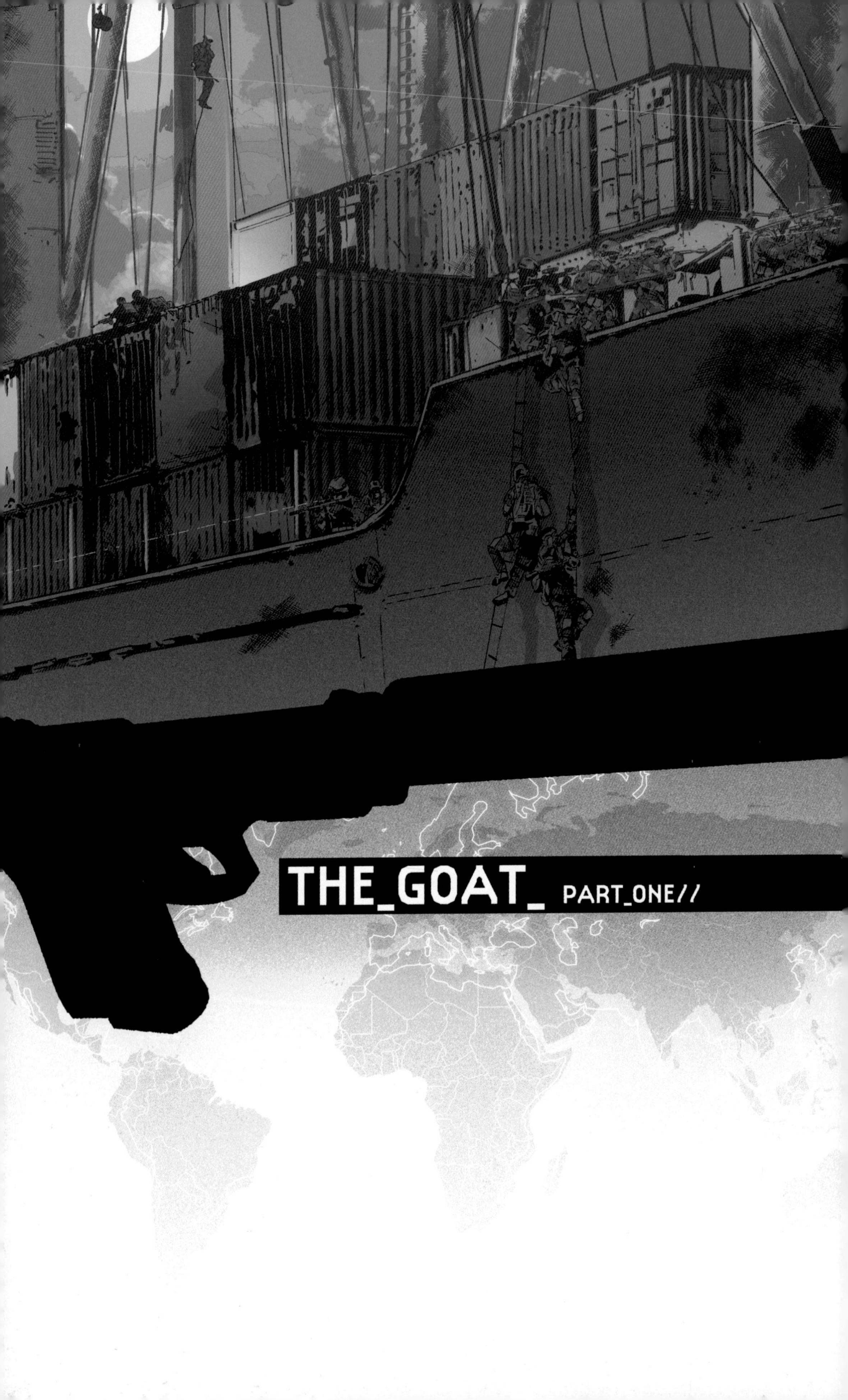
THE_GOAT_ PART_ONE//

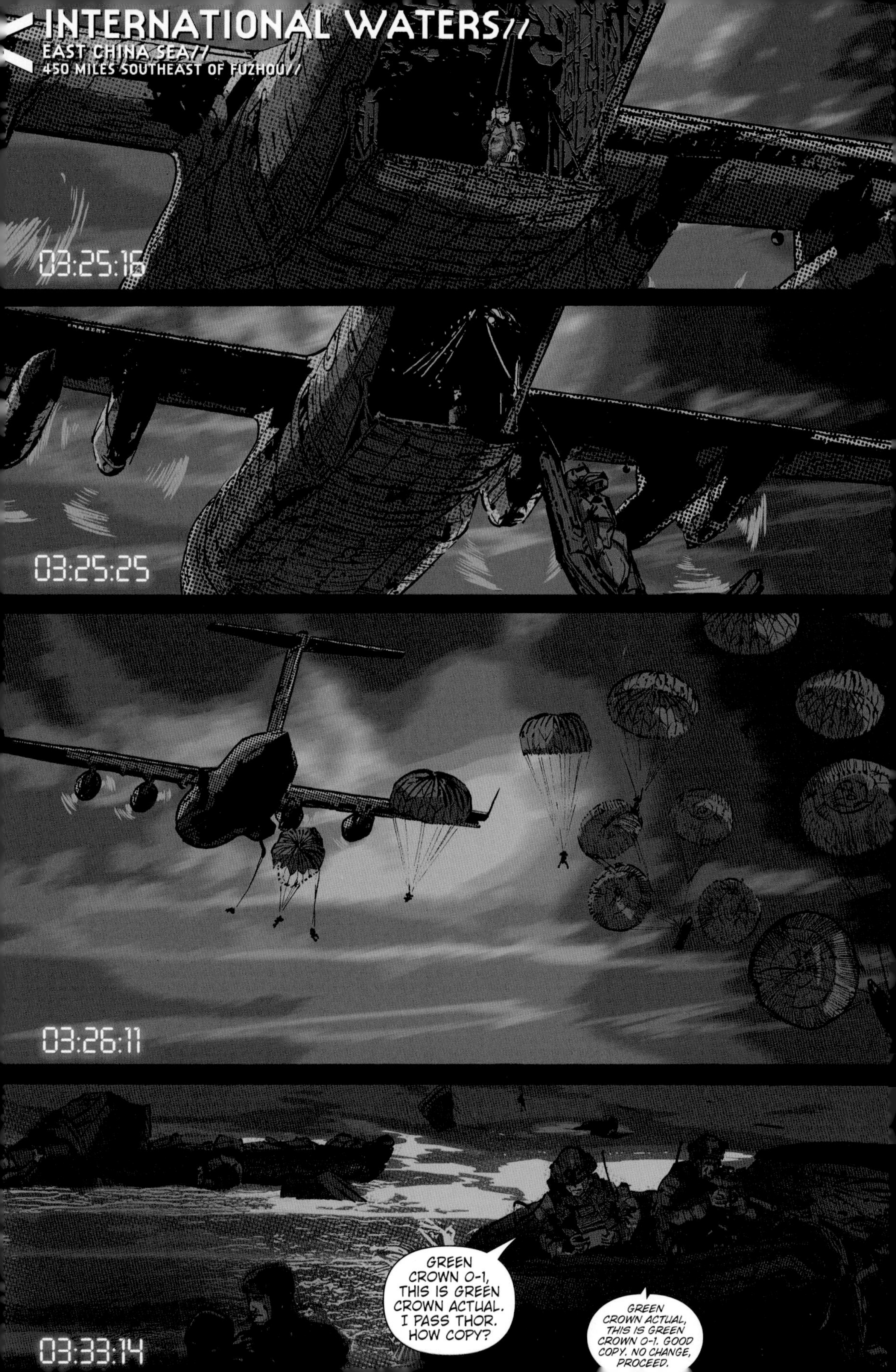
INTERNATIONAL WATERS//
EAST CHINA SEA//
450 MILES SOUTHEAST OF FUZHOU//
03:25:16
03:25:25
03:26:11
03:33:14
GREEN CROWN O-1, THIS IS GREEN CROWN ACTUAL. I PASS THOR. HOW COPY?
GREEN CROWN ACTUAL, THIS IS GREEN CROWN O-1. GOOD COPY. NO CHANGE, PROCEED.

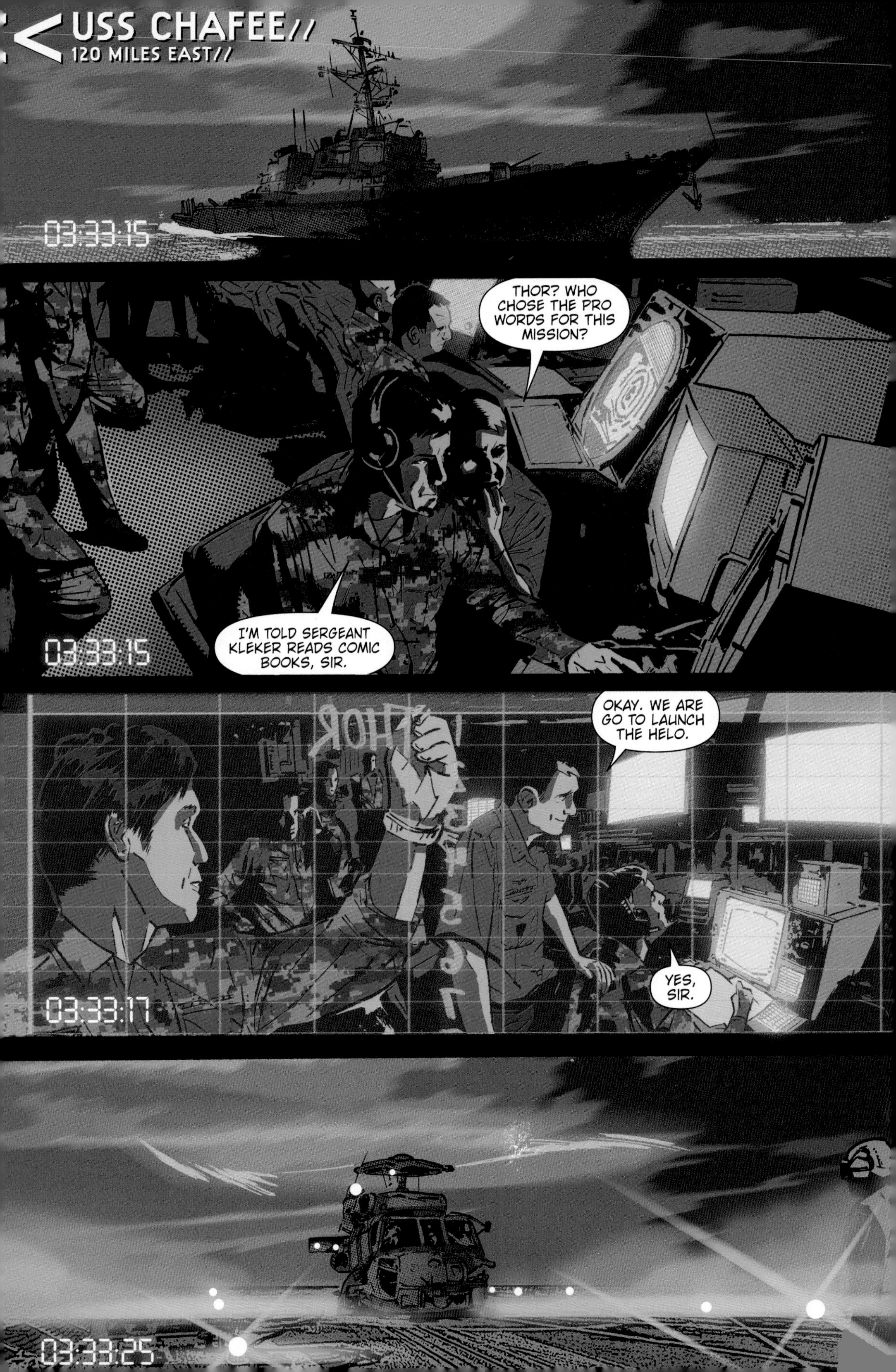
USS CHAFEE//
120 MILES EAST//
03:33:15
THOR? WHO CHOSE THE PRO WORDS FOR THIS MISSION?
I'M TOLD SERGEANT KLEKER READS COMIC BOOKS, SIR.
03:33:15
OKAY. WE ARE GO TO LAUNCH THE HELO.
YES, SIR.
03:33:17
03:33:25

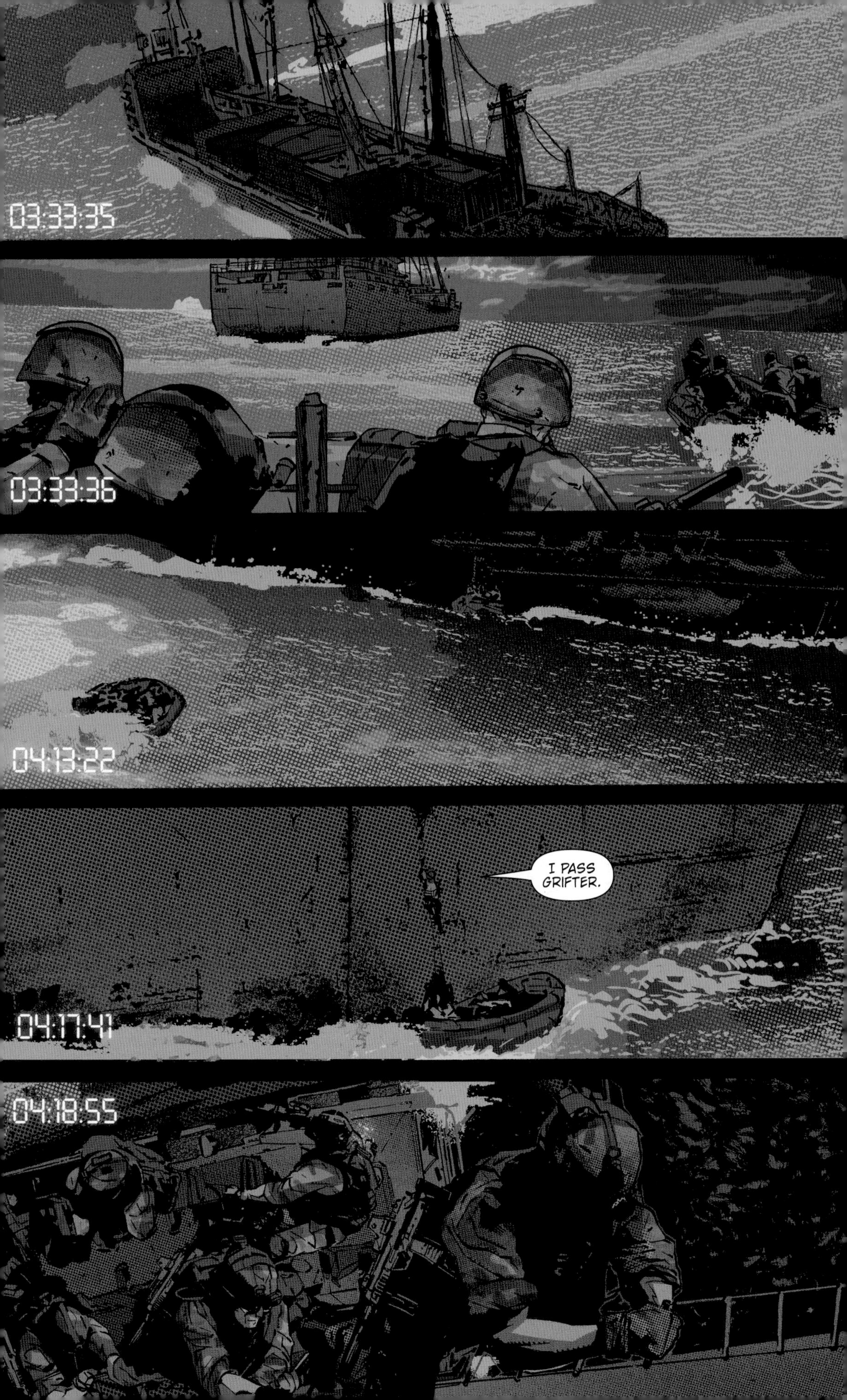
03:33:35
03:33:36
04:13:22
I PASS GRIFTER.
04:17:41
04:18:55

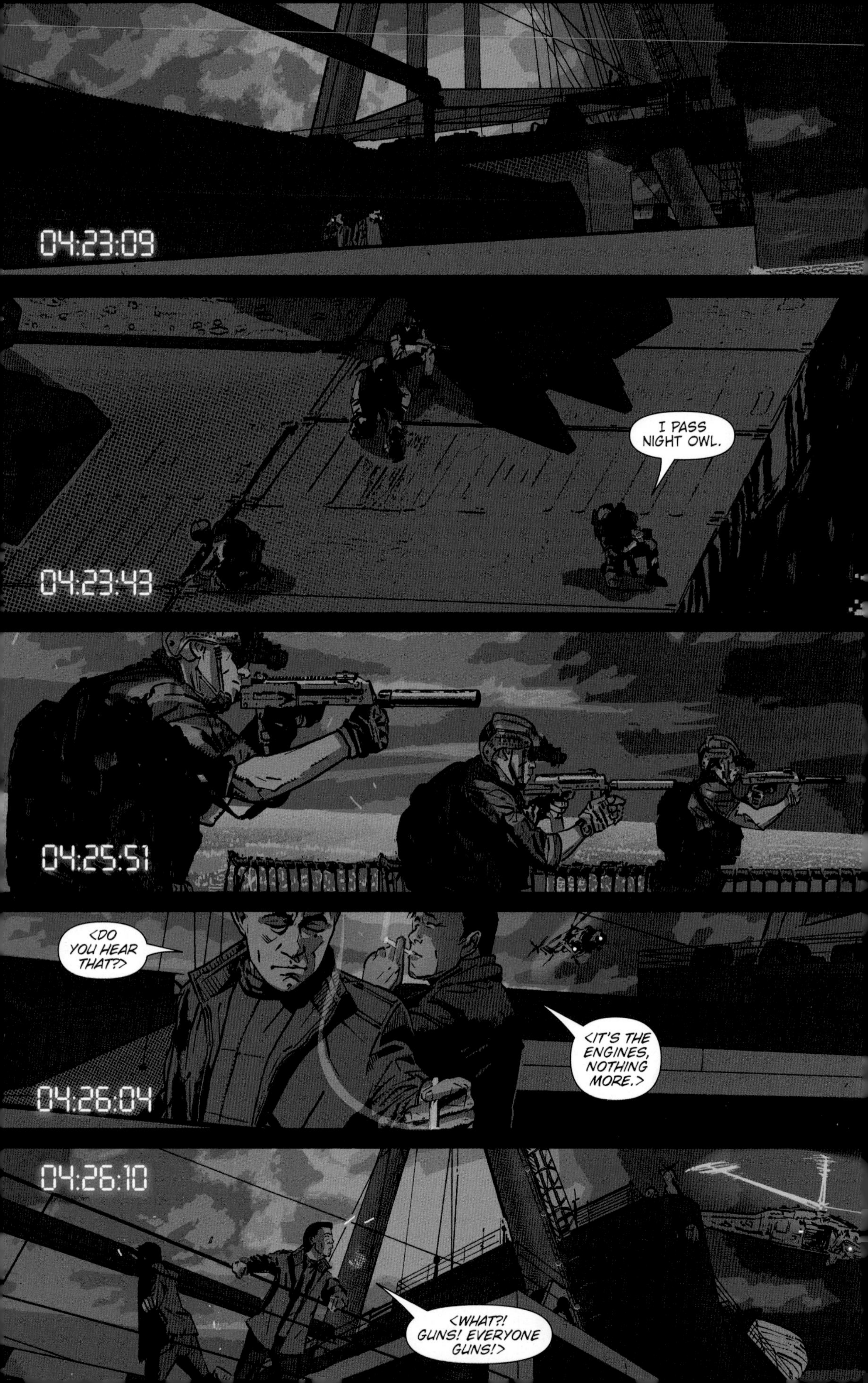
04:23:09
04:23:43
I PASS NIGHT OWL.
04:25:51
<DO YOU HEAR THAT?>
<IT'S THE ENGINES, NOTHING MORE.>
04:26:04
04:26:10
<WHAT?! GUNS! EVERYONE GUNS!>

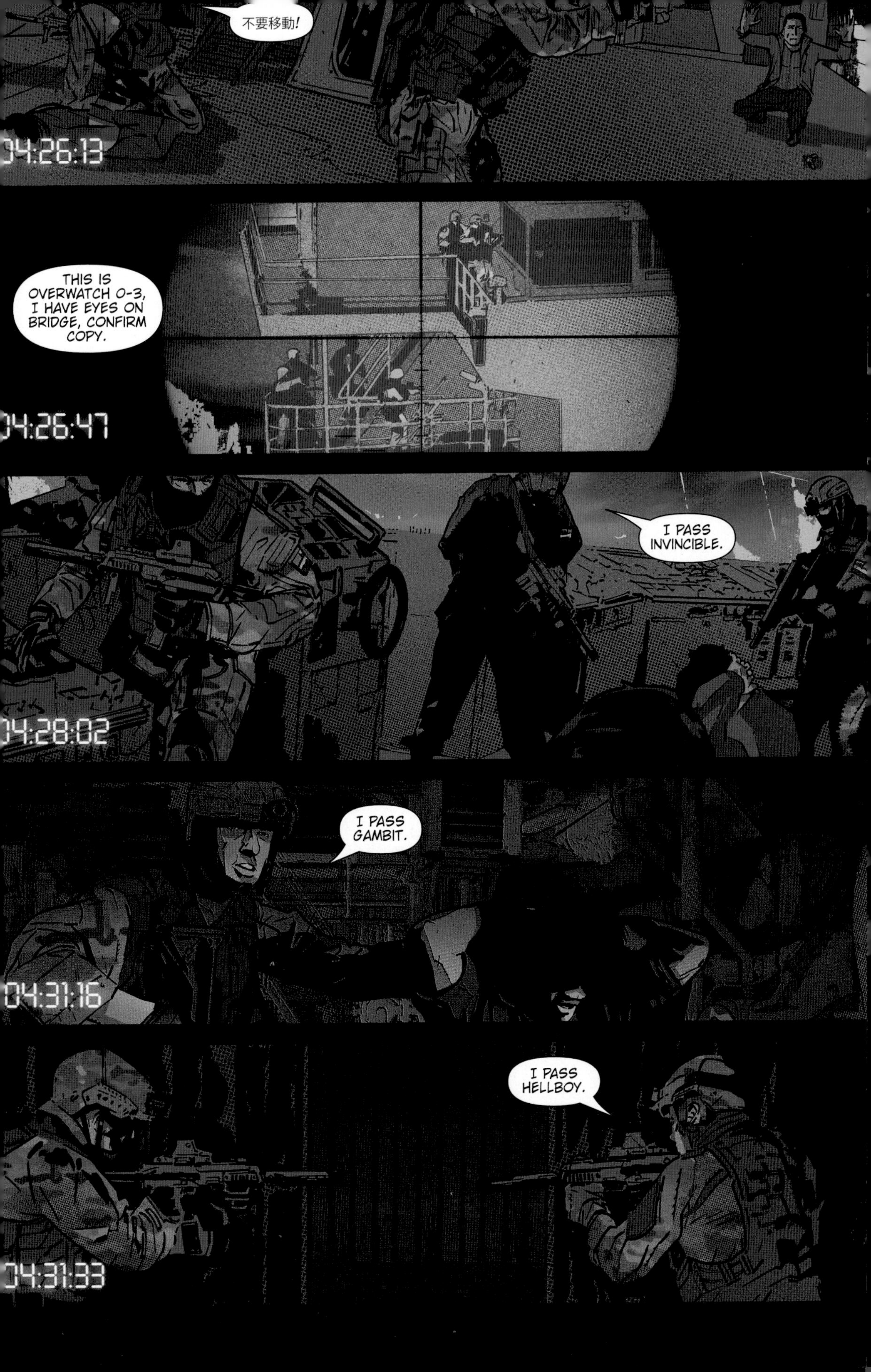
不要移動!
04:26:13
THIS IS OVERWATCH 0-3, I HAVE EYES ON BRIDGE, CONFIRM COPY.
04:26:47
I PASS INVINCIBLE.
04:28:02
I PASS GAMBIT.
04:31:16
I PASS HELLBOY.
04:31:33

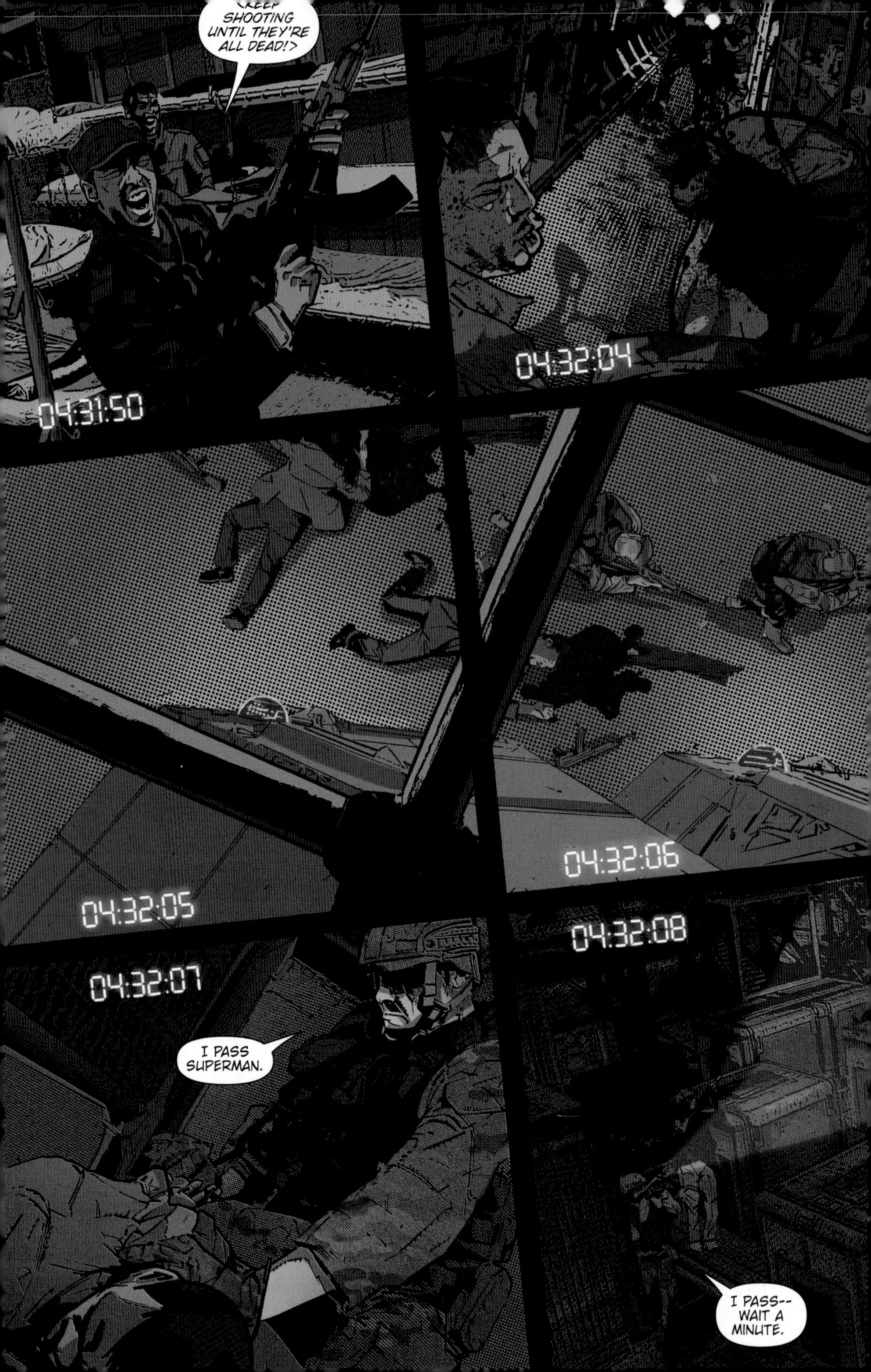
<KEEP SHOOTING UNTIL THEY'RE ALL DEAD!>
04:31:50
04:32:04
04:32:05
04:32:06
04:32:07
I PASS SUPERMAN.
04:32:08
I PASS-- WAIT A MINUTE.

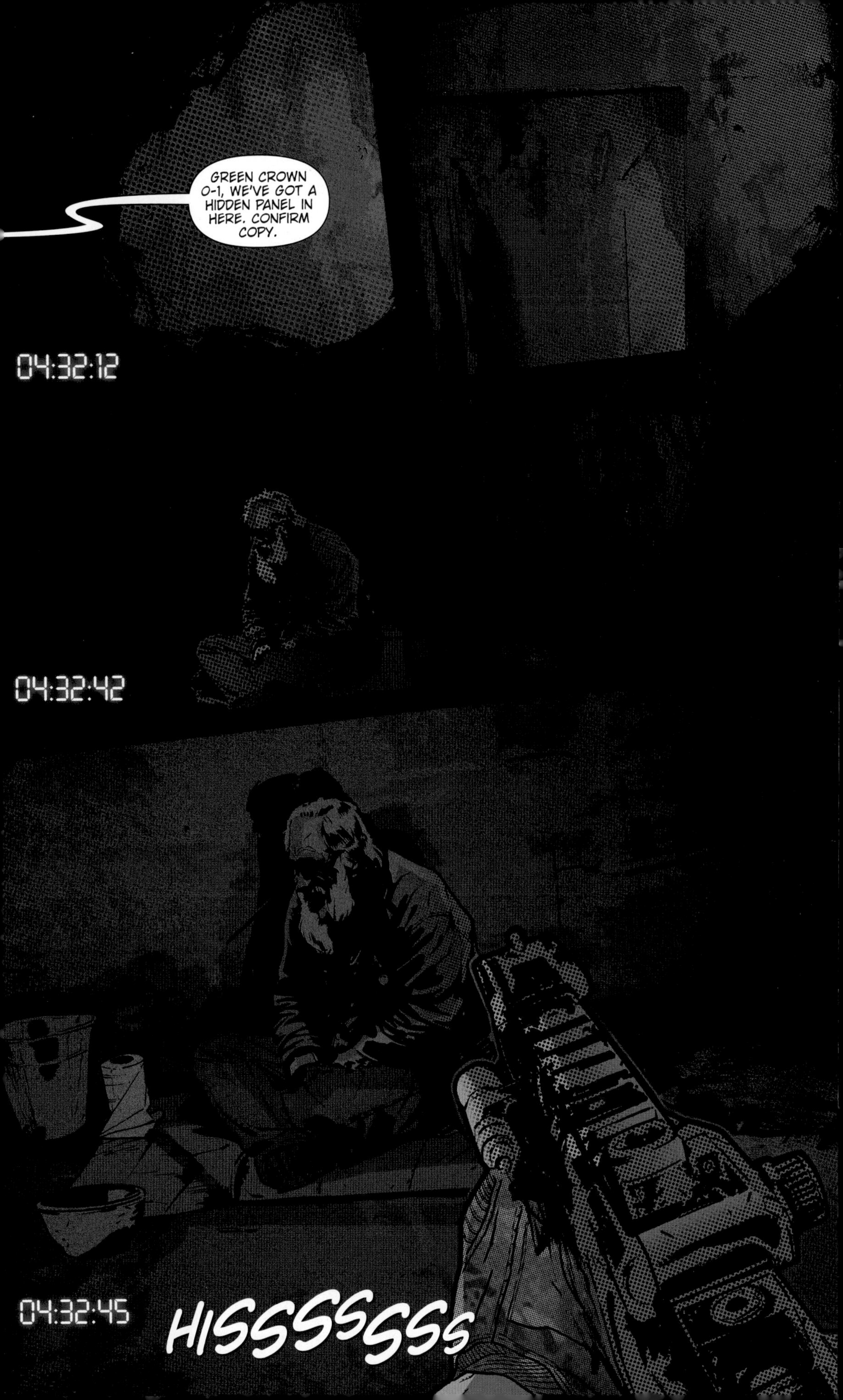
GREEN CROWN O-1, WE'VE GOT A HIDDEN PANEL IN HERE. CONFIRM COPY.
04:32:12
04:32:42
04:32:45
HISSSSSSs

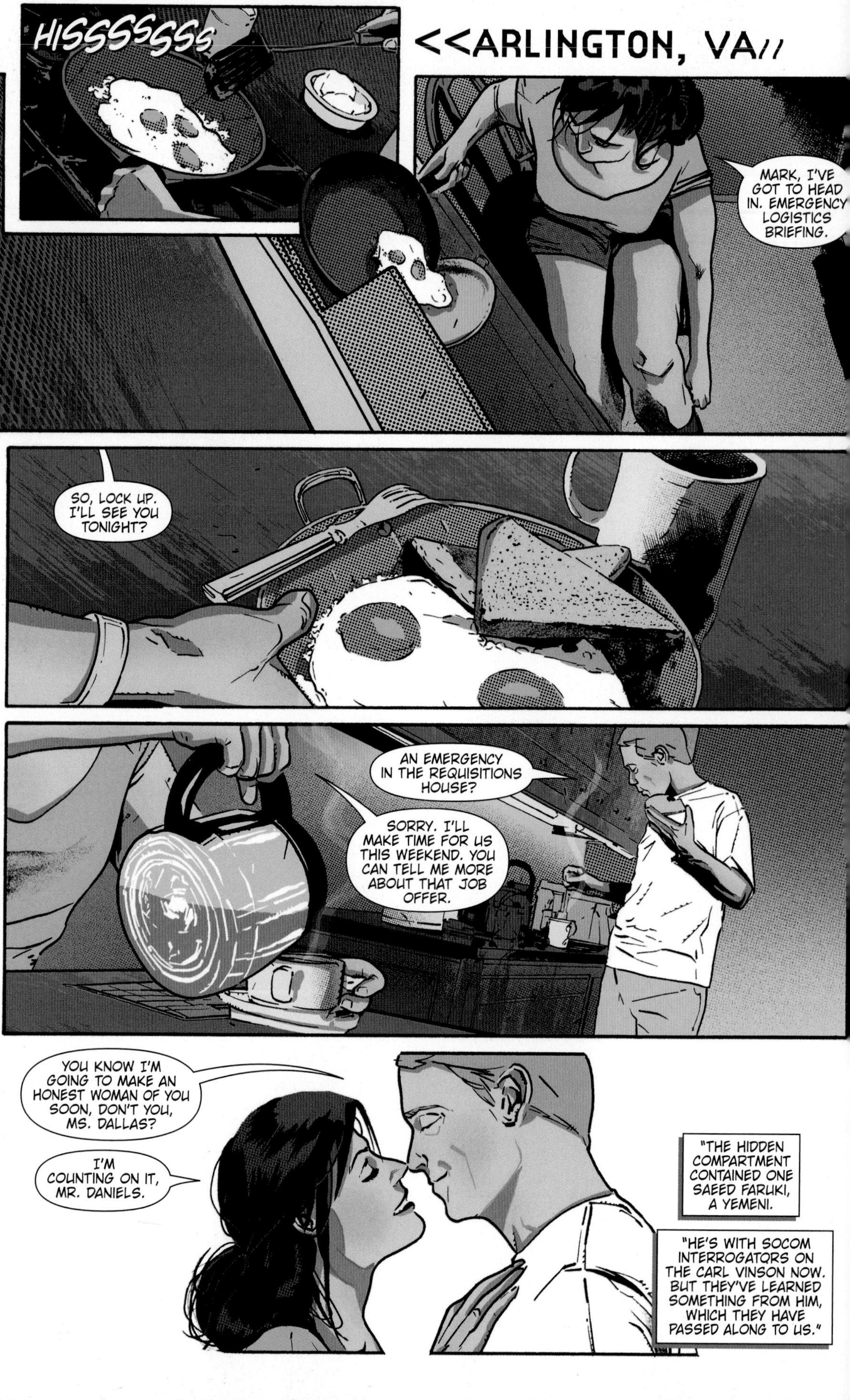
HISSSSSSs
<<ARLINGTON, VA//
MARK, I'VE GOT TO HEAD IN. EMERGENCY LOGISTICS BRIEFING.
SO, LOCK UP. I'LL SEE YOU TONIGHT?
AN EMERGENCY IN THE REQUISITIONS HOUSE?
SORRY. I'LL MAKE TIME FOR US THIS WEEKEND. YOU CAN TELL ME MORE ABOUT THAT JOB OFFER.
YOU KNOW I'M GOING TO MAKE AN HONEST WOMAN OF YOU SOON, DON'T YOU, MS. DALLAS?
I'M COUNTING ON IT, MR. DANIELS.
"THE HIDDEN COMPARTMENT CONTAINED ONE SAEED FARUKI, A YEMENI.
"HE'S WITH SOCOM INTERROGATORS ON THE CARL VINSON NOW. BUT THEY'VE LEARNED SOMETHING FROM HIM, WHICH THEY HAVE PASSED ALONG TO US."

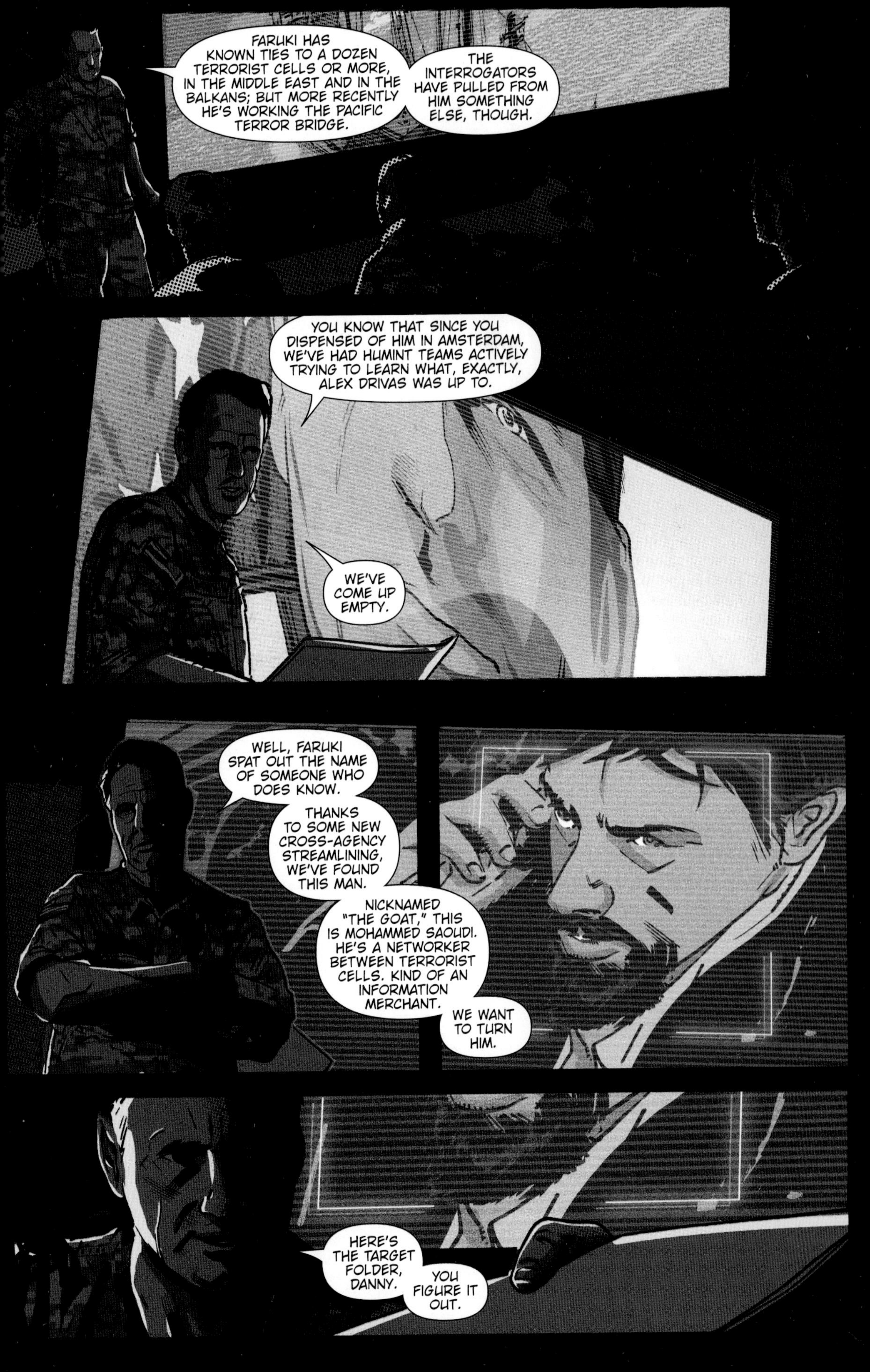
FARUKI HAS KNOWN TIES TO A DOZEN TERRORIST CELLS OR MORE, IN THE MIDDLE EAST AND IN THE BALKANS; BUT MORE RECENTLY HE'S WORKING THE PACIFIC TERROR BRIDGE.
THE INTERROGATORS HAVE PULLED FROM HIM SOMETHING ELSE, THOUGH.
YOU KNOW THAT SINCE YOU DISPENSED OF HIM IN AMSTERDAM, WE'VE HAD HUMINT TEAMS ACTIVELY TRYING TO LEARN WHAT, EXACTLY, ALEX DRIVAS WAS UP TO.
WE'VE COME UP EMPTY.
WELL, FARUKI SPAT OUT THE NAME OF SOMEONE WHO DOES KNOW.
THANKS TO SOME NEW CROSS-AGENCY STREAMLINING, WE'VE FOUND THIS MAN.
NICKNAMED "THE GOAT," THIS IS MOHAMMED SAOUDI. HE'S A NETWORKER BETWEEN TERRORIST CELLS. KIND OF AN INFORMATION MERCHANT.
WE WANT TO TURN HIM.
HERE'S THE TARGET FOLDER, DANNY.
YOU FIGURE IT OUT.

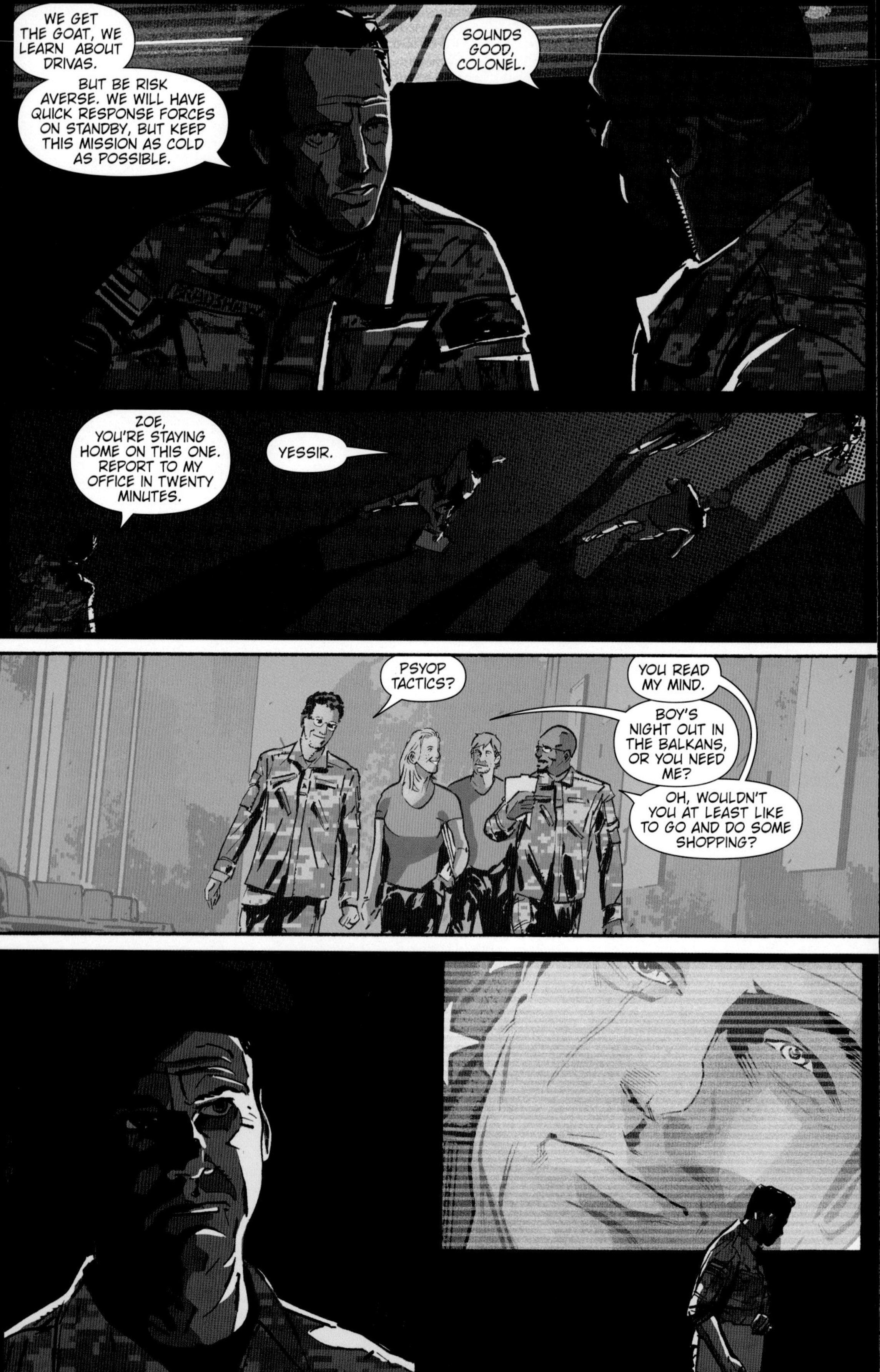
WE GET THE GOAT, WE LEARN ABOUT DRIVAS.
BUT BE RISK AVERSE. WE WILL HAVE QUICK RESPONSE FORCES ON STANDBY, BUT KEEP THIS MISSION AS COLD AS POSSIBLE.
SOUNDS GOOD, COLONEL.
ZOE, YOU'RE STAYING HOME ON THIS ONE. REPORT TO MY OFFICE IN TWENTY MINUTES.
YESSIR.
PSYOP TACTICS?
YOU READ MY MIND.
BOY'S NIGHT OUT IN THE BALKANS, OR YOU NEED ME?
OH, WOULDN'T YOU AT LEAST LIKE TO GO AND DO SOME SHOPPING?

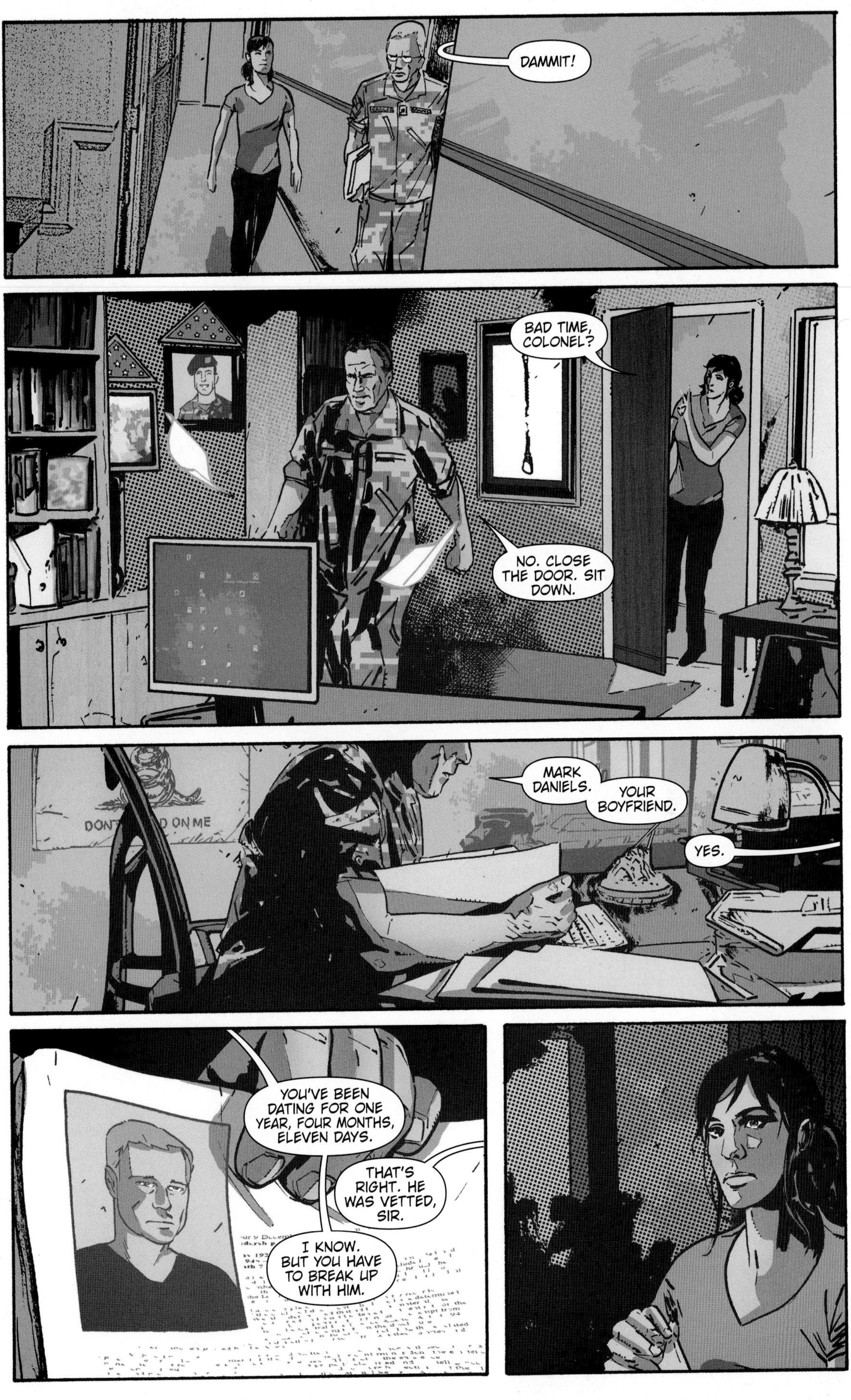
DAMMIT!
BAD TIME, COLONEL?
NO. CLOSE THE DOOR. SIT DOWN.
MARK DANIELS.
YOUR BOYFRIEND.
YES.
YOU'VE BEEN DATING FOR ONE YEAR, FOUR MONTHS, ELEVEN DAYS.
THAT'S RIGHT. HE WAS VETTED, SIR.
I KNOW. BUT YOU HAVE TO BREAK UP WITH HIM.

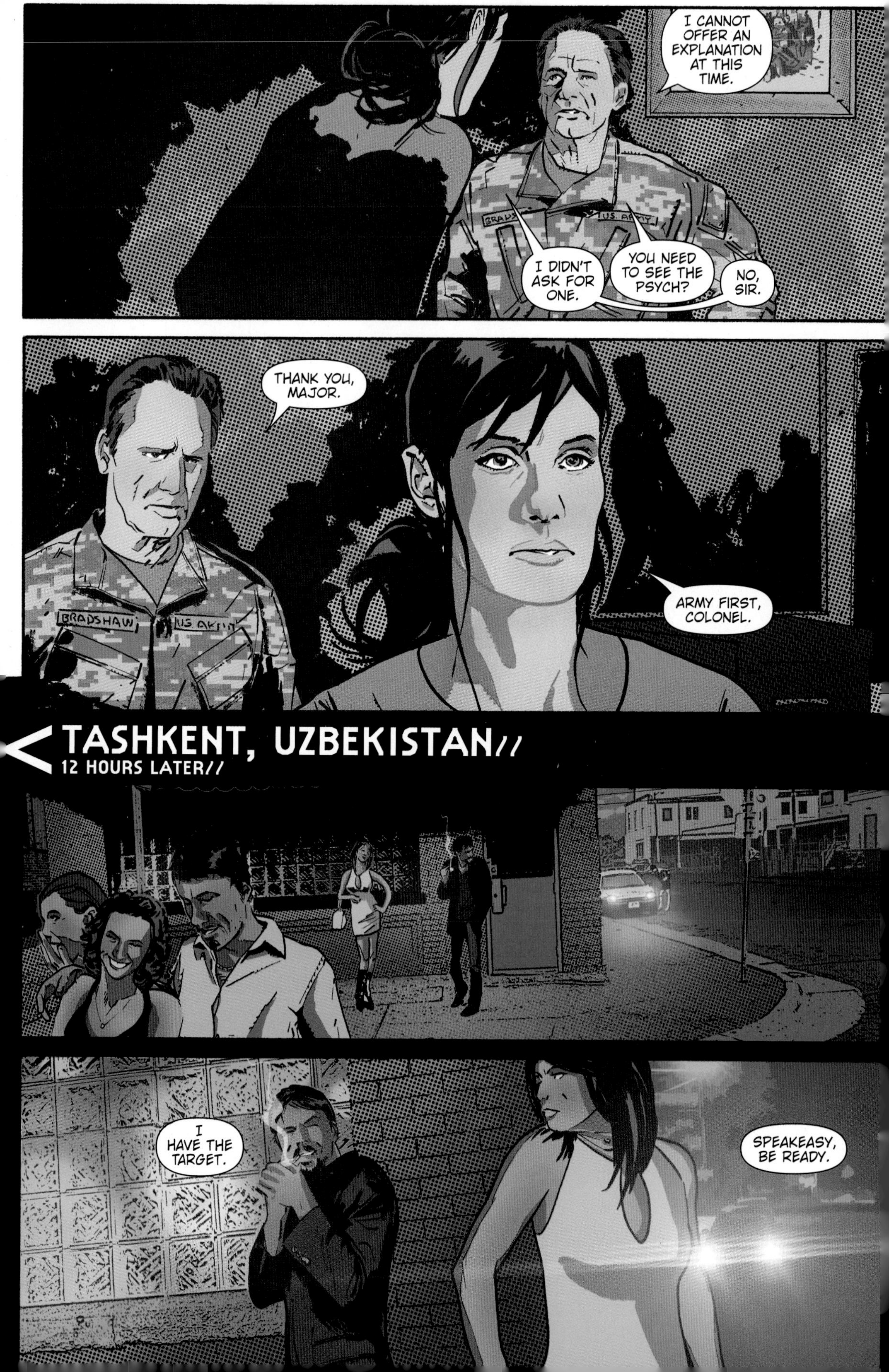
I CANNOT OFFER AN EXPLANATION AT THIS TIME.
I DIDN'T ASK FOR ONE.
YOU NEED TO SEE THE PSYCH?
NO, SIR.
THANK YOU, MAJOR.
BRADSHAW
ARMY FIRST, COLONEL.
TASHKENT, UZBEKISTAN//
12 HOURS LATER//
I HAVE THE TARGET.
SPEAKEASY, BE READY.

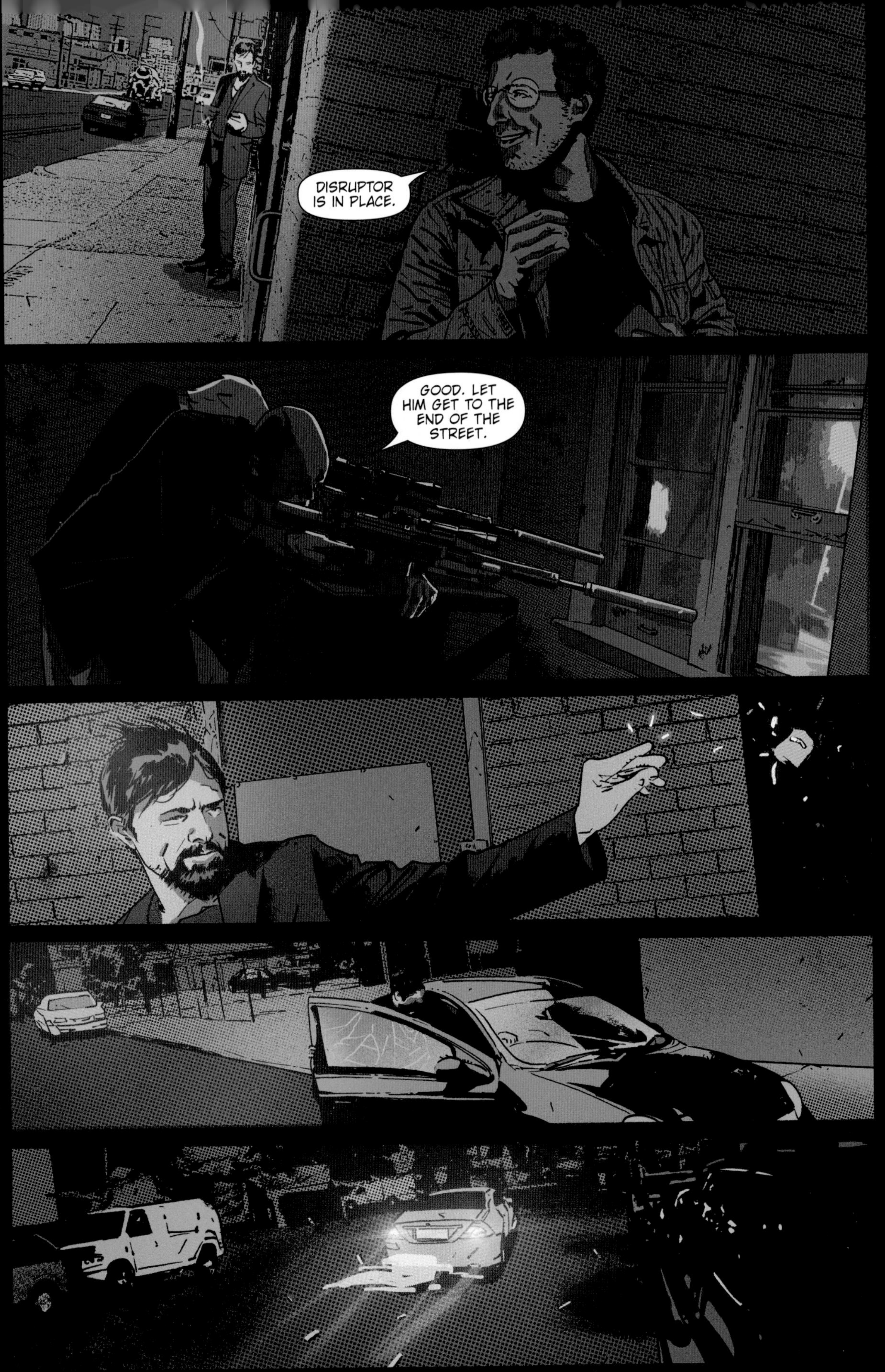
DISRUPTOR IS IN PLACE.
GOOD. LET HIM GET TO THE END OF THE STREET.

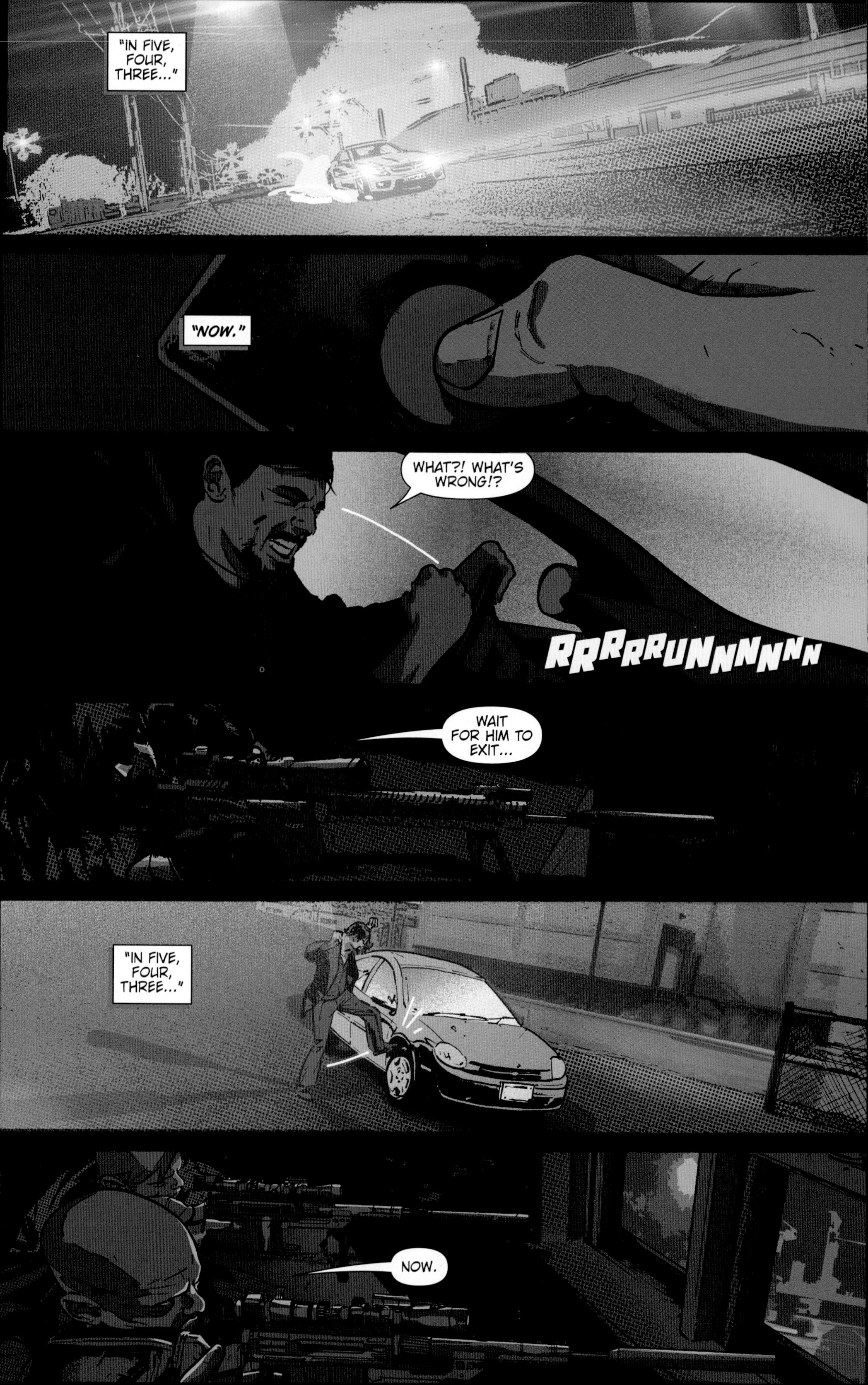
"IN FIVE, FOUR, THREE..."
"NOW."
WHAT?! WHAT'S WRONG!?
RRRRRUNNNNNN
WAIT FOR HIM TO EXIT...
"IN FIVE, FOUR, THREE..."
NOW.

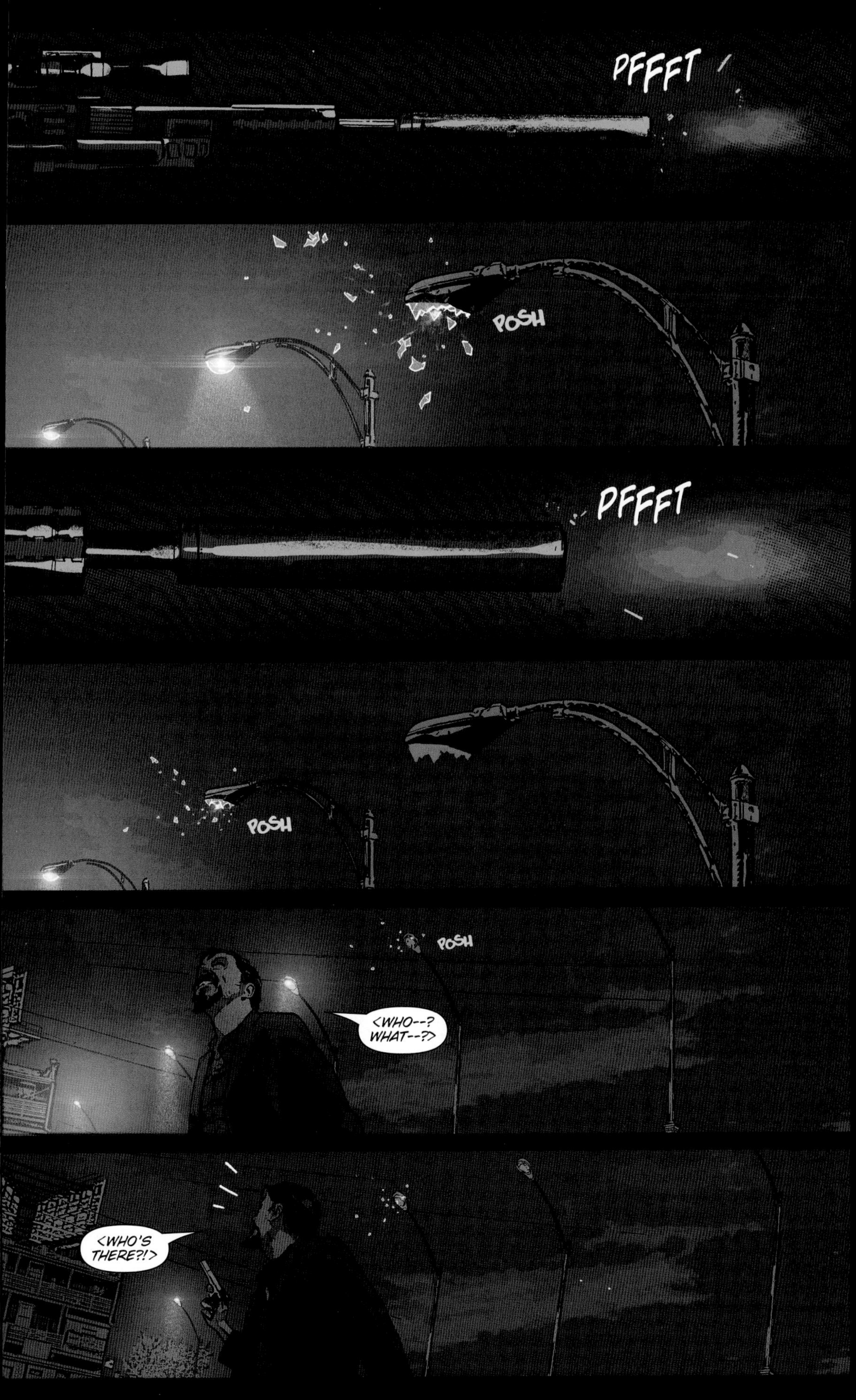
PFFFT
POSH
PFFFT
POSH
POSH
<WHO--? WHAT--?>
<WHO'S THERE?!>

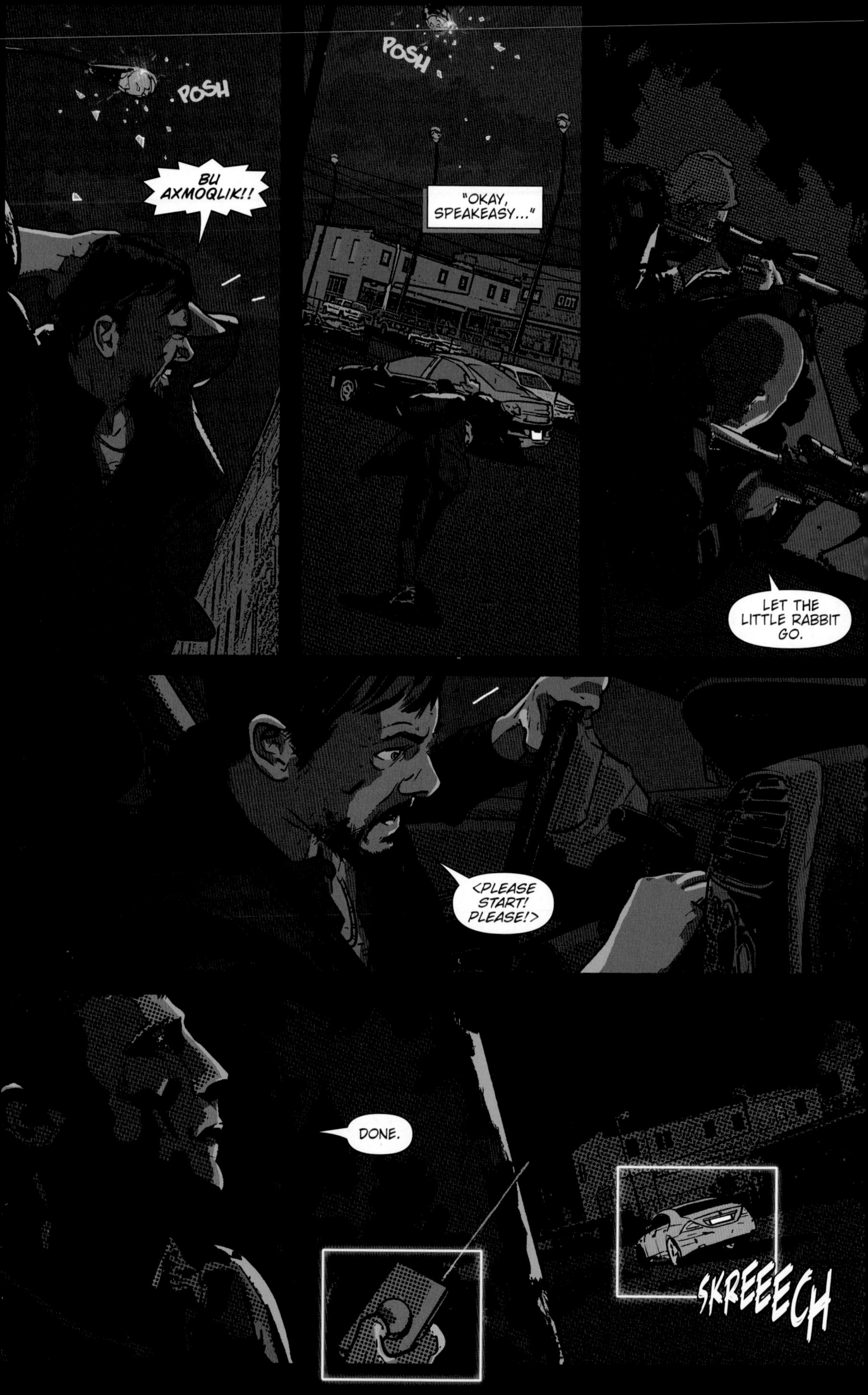
POSH
BU AXMOQLIK!!
POSH
"OKAY, SPEAKEASY..."
LET THE LITTLE RABBIT GO.
<PLEASE START! PLEASE!>
DONE.
SKREEECH

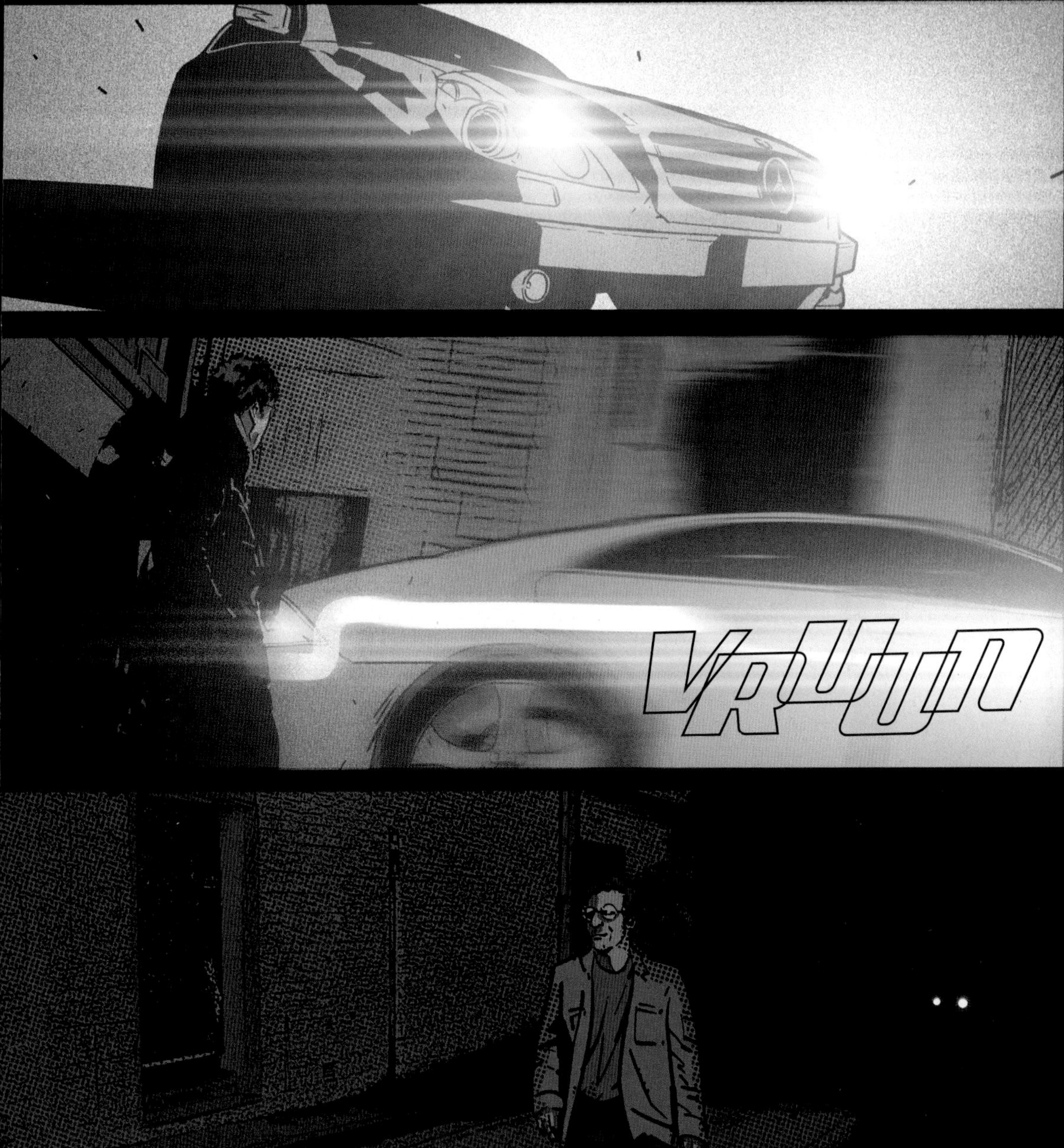
VRUUUN

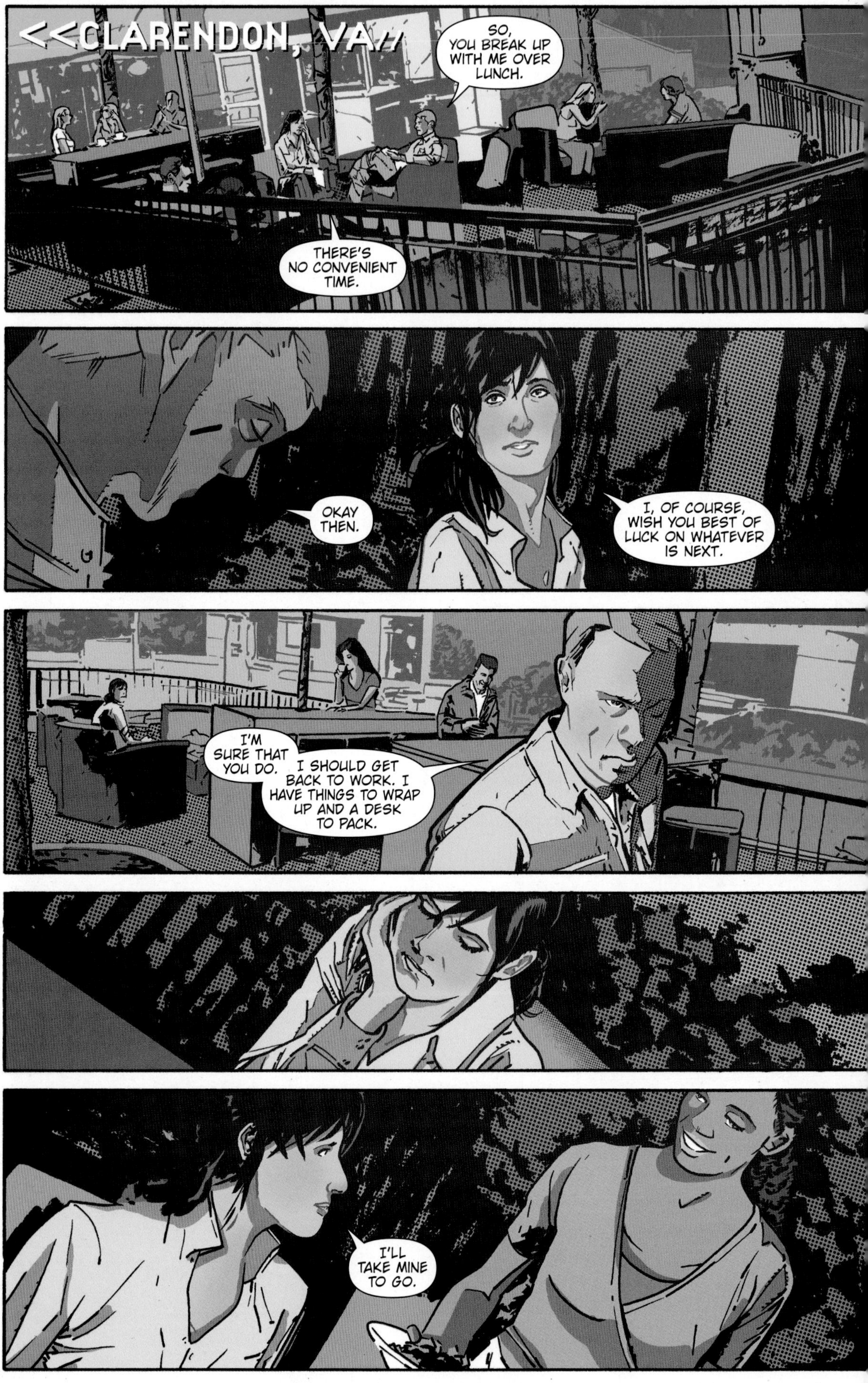

<<CLARENDON, VA//
SO, YOU BREAK UP WITH ME OVER LUNCH.
THERE'S NO CONVENIENT TIME.
OKAY THEN.
I, OF COURSE, WISH YOU BEST OF LUCK ON WHATEVER IS NEXT.
I'M SURE THAT YOU DO.
I SHOULD GET BACK TO WORK. I HAVE THINGS TO WRAP UP AND A DESK TO PACK.
I'LL TAKE MINE TO GO.

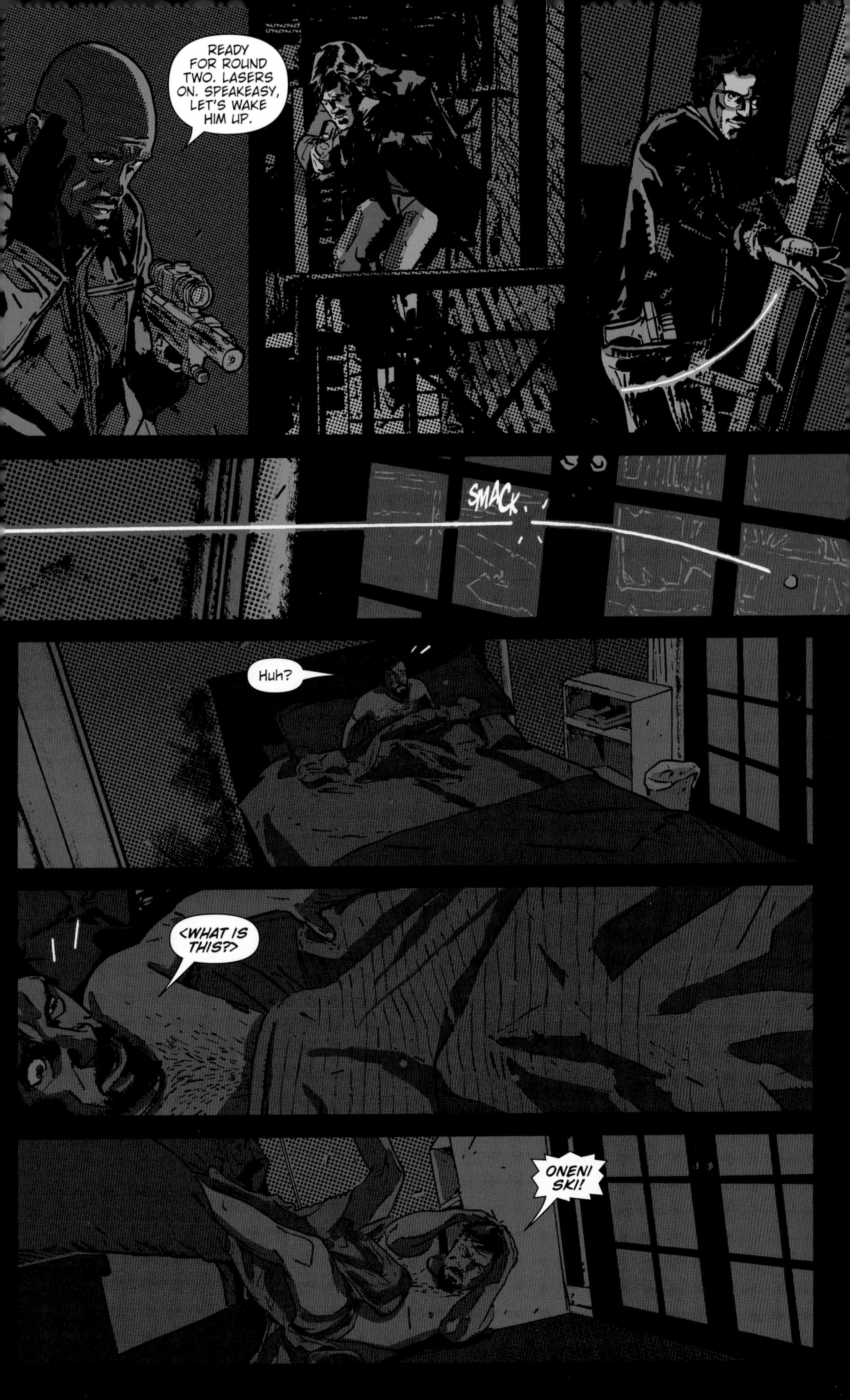
READY FOR ROUND TWO. LASERS ON. SPEAKEASY, LET'S WAKE HIM UP.
SMACK
Huh?
<WHAT IS THIS?>
ONENI SKI!

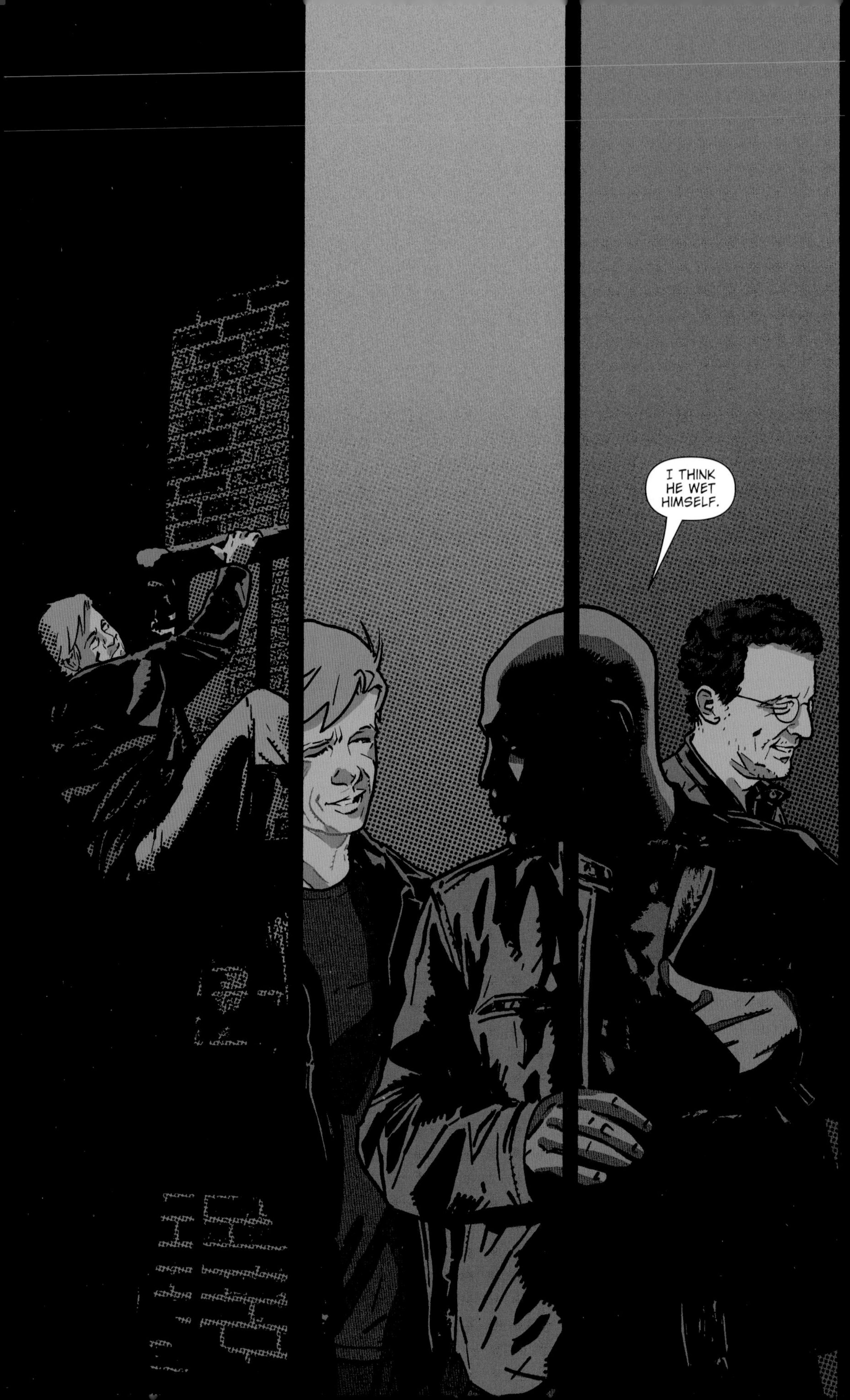
I THINK HE WET HIMSELF.

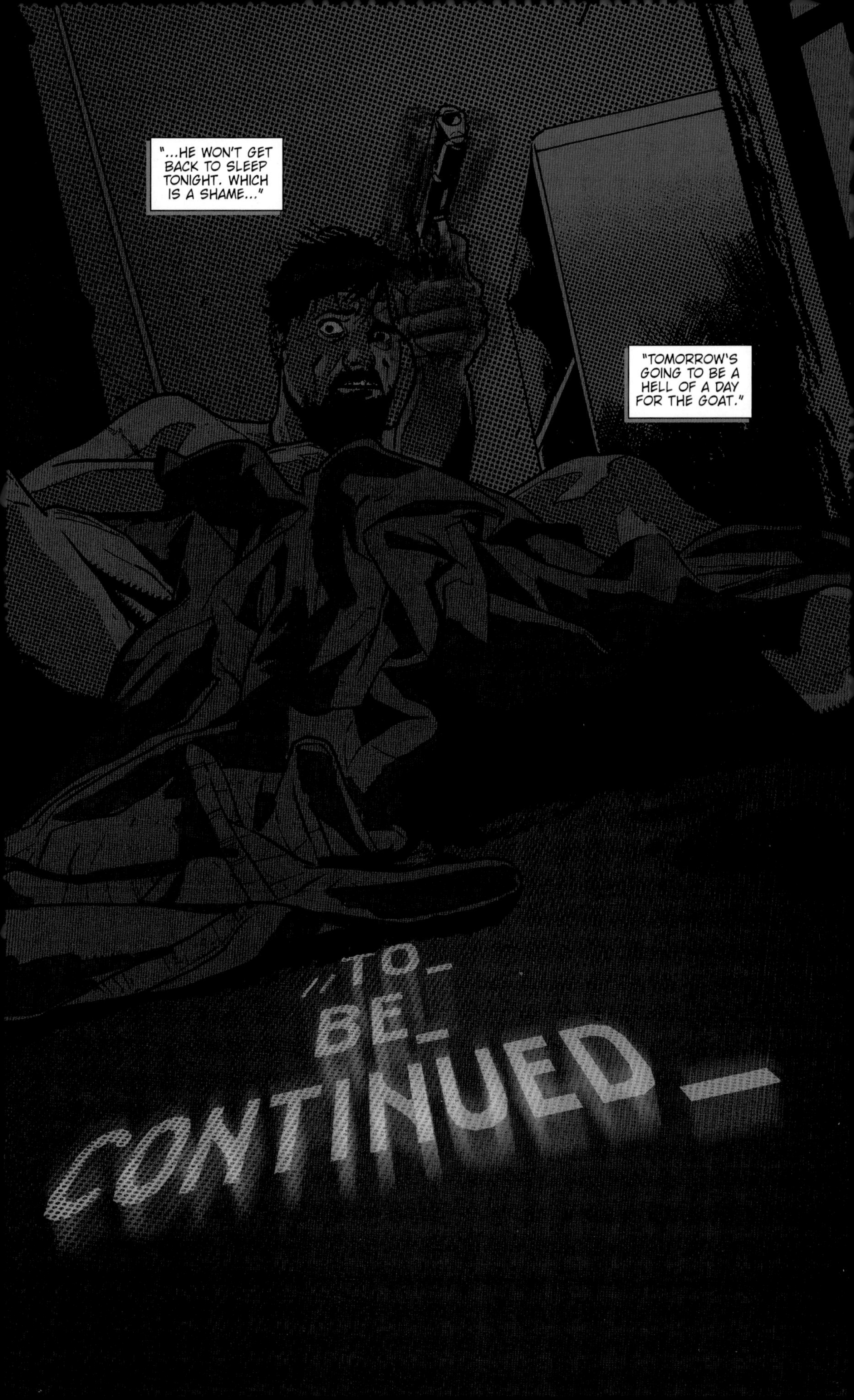
"...HE WON'T GET BACK TO SLEEP TONIGHT. WHICH IS A SHAME..."
"TOMORROW'S GOING TO BE A HELL OF A DAY FOR THE GOAT."
--TO--
BE--
CONTINUED--

UNCLASSIFIED

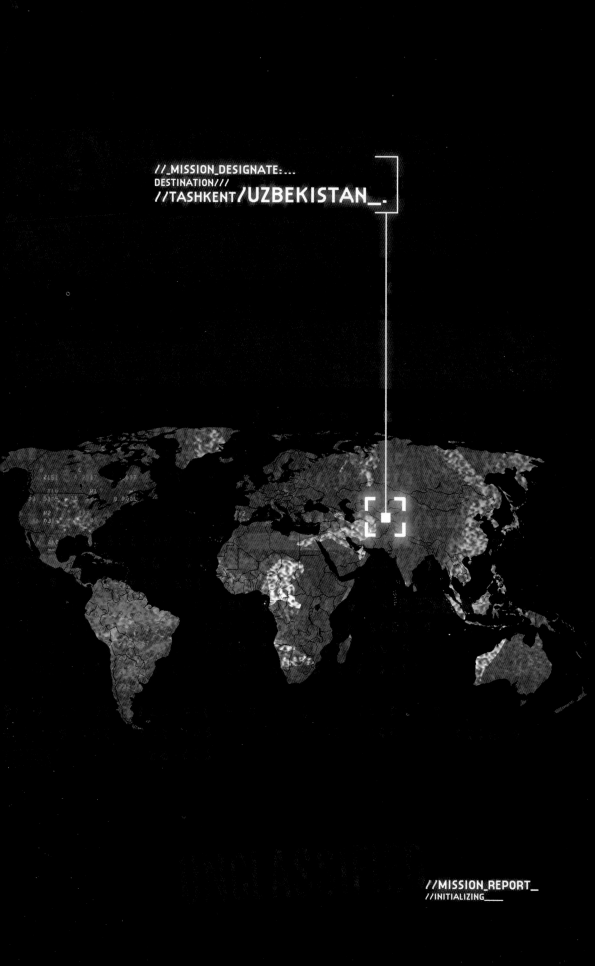

//_MISSION_DESIGNATE:...
DESTINATION///
//TASHKENT/UZBEKISTAN_.

//MISSION_REPORT_
//INITIALIZING____

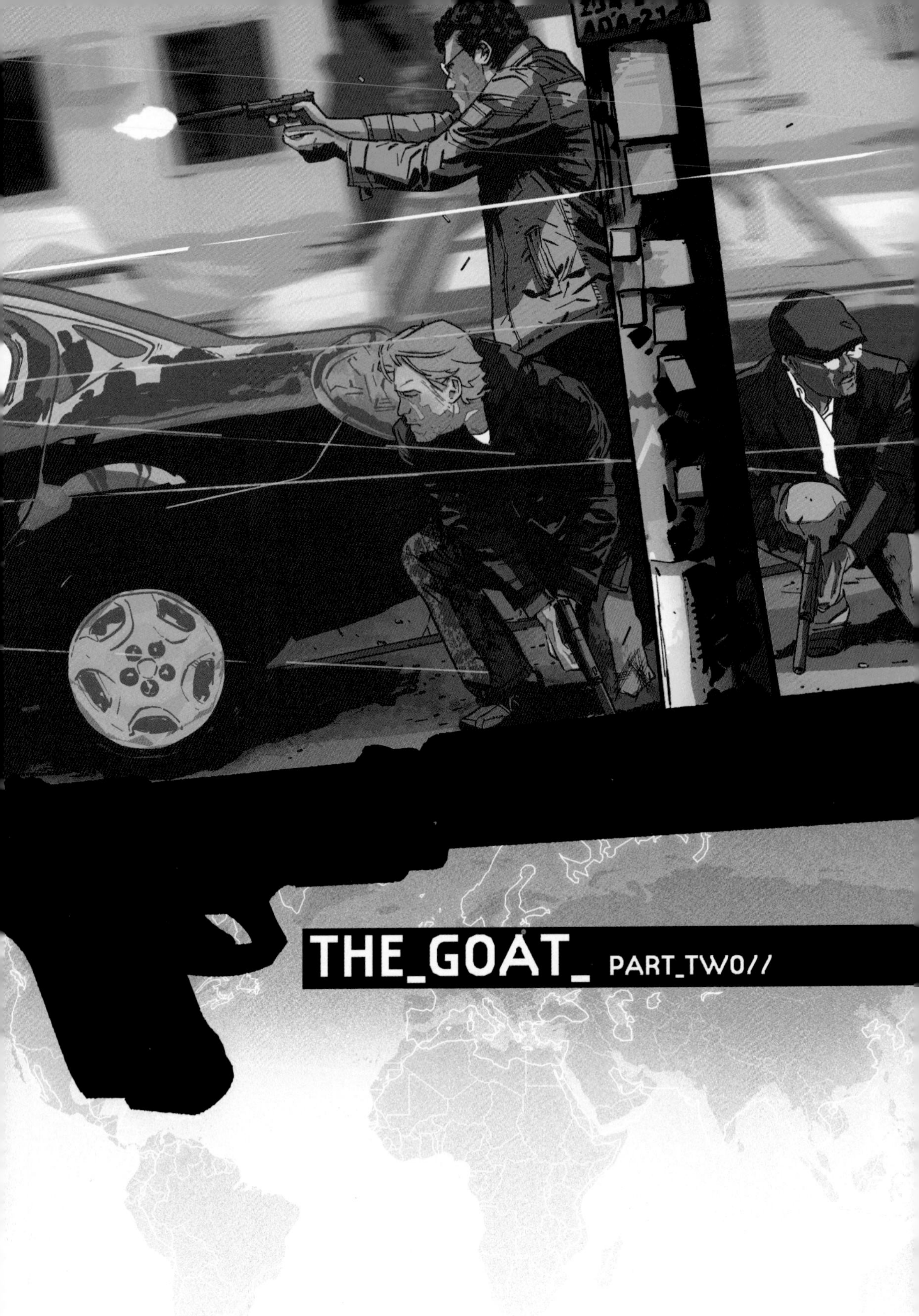

THE_GOAT_ PART_TWO//

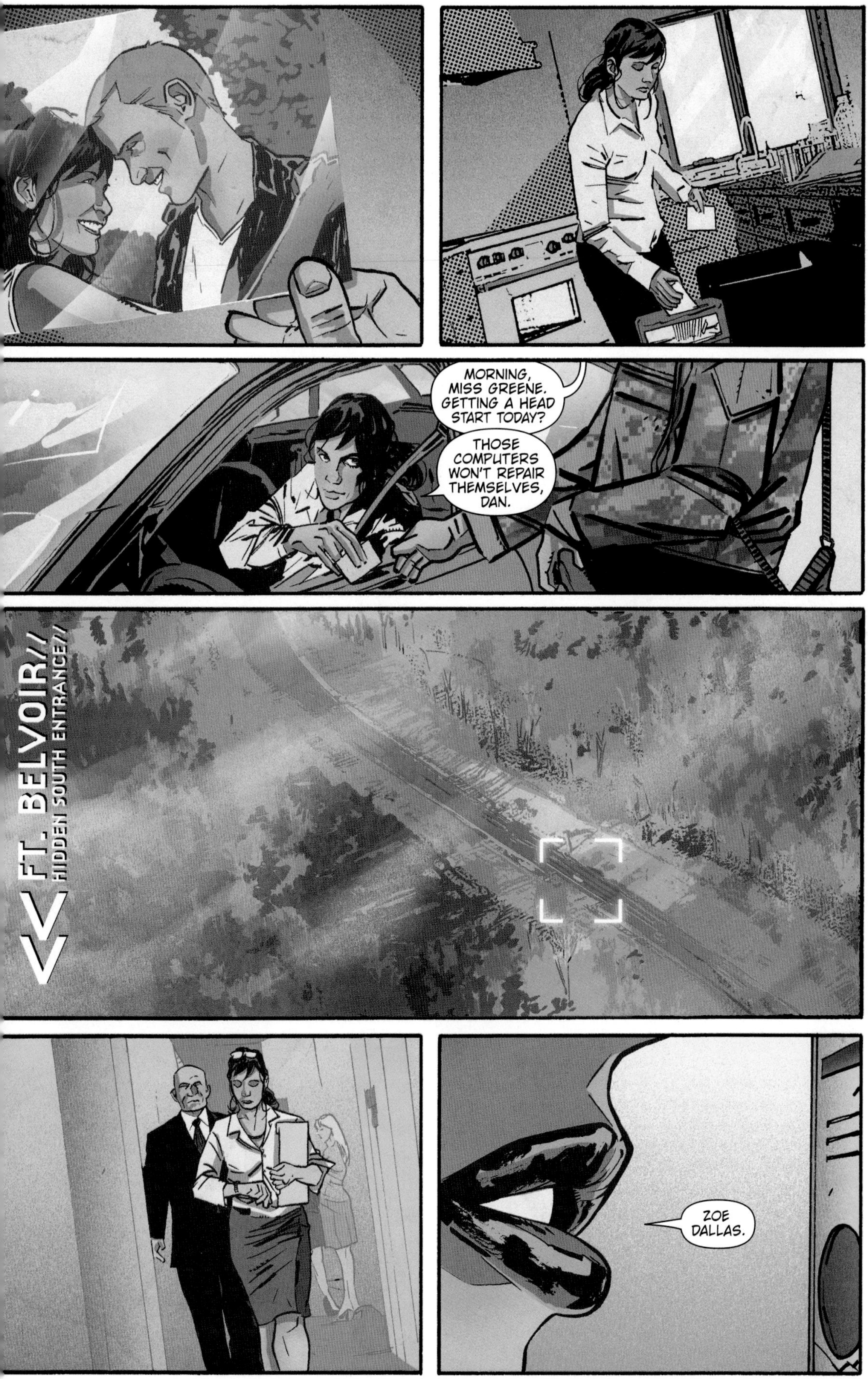
MORNING, MISS GREENE. GETTING A HEAD START TODAY?
THOSE COMPUTERS WON'T REPAIR THEMSELVES, DAN.
FT. BELVOIR//
HIDDEN SOUTH ENTRANCE//
ZOE DALLAS.

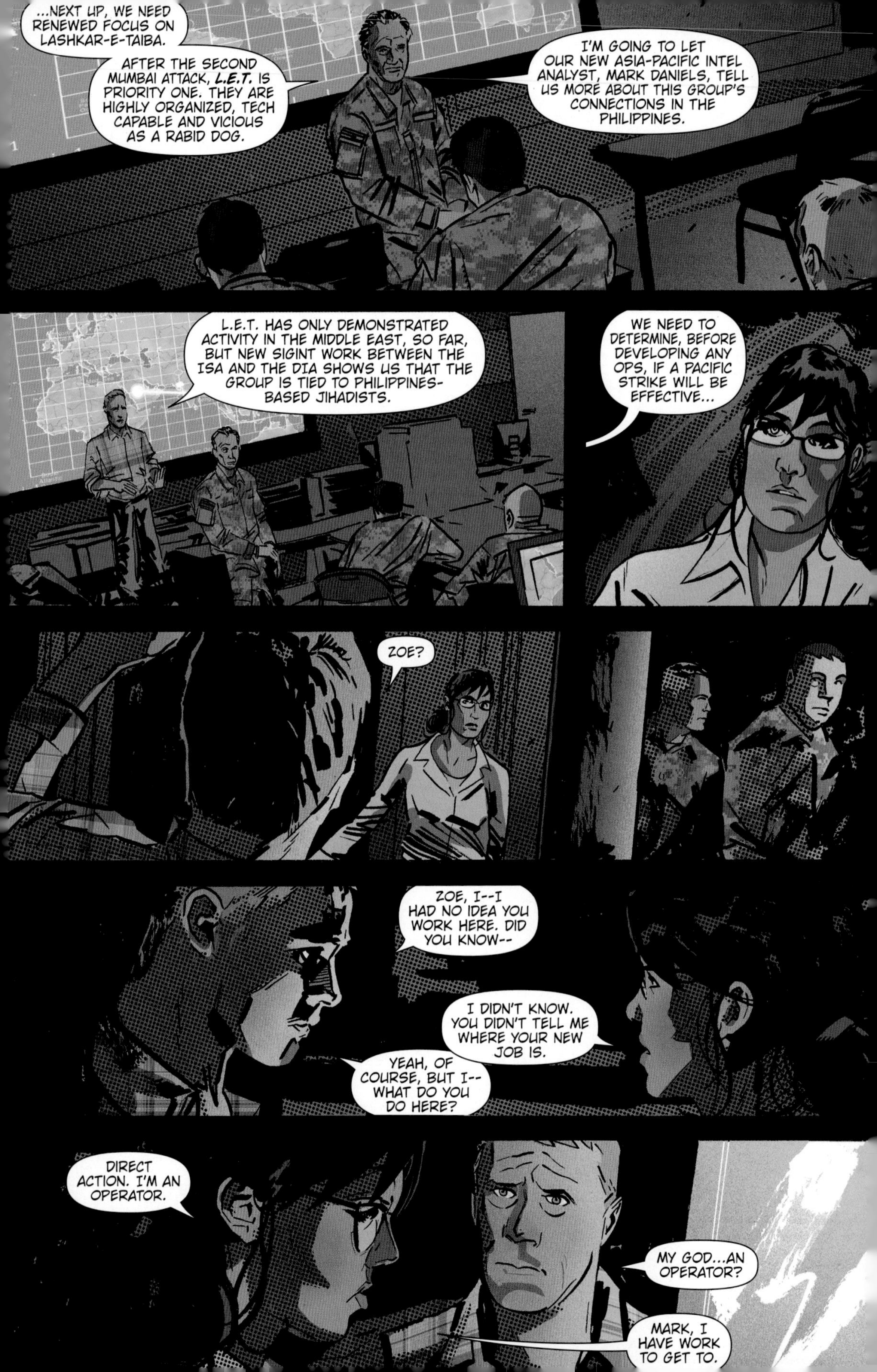
...NEXT UP, WE NEED RENEWED FOCUS ON LASHKAR-E-TAIBA.
AFTER THE SECOND MUMBAI ATTACK, L.E.T. IS PRIORITY ONE. THEY ARE HIGHLY ORGANIZED, TECH CAPABLE AND VICIOUS AS A RABID DOG.
I'M GOING TO LET OUR NEW ASIA-PACIFIC INTEL ANALYST, MARK DANIELS, TELL US MORE ABOUT THIS GROUP'S CONNECTIONS IN THE PHILIPPINES.
L.E.T. HAS ONLY DEMONSTRATED ACTIVITY IN THE MIDDLE EAST, SO FAR, BUT NEW SIGINT WORK BETWEEN THE ISA AND THE DIA SHOWS US THAT THE GROUP IS TIED TO PHILIPPINES-BASED JIHADISTS.
WE NEED TO DETERMINE, BEFORE DEVELOPING ANY OPS, IF A PACIFIC STRIKE WILL BE EFFECTIVE...
ZOE?
ZOE, I--I HAD NO IDEA YOU WORK HERE. DID YOU KNOW--
I DIDN'T KNOW. YOU DIDN'T TELL ME WHERE YOUR NEW JOB IS.
YEAH, OF COURSE, BUT I-- WHAT DO YOU DO HERE?
DIRECT ACTION. I'M AN OPERATOR.
MY GOD...AN OPERATOR?
MARK, I HAVE WORK TO GET TO.

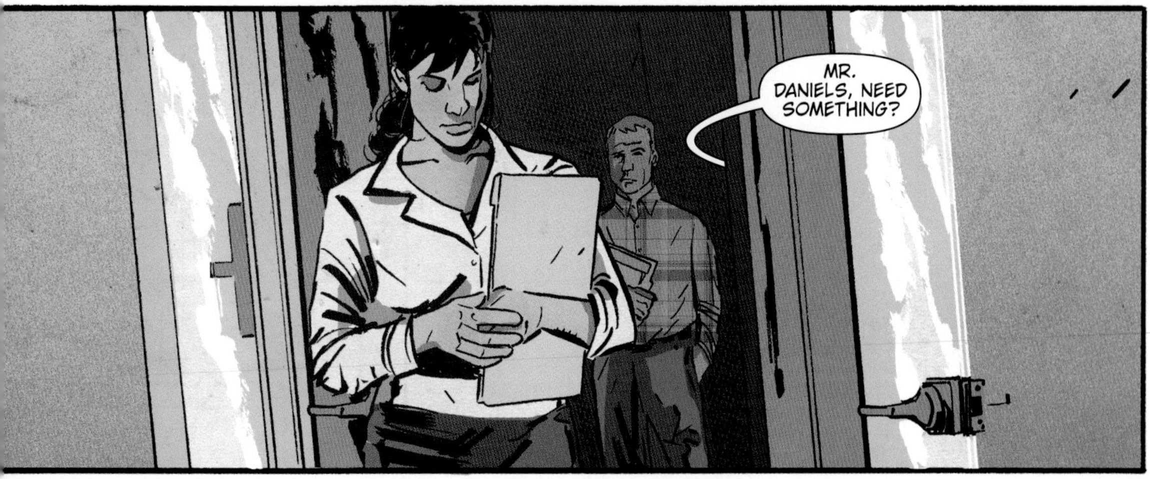
MR. DANIELS, NEED SOMETHING?

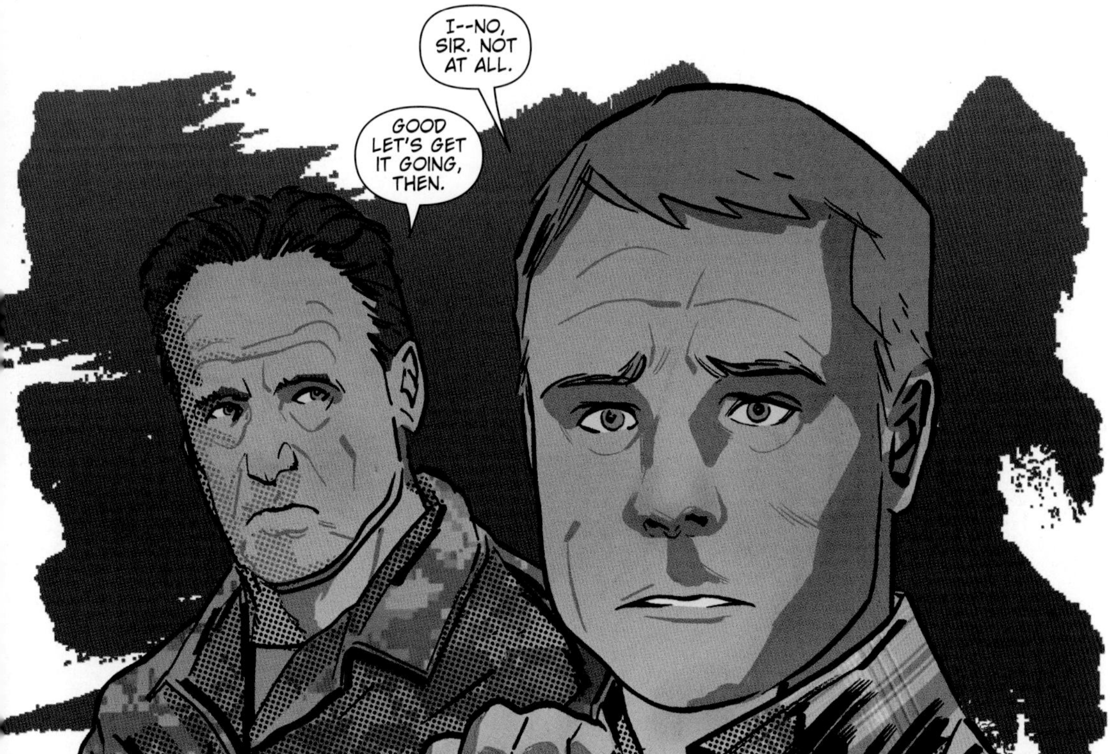
I--NO, SIR. NOT AT ALL.
GOOD LET'S GET IT GOING, THEN.

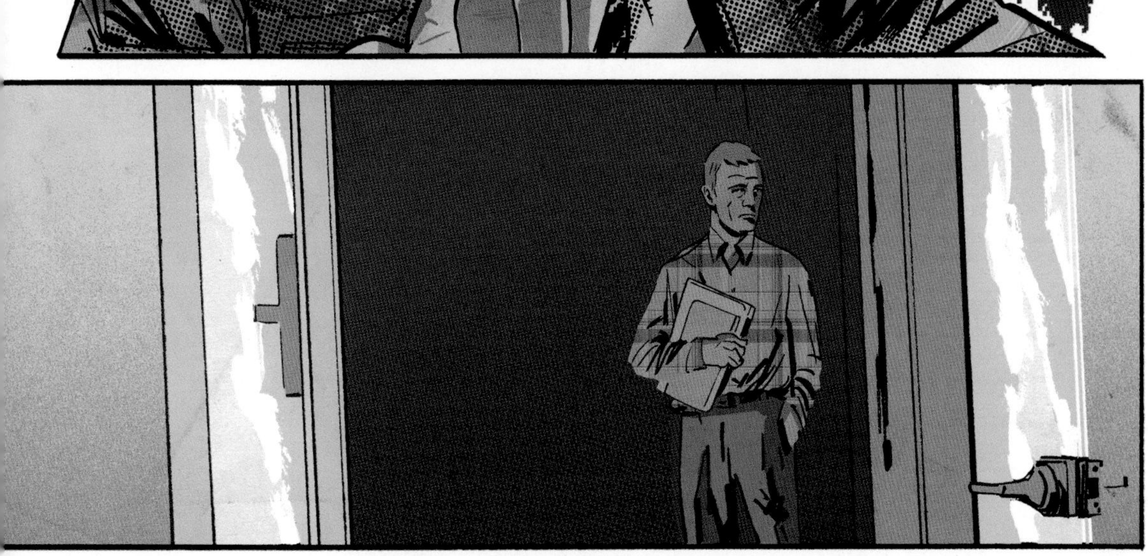

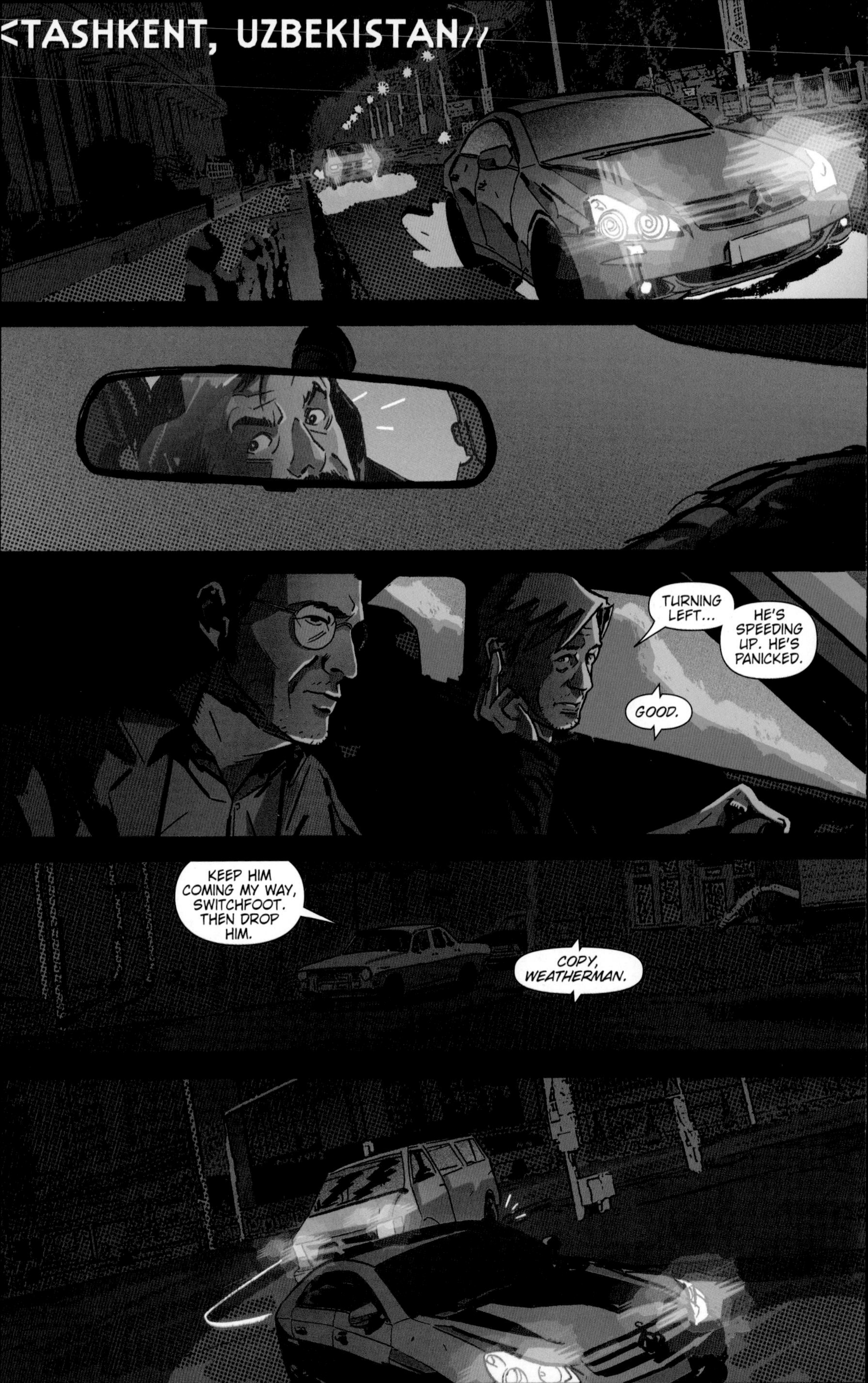
<TASHKENT, UZBEKISTAN//
TURNING LEFT...
HE'S SPEEDING UP. HE'S PANICKED.
GOOD.
KEEP HIM COMING MY WAY, SWITCHFOOT. THEN DROP HIM.
COPY, WEATHERMAN.

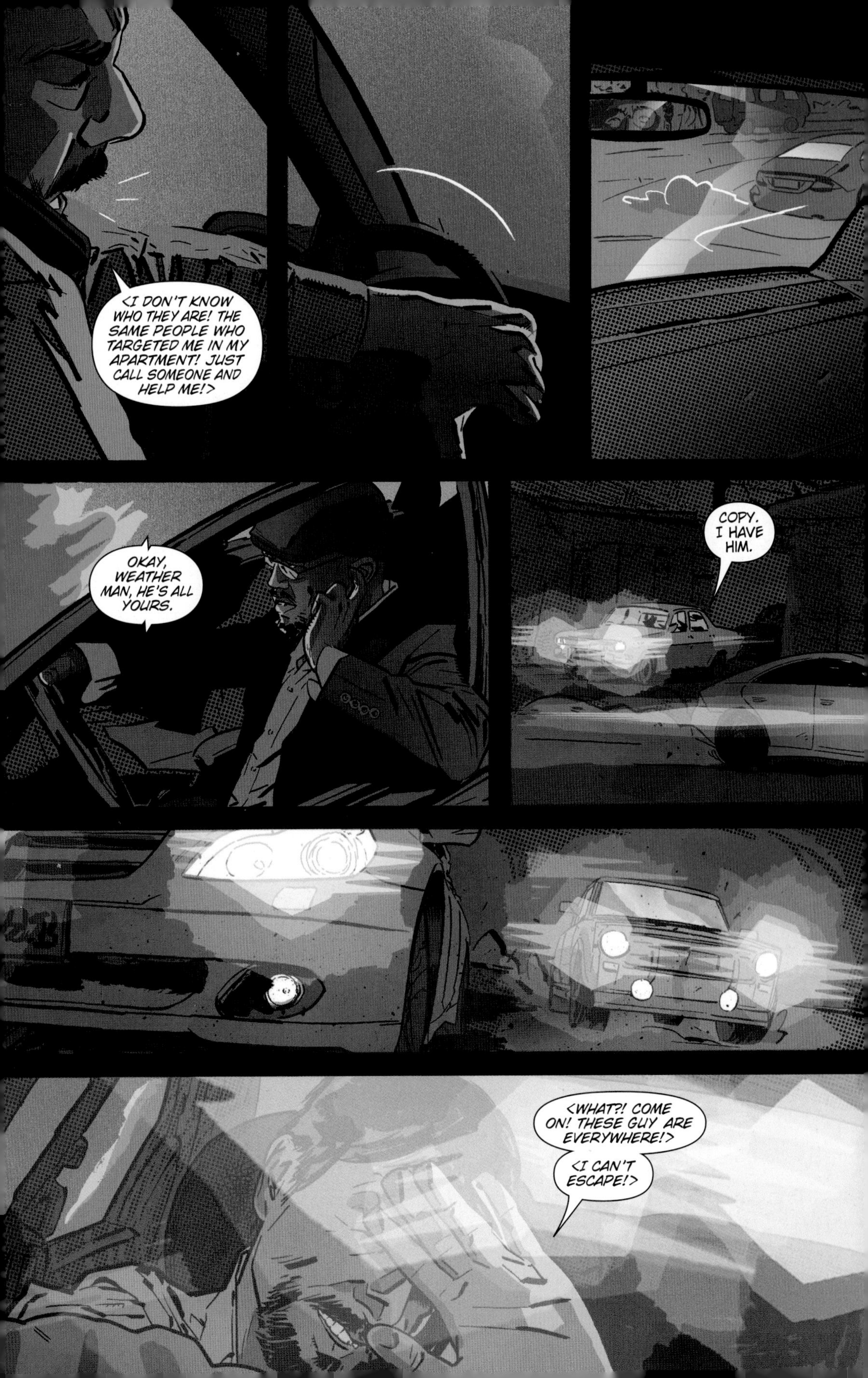
<I DON'T KNOW WHO THEY ARE! THE SAME PEOPLE WHO TARGETED ME IN MY APARTMENT! JUST CALL SOMEONE AND HELP ME!>
OKAY, WEATHER MAN, HE'S ALL YOURS.
COPY. I HAVE HIM.
<WHAT?! COME ON! THESE GUY ARE EVERYWHERE!>
<I CAN'T ESCAPE!>

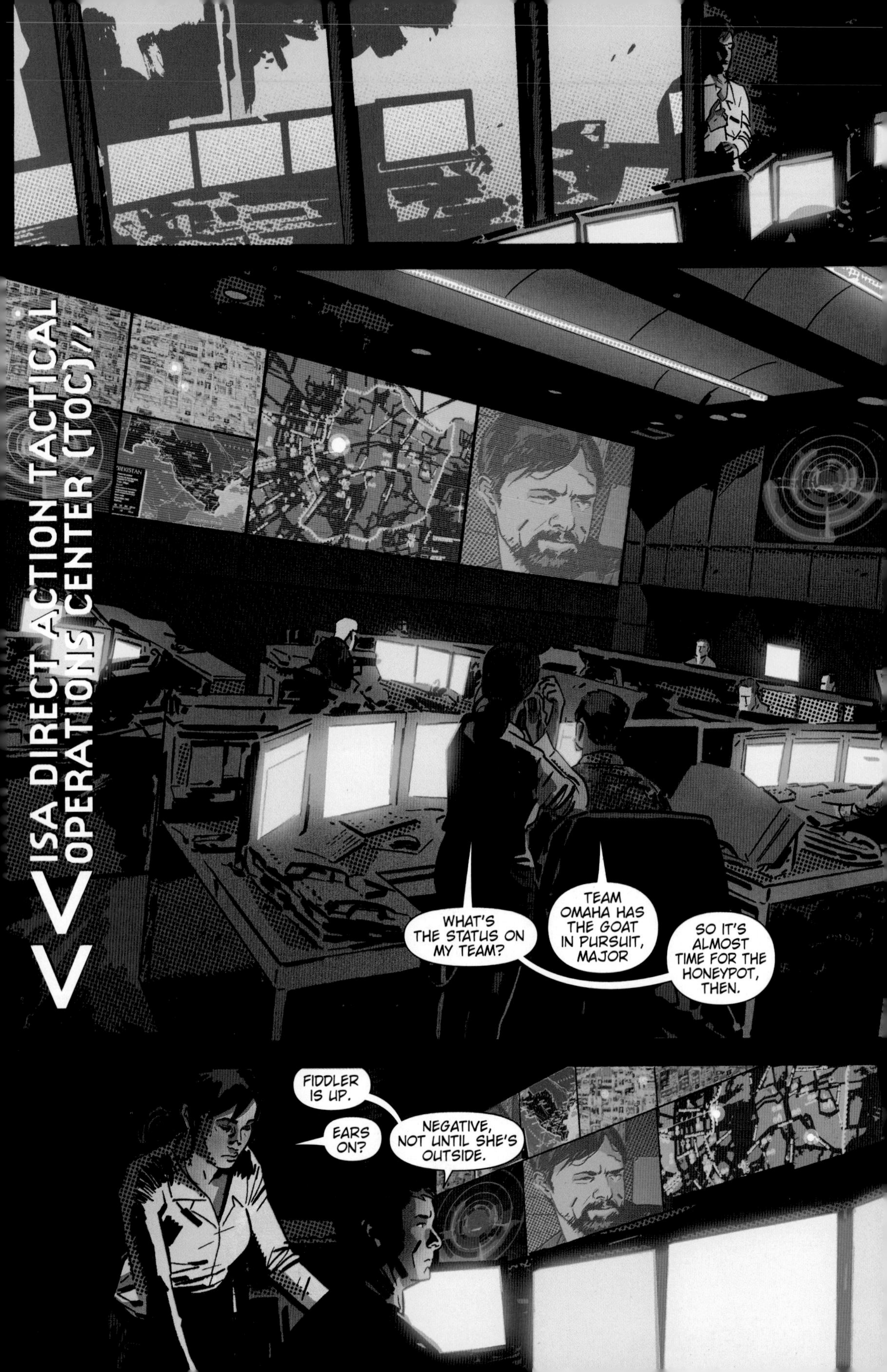
ISA DIRECT ACTION TACTICAL OPERATIONS CENTER (TOC)//
WHAT'S THE STATUS ON MY TEAM?
TEAM OMAHA HAS THE GOAT IN PURSUIT, MAJOR
SO IT'S ALMOST TIME FOR THE HONEYPOT, THEN.
FIDDLER IS UP.
EARS ON?
NEGATIVE, NOT UNTIL SHE'S OUTSIDE.

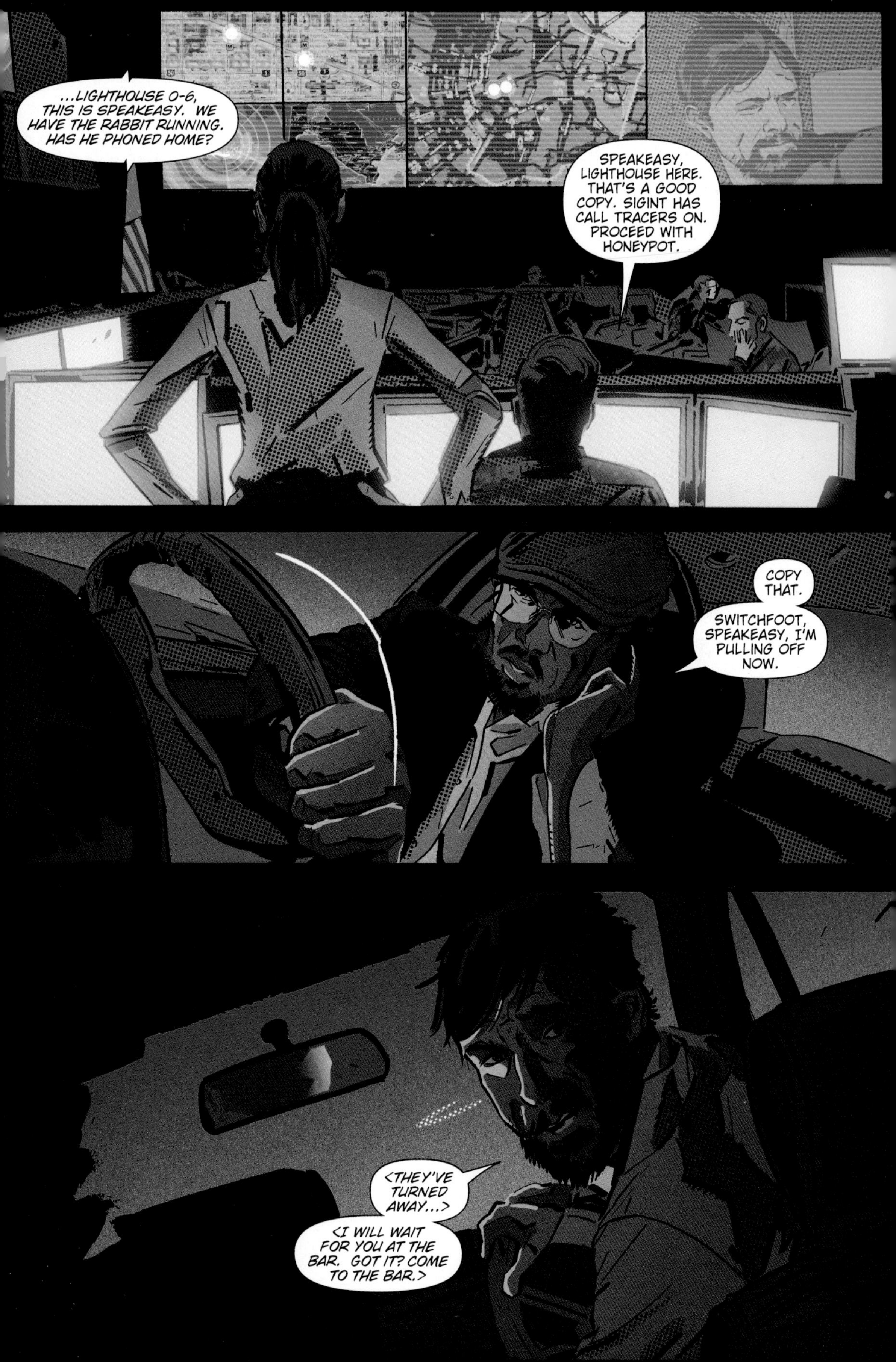
...LIGHTHOUSE 0-6, THIS IS SPEAKEASY. WE HAVE THE RABBIT RUNNING. HAS HE PHONED HOME?
SPEAKEASY, LIGHTHOUSE HERE. THAT'S A GOOD COPY. SIGINT HAS CALL TRACERS ON. PROCEED WITH HONEYPOT.
COPY THAT.
SWITCHFOOT, SPEAKEASY, I'M PULLING OFF NOW.
<THEY'VE TURNED AWAY...>
<I WILL WAIT FOR YOU AT THE BAR. GOT IT? COME TO THE BAR.>

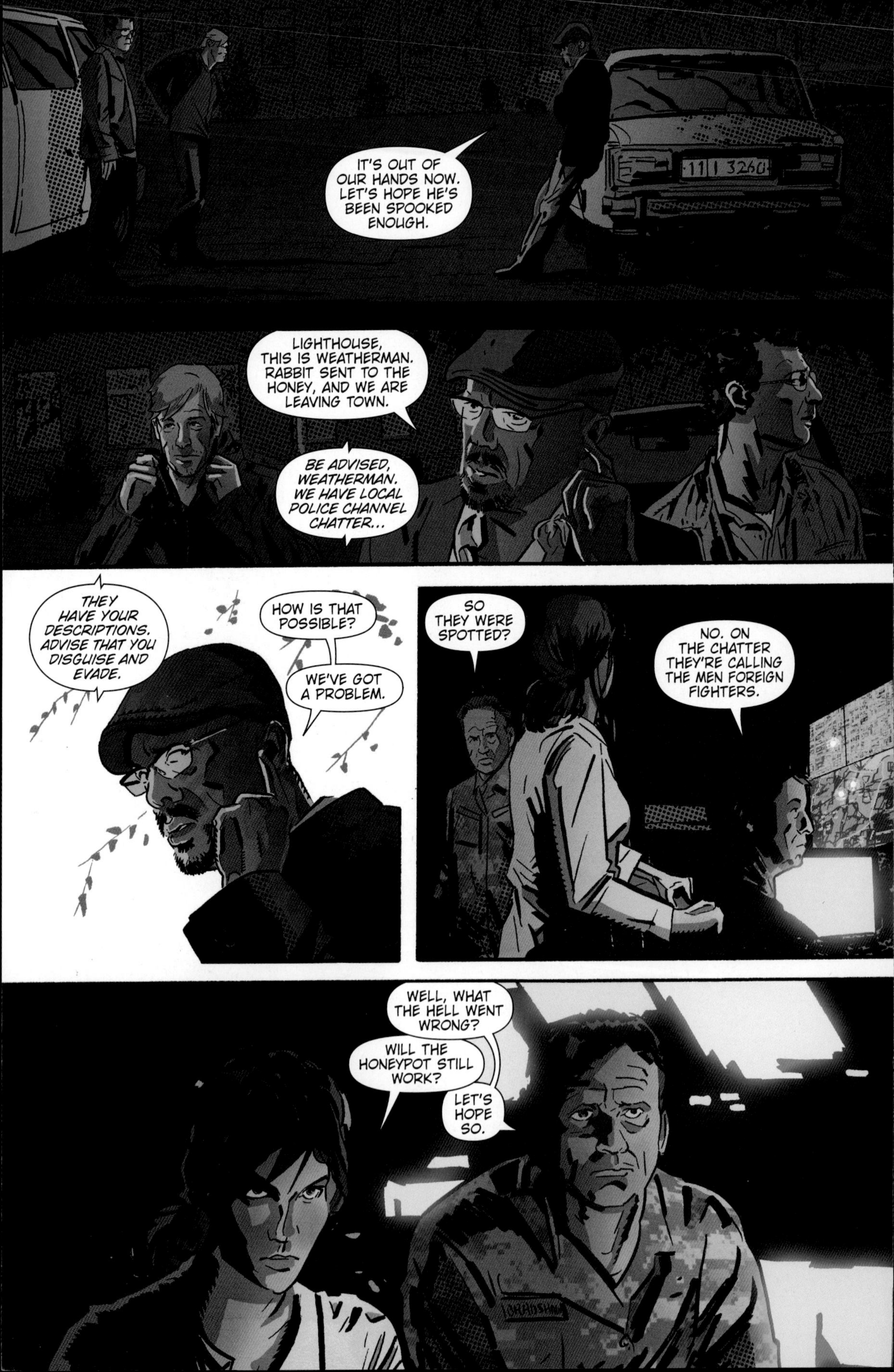
IT'S OUT OF OUR HANDS NOW. LET'S HOPE HE'S BEEN SPOOKED ENOUGH.
11 I 3260
LIGHTHOUSE, THIS IS WEATHERMAN. RABBIT SENT TO THE HONEY, AND WE ARE LEAVING TOWN.
BE ADVISED, WEATHERMAN. WE HAVE LOCAL POLICE CHANNEL CHATTER...
THEY HAVE YOUR DESCRIPTIONS. ADVISE THAT YOU DISGUISE AND EVADE.
HOW IS THAT POSSIBLE?
WE'VE GOT A PROBLEM.
SO THEY WERE SPOTTED?
NO. ON THE CHATTER THEY'RE CALLING THE MEN FOREIGN FIGHTERS.
WELL, WHAT THE HELL WENT WRONG?
WILL THE HONEYPOT STILL WORK?
LET'S HOPE SO.

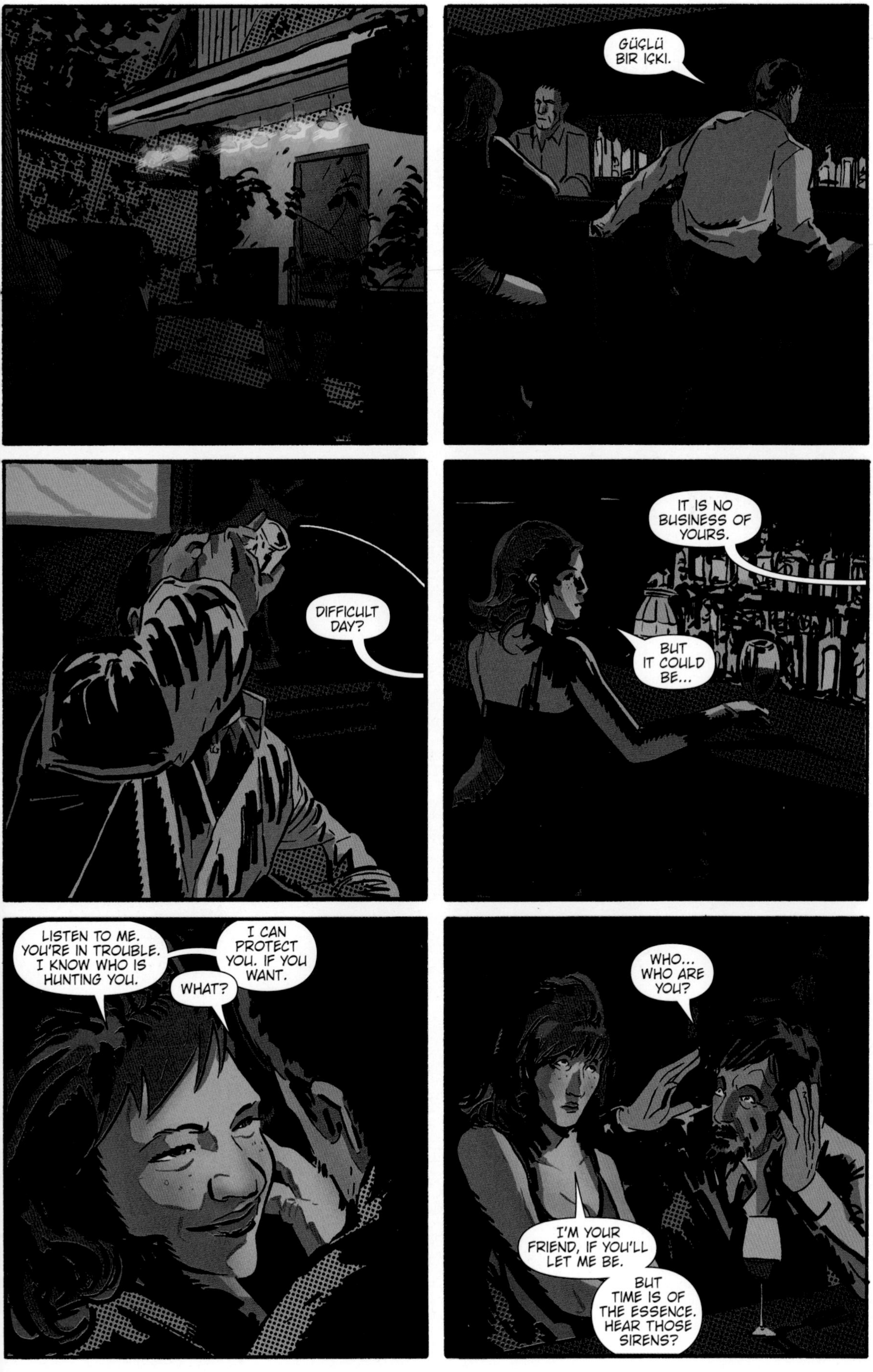
GÜÇLÜ BIR IÇKI.
DIFFICULT DAY?
IT IS NO BUSINESS OF YOURS.
BUT IT COULD BE...
LISTEN TO ME. YOU'RE IN TROUBLE. I KNOW WHO IS HUNTING YOU.
I CAN PROTECT YOU. IF YOU WANT.
WHAT?
WHO... WHO ARE YOU?
I'M YOUR FRIEND, IF YOU'LL LET ME BE.
BUT TIME IS OF THE ESSENCE. HEAR THOSE SIRENS?

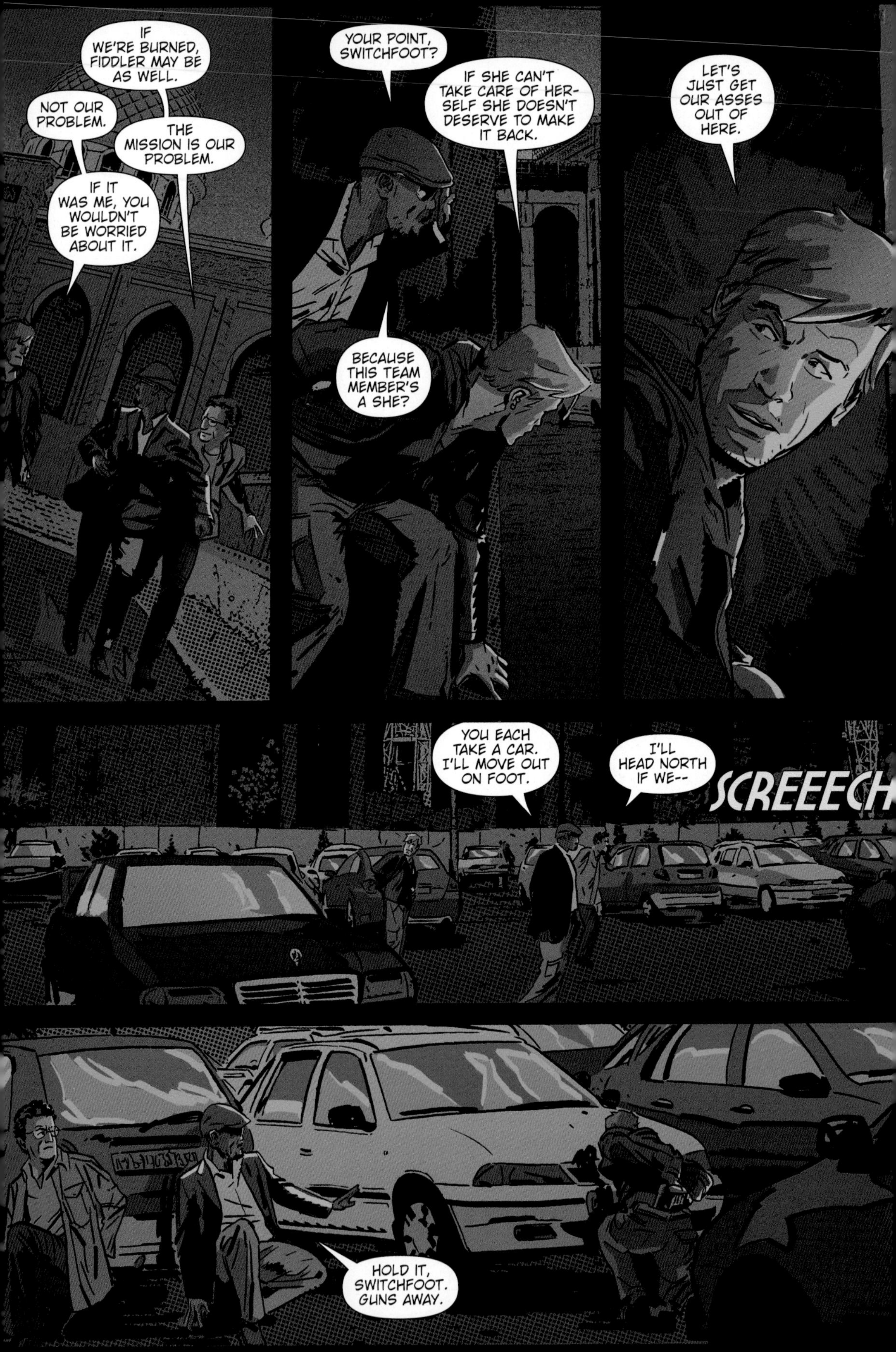
IF WE'RE BURNED, FIDDLER MAY BE AS WELL.
NOT OUR PROBLEM.
THE MISSION IS OUR PROBLEM.
IF IT WAS ME, YOU WOULDN'T BE WORRIED ABOUT IT.
YOUR POINT, SWITCHFOOT?
IF SHE CAN'T TAKE CARE OF HER-SELF SHE DOESN'T DESERVE TO MAKE IT BACK.
BECAUSE THIS TEAM MEMBER'S A SHE?
LET'S JUST GET OUR ASSES OUT OF HERE.
YOU EACH TAKE A CAR. I'LL MOVE OUT ON FOOT.
I'LL HEAD NORTH IF WE--
SCREEECH
HOLD IT, SWITCHFOOT. GUNS AWAY.

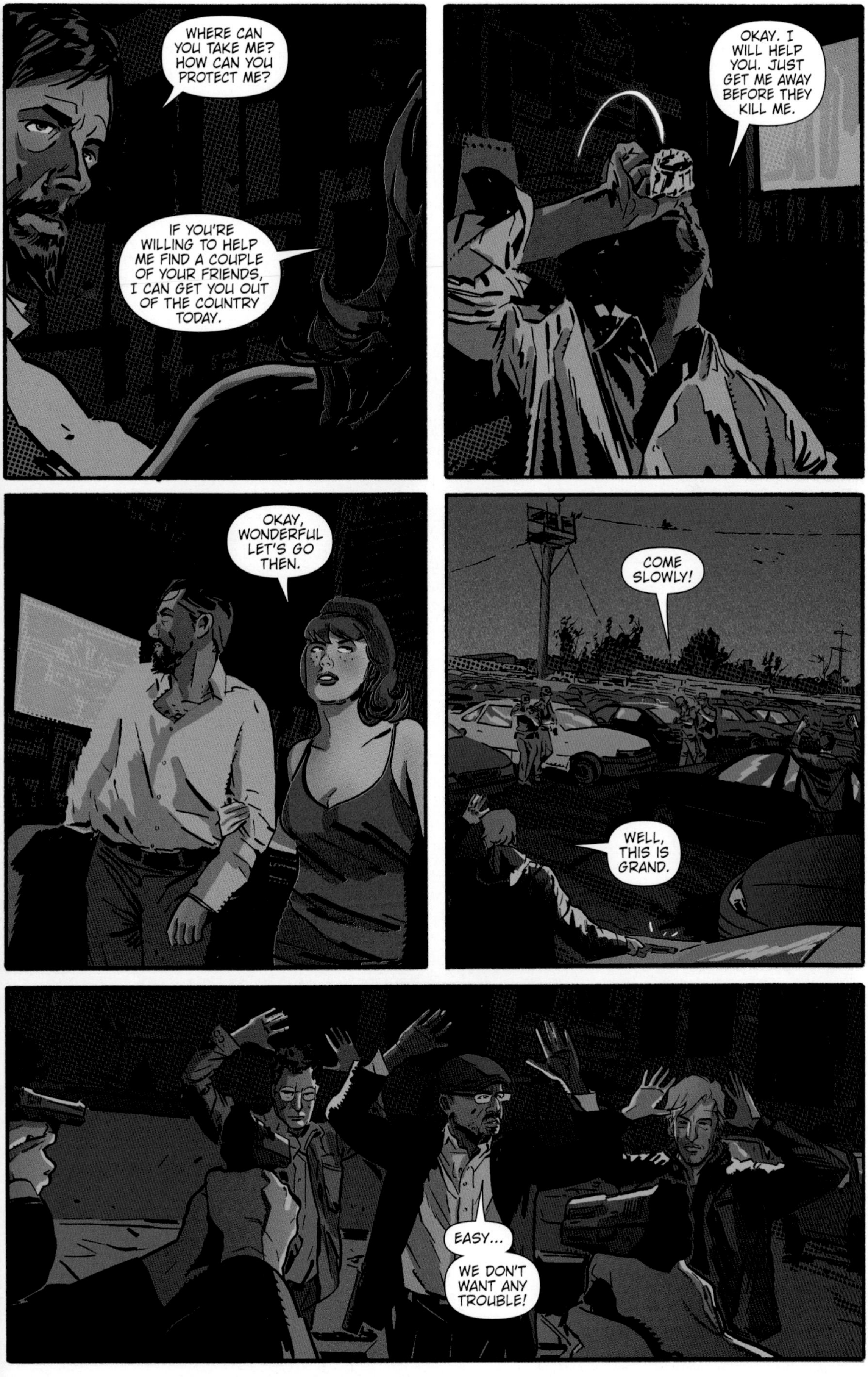
WHERE CAN YOU TAKE ME? HOW CAN YOU PROTECT ME?
IF YOU'RE WILLING TO HELP ME FIND A COUPLE OF YOUR FRIENDS, I CAN GET YOU OUT OF THE COUNTRY TODAY.
OKAY. I WILL HELP YOU. JUST GET ME AWAY BEFORE THEY KILL ME.
OKAY, WONDERFUL LET'S GO THEN.
COME SLOWLY!
WELL, THIS IS GRAND.
EASY...
WE DON'T WANT ANY TROUBLE!

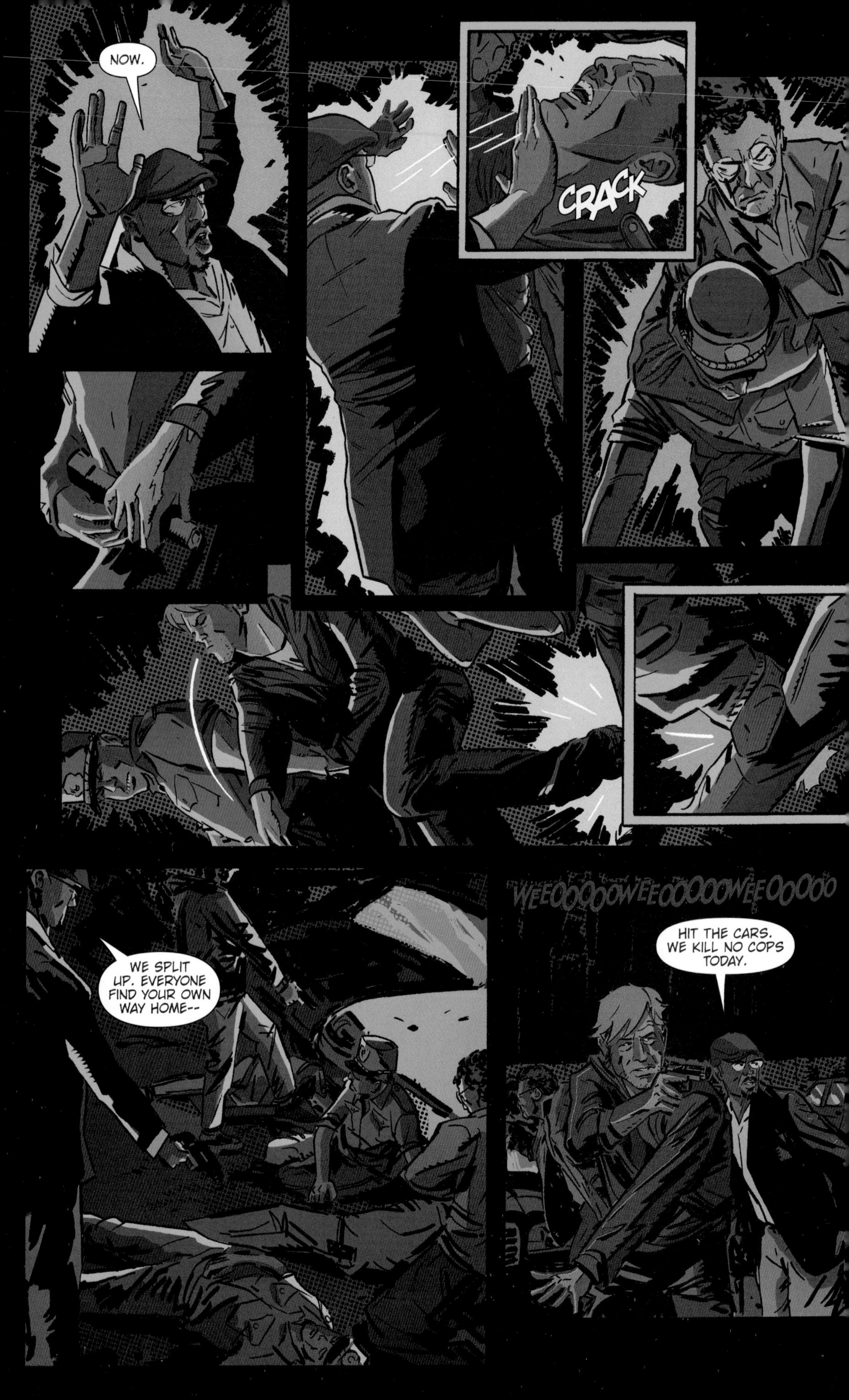
NOW.
CRACK
WE SPLIT UP. EVERYONE FIND YOUR OWN WAY HOME--
WEEOOOOOWEEOOOOOWEEOOOOO
HIT THE CARS. WE KILL NO COPS TODAY.

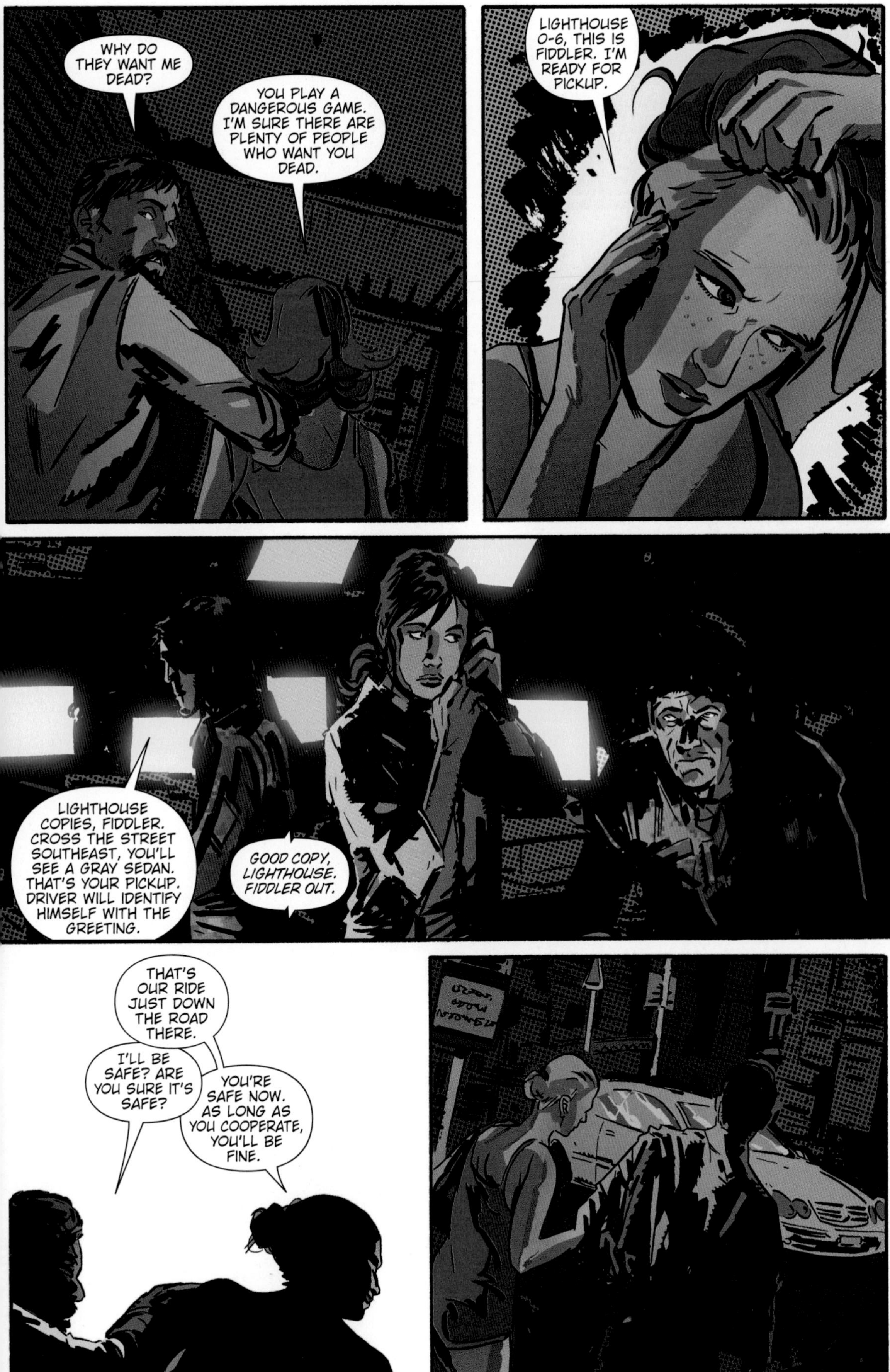
WHY DO THEY WANT ME DEAD?
YOU PLAY A DANGEROUS GAME. I'M SURE THERE ARE PLENTY OF PEOPLE WHO WANT YOU DEAD.
LIGHTHOUSE O-6, THIS IS FIDDLER. I'M READY FOR PICKUP.
LIGHTHOUSE COPIES, FIDDLER. CROSS THE STREET SOUTHEAST, YOU'LL SEE A GRAY SEDAN. THAT'S YOUR PICKUP. DRIVER WILL IDENTIFY HIMSELF WITH THE GREETING.
GOOD COPY, LIGHTHOUSE. FIDDLER OUT.
THAT'S OUR RIDE JUST DOWN THE ROAD THERE.
I'LL BE SAFE? ARE YOU SURE IT'S SAFE?
YOU'RE SAFE NOW. AS LONG AS YOU COOPERATE, YOU'LL BE FINE.

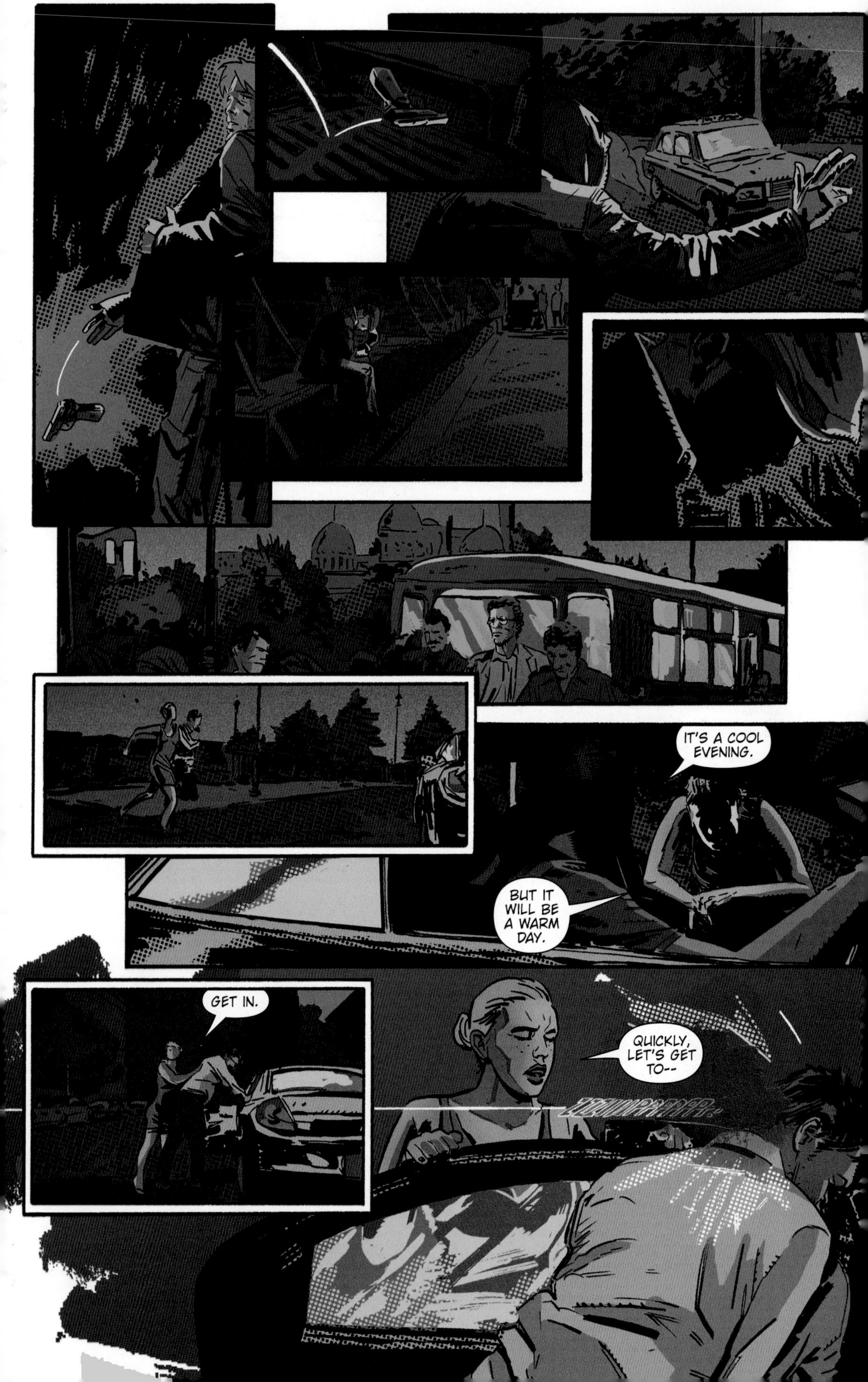

IT'S A COOL EVENING.
BUT IT WILL BE A WARM DAY.
GET IN.
QUICKLY, LET'S GET TO--

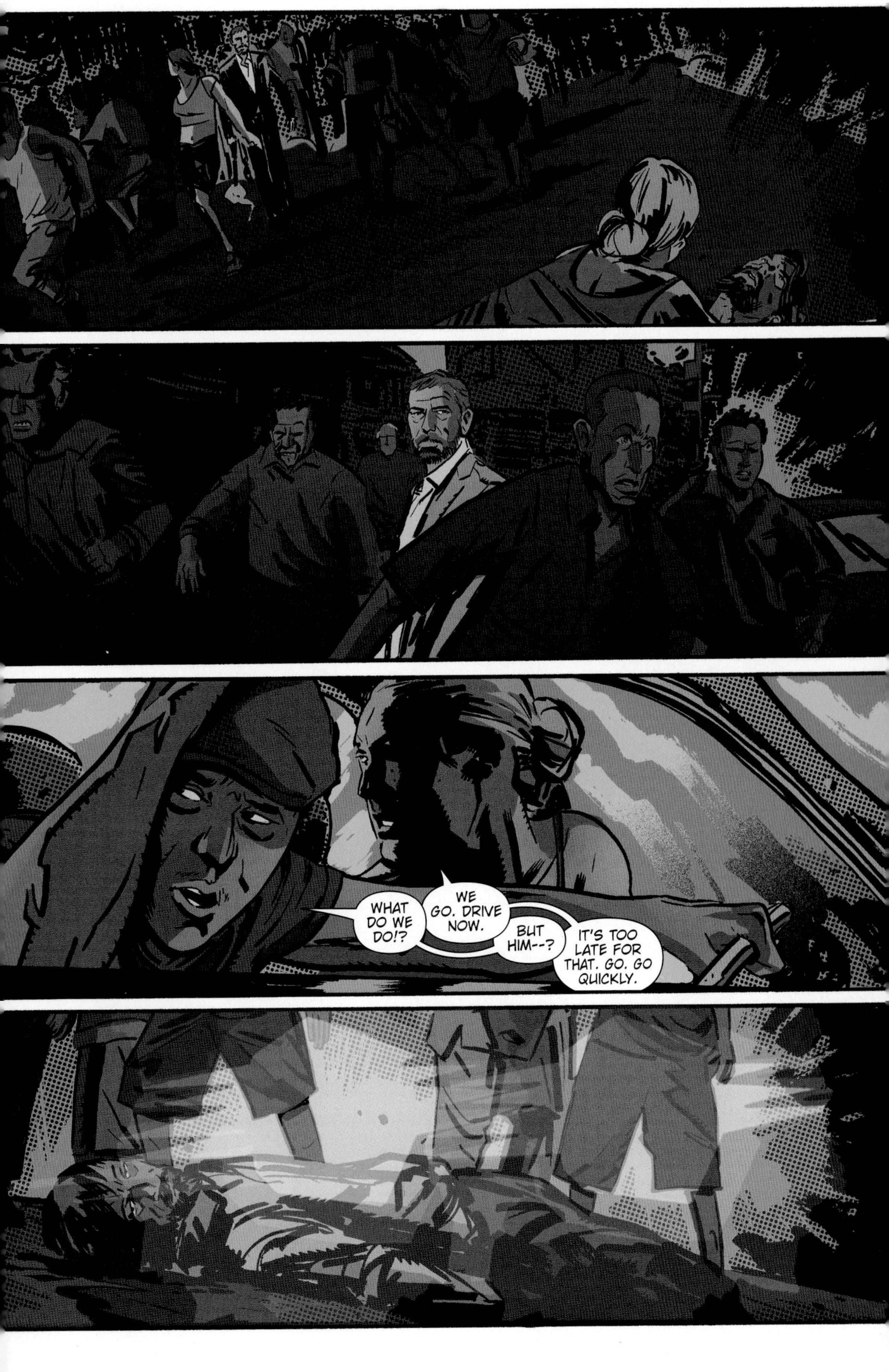
WHAT DO WE DO!?
WE GO. DRIVE NOW.
BUT HIM--?
IT'S TOO LATE FOR THAT. GO. GO QUICKLY.

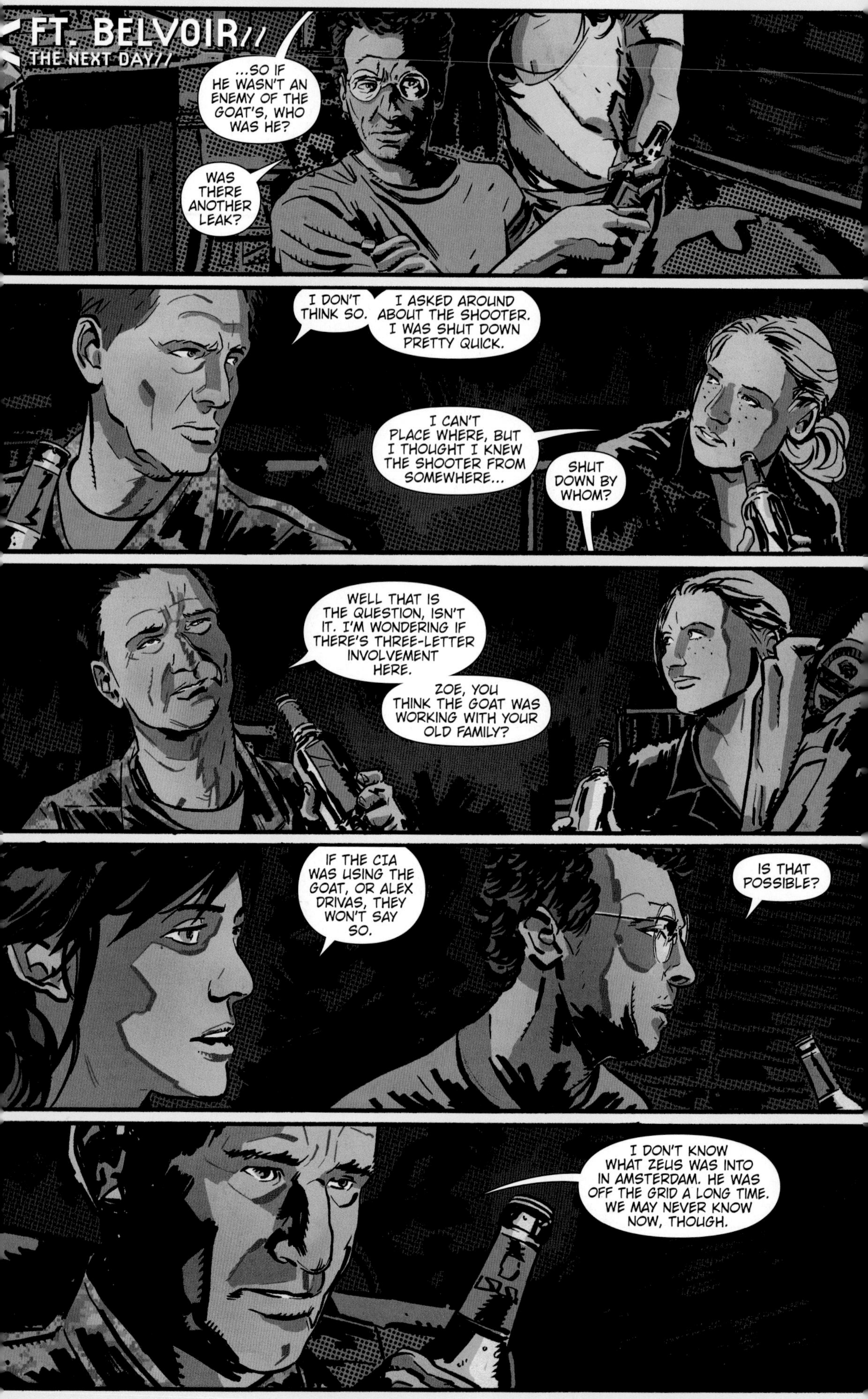
FT. BELVOIR//
THE NEXT DAY//
...SO IF HE WASN'T AN ENEMY OF THE GOAT'S, WHO WAS HE?
WAS THERE ANOTHER LEAK?
I DON'T THINK SO.
I ASKED AROUND ABOUT THE SHOOTER. I WAS SHUT DOWN PRETTY QUICK.
I CAN'T PLACE WHERE, BUT I THOUGHT I KNEW THE SHOOTER FROM SOMEWHERE...
SHUT DOWN BY WHOM?
WELL THAT IS THE QUESTION, ISN'T IT. I'M WONDERING IF THERE'S THREE-LETTER INVOLVEMENT HERE.
ZOE, YOU THINK THE GOAT WAS WORKING WITH YOUR OLD FAMILY?
IF THE CIA WAS USING THE GOAT, OR ALEX DRIVAS, THEY WON'T SAY SO.
IS THAT POSSIBLE?
I DON'T KNOW WHAT ZEUS WAS INTO IN AMSTERDAM. HE WAS OFF THE GRID A LONG TIME. WE MAY NEVER KNOW NOW, THOUGH.

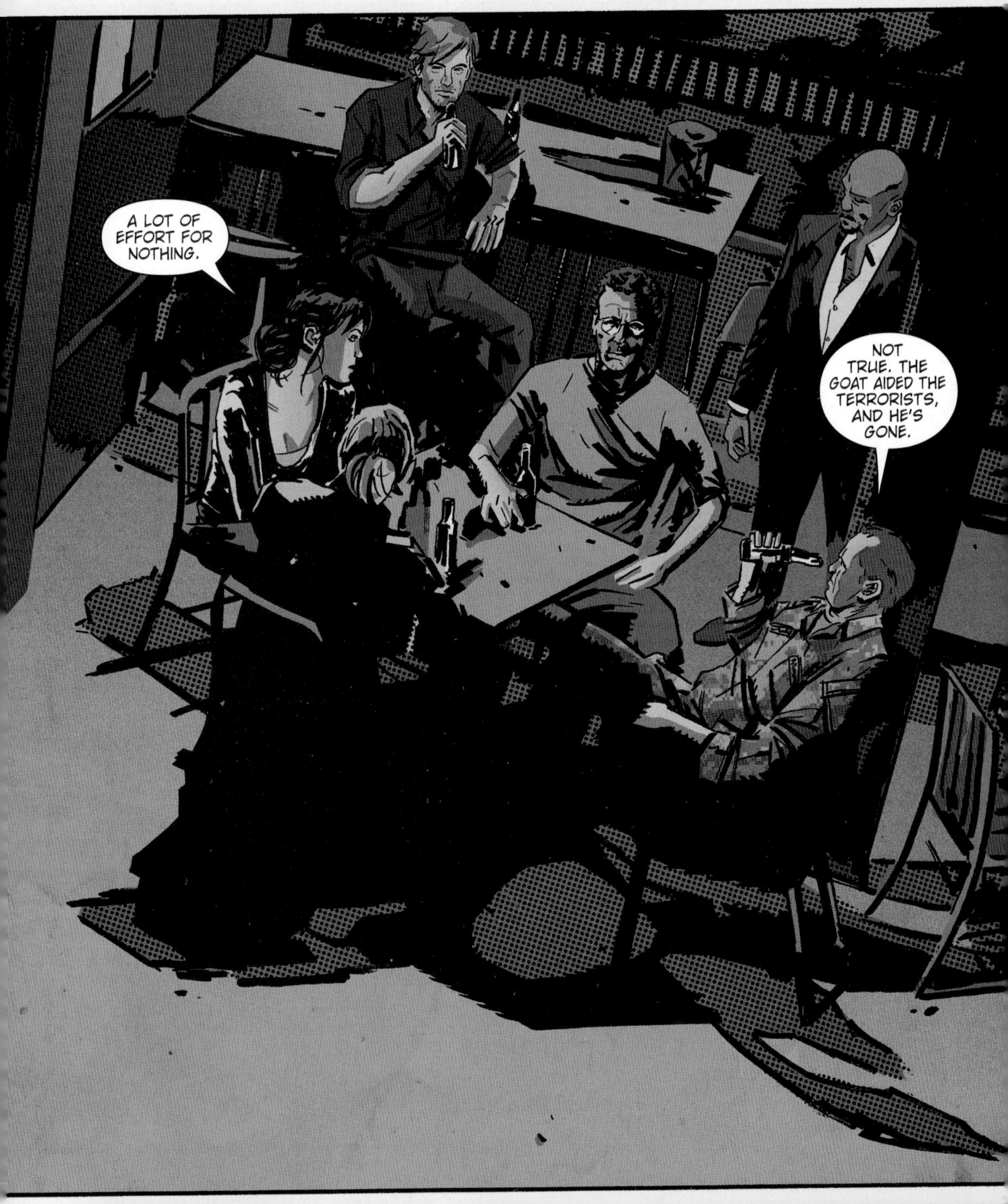
A LOT OF EFFORT FOR NOTHING.
NOT TRUE. THE GOAT AIDED THE TERRORISTS, AND HE'S GONE.

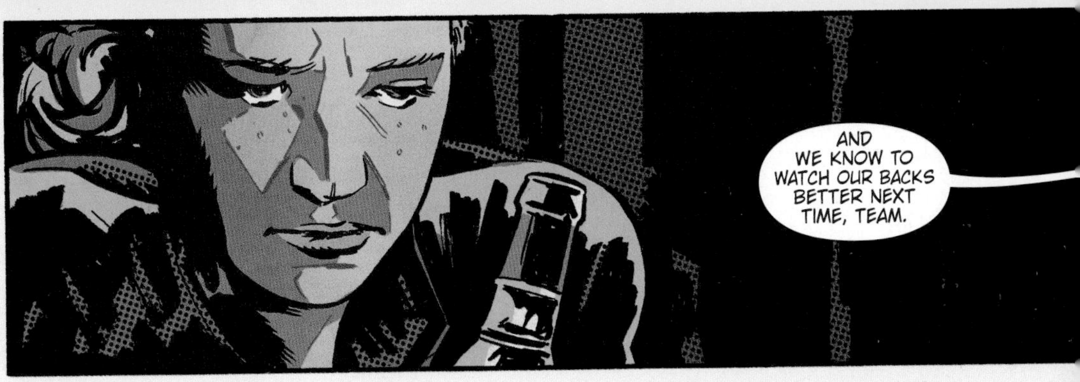
AND WE KNOW TO WATCH OUR BACKS BETTER NEXT TIME, TEAM.

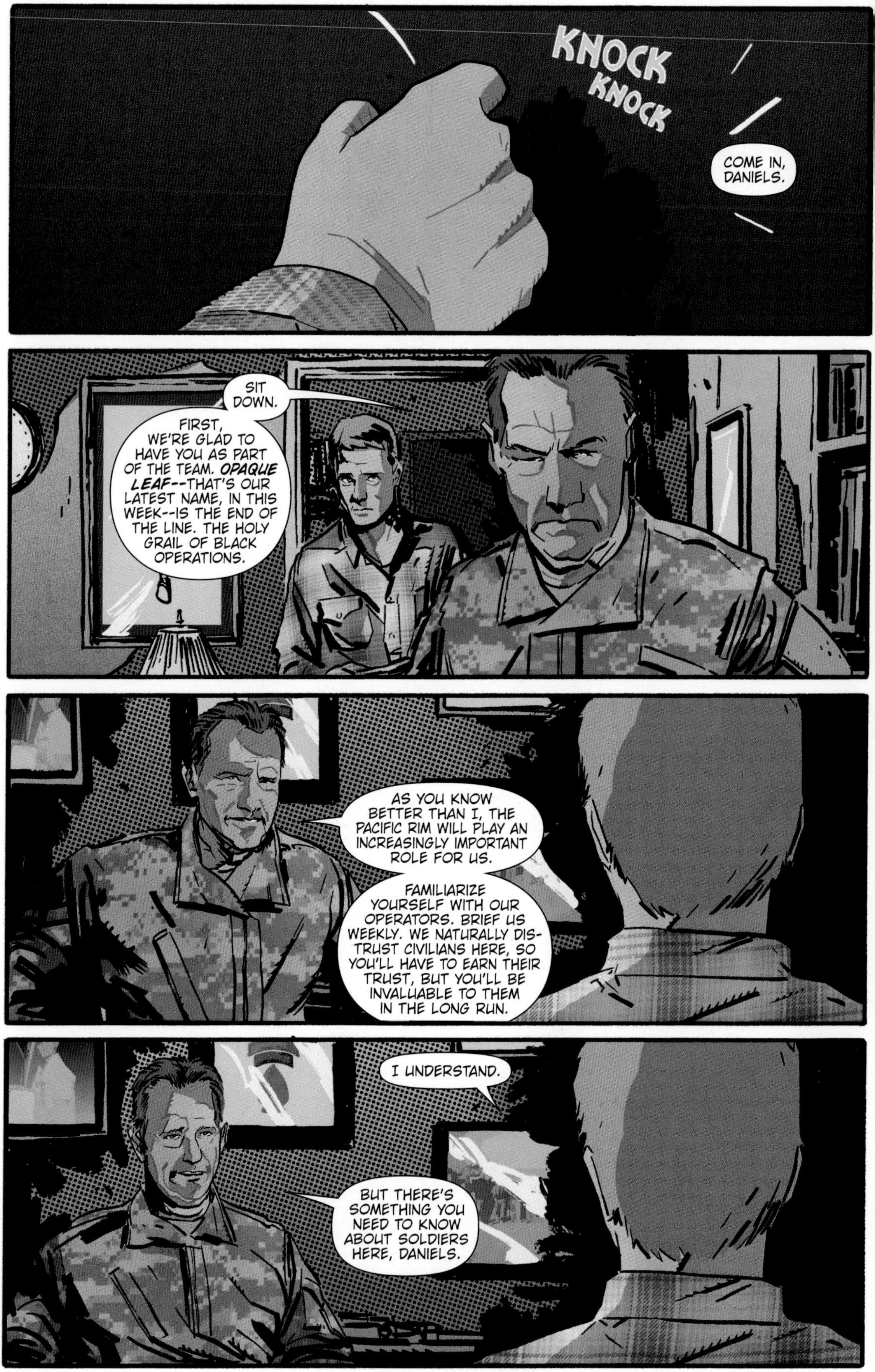
KNOCK KNOCK
COME IN, DANIELS.
SIT DOWN.
FIRST, WE'RE GLAD TO HAVE YOU AS PART OF THE TEAM. *OPAQUE LEAF*--THAT'S OUR LATEST NAME, IN THIS WEEK--IS THE END OF THE LINE. THE HOLY GRAIL OF BLACK OPERATIONS.
AS YOU KNOW BETTER THAN I, THE PACIFIC RIM WILL PLAY AN INCREASINGLY IMPORTANT ROLE FOR US.
FAMILIARIZE YOURSELF WITH OUR OPERATORS. BRIEF US WEEKLY. WE NATURALLY DIS-TRUST CIVILIANS HERE, SO YOU'LL HAVE TO EARN THEIR TRUST, BUT YOU'LL BE INVALUABLE TO THEM IN THE LONG RUN.
I UNDERSTAND.
BUT THERE'S SOMETHING YOU NEED TO KNOW ABOUT SOLDIERS HERE, DANIELS.

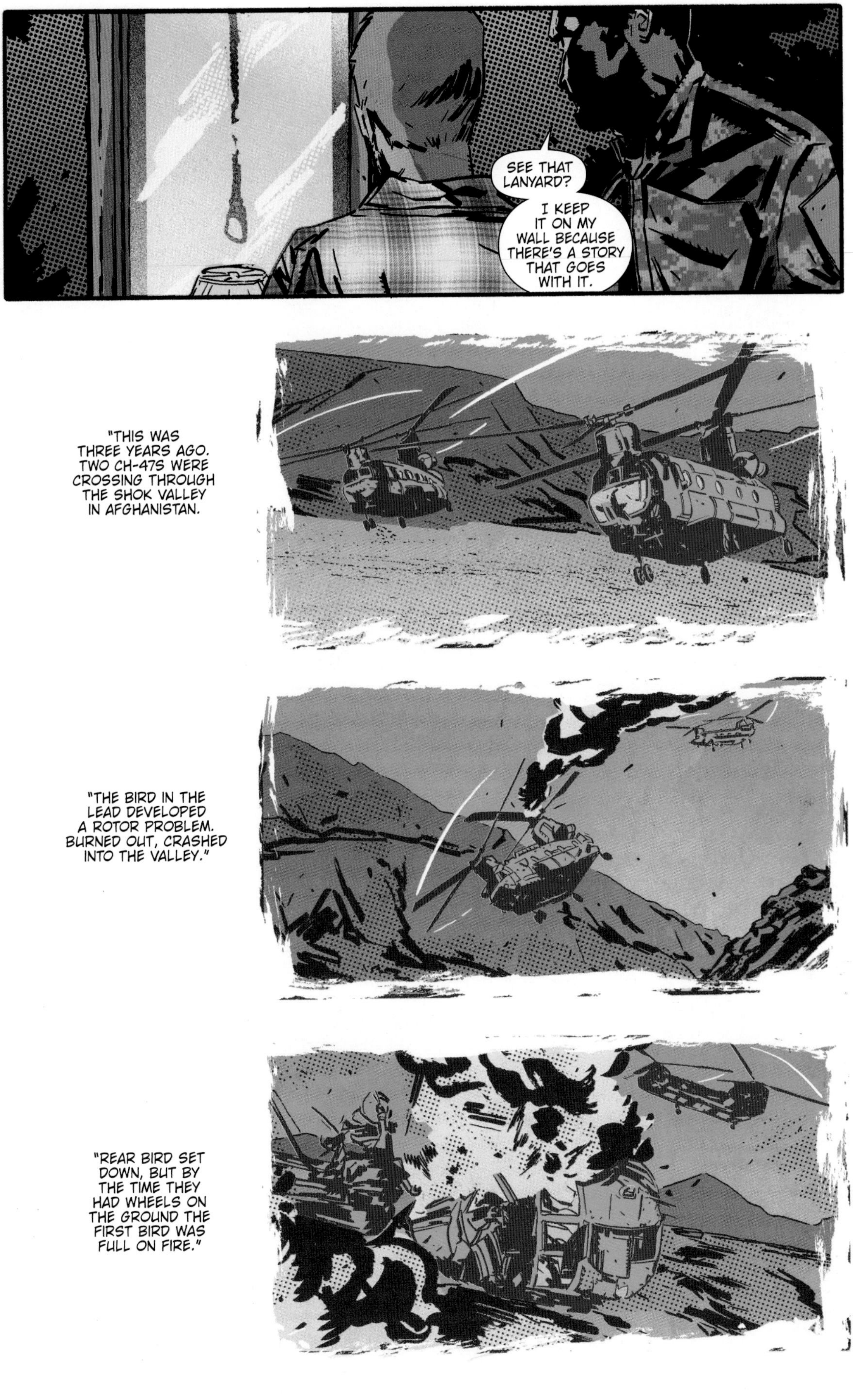
SEE THAT LANYARD?
I KEEP IT ON MY WALL BECAUSE THERE'S A STORY THAT GOES WITH IT.
"THIS WAS THREE YEARS AGO. TWO CH-47S WERE CROSSING THROUGH THE SHOK VALLEY IN AFGHANISTAN.
"THE BIRD IN THE LEAD DEVELOPED A ROTOR PROBLEM. BURNED OUT, CRASHED INTO THE VALLEY."
"REAR BIRD SET DOWN, BUT BY THE TIME THEY HAD WHEELS ON THE GROUND THE FIRST BIRD WAS FULL ON FIRE."

"ONE SOLDIER RAN AHEAD.

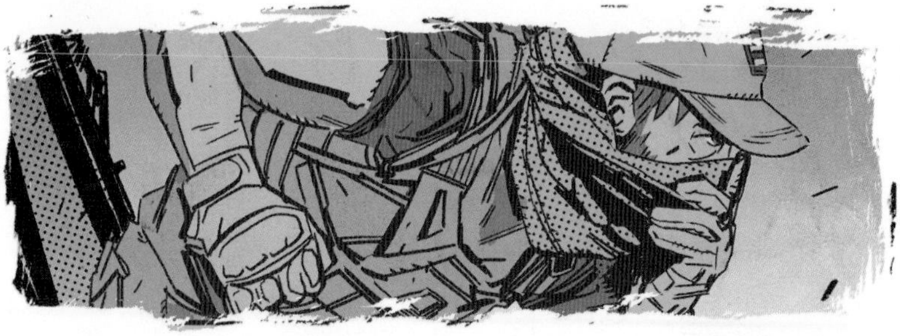

"HE RAN INTO THE FLAMES. THE HELO WAS JUST AN OVEN AT THIS POINT.

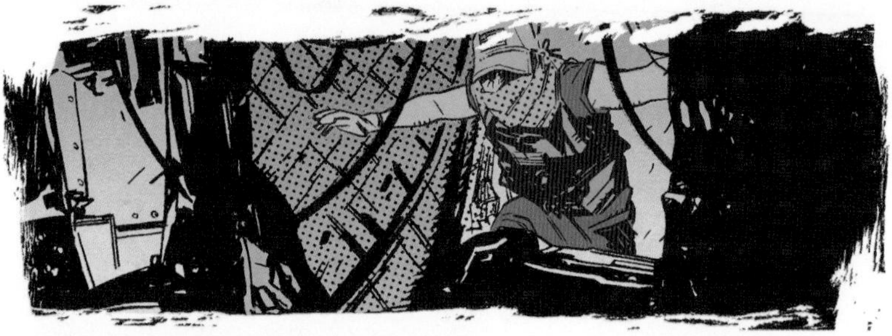

"MOST OF THE SOLDIERS DIED QUICKLY, BUT ONE WAS STUCK, HANGING BY HIS LANYARD FROM THE FLOOR OF THE CHINOOK.

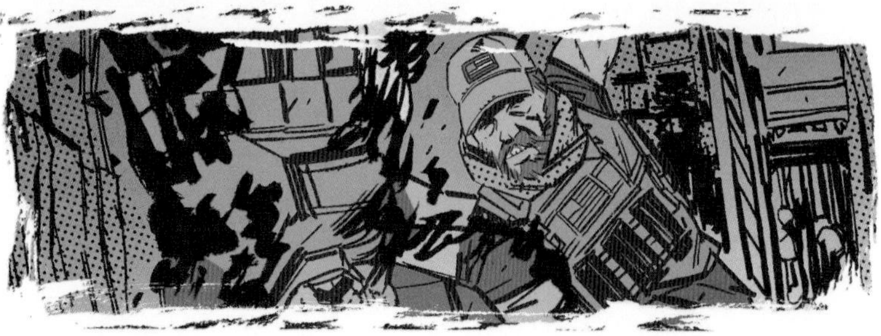

"THE SOLDIER CLIMBED UP TO FREE THE DYING RANGER."

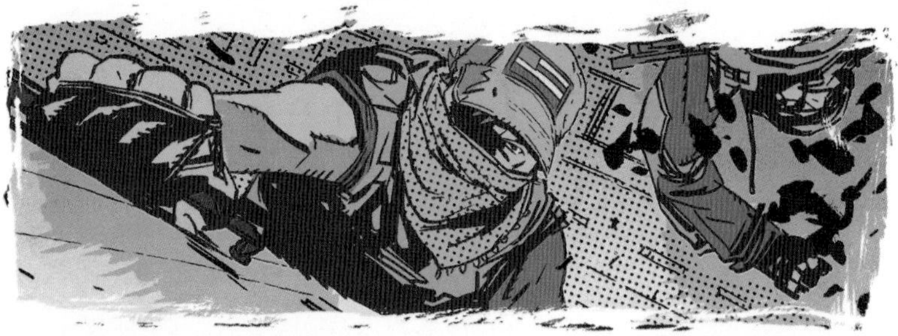

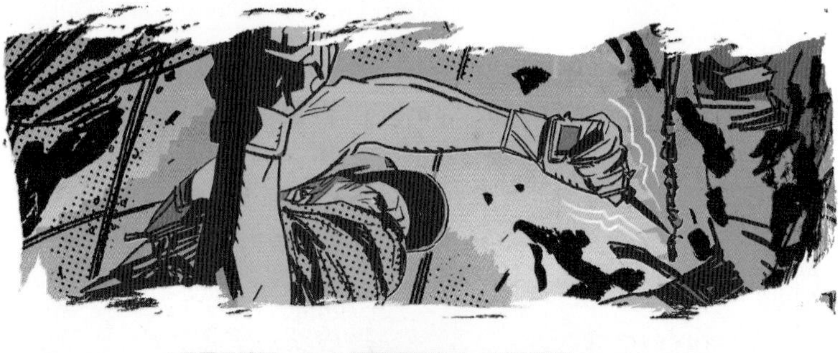

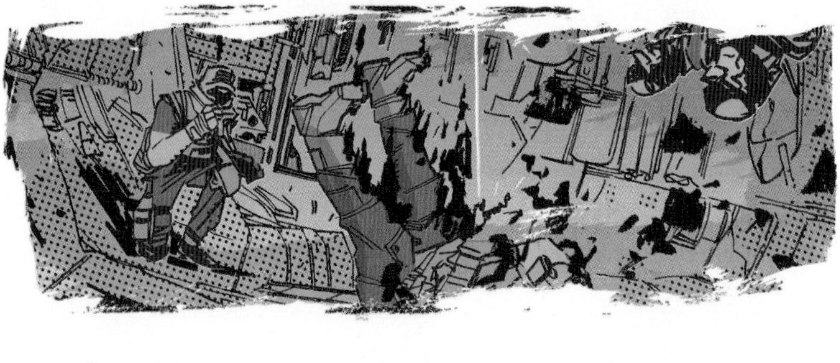

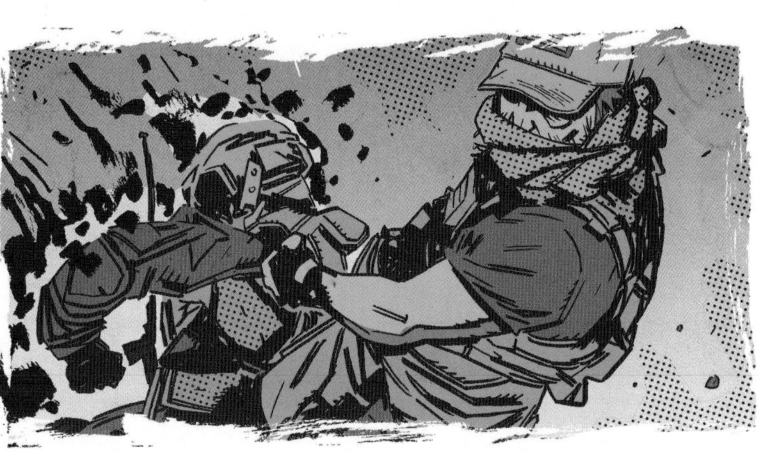

"JET FUEL WAS EVERYWHERE. HE COULDN'T JUST PUT THE FLAMES OUT. SO THE SOLDIER CARRIED THIS MAN TWO HUNDRED YARDS OVER STEEP ROCKS TO A STREAM.

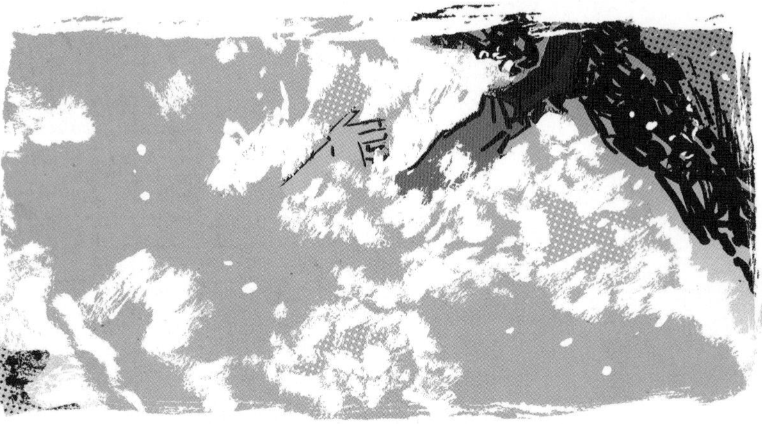

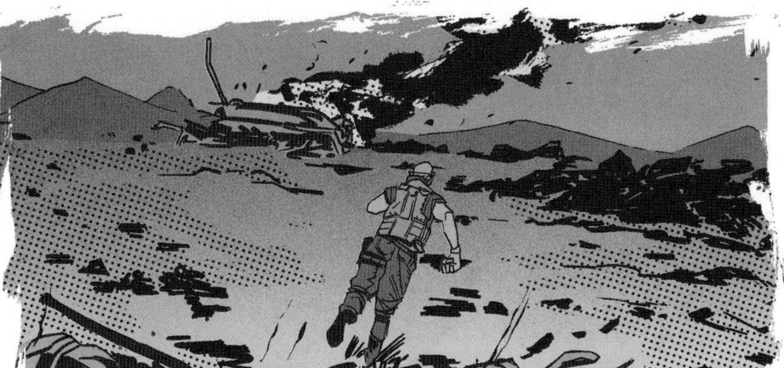

"HE RAN BACK UP THE HILL TO PULL THE REST OF THE BODIES OUT OF THE HELICOPTER, BEFORE THE FIRE TOOK THEM ALL.

"THAT WAS AN ISA OPERATOR. THE RANGER WHOSE LIFE HE SAVED WILL NEVER KNOW HIS SAVIOR'S NAME NEITHER WILL ANYONE ELSE."

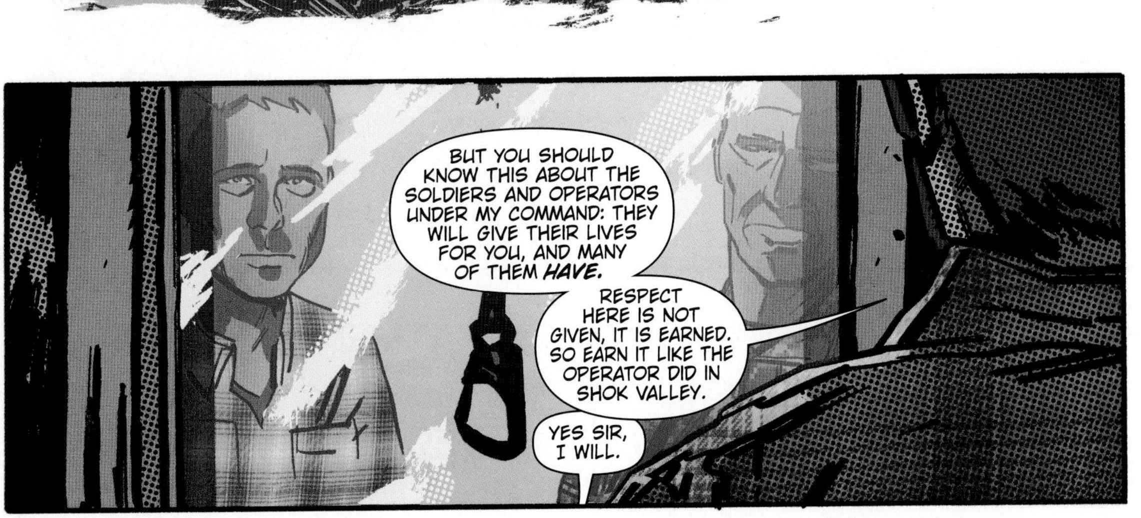
BUT YOU SHOULD KNOW THIS ABOUT THE SOLDIERS AND OPERATORS UNDER MY COMMAND: THEY WILL GIVE THEIR LIVES FOR YOU, AND MANY OF THEM ***HAVE.***
RESPECT HERE IS NOT GIVEN, IT IS EARNED. SO EARN IT LIKE THE OPERATOR DID IN SHOK VALLEY.
YES SIR, I WILL.

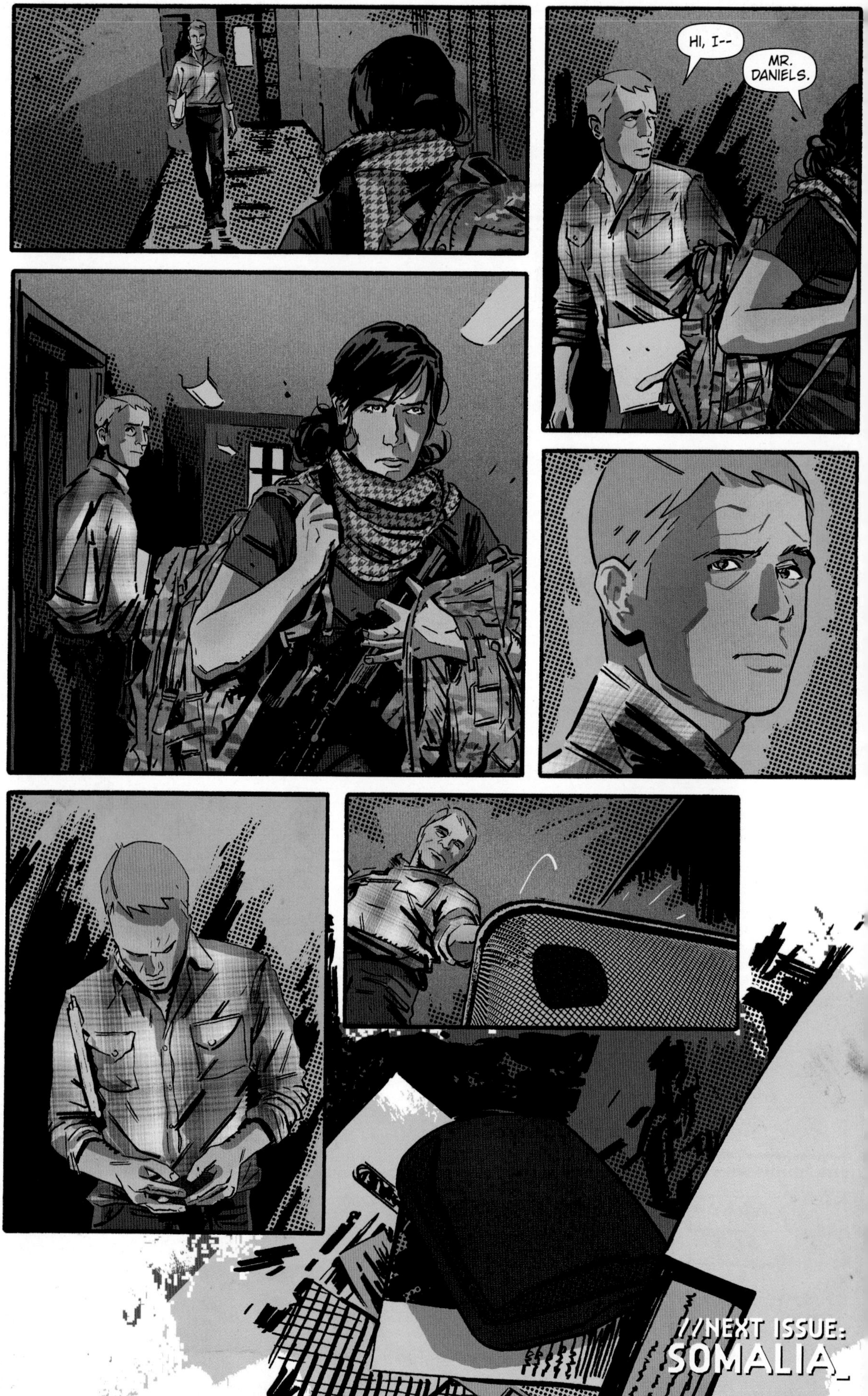
HI, I--
MR. DANIELS.
//NEXT ISSUE:
SOMALIA_

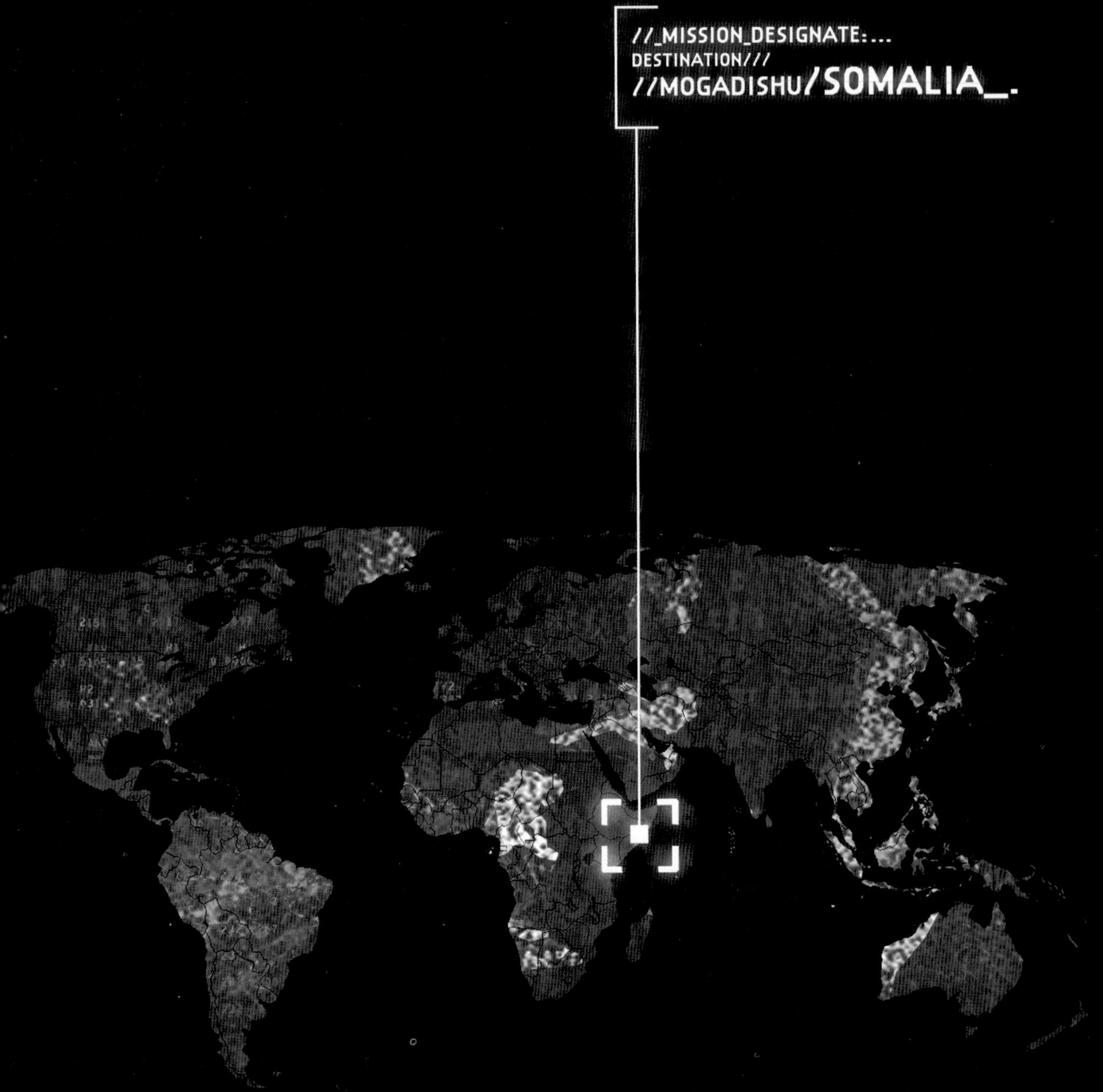
//_MISSION_DESIGNATE:...
DESTINATION///
//MOGADISHU/SOMALIA_.

//MISSION_REPORT_
//INITIALIZING____

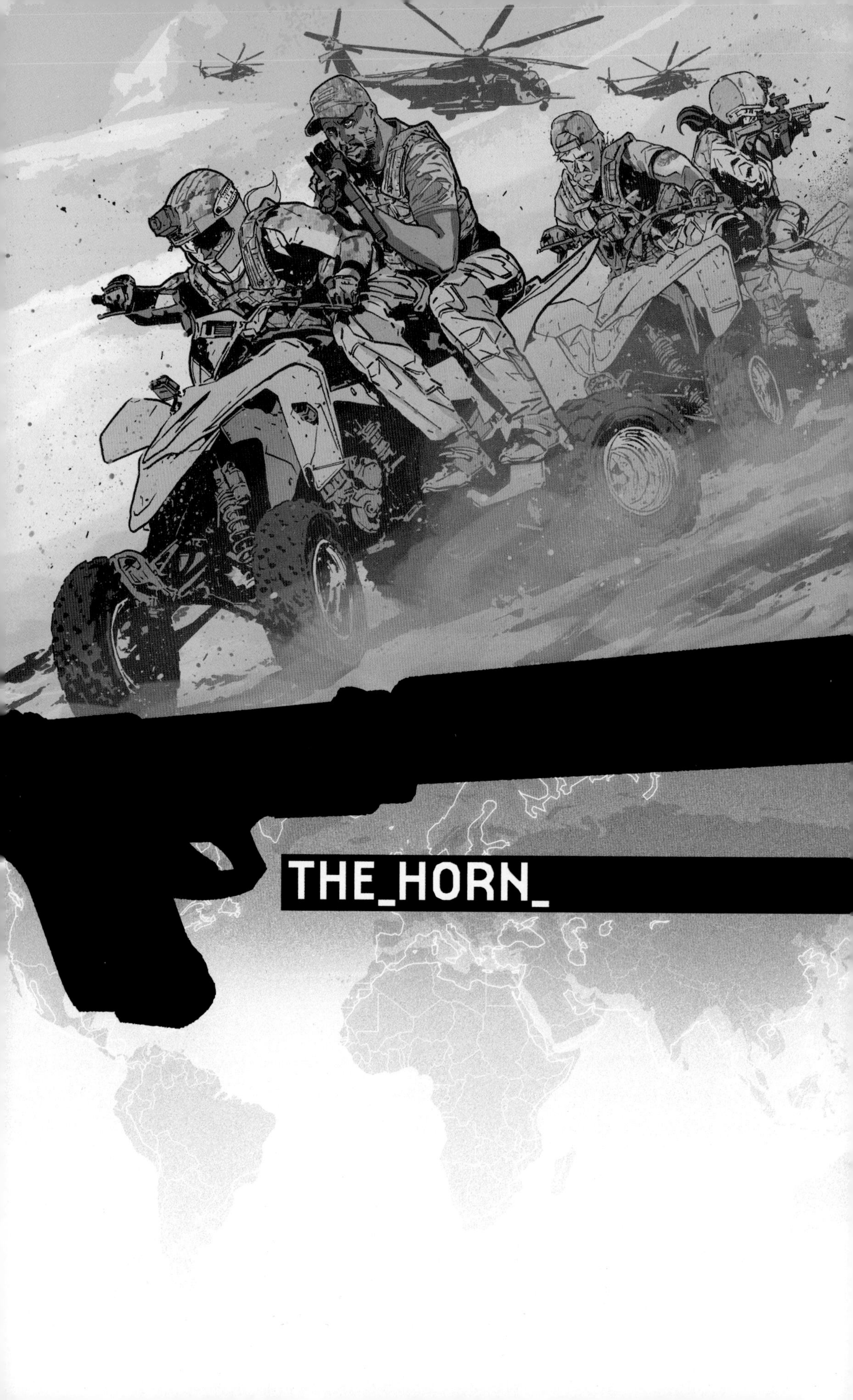
THE_HORN_

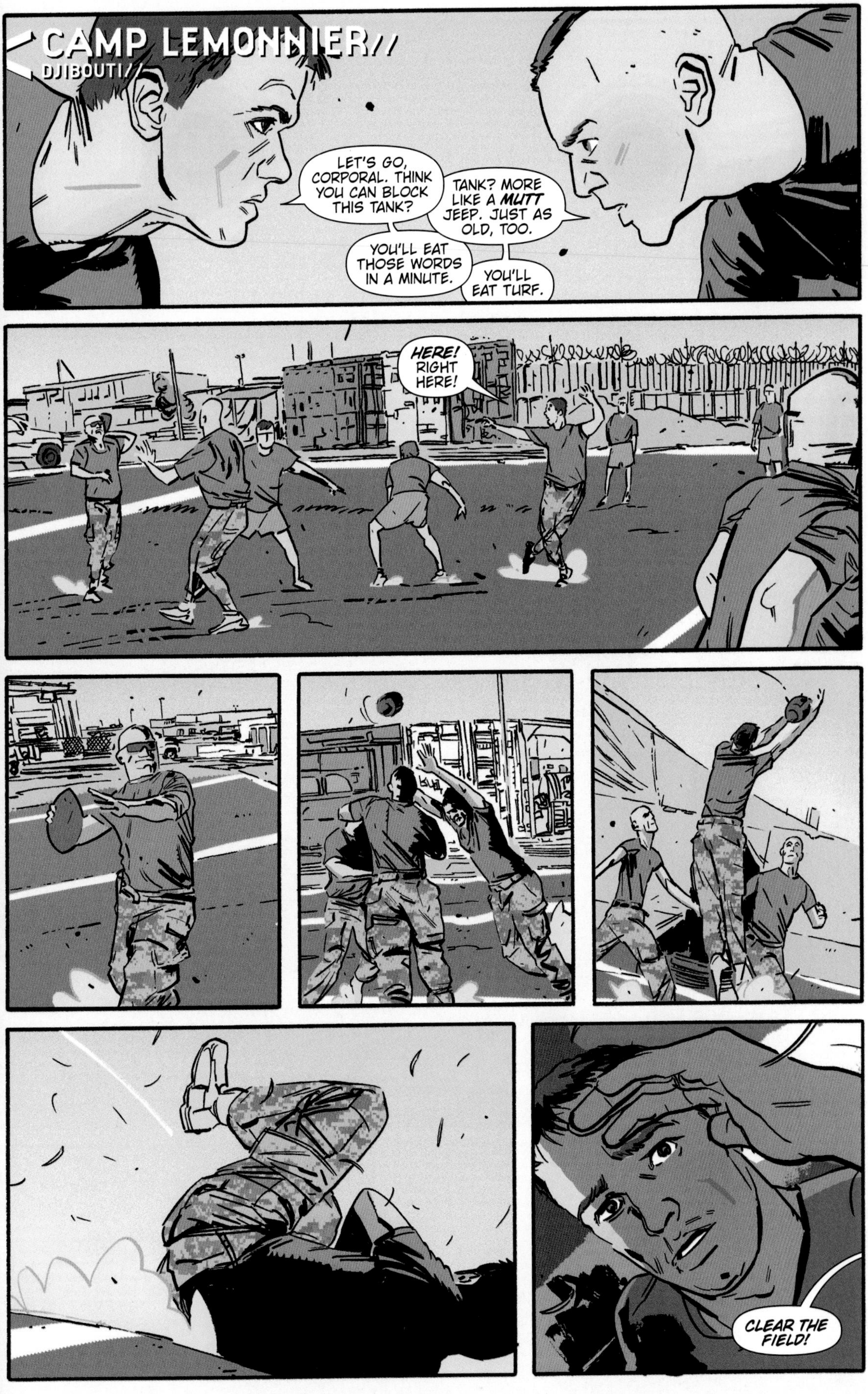
CAMP LEMONNIER//
DJIBOUTI//
LET'S GO, CORPORAL. THINK YOU CAN BLOCK THIS TANK?
TANK? MORE LIKE A MUTT JEEP. JUST AS OLD, TOO.
YOU'LL EAT THOSE WORDS IN A MINUTE.
YOU'LL EAT TURF.
HERE! RIGHT HERE!
CLEAR THE FIELD!

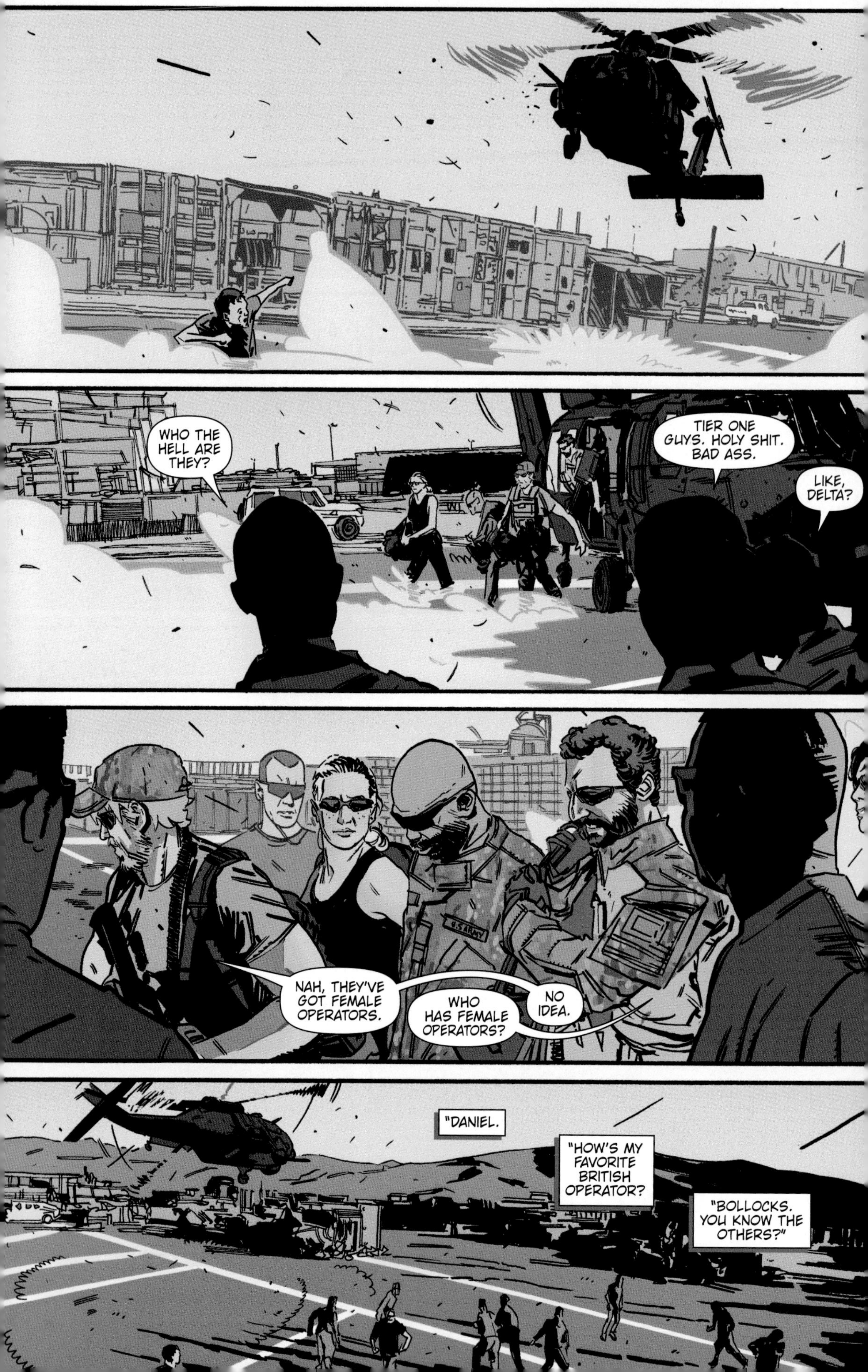
WHO THE HELL ARE THEY?
TIER ONE GUYS. HOLY SHIT. BAD ASS.
LIKE, DELTA?
NAH, THEY'VE GOT FEMALE OPERATORS.
WHO HAS FEMALE OPERATORS?
NO IDEA.
"DANIEL.
"HOW'S MY FAVORITE BRITISH OPERATOR?
"BOLLOCKS. YOU KNOW THE OTHERS?"

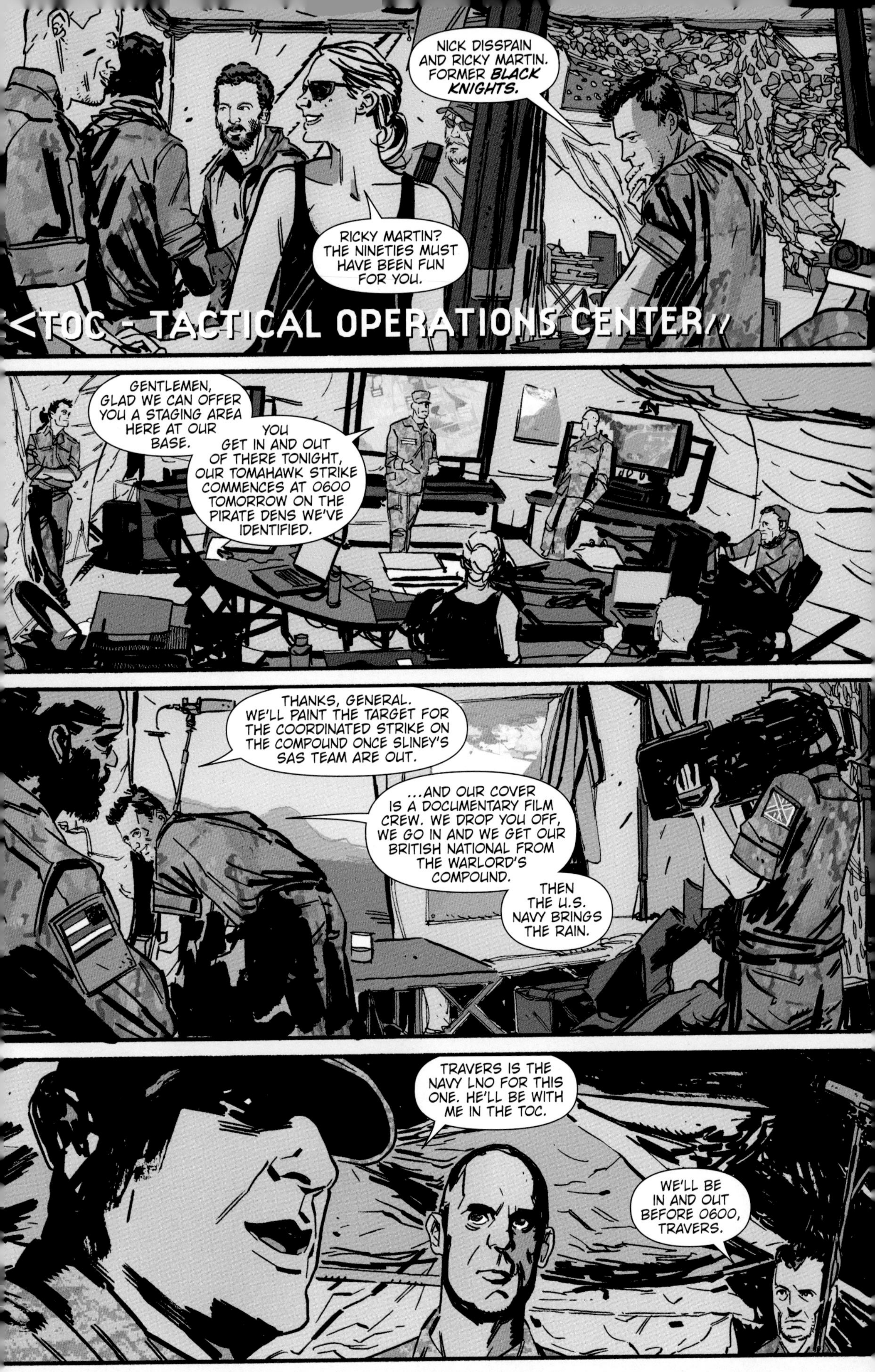
NICK DISSPAIN AND RICKY MARTIN. FORMER *BLACK KNIGHTS.*
RICKY MARTIN? THE NINETIES MUST HAVE BEEN FUN FOR YOU.
<TOC - TACTICAL OPERATIONS CENTER//
GENTLEMEN, GLAD WE CAN OFFER YOU A STAGING AREA HERE AT OUR BASE.
YOU GET IN AND OUT OF THERE TONIGHT, OUR TOMAHAWK STRIKE COMMENCES AT 0600 TOMORROW ON THE PIRATE DENS WE'VE IDENTIFIED.
THANKS, GENERAL. WE'LL PAINT THE TARGET FOR THE COORDINATED STRIKE ON THE COMPOUND ONCE SLINEY'S SAS TEAM ARE OUT.
...AND OUR COVER IS A DOCUMENTARY FILM CREW. WE DROP YOU OFF, WE GO IN AND WE GET OUR BRITISH NATIONAL FROM THE WARLORD'S COMPOUND.
THEN THE U.S. NAVY BRINGS THE RAIN.
TRAVERS IS THE NAVY LNO FOR THIS ONE. HE'LL BE WITH ME IN THE TOC.
WE'LL BE IN AND OUT BEFORE 0600, TRAVERS.

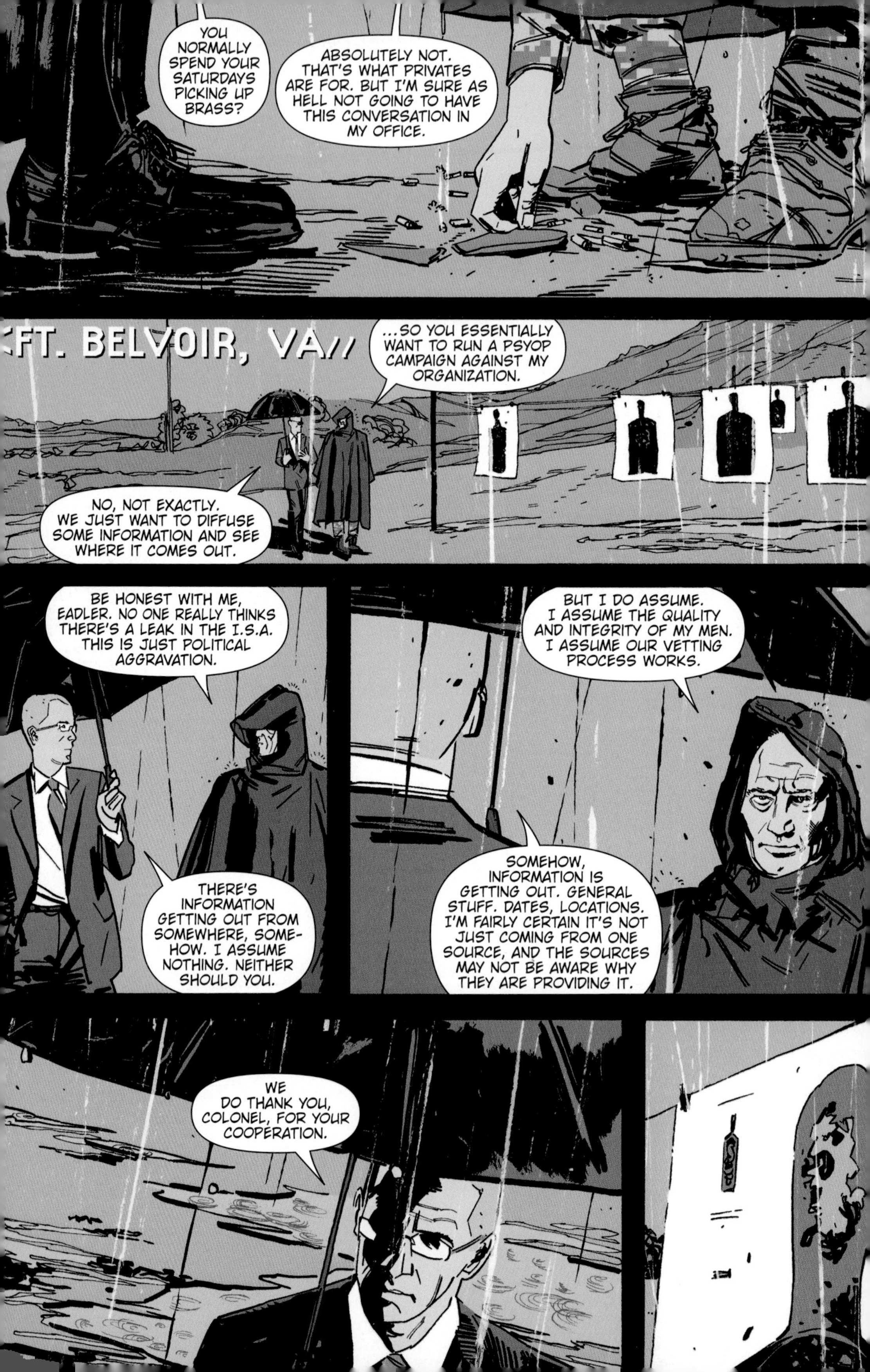
YOU NORMALLY SPEND YOUR SATURDAYS PICKING UP BRASS?
ABSOLUTELY NOT. THAT'S WHAT PRIVATES ARE FOR. BUT I'M SURE AS HELL NOT GOING TO HAVE THIS CONVERSATION IN MY OFFICE.
FT. BELVOIR, VA
...SO YOU ESSENTIALLY WANT TO RUN A PSYOP CAMPAIGN AGAINST MY ORGANIZATION.
NO, NOT EXACTLY. WE JUST WANT TO DIFFUSE SOME INFORMATION AND SEE WHERE IT COMES OUT.
BE HONEST WITH ME, EADLER. NO ONE REALLY THINKS THERE'S A LEAK IN THE I.S.A. THIS IS JUST POLITICAL AGGRAVATION.
THERE'S INFORMATION GETTING OUT FROM SOMEWHERE, SOME-HOW. I ASSUME NOTHING. NEITHER SHOULD YOU.
BUT I DO ASSUME. I ASSUME THE QUALITY AND INTEGRITY OF MY MEN. I ASSUME OUR VETTING PROCESS WORKS.
SOMEHOW, INFORMATION IS GETTING OUT. GENERAL STUFF. DATES, LOCATIONS. I'M FAIRLY CERTAIN IT'S NOT JUST COMING FROM ONE SOURCE, AND THE SOURCES MAY NOT BE AWARE WHY THEY ARE PROVIDING IT.
WE DO THANK YOU, COLONEL, FOR YOUR COOPERATION.

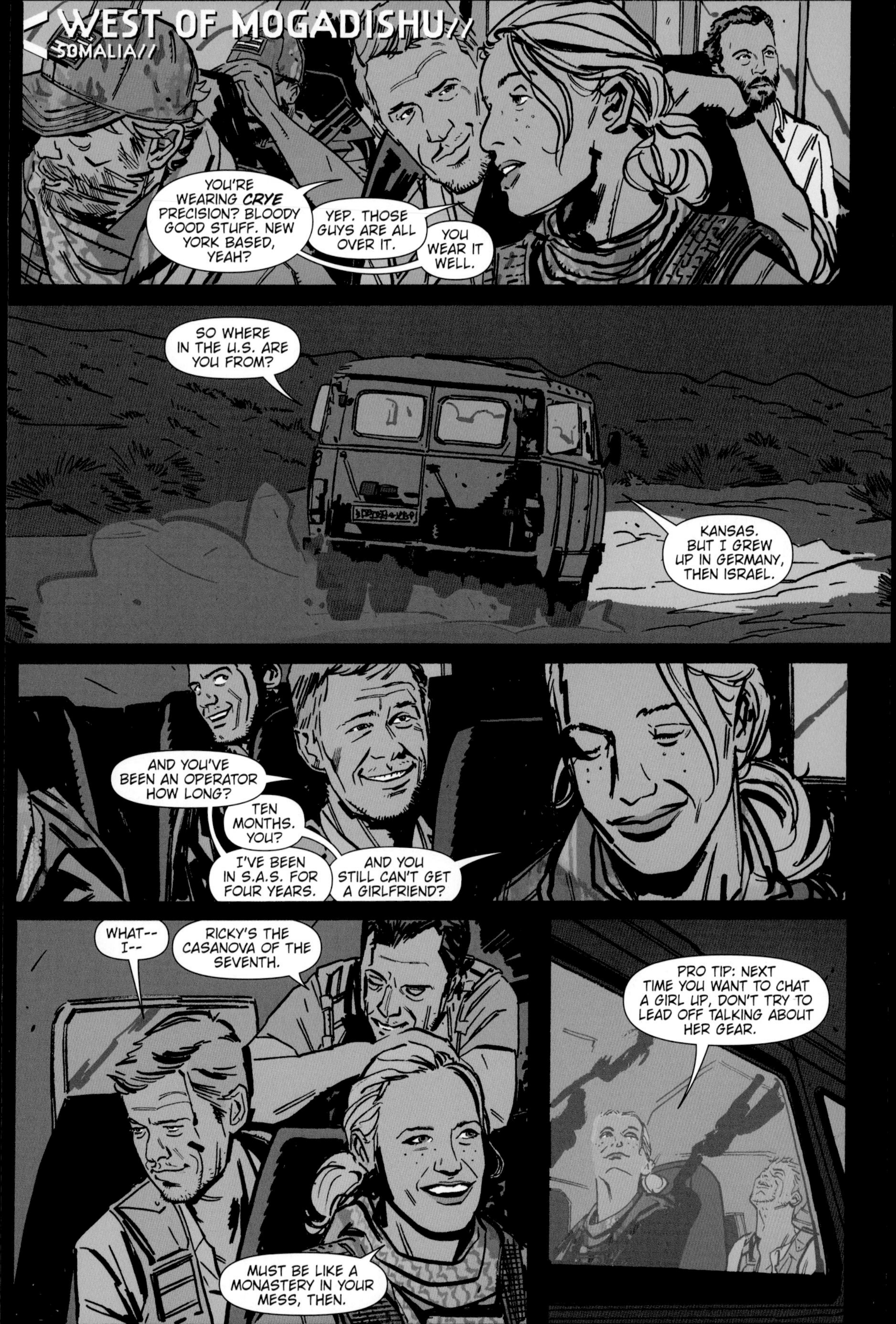
WEST OF MOGADISHU//
SOMALIA//
YOU'RE WEARING CRYE PRECISION? BLOODY GOOD STUFF. NEW YORK BASED, YEAH?
YEP. THOSE GUYS ARE ALL OVER IT.
YOU WEAR IT WELL.
SO WHERE IN THE U.S. ARE YOU FROM?
KANSAS. BUT I GREW UP IN GERMANY, THEN ISRAEL.
AND YOU'VE BEEN AN OPERATOR HOW LONG?
TEN MONTHS. YOU?
I'VE BEEN IN S.A.S. FOR FOUR YEARS.
AND YOU STILL CAN'T GET A GIRLFRIEND?
WHAT-- I--
RICKY'S THE CASANOVA OF THE SEVENTH.
MUST BE LIKE A MONASTERY IN YOUR MESS, THEN.
PRO TIP: NEXT TIME YOU WANT TO CHAT A GIRL UP, DON'T TRY TO LEAD OFF TALKING ABOUT HER GEAR.

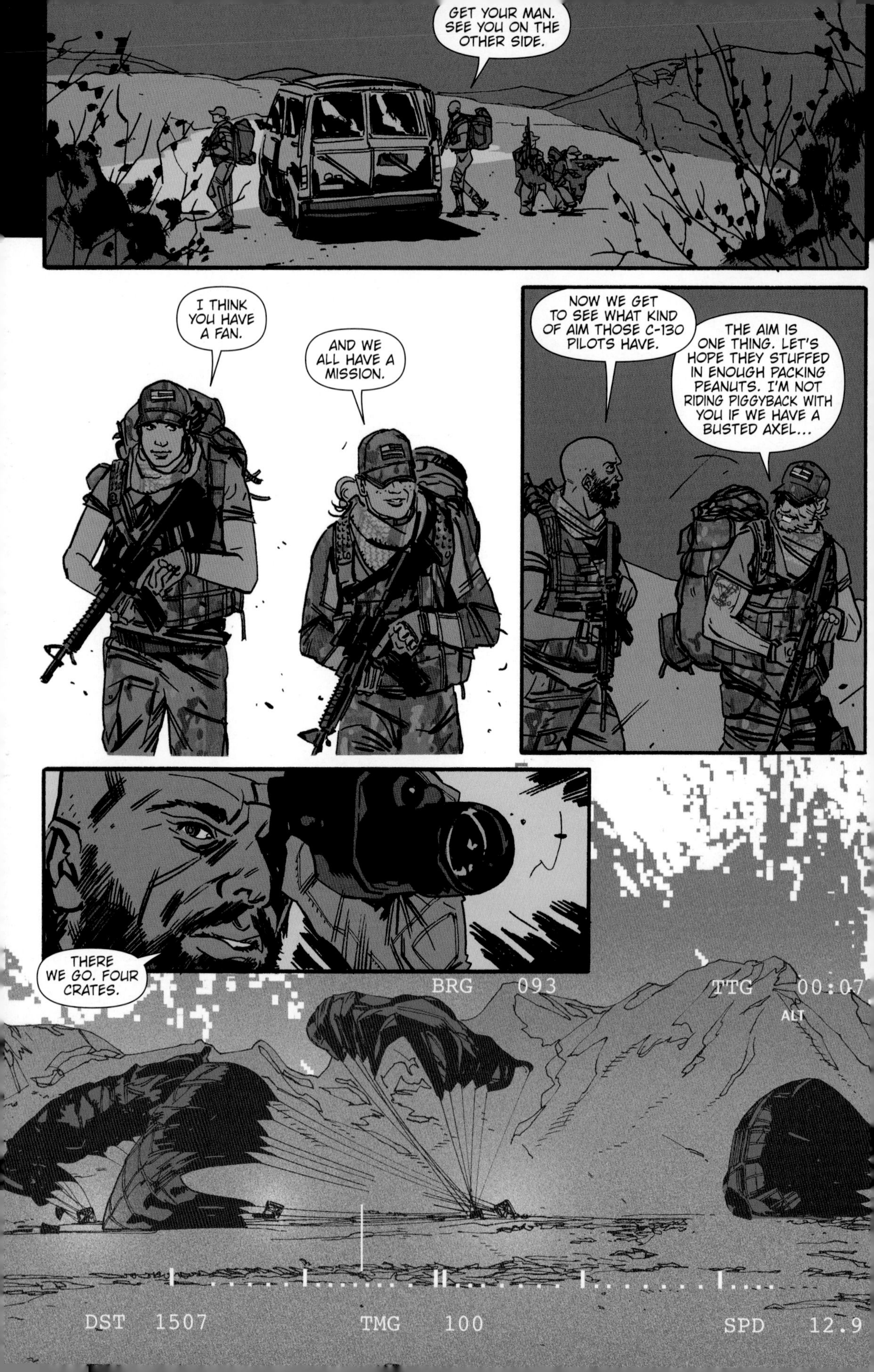
GET YOUR MAN. SEE YOU ON THE OTHER SIDE.
I THINK YOU HAVE A FAN.
AND WE ALL HAVE A MISSION.
NOW WE GET TO SEE WHAT KIND OF AIM THOSE C-130 PILOTS HAVE.
THE AIM IS ONE THING. LET'S HOPE THEY STUFFED IN ENOUGH PACKING PEANUTS. I'M NOT RIDING PIGGYBACK WITH YOU IF WE HAVE A BUSTED AXEL...
THERE WE GO. FOUR CRATES.
BRG 093
TTG 00:07
ALT
DST 1507
TMG 100
SPD 12.9

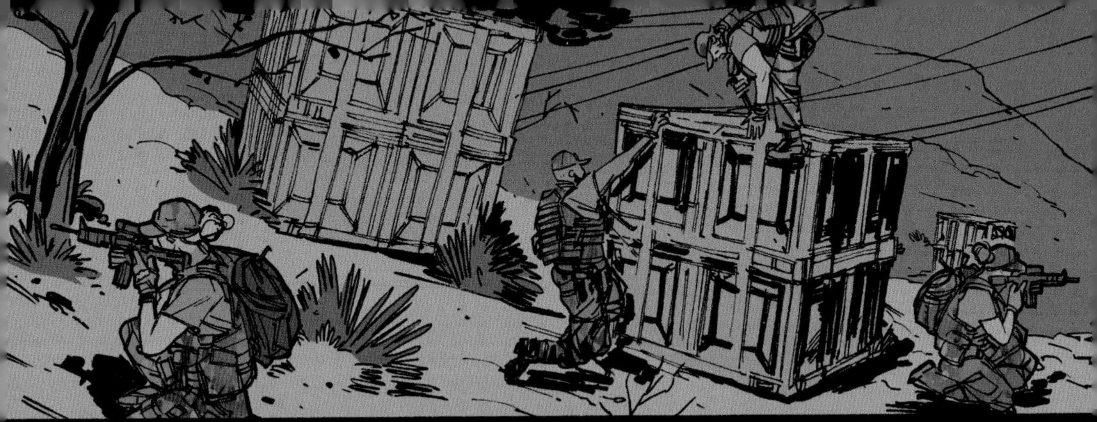

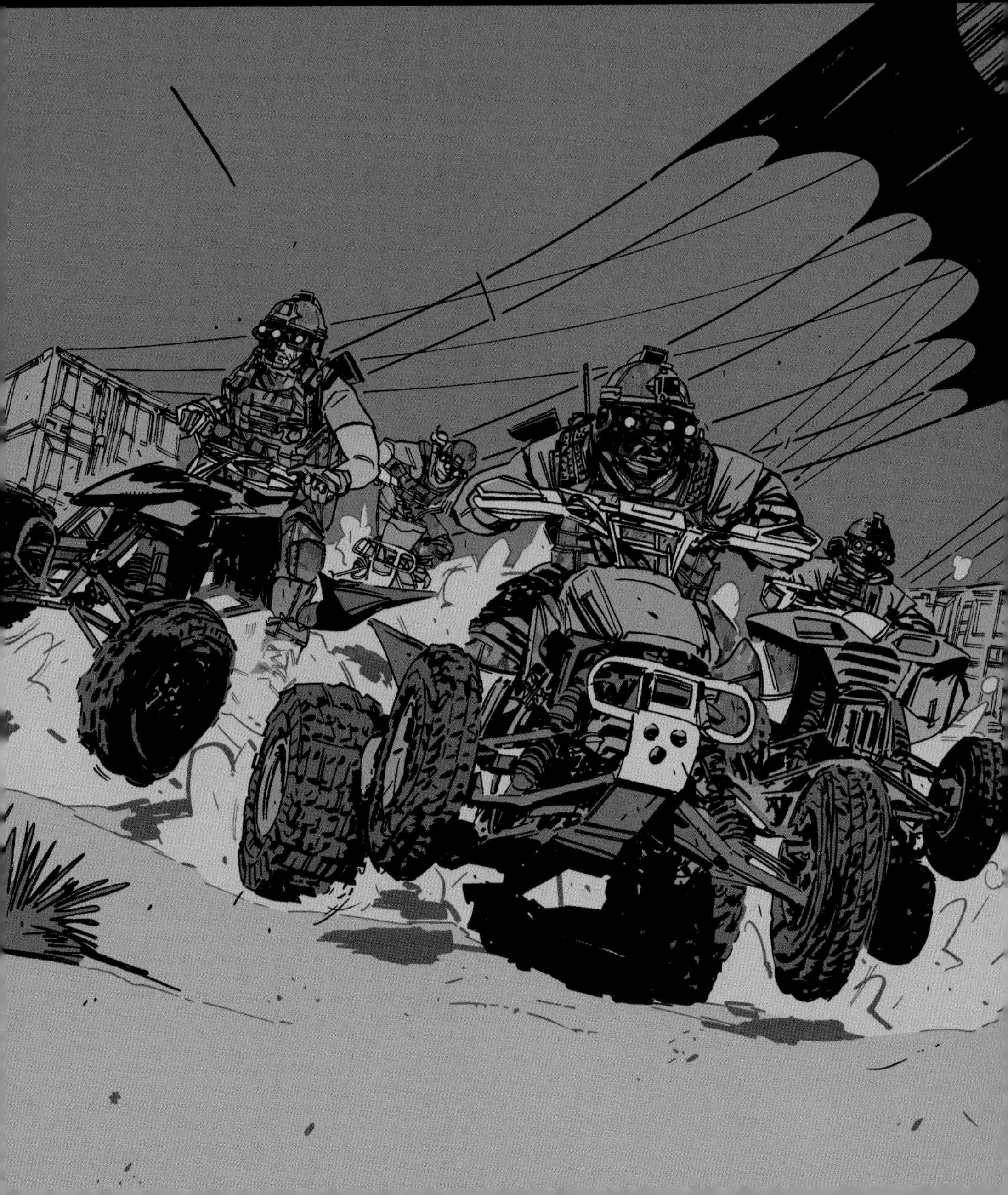

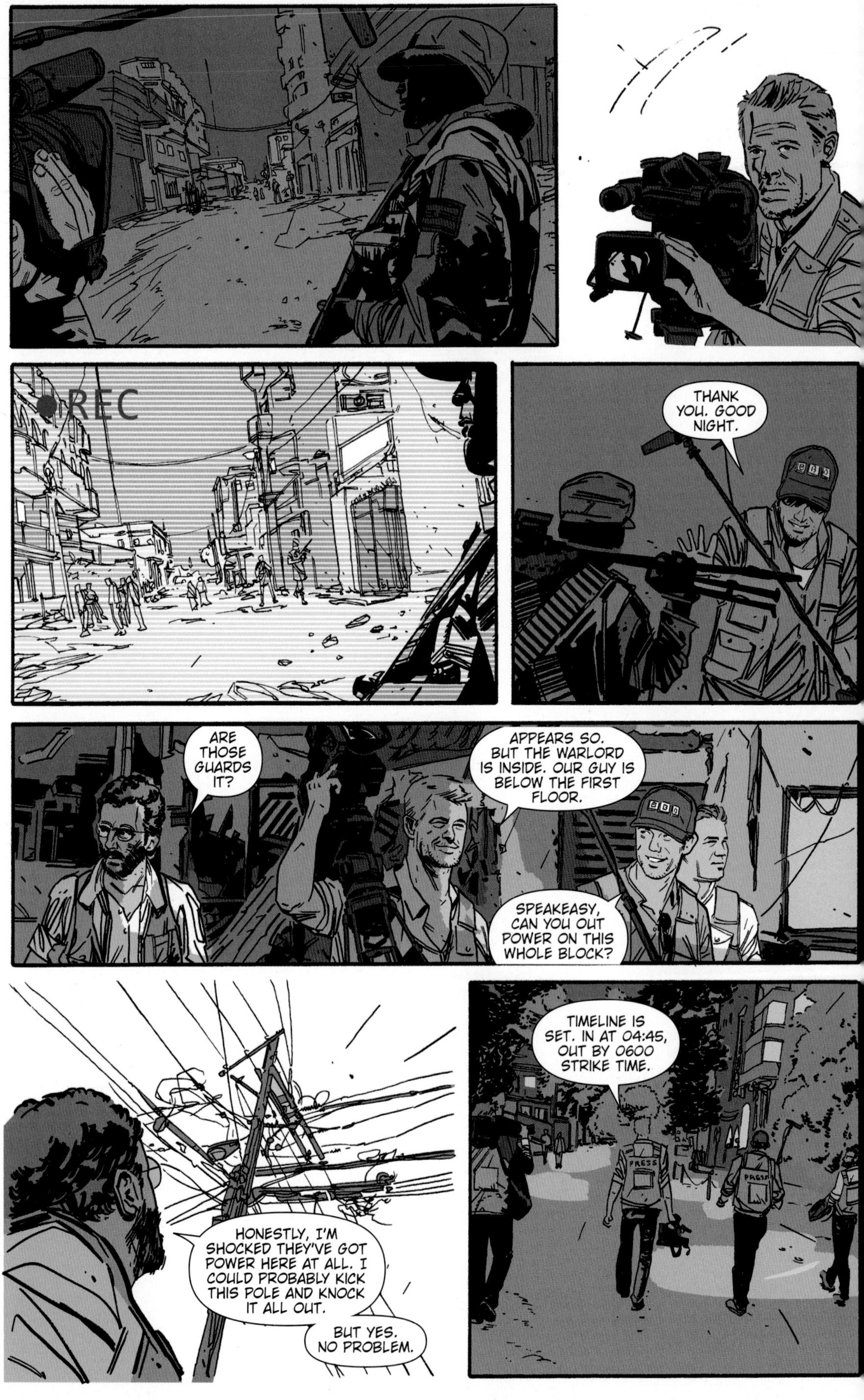
REC
THANK YOU. GOOD NIGHT.
ARE THOSE GUARDS IT?
APPEARS SO. BUT THE WARLORD IS INSIDE. OUR GUY IS BELOW THE FIRST FLOOR.
SPEAKEASY, CAN YOU OUT POWER ON THIS WHOLE BLOCK?
HONESTLY, I'M SHOCKED THEY'VE GOT POWER HERE AT ALL. I COULD PROBABLY KICK THIS POLE AND KNOCK IT ALL OUT.
BUT YES. NO PROBLEM.
TIMELINE IS SET. IN AT 04:45, OUT BY 0600 STRIKE TIME.
PRESS
PRESS

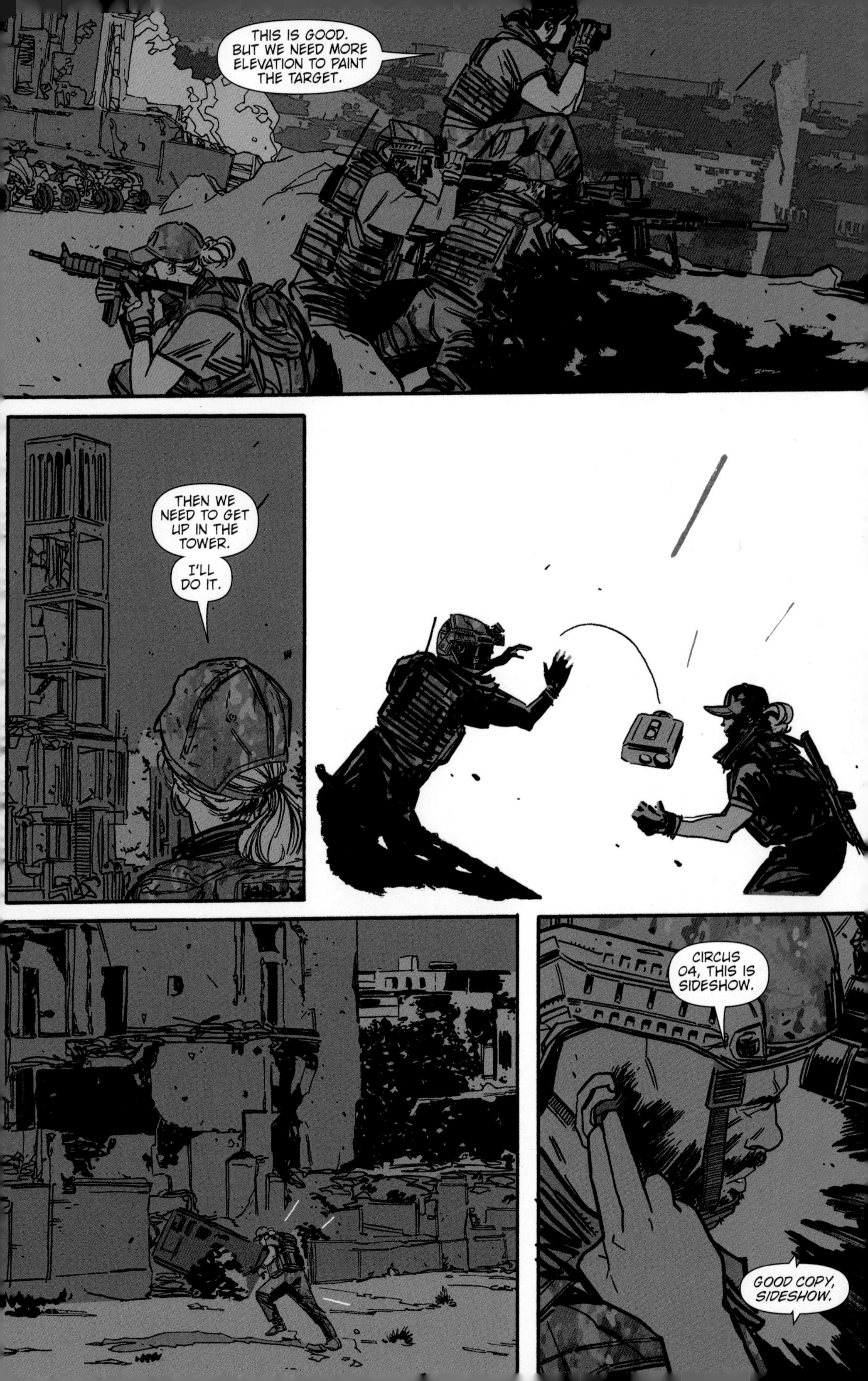
THIS IS GOOD. BUT WE NEED MORE ELEVATION TO PAINT THE TARGET.
THEN WE NEED TO GET UP IN THE TOWER.
I'LL DO IT.
CIRCUS 04, THIS IS SIDESHOW.
GOOD COPY, SIDESHOW.

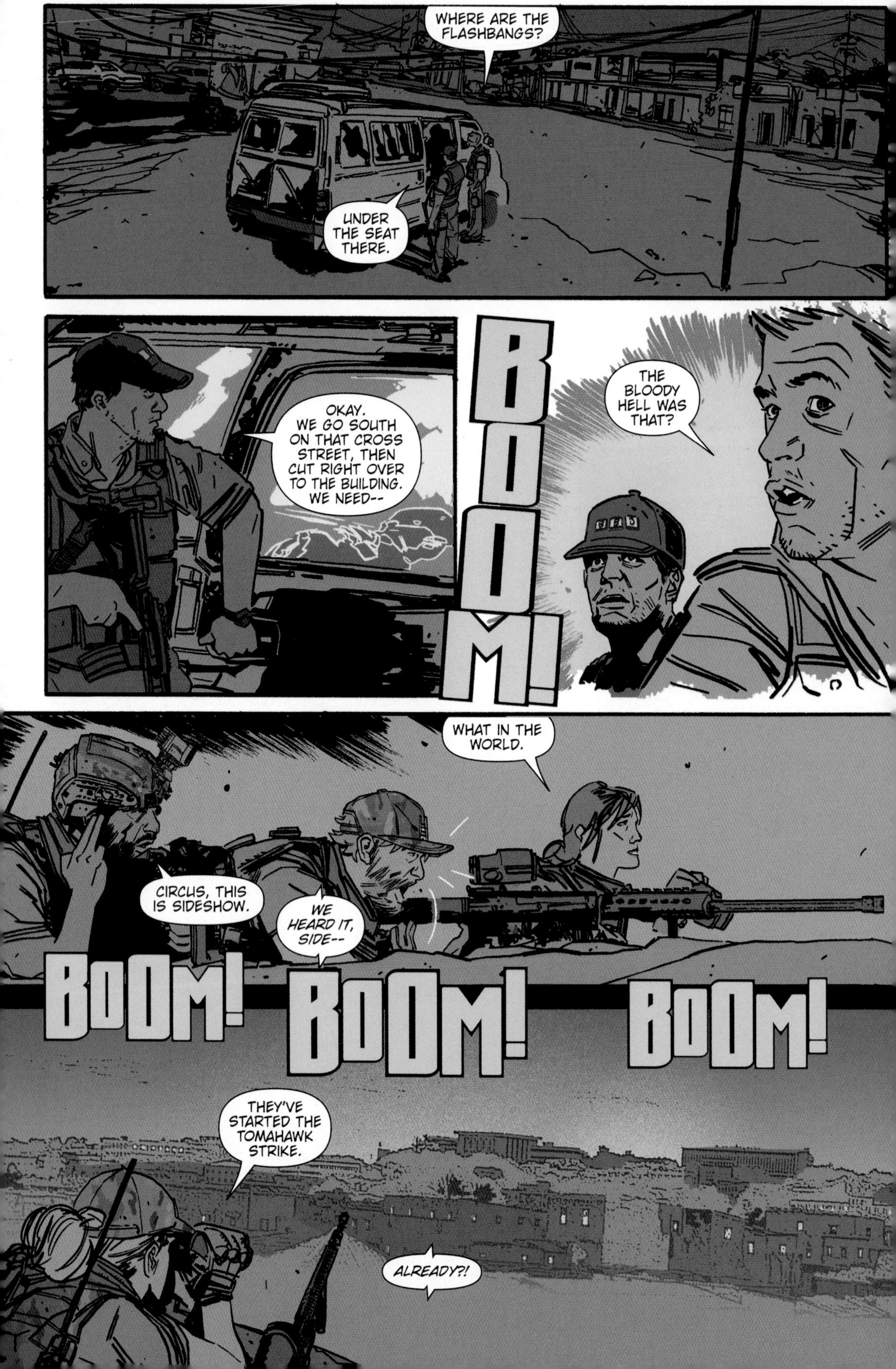
WHERE ARE THE FLASHBANGS?
UNDER THE SEAT THERE.
OKAY. WE GO SOUTH ON THAT CROSS STREET, THEN CUT RIGHT OVER TO THE BUILDING. WE NEED--
BOOM!
THE BLOODY HELL WAS THAT?
WHAT IN THE WORLD.
CIRCUS, THIS IS SIDESHOW.
WE HEARD IT, SIDE--
BOOM!
BOOM!
BOOM!
THEY'VE STARTED THE TOMAHAWK STRIKE.
ALREADY?!

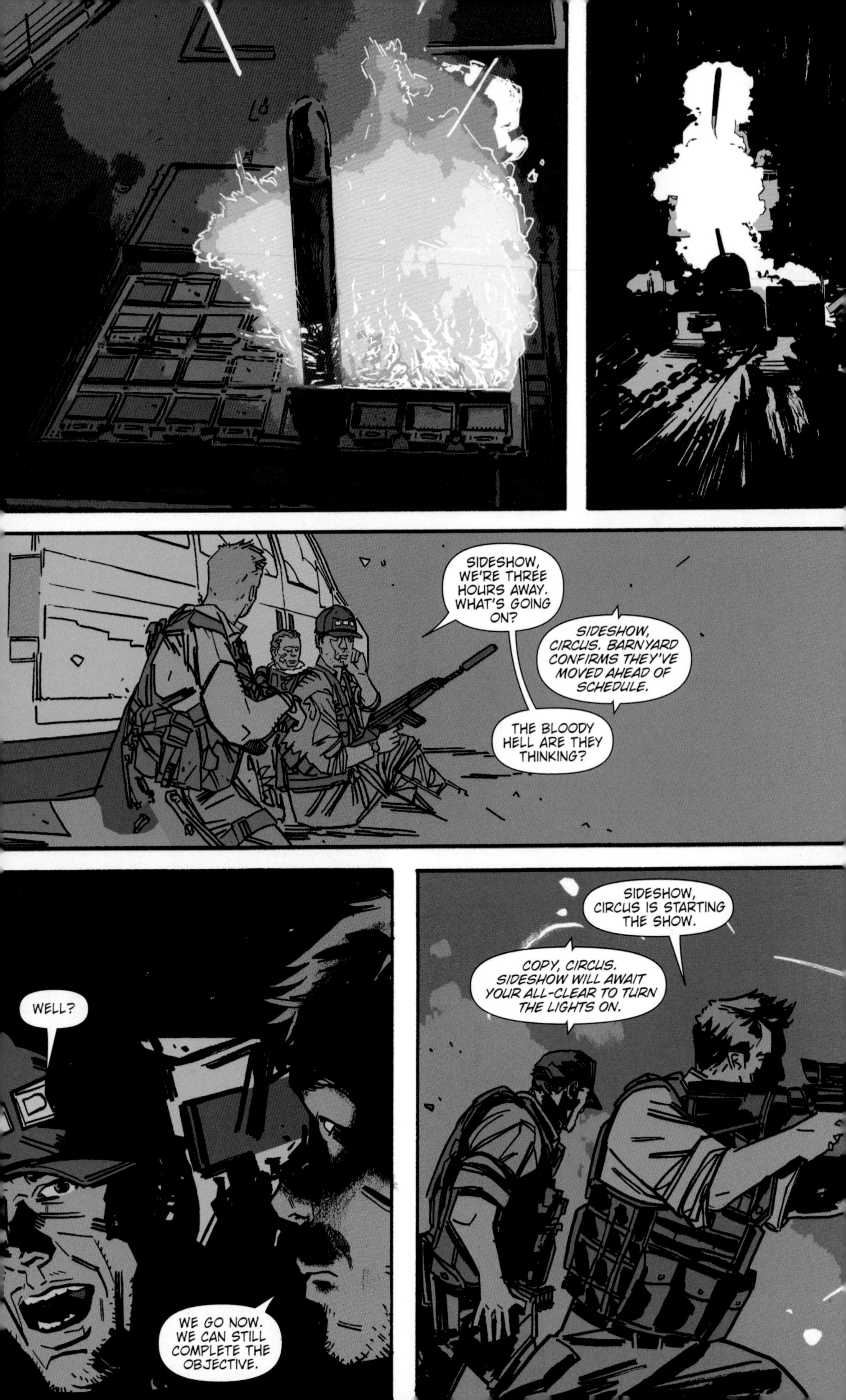
SIDESHOW, WE'RE THREE HOURS AWAY. WHAT'S GOING ON?
SIDESHOW, CIRCUS. BARNYARD CONFIRMS THEY'VE MOVED AHEAD OF SCHEDULE.
THE BLOODY HELL ARE THEY THINKING?
WELL?
WE GO NOW. WE CAN STILL COMPLETE THE OBJECTIVE.
SIDESHOW, CIRCUS IS STARTING THE SHOW.
COPY, CIRCUS. SIDESHOW WILL AWAIT YOUR ALL-CLEAR TO TURN THE LIGHTS ON.

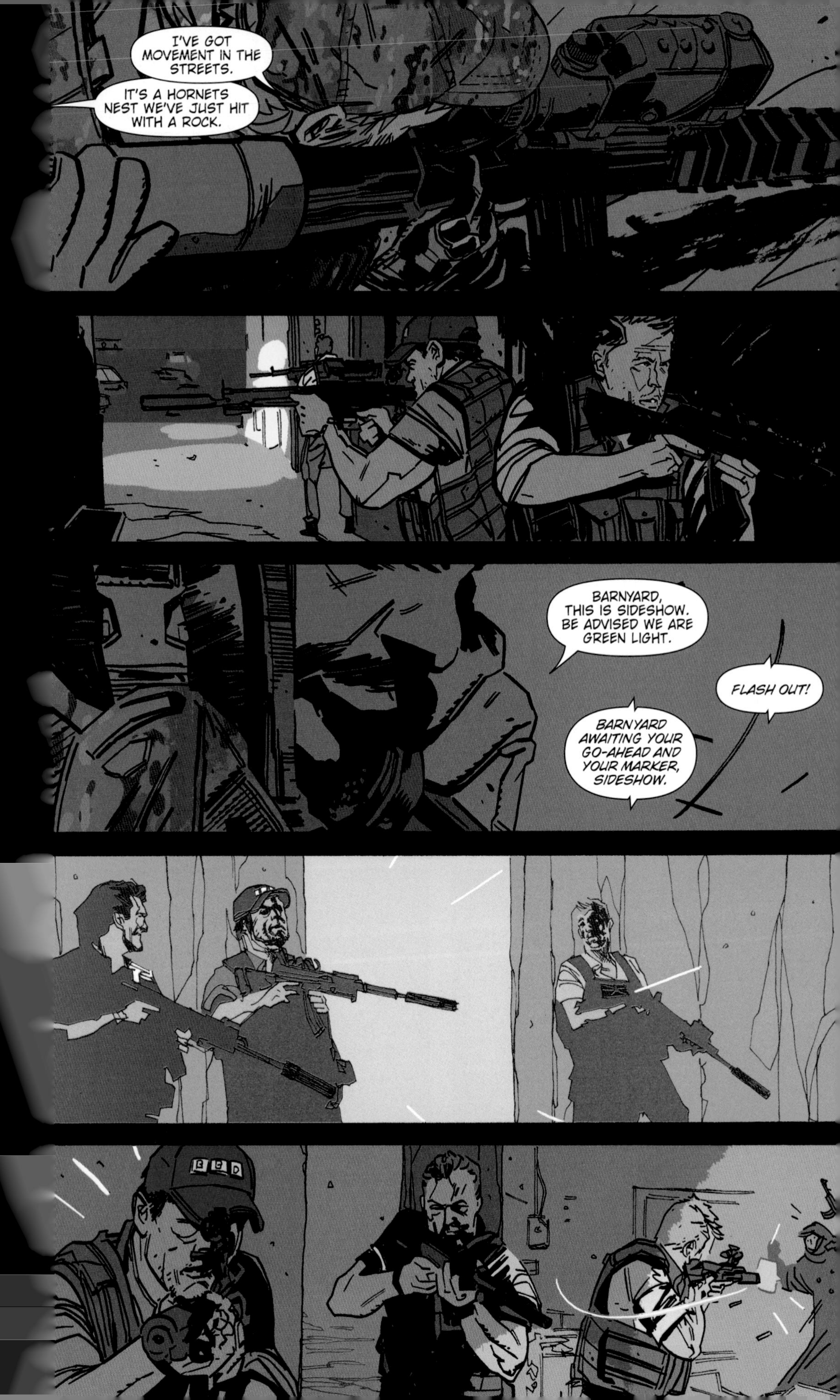
I'VE GOT MOVEMENT IN THE STREETS.
IT'S A HORNETS NEST WE'VE JUST HIT WITH A ROCK.
BARNYARD, THIS IS SIDESHOW. BE ADVISED WE ARE GREEN LIGHT.
BARNYARD AWAITING YOUR GO-AHEAD AND YOUR MARKER, SIDESHOW.
FLASH OUT!
BBD

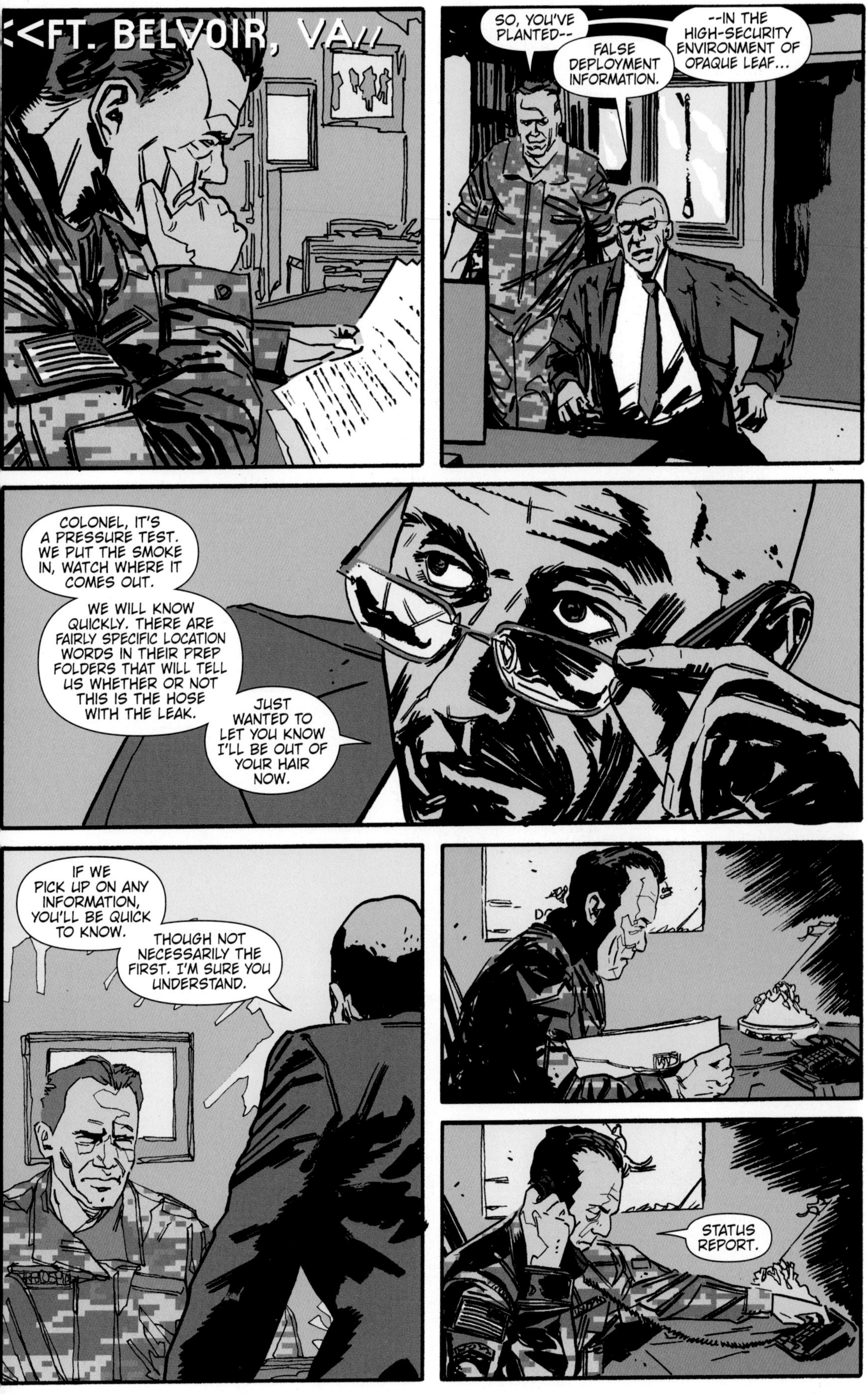

<<FT. BELVOIR, VA//
SO, YOU'VE PLANTED--
FALSE DEPLOYMENT INFORMATION.
--IN THE HIGH-SECURITY ENVIRONMENT OF OPAQUE LEAF...
COLONEL, IT'S A PRESSURE TEST. WE PUT THE SMOKE IN, WATCH WHERE IT COMES OUT.
WE WILL KNOW QUICKLY. THERE ARE FAIRLY SPECIFIC LOCATION WORDS IN THEIR PREP FOLDERS THAT WILL TELL US WHETHER OR NOT THIS IS THE HOSE WITH THE LEAK.
JUST WANTED TO LET YOU KNOW I'LL BE OUT OF YOUR HAIR NOW.
IF WE PICK UP ON ANY INFORMATION, YOU'LL BE QUICK TO KNOW.
THOUGH NOT NECESSARILY THE FIRST. I'M SURE YOU UNDERSTAND.
STATUS REPORT.

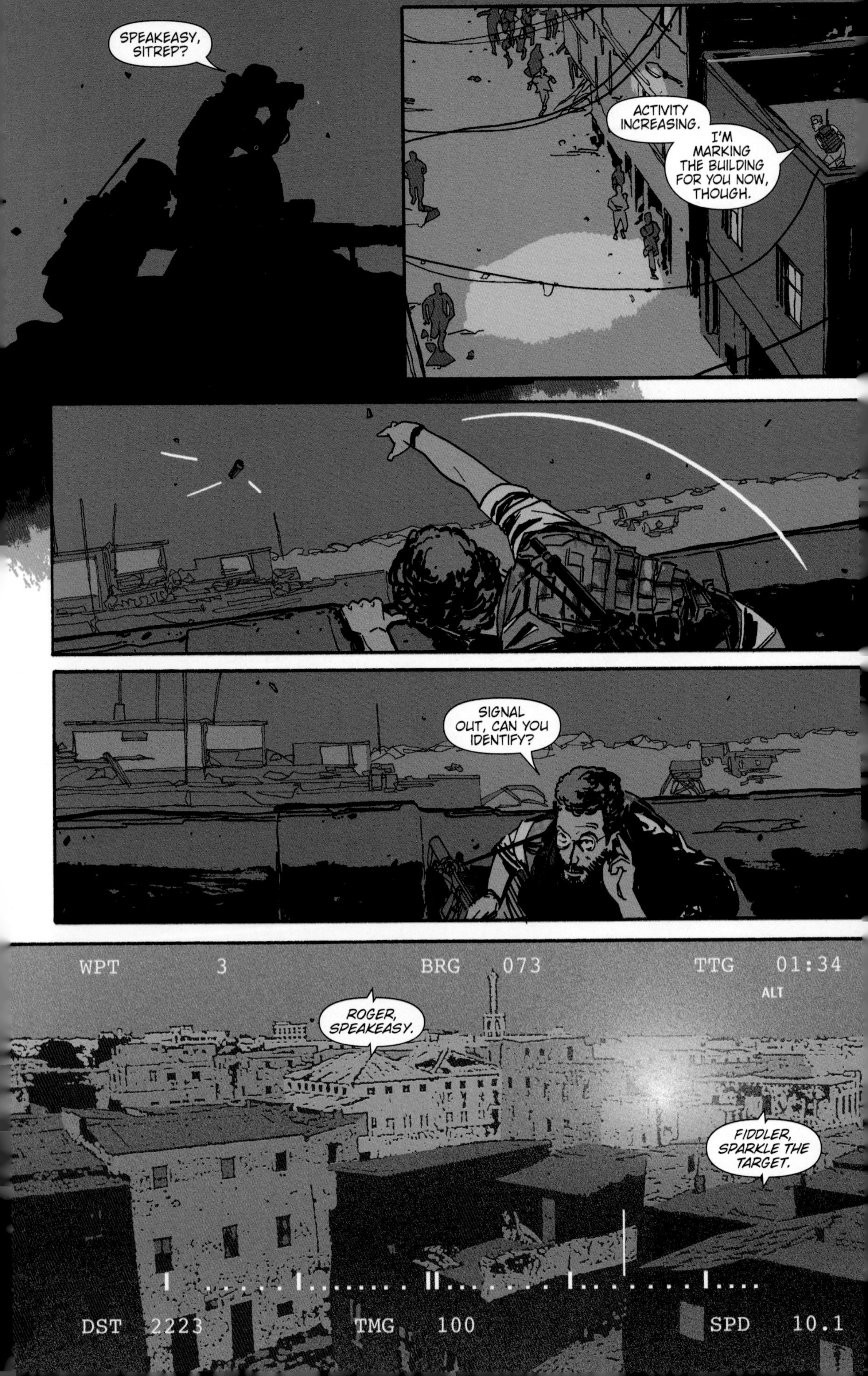
SPEAKEASY, SITREP?
ACTIVITY INCREASING.
I'M MARKING THE BUILDING FOR YOU NOW, THOUGH.
SIGNAL OUT, CAN YOU IDENTIFY?
WPT 3
BRG 073
TTG 01:34
ALT
ROGER, SPEAKEASY.
FIDDLER, SPARKLE THE TARGET.
DST 2223
TMG 100
SPD 10.1

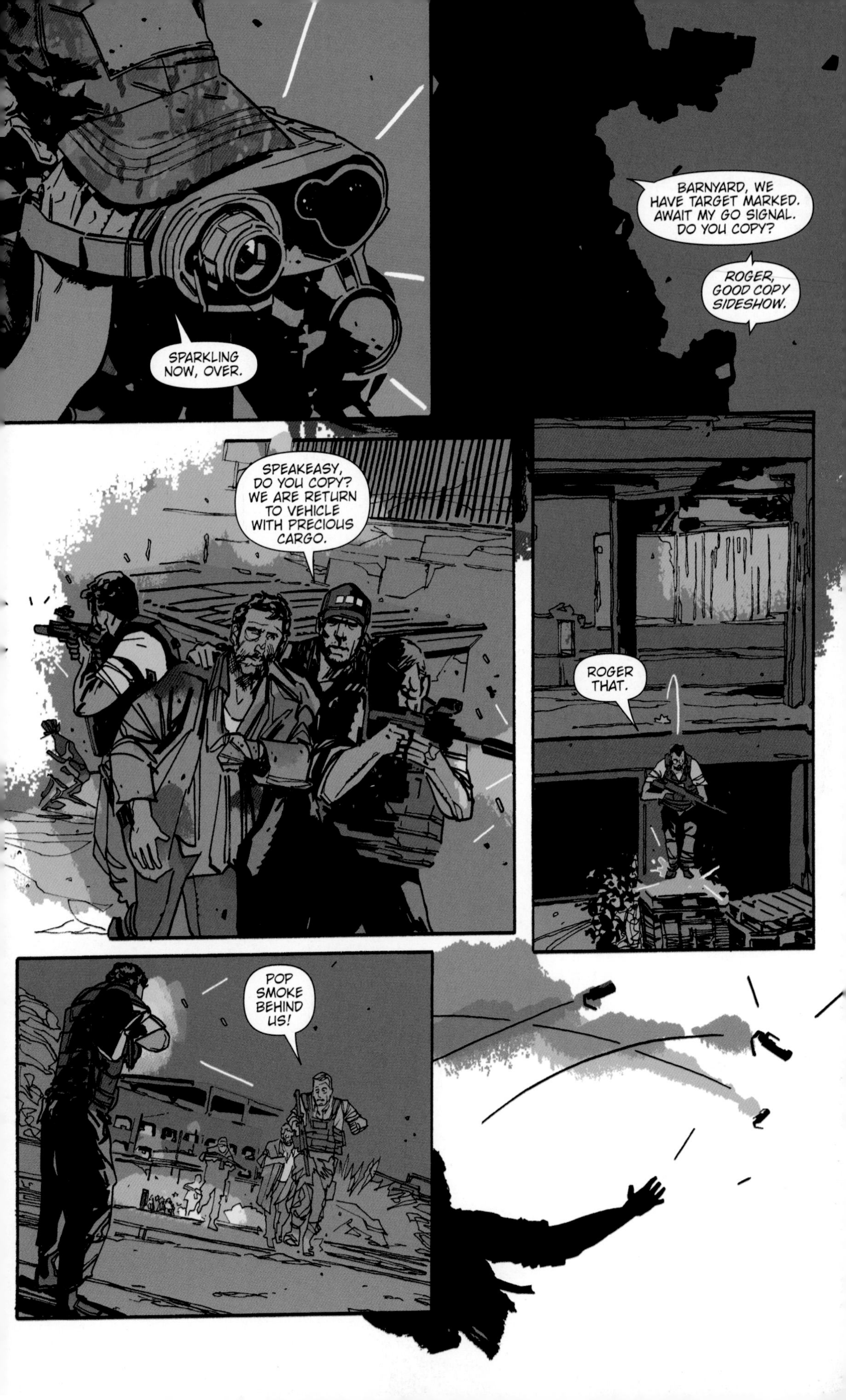
SPARKLING NOW, OVER.
BARNYARD, WE HAVE TARGET MARKED. AWAIT MY GO SIGNAL. DO YOU COPY?
ROGER, GOOD COPY SIDESHOW.
SPEAKEASY, DO YOU COPY? WE ARE RETURN TO VEHICLE WITH PRECIOUS CARGO.
ROGER THAT.
POP SMOKE BEHIND US!

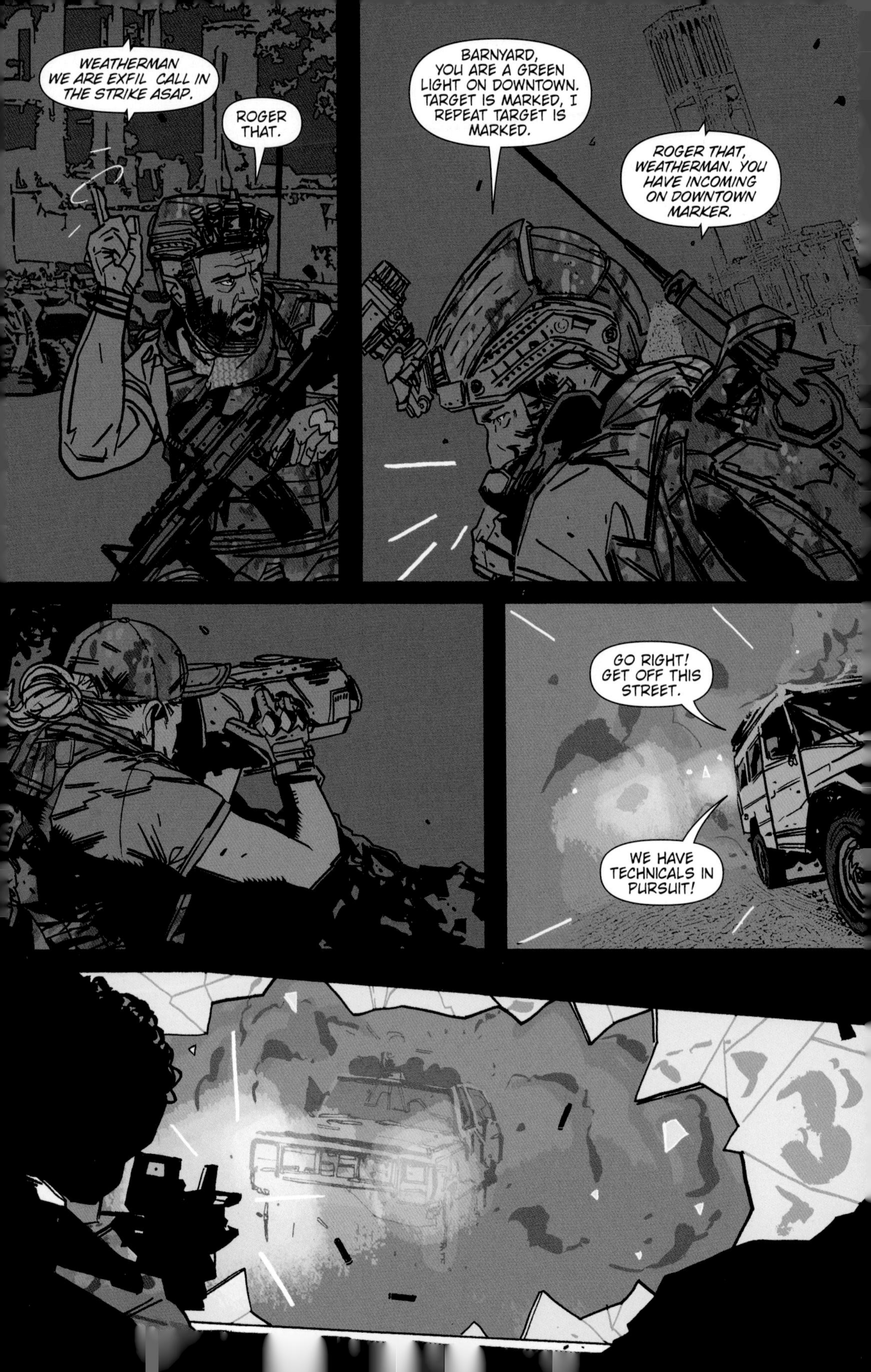
WEATHERMAN WE ARE EXFIL CALL IN THE STRIKE ASAP.
ROGER THAT.
BARNYARD, YOU ARE A GREEN LIGHT ON DOWNTOWN. TARGET IS MARKED, I REPEAT TARGET IS MARKED.
ROGER THAT, WEATHERMAN. YOU HAVE INCOMING ON DOWNTOWN MARKER.
GO RIGHT! GET OFF THIS STREET.
WE HAVE TECHNICALS IN PURSUIT!

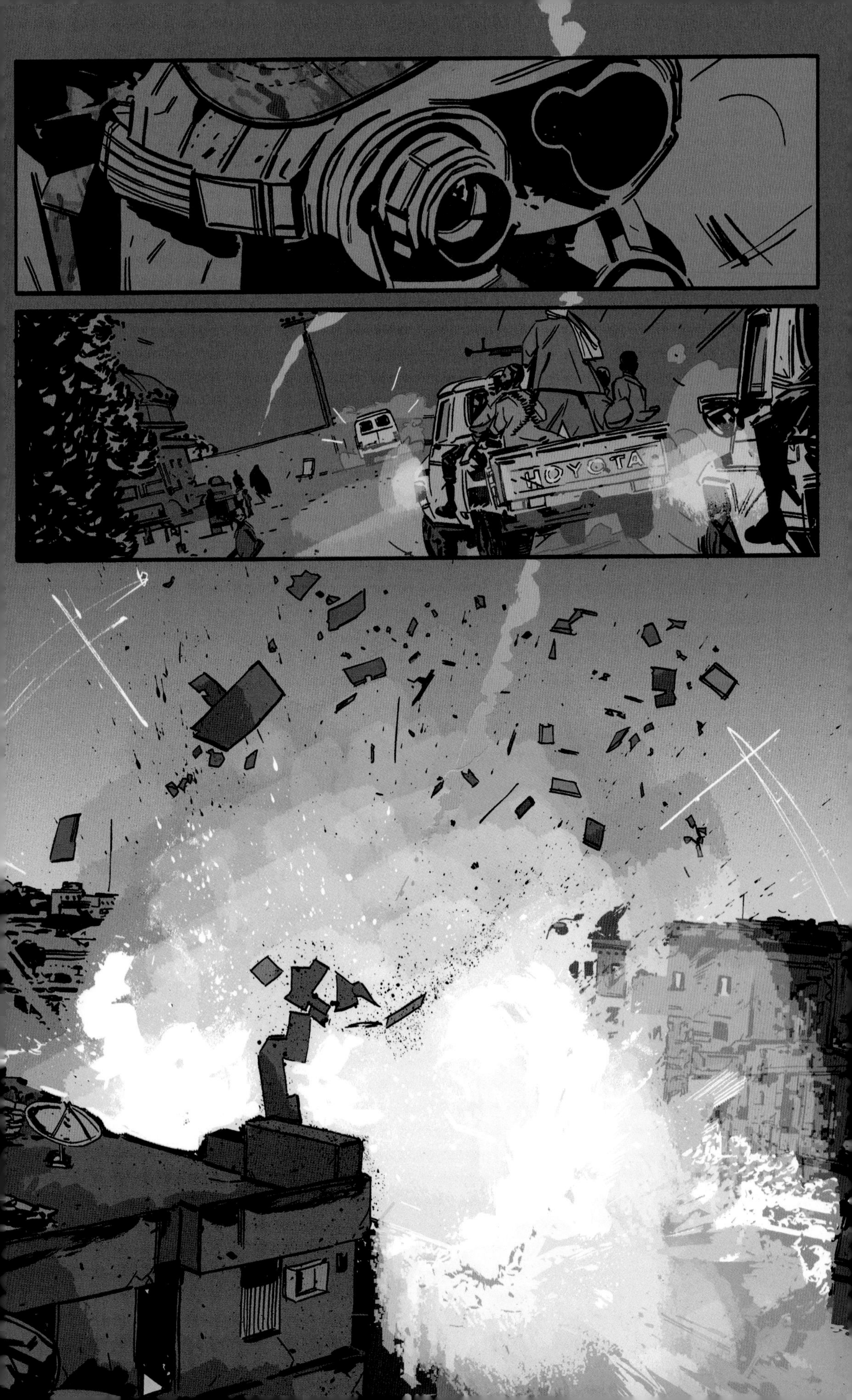

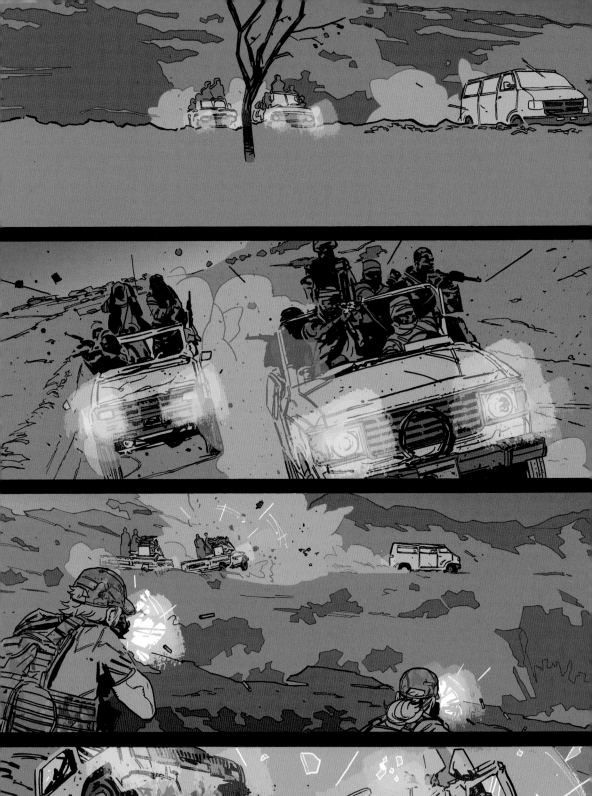

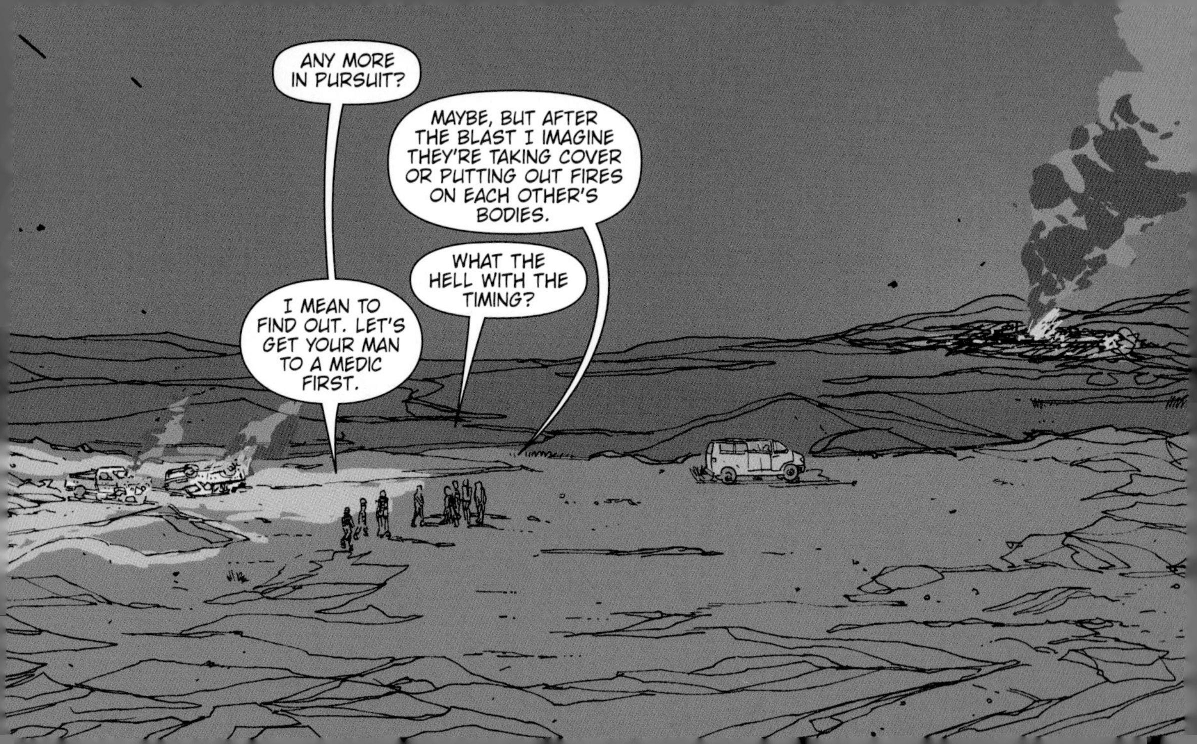
ANY MORE IN PURSUIT?
MAYBE, BUT AFTER THE BLAST I IMAGINE THEY'RE TAKING COVER OR PUTTING OUT FIRES ON EACH OTHER'S BODIES.
I MEAN TO FIND OUT. LET'S GET YOUR MAN TO A MEDIC FIRST.
WHAT THE HELL WITH THE TIMING?

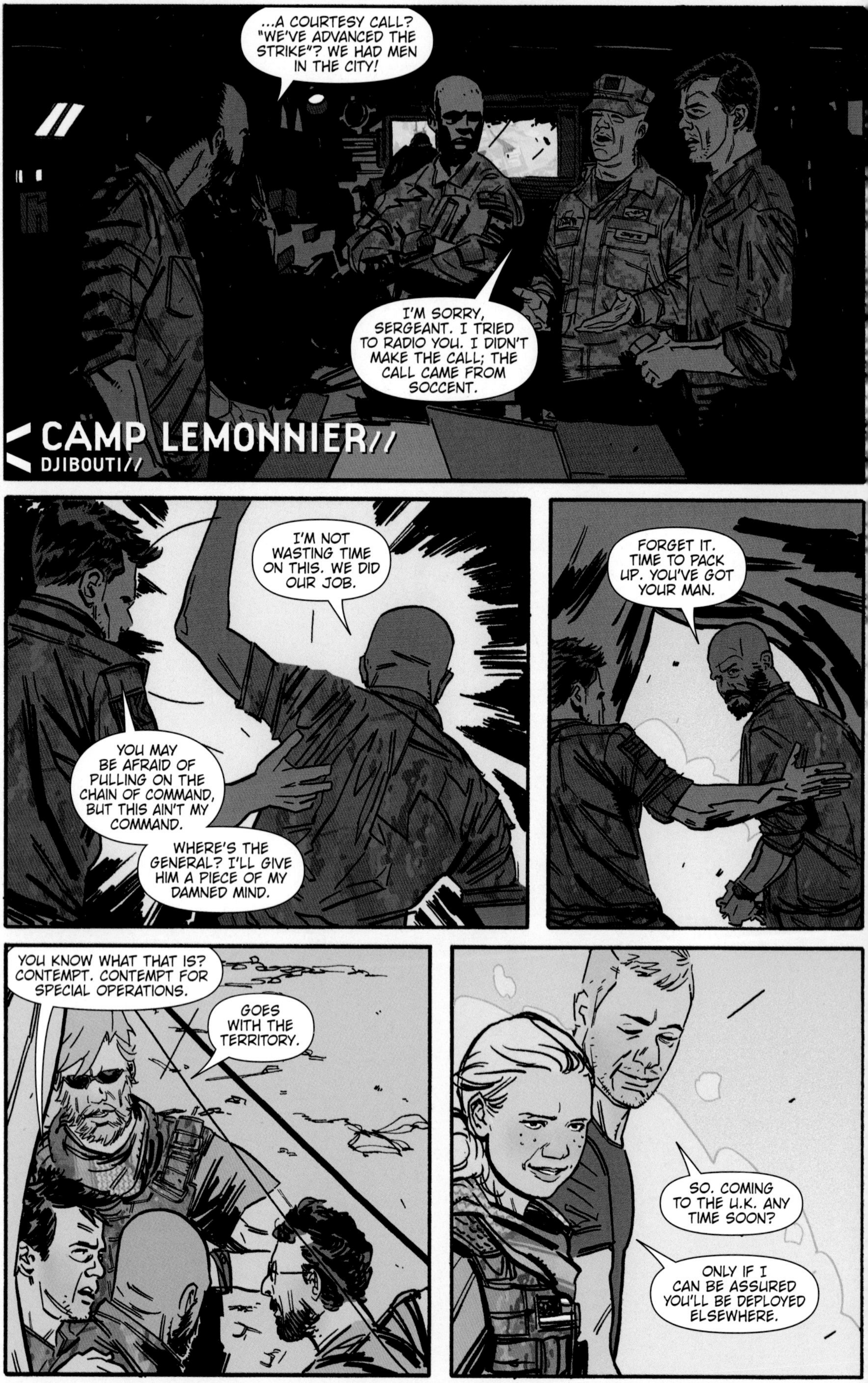

...A COURTESY CALL? "WE'VE ADVANCED THE STRIKE"? WE HAD MEN IN THE CITY!
I'M SORRY, SERGEANT. I TRIED TO RADIO YOU. I DIDN'T MAKE THE CALL; THE CALL CAME FROM SOCCENT.
CAMP LEMONNIER//
DJIBOUTI//
I'M NOT WASTING TIME ON THIS. WE DID OUR JOB.
YOU MAY BE AFRAID OF PULLING ON THE CHAIN OF COMMAND, BUT THIS AIN'T MY COMMAND.
WHERE'S THE GENERAL? I'LL GIVE HIM A PIECE OF MY DAMNED MIND.
FORGET IT. TIME TO PACK UP. YOU'VE GOT YOUR MAN.
YOU KNOW WHAT THAT IS? CONTEMPT. CONTEMPT FOR SPECIAL OPERATIONS.
GOES WITH THE TERRITORY.
SO. COMING TO THE U.K. ANY TIME SOON?
ONLY IF I CAN BE ASSURED YOU'LL BE DEPLOYED ELSEWHERE.

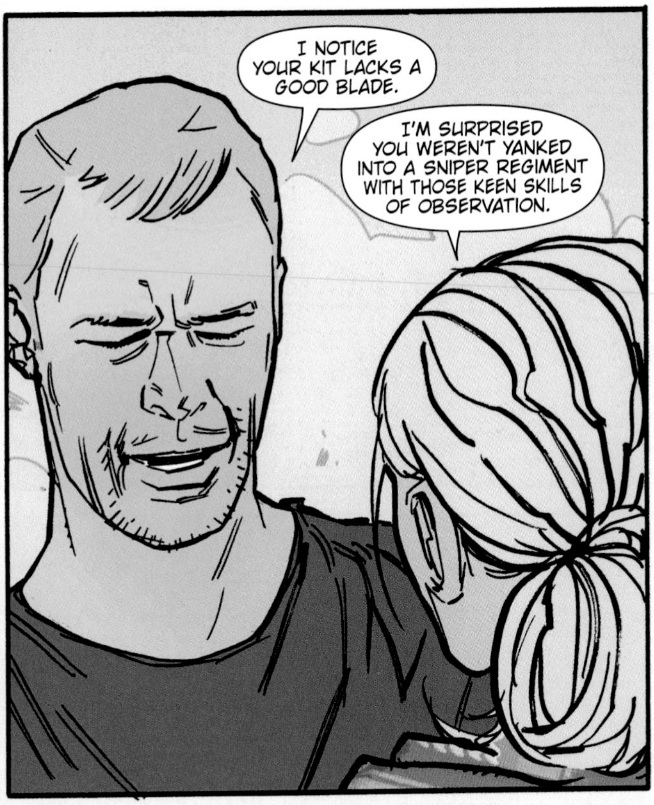
I NOTICE YOUR KIT LACKS A GOOD BLADE.
I'M SURPRISED YOU WEREN'T YANKED INTO A SNIPER REGIMENT WITH THOSE KEEN SKILLS OF OBSERVATION.

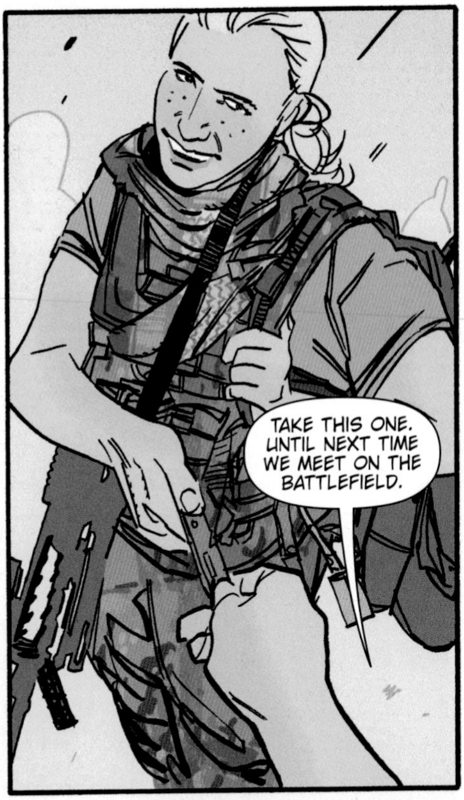
TAKE THIS ONE. UNTIL NEXT TIME WE MEET ON THE BATTLEFIELD.

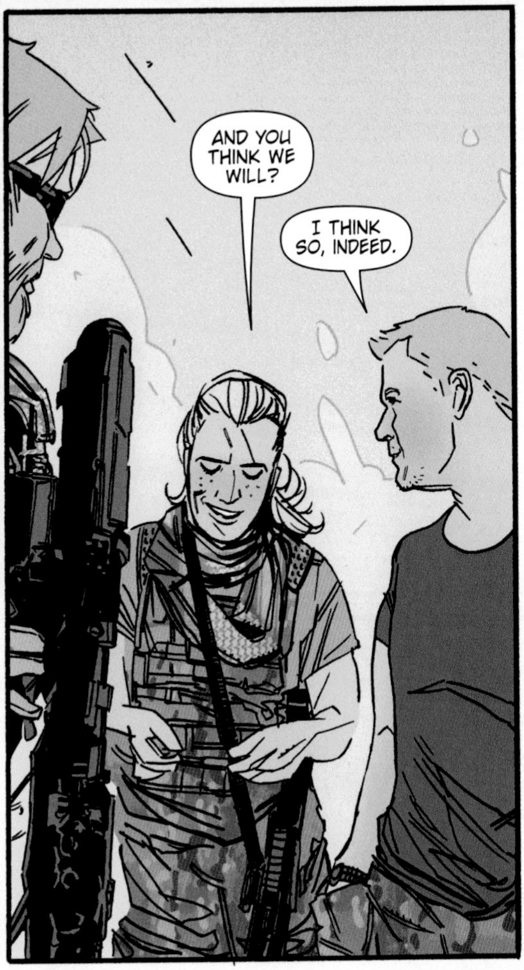
AND YOU THINK WE WILL?
I THINK SO, INDEED.

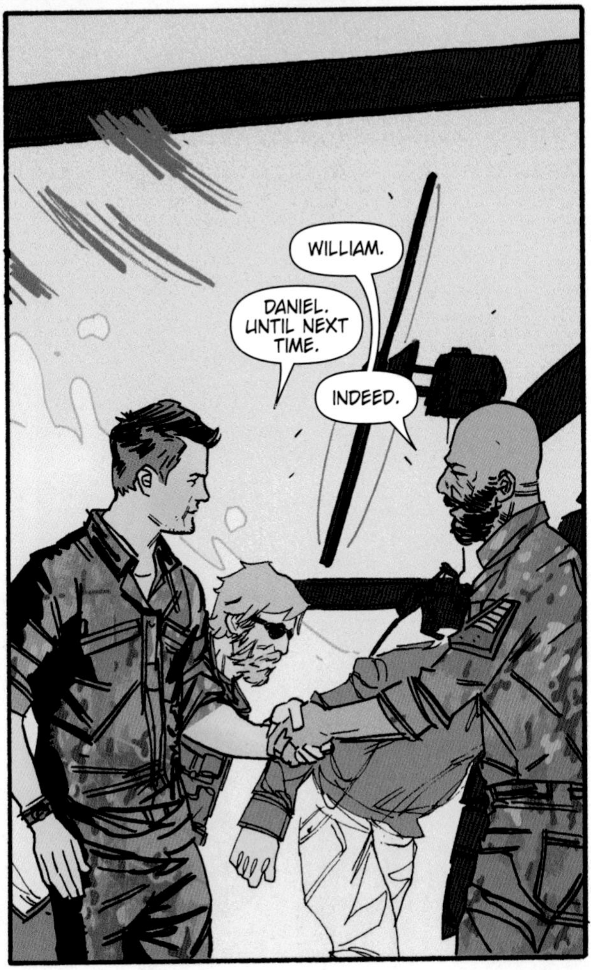
WILLIAM.
DANIEL. UNTIL NEXT TIME.
INDEED.

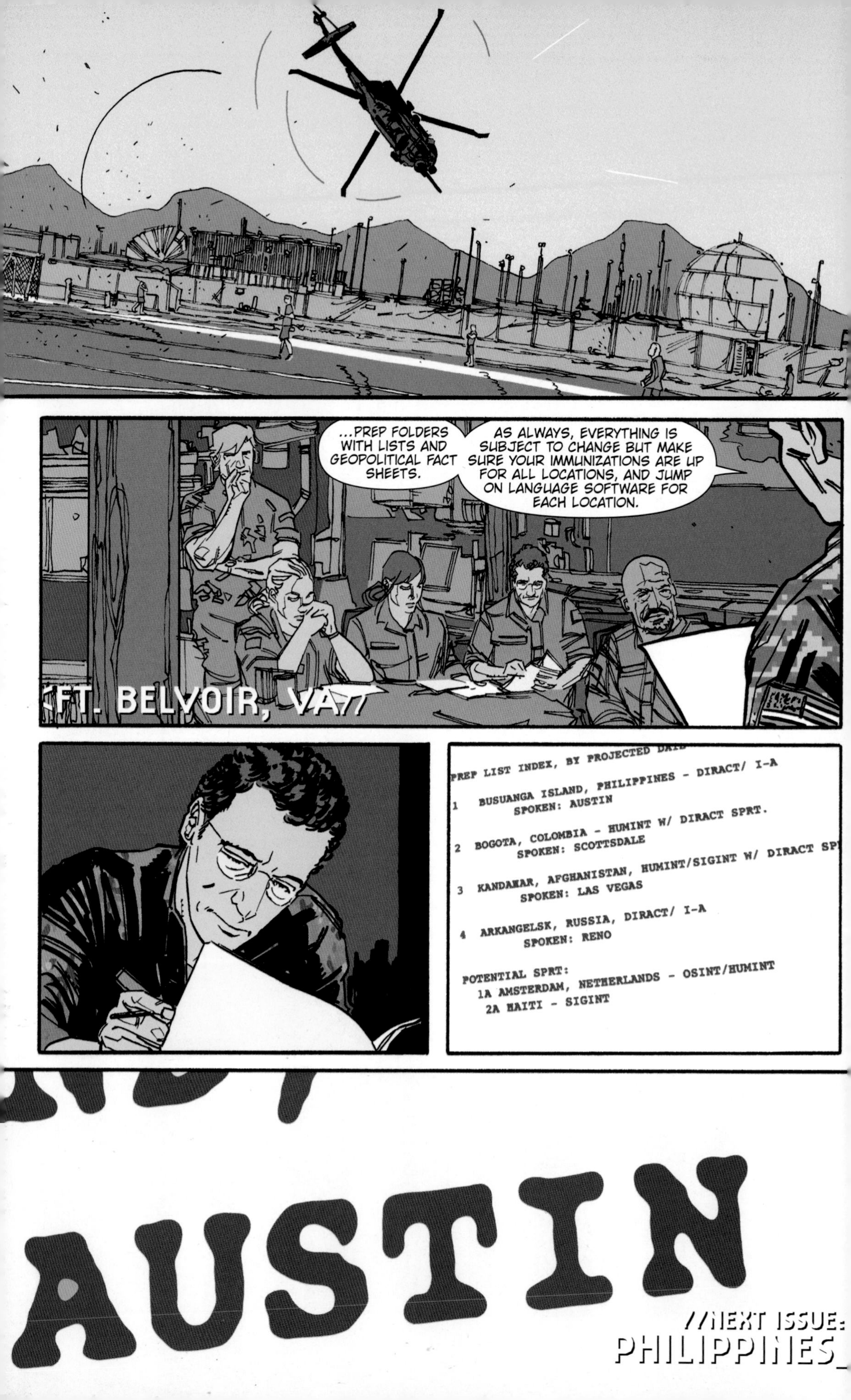
...PREP FOLDERS WITH LISTS AND GEOPOLITICAL FACT SHEETS.
AS ALWAYS, EVERYTHING IS SUBJECT TO CHANGE BUT MAKE SURE YOUR IMMUNIZATIONS ARE UP FOR ALL LOCATIONS, AND JUMP ON LANGUAGE SOFTWARE FOR EACH LOCATION.
<FT. BELVOIR, VA//
PREP LIST INDEX, BY PROJECTED DATE
1 BUSUANGA ISLAND, PHILIPPINES - DIRACT/ I-A
SPOKEN: AUSTIN
2 BOGOTA, COLOMBIA - HUMINT W/ DIRACT SPRT.
SPOKEN: SCOTTSDALE
3 KANDAHAR, AFGHANISTAN, HUMINT/SIGINT W/ DIRACT SP
SPOKEN: LAS VEGAS
4 ARKANGELSK, RUSSIA, DIRACT/ I-A
SPOKEN: RENO
POTENTIAL SPRT:
1A AMSTERDAM, NETHERLANDS - OSINT/HUMINT
2A HAITI - SIGINT
AUSTIN
//NEXT ISSUE:
PHILIPPINES_

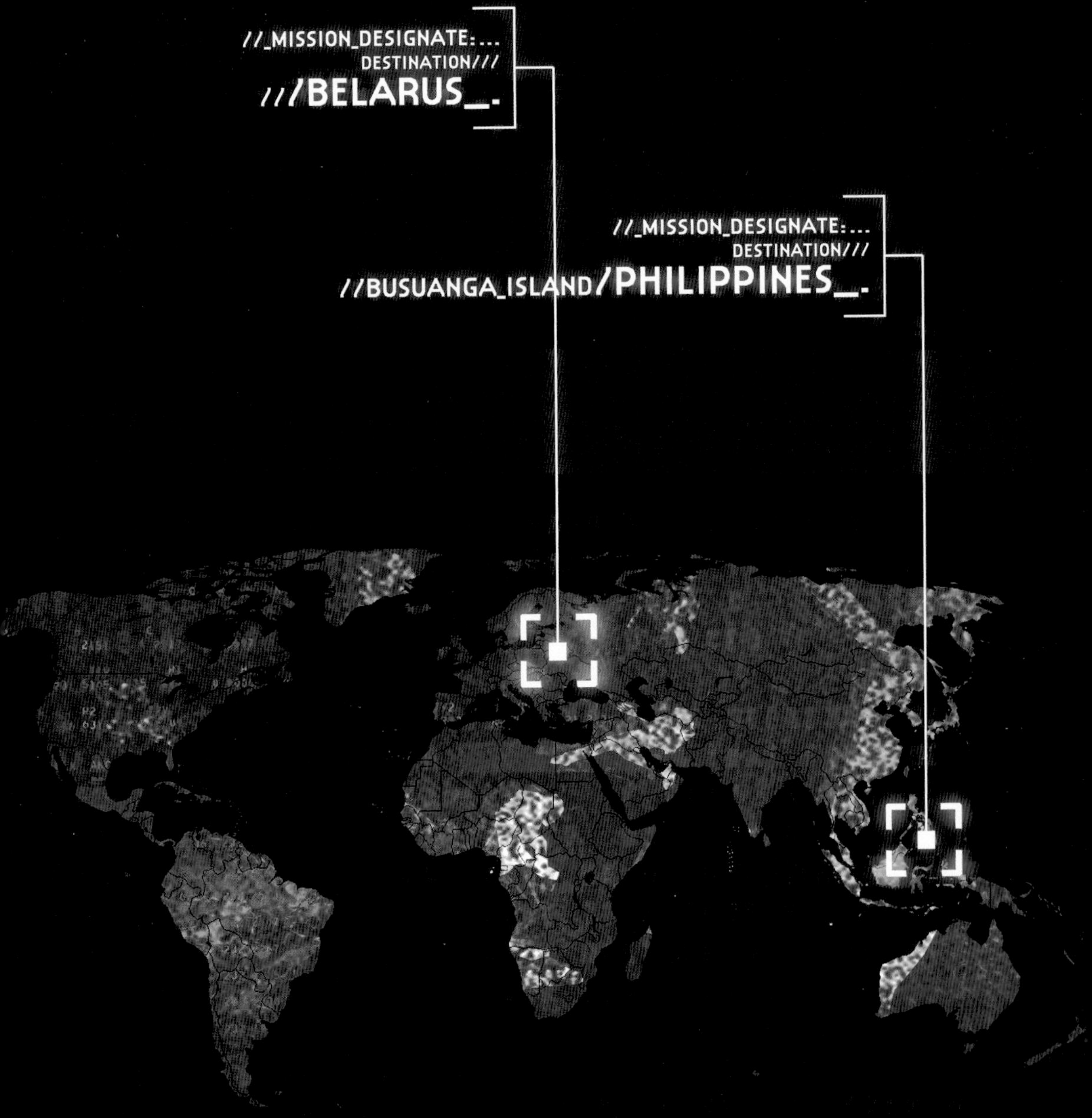
//_MISSION_DESIGNATE:...
DESTINATION///
///BELARUS_.
//_MISSION_DESIGNATE:...
DESTINATION///
//BUSUANGA_ISLAND/PHILIPPINES_.

//MISSION_REPORT_
//INITIALIZING____

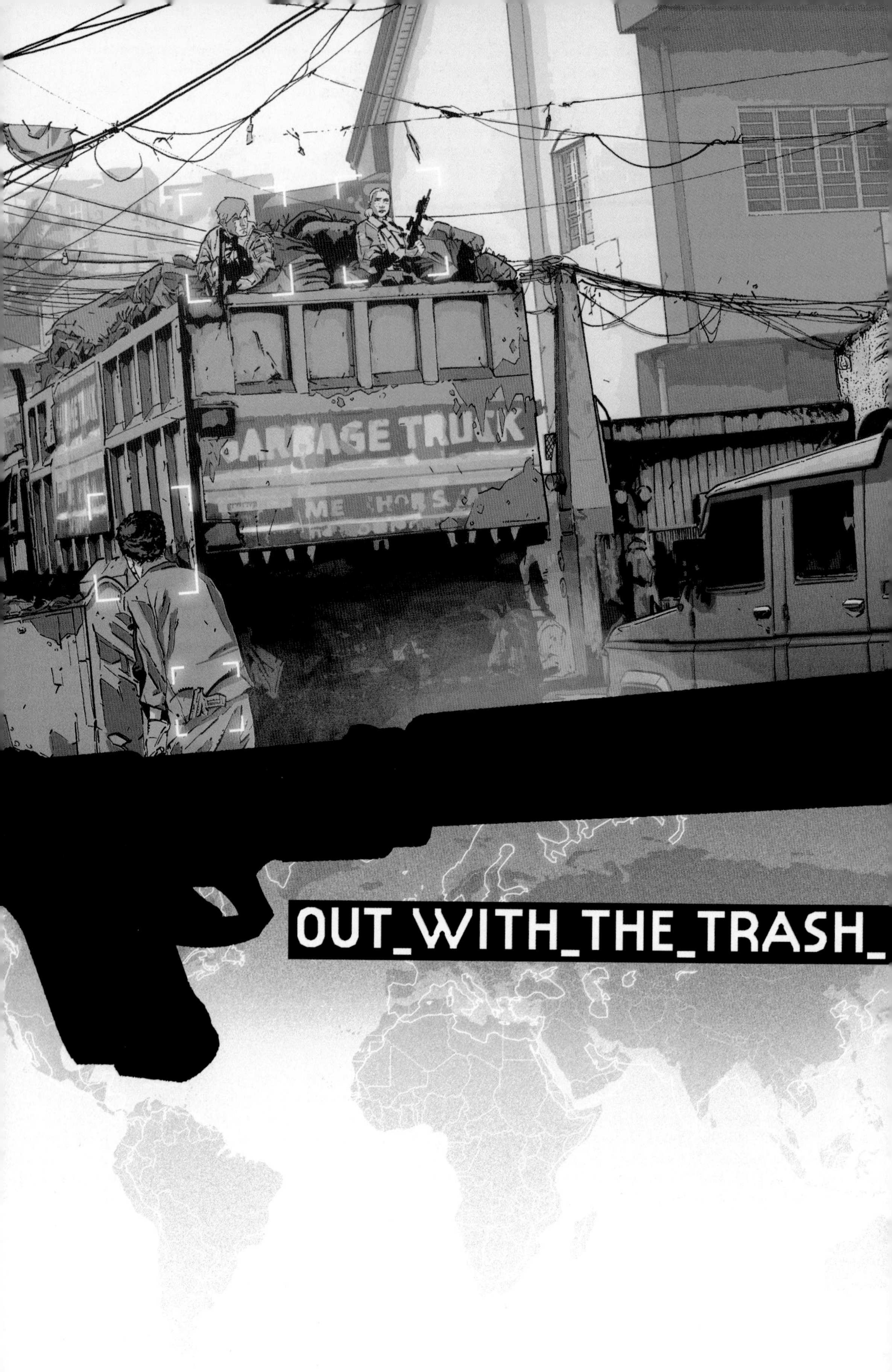
GARBAGE TRUCK

OUT_WITH_THE_TRASH_

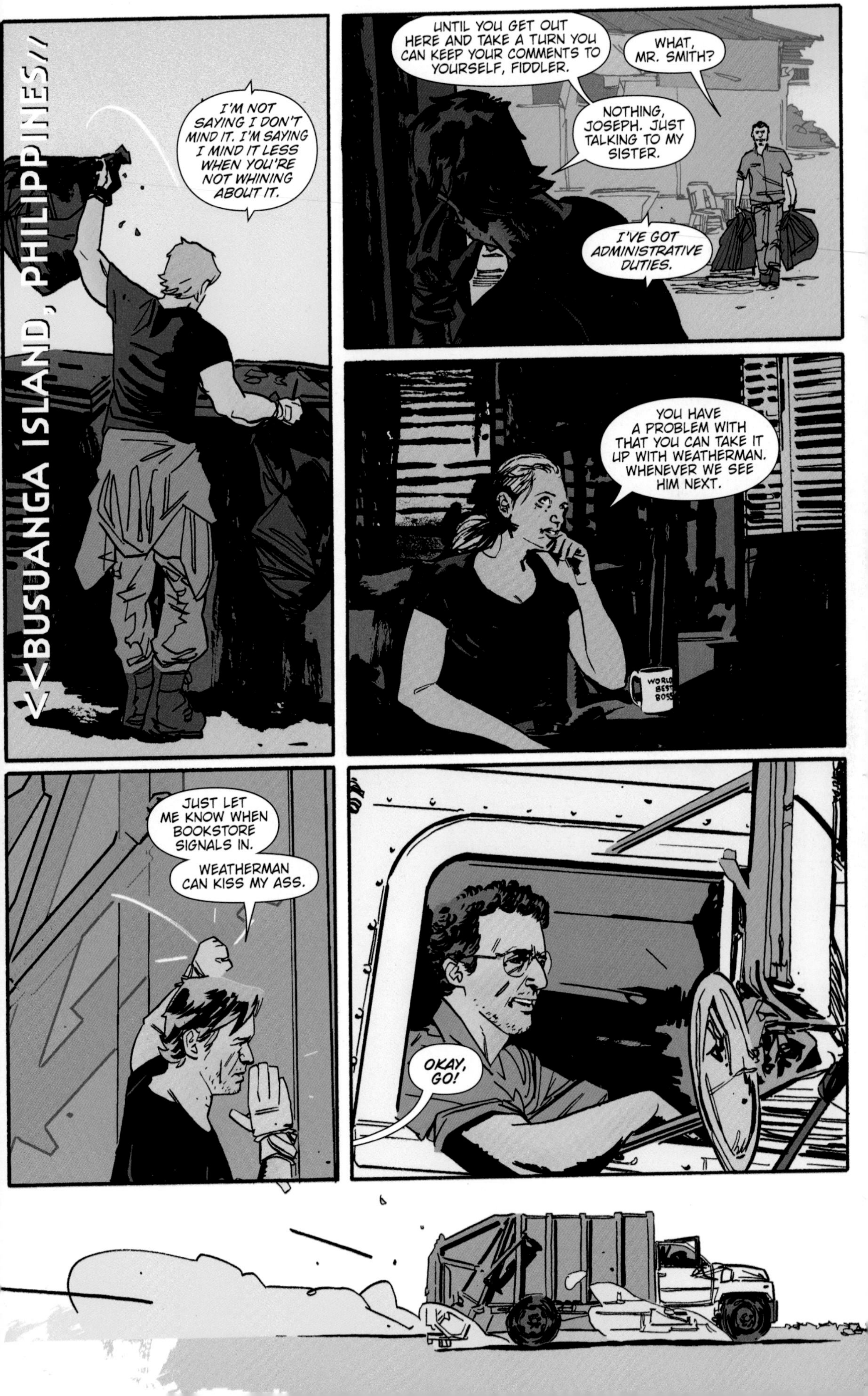

<<BUSUANGA ISLAND, PHILIPPINES//
I'M NOT SAYING I DON'T MIND IT. I'M SAYING I MIND IT LESS WHEN YOU'RE NOT WHINING ABOUT IT.
UNTIL YOU GET OUT HERE AND TAKE A TURN YOU CAN KEEP YOUR COMMENTS TO YOURSELF, FIDDLER.
WHAT, MR. SMITH?
NOTHING, JOSEPH. JUST TALKING TO MY SISTER.
I'VE GOT ADMINISTRATIVE DUTIES.
YOU HAVE A PROBLEM WITH THAT YOU CAN TAKE IT UP WITH WEATHERMAN. WHENEVER WE SEE HIM NEXT.
JUST LET ME KNOW WHEN BOOKSTORE SIGNALS IN.
WEATHERMAN CAN KISS MY ASS.
OKAY, GO!

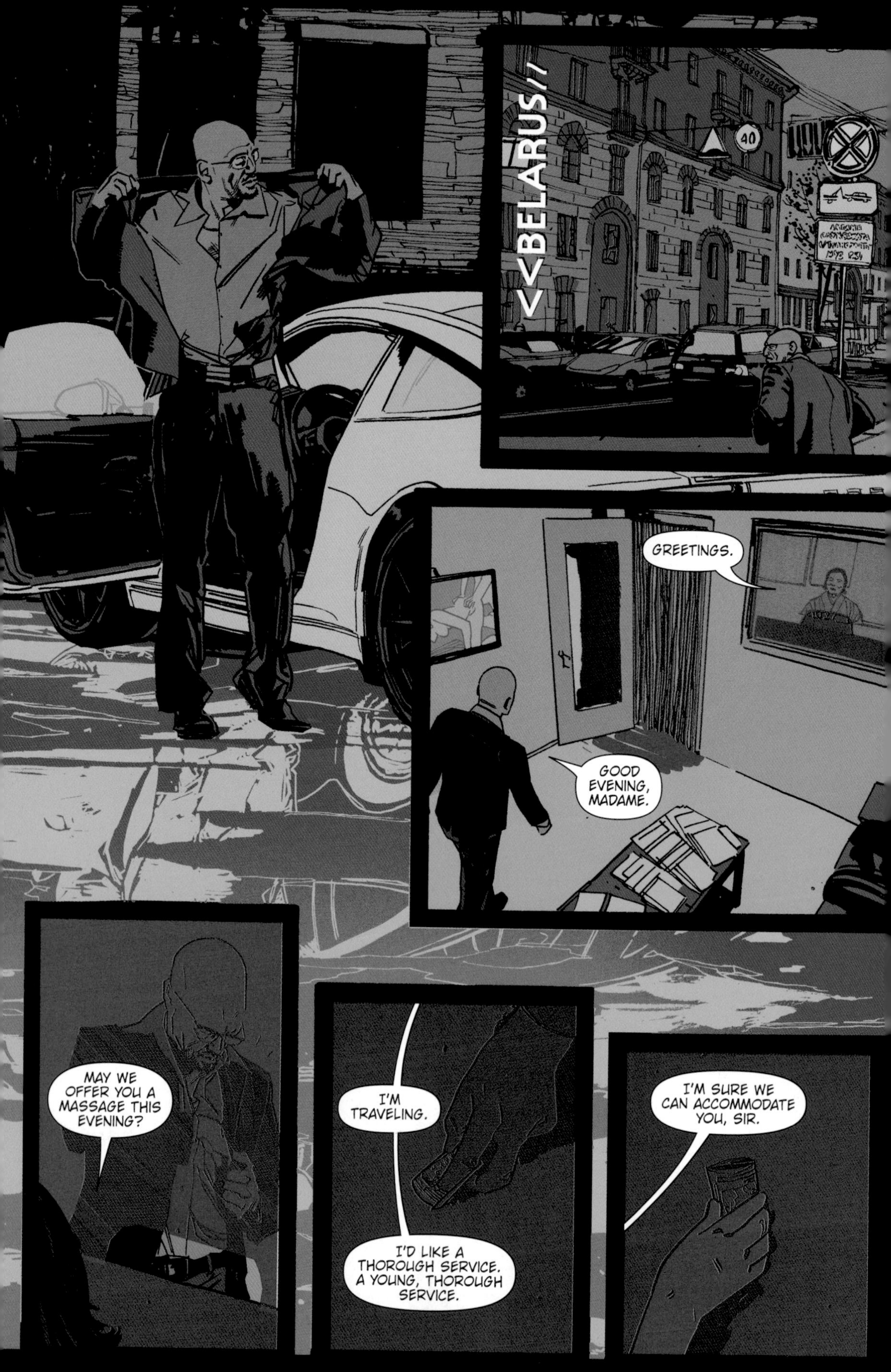

<<BELARUS//
GREETINGS.
GOOD EVENING, MADAME.
MAY WE OFFER YOU A MASSAGE THIS EVENING?
I'M TRAVELING.
I'D LIKE A THOROUGH SERVICE. A YOUNG, THOROUGH SERVICE.
I'M SURE WE CAN ACCOMMODATE YOU, SIR.

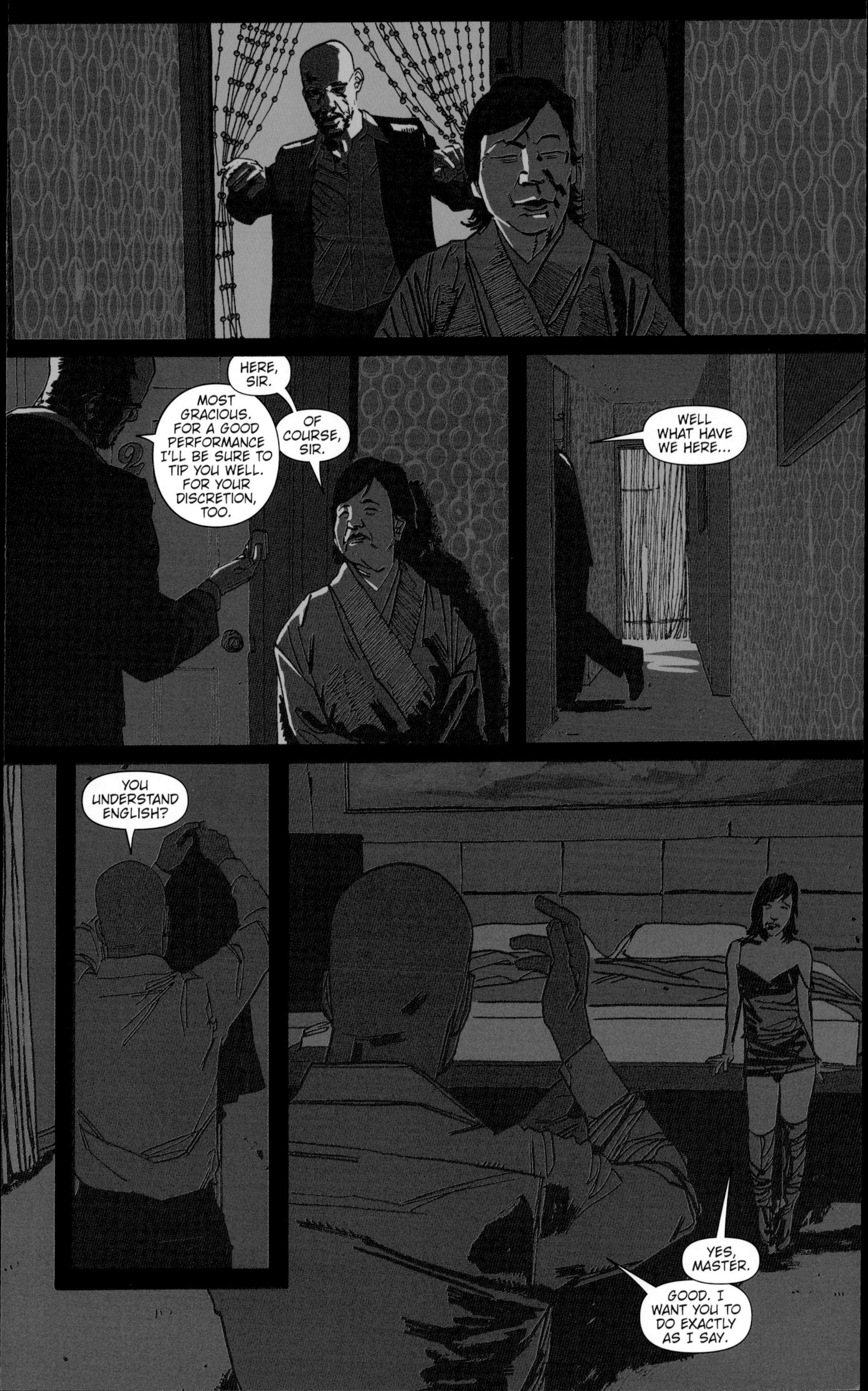
HERE, SIR.
MOST GRACIOUS. FOR A GOOD PERFORMANCE I'LL BE SURE TO TIP YOU WELL. FOR YOUR DISCRETION, TOO.
OF COURSE, SIR.
WELL WHAT HAVE WE HERE...
YOU UNDERSTAND ENGLISH?
YES, MASTER.
GOOD. I WANT YOU TO DO EXACTLY AS I SAY.

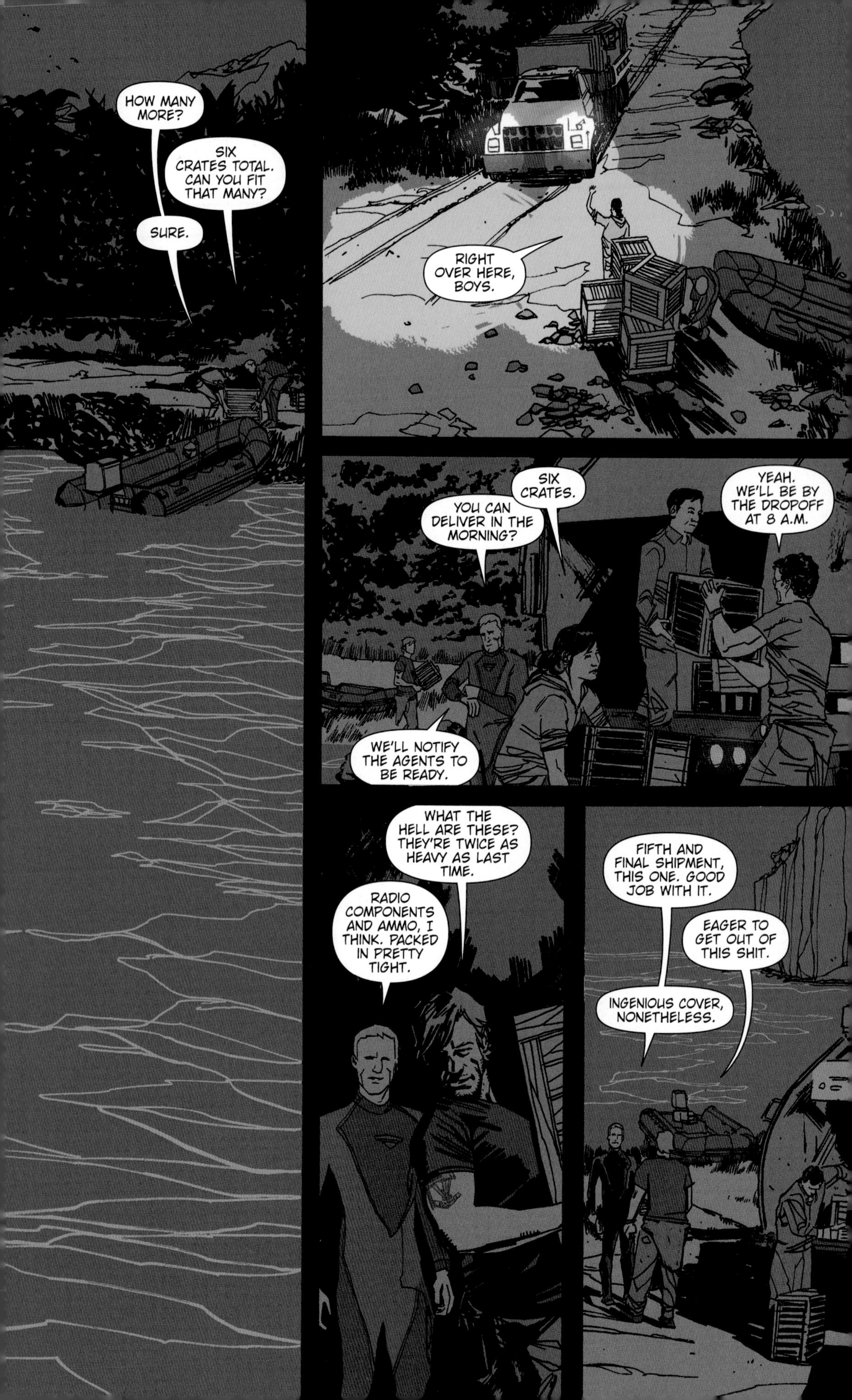
HOW MANY MORE?
SIX CRATES TOTAL. CAN YOU FIT THAT MANY?
SURE.
RIGHT OVER HERE, BOYS.
YOU CAN DELIVER IN THE MORNING?
SIX CRATES.
YEAH. WE'LL BE BY THE DROPOFF AT 8 A.M.
WE'LL NOTIFY THE AGENTS TO BE READY.
WHAT THE HELL ARE THESE? THEY'RE TWICE AS HEAVY AS LAST TIME.
RADIO COMPONENTS AND AMMO, I THINK. PACKED IN PRETTY TIGHT.
FIFTH AND FINAL SHIPMENT, THIS ONE. GOOD JOB WITH IT.
EAGER TO GET OUT OF THIS SHIT.
INGENIOUS COVER, NONETHELESS.

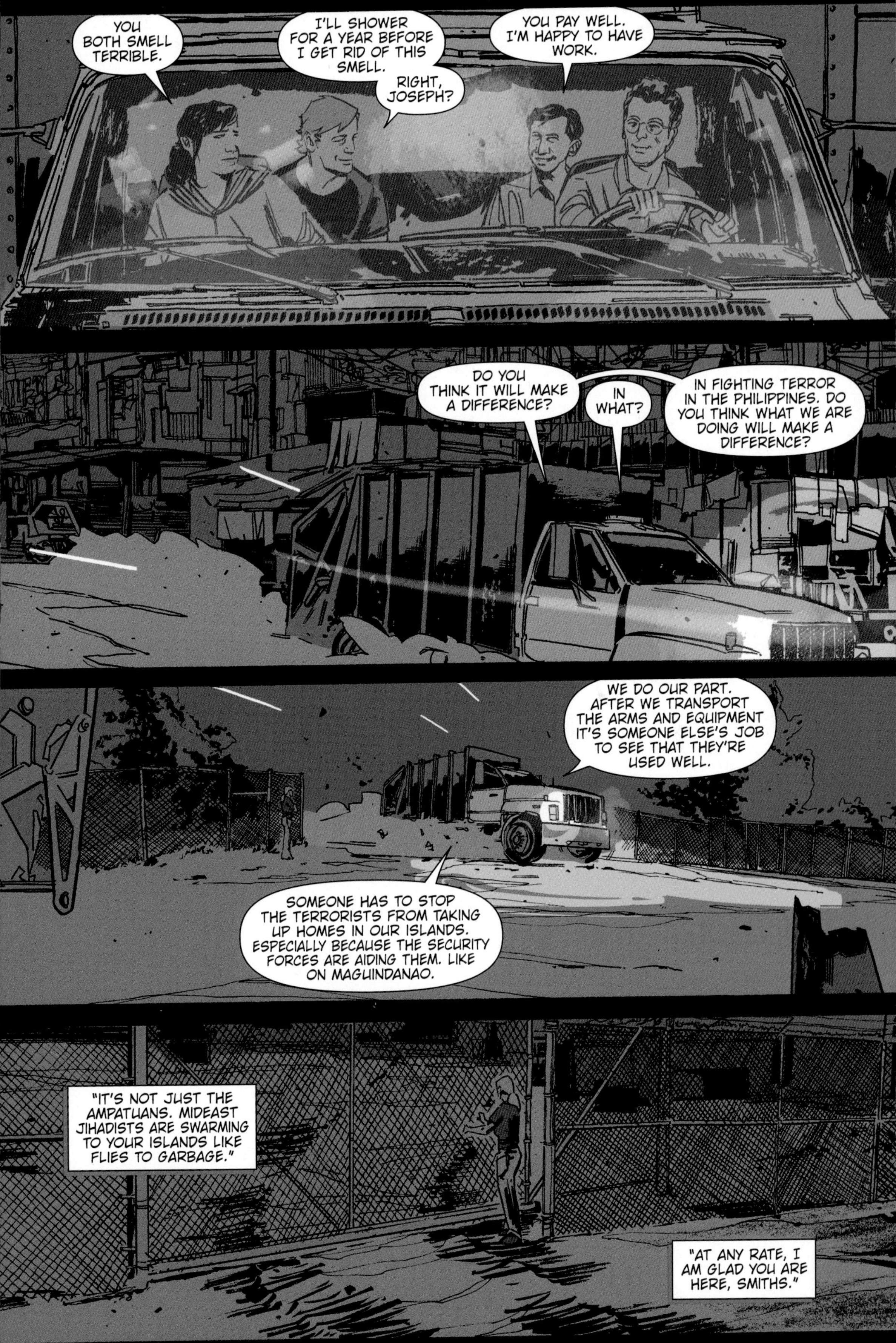
YOU BOTH SMELL TERRIBLE.
I'LL SHOWER FOR A YEAR BEFORE I GET RID OF THIS SMELL.
RIGHT, JOSEPH?
YOU PAY WELL. I'M HAPPY TO HAVE WORK.
DO YOU THINK IT WILL MAKE A DIFFERENCE?
IN WHAT?
IN FIGHTING TERROR IN THE PHILIPPINES. DO YOU THINK WHAT WE ARE DOING WILL MAKE A DIFFERENCE?
WE DO OUR PART. AFTER WE TRANSPORT THE ARMS AND EQUIPMENT IT'S SOMEONE ELSE'S JOB TO SEE THAT THEY'RE USED WELL.
SOMEONE HAS TO STOP THE TERRORISTS FROM TAKING UP HOMES IN OUR ISLANDS. ESPECIALLY BECAUSE THE SECURITY FORCES ARE AIDING THEM. LIKE ON MAGUINDANAO.
"IT'S NOT JUST THE AMPATUANS. MIDEAST JIHADISTS ARE SWARMING TO YOUR ISLANDS LIKE FLIES TO GARBAGE."
"AT ANY RATE, I AM GLAD YOU ARE HERE, SMITHS."

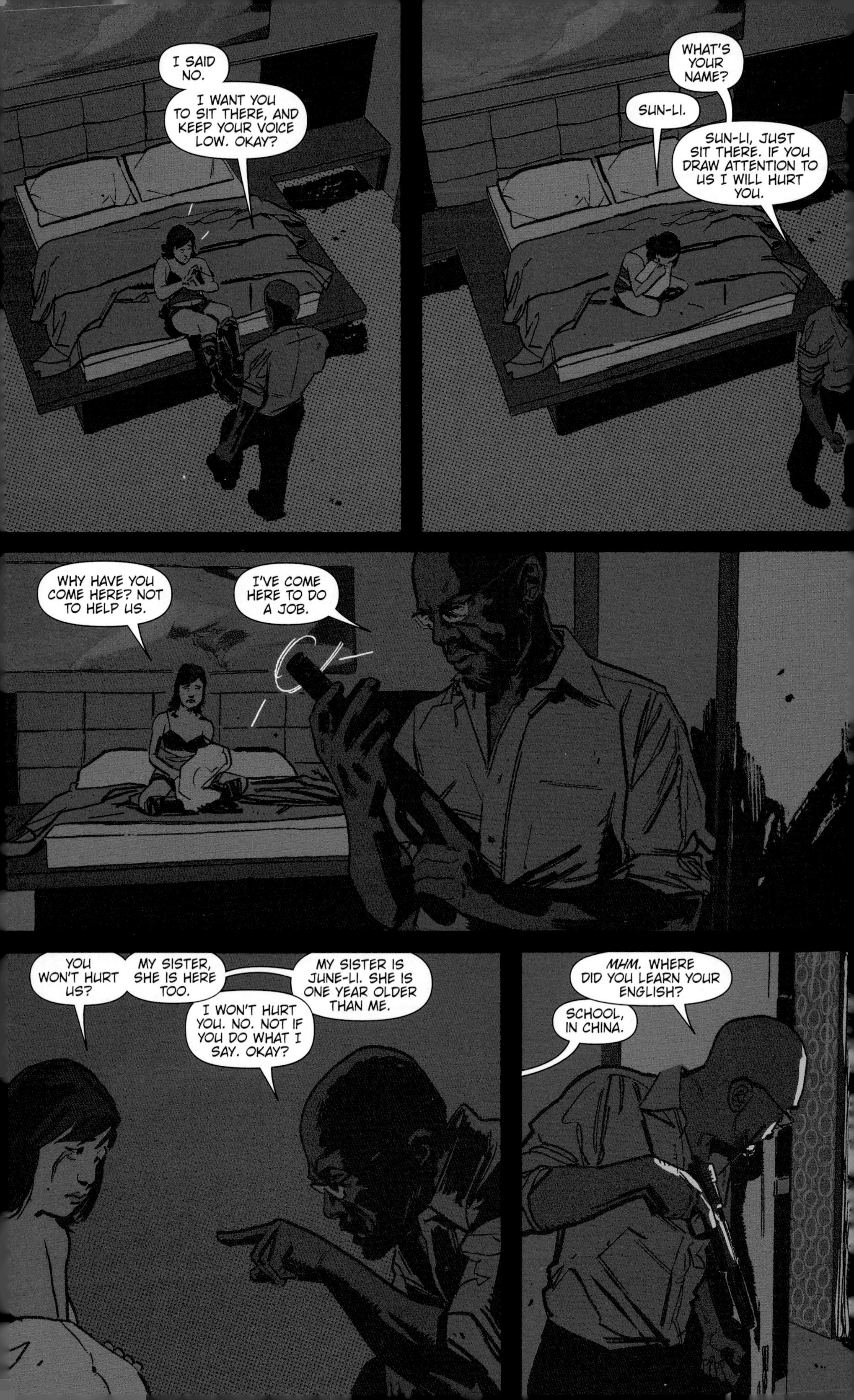

I SAID NO.
I WANT YOU TO SIT THERE, AND KEEP YOUR VOICE LOW. OKAY?
WHAT'S YOUR NAME?
SUN-LI.
SUN-LI, JUST SIT THERE. IF YOU DRAW ATTENTION TO US I WILL HURT YOU.
WHY HAVE YOU COME HERE? NOT TO HELP US.
I'VE COME HERE TO DO A JOB.
YOU WON'T HURT US?
I WON'T HURT YOU. NO. NOT IF YOU DO WHAT I SAY. OKAY?
MY SISTER, SHE IS HERE TOO.
MY SISTER IS JUNE-LI. SHE IS ONE YEAR OLDER THAN ME.
MHM. WHERE DID YOU LEARN YOUR ENGLISH?
SCHOOL, IN CHINA.

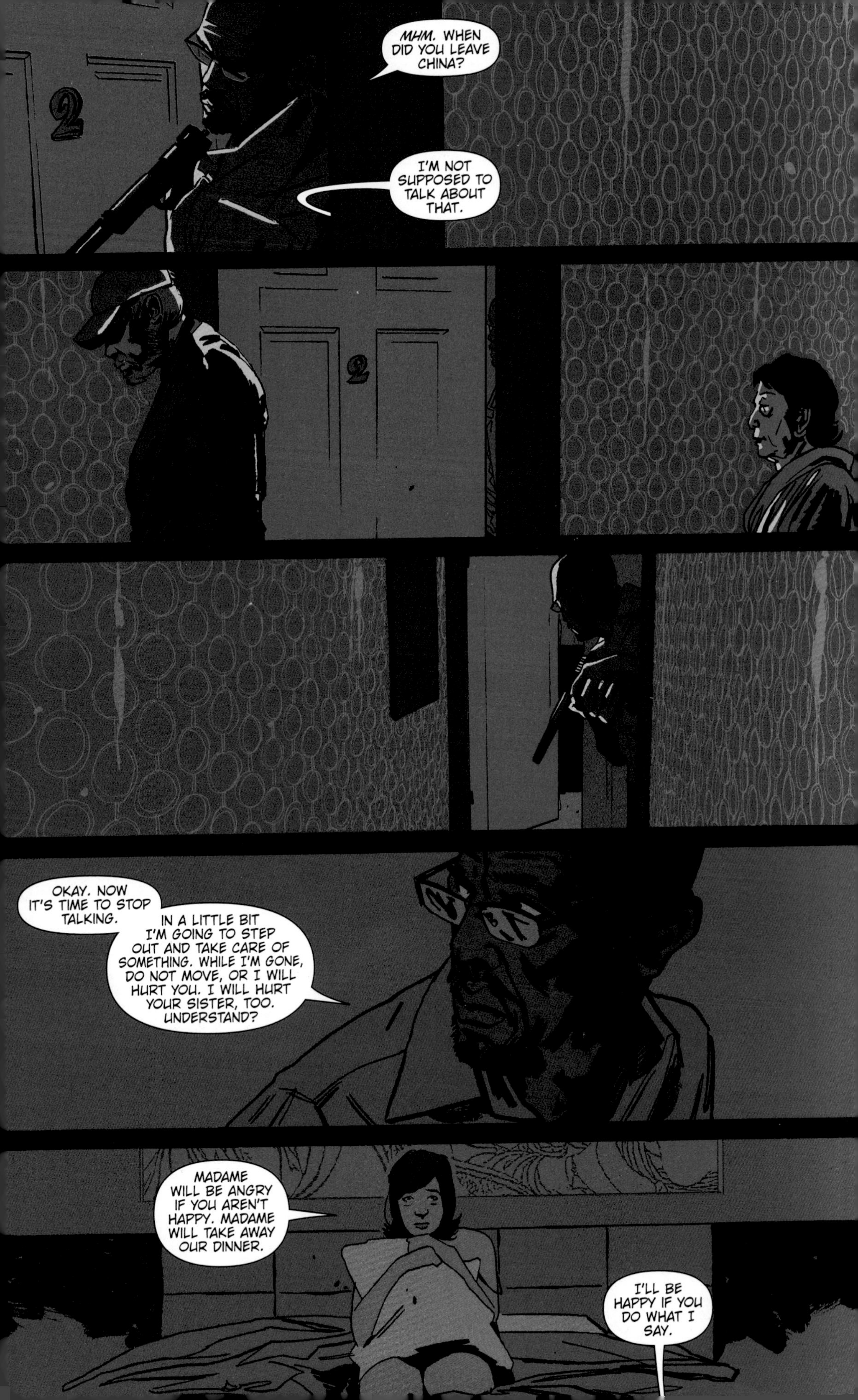

MHM. WHEN DID YOU LEAVE CHINA?
I'M NOT SUPPOSED TO TALK ABOUT THAT.
OKAY. NOW IT'S TIME TO STOP TALKING.
IN A LITTLE BIT I'M GOING TO STEP OUT AND TAKE CARE OF SOMETHING. WHILE I'M GONE, DO NOT MOVE, OR I WILL HURT YOU. I WILL HURT YOUR SISTER, TOO. UNDERSTAND?
MADAME WILL BE ANGRY IF YOU AREN'T HAPPY. MADAME WILL TAKE AWAY OUR DINNER.
I'LL BE HAPPY IF YOU DO WHAT I SAY.

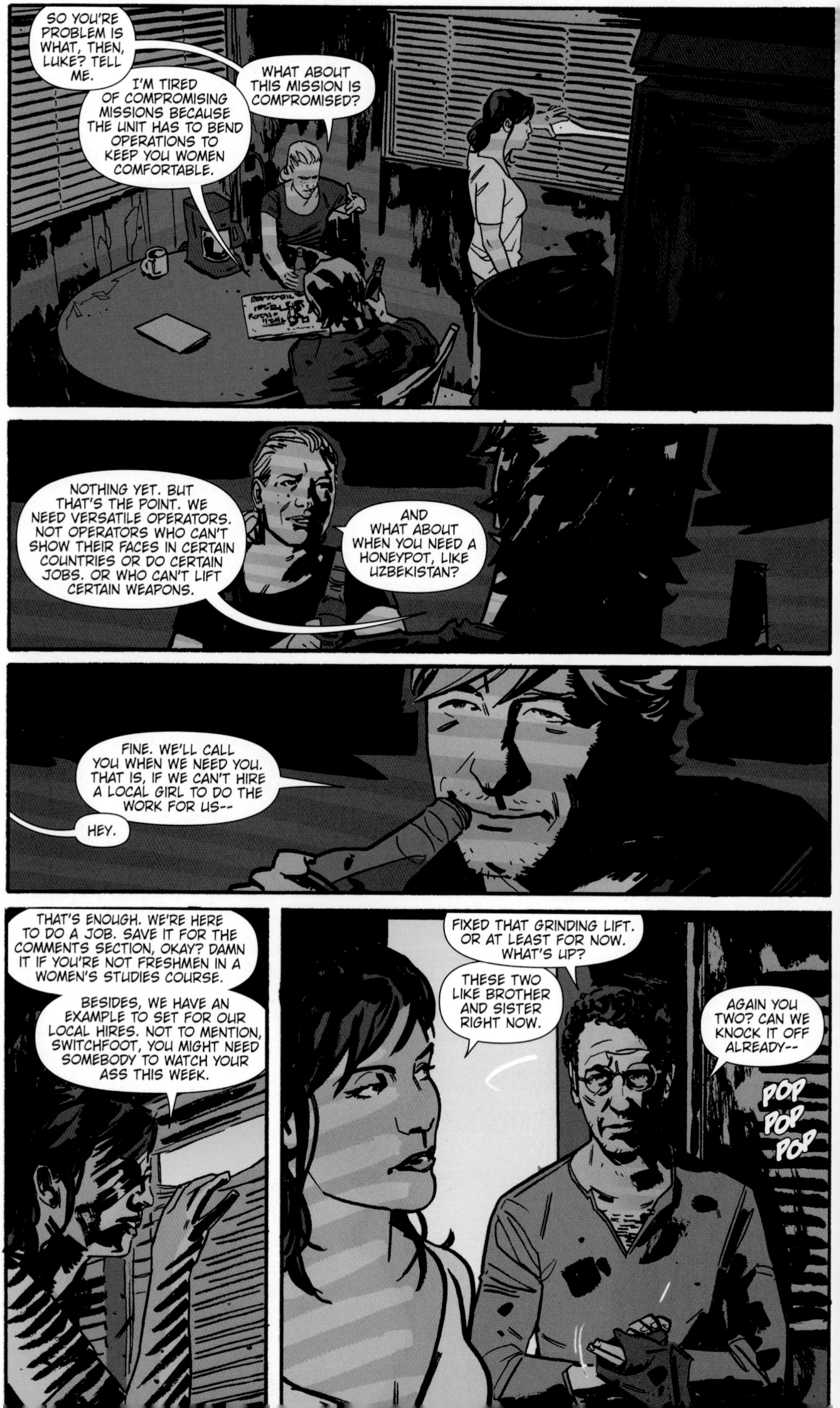
SO YOU'RE PROBLEM IS WHAT, THEN, LUKE? TELL ME.
I'M TIRED OF COMPROMISING MISSIONS BECAUSE THE UNIT HAS TO BEND OPERATIONS TO KEEP YOU WOMEN COMFORTABLE.
WHAT ABOUT THIS MISSION IS COMPROMISED?
NOTHING YET. BUT THAT'S THE POINT. WE NEED VERSATILE OPERATORS. NOT OPERATORS WHO CAN'T SHOW THEIR FACES IN CERTAIN COUNTRIES OR DO CERTAIN JOBS. OR WHO CAN'T LIFT CERTAIN WEAPONS.
AND WHAT ABOUT WHEN YOU NEED A HONEYPOT, LIKE UZBEKISTAN?
FINE. WE'LL CALL YOU WHEN WE NEED YOU. THAT IS, IF WE CAN'T HIRE A LOCAL GIRL TO DO THE WORK FOR US--
HEY.
THAT'S ENOUGH. WE'RE HERE TO DO A JOB. SAVE IT FOR THE COMMENTS SECTION, OKAY? DAMN IT IF YOU'RE NOT FRESHMEN IN A WOMEN'S STUDIES COURSE.
BESIDES, WE HAVE AN EXAMPLE TO SET FOR OUR LOCAL HIRES. NOT TO MENTION, SWITCHFOOT, YOU MIGHT NEED SOMEBODY TO WATCH YOUR ASS THIS WEEK.
FIXED THAT GRINDING LIFT. OR AT LEAST FOR NOW. WHAT'S UP?
THESE TWO LIKE BROTHER AND SISTER RIGHT NOW.
AGAIN YOU TWO? CAN WE KNOCK IT OFF ALREADY--
POP
POP
POP

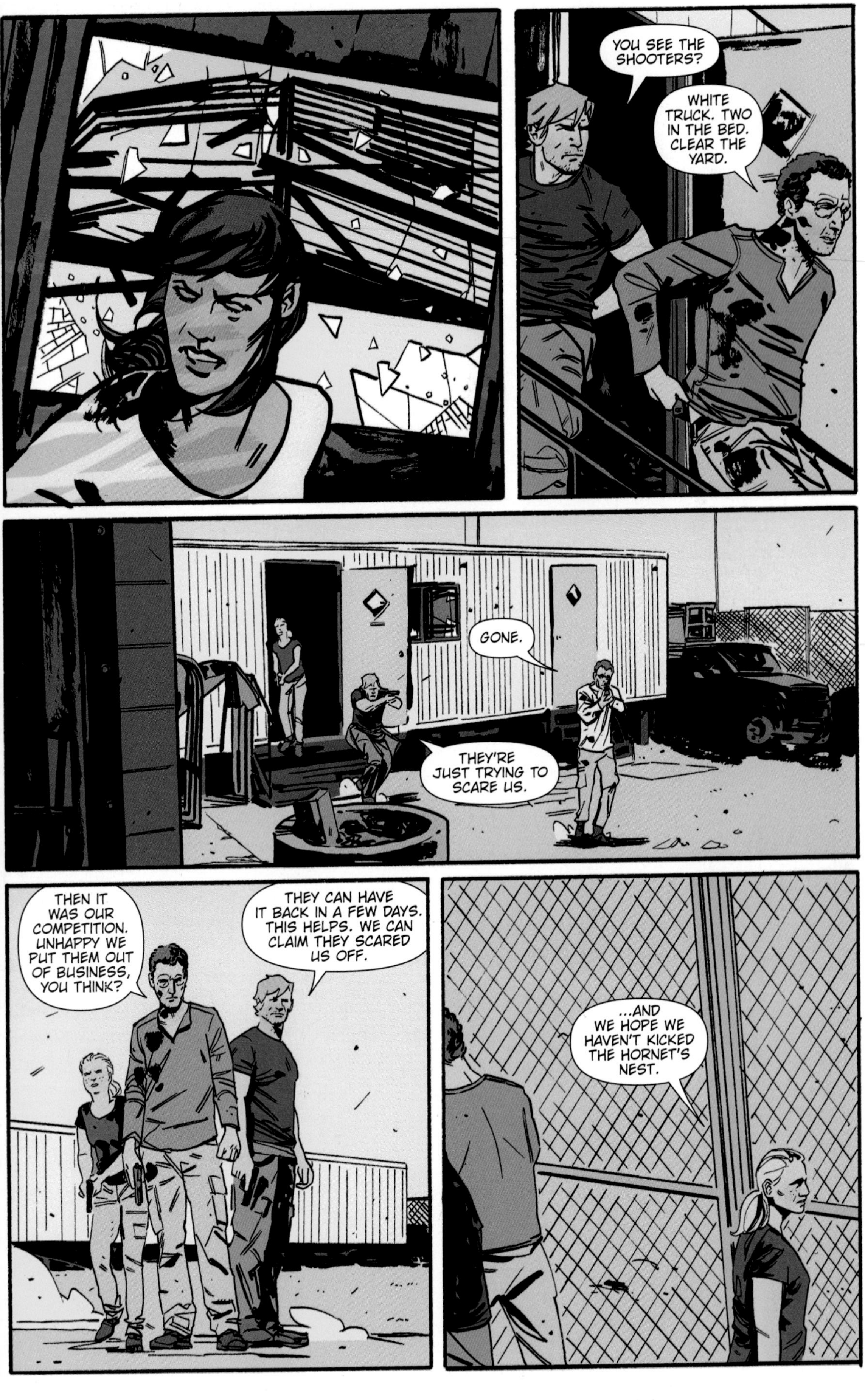
YOU SEE THE SHOOTERS?
WHITE TRUCK. TWO IN THE BED. CLEAR THE YARD.
GONE.
THEY'RE JUST TRYING TO SCARE US.
THEN IT WAS OUR COMPETITION. UNHAPPY WE PUT THEM OUT OF BUSINESS, YOU THINK?
THEY CAN HAVE IT BACK IN A FEW DAYS. THIS HELPS. WE CAN CLAIM THEY SCARED US OFF.
...AND WE HOPE WE HAVEN'T KICKED THE HORNET'S NEST.

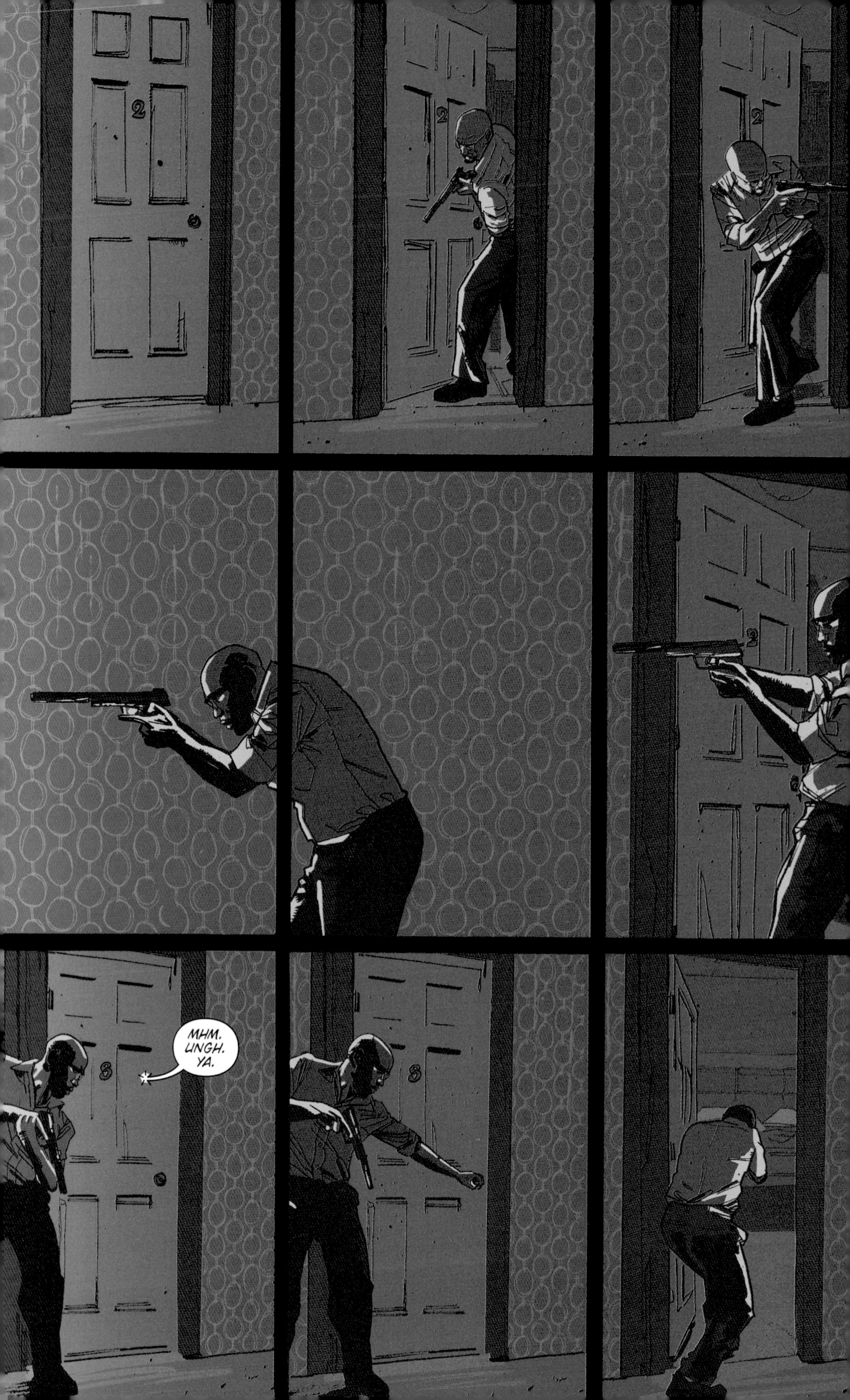
MHM. UNGH. YA.

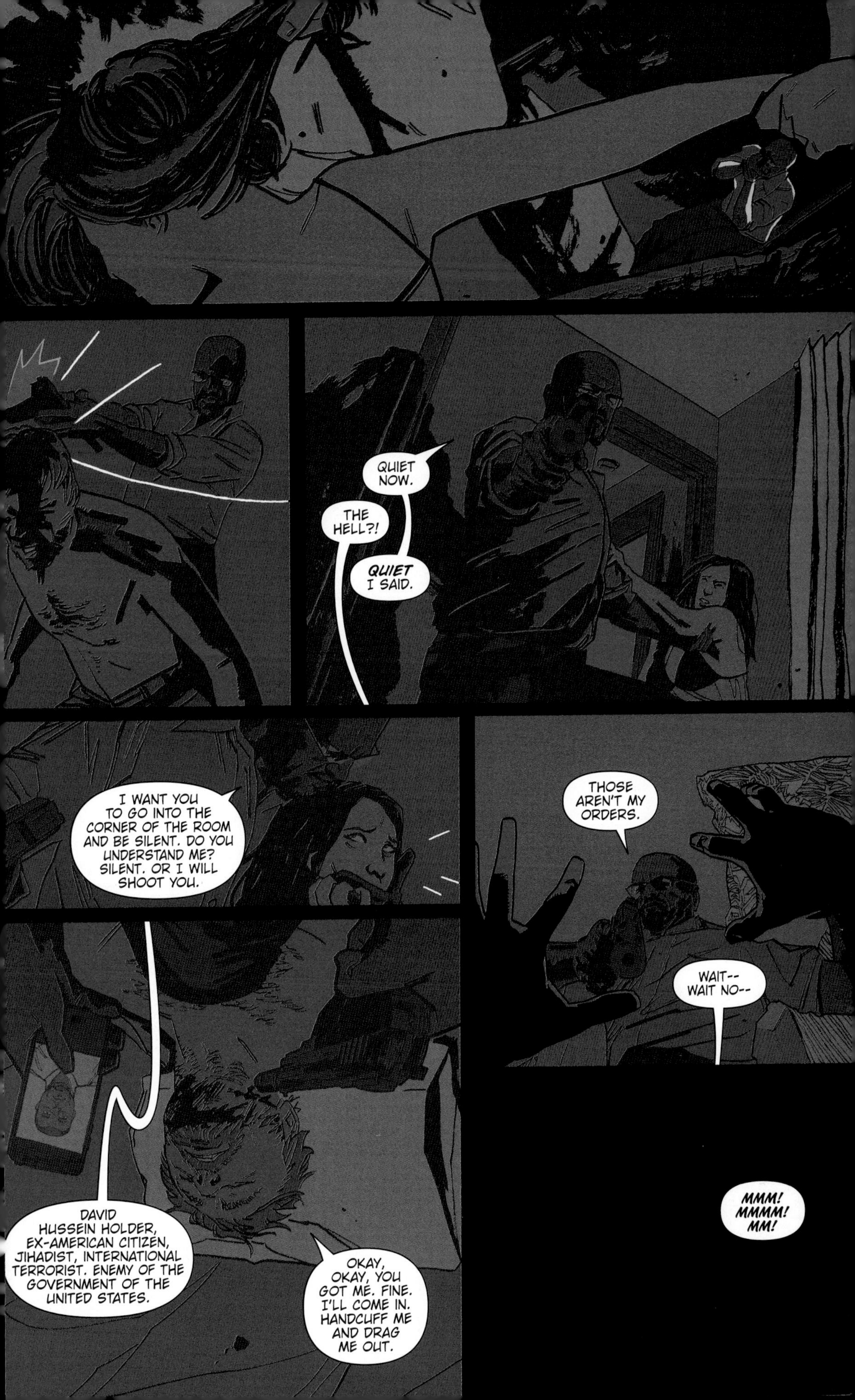
QUIET NOW.
THE HELL?!
QUIET I SAID.
I WANT YOU TO GO INTO THE CORNER OF THE ROOM AND BE SILENT. DO YOU UNDERSTAND ME? SILENT. OR I WILL SHOOT YOU.
DAVID HUSSEIN HOLDER, EX-AMERICAN CITIZEN, JIHADIST, INTERNATIONAL TERRORIST. ENEMY OF THE GOVERNMENT OF THE UNITED STATES.
OKAY, OKAY, YOU GOT ME. FINE. I'LL COME IN. HANDCUFF ME AND DRAG ME OUT.
THOSE AREN'T MY ORDERS.
WAIT-- WAIT NO--
MMM! MMMM! MM!

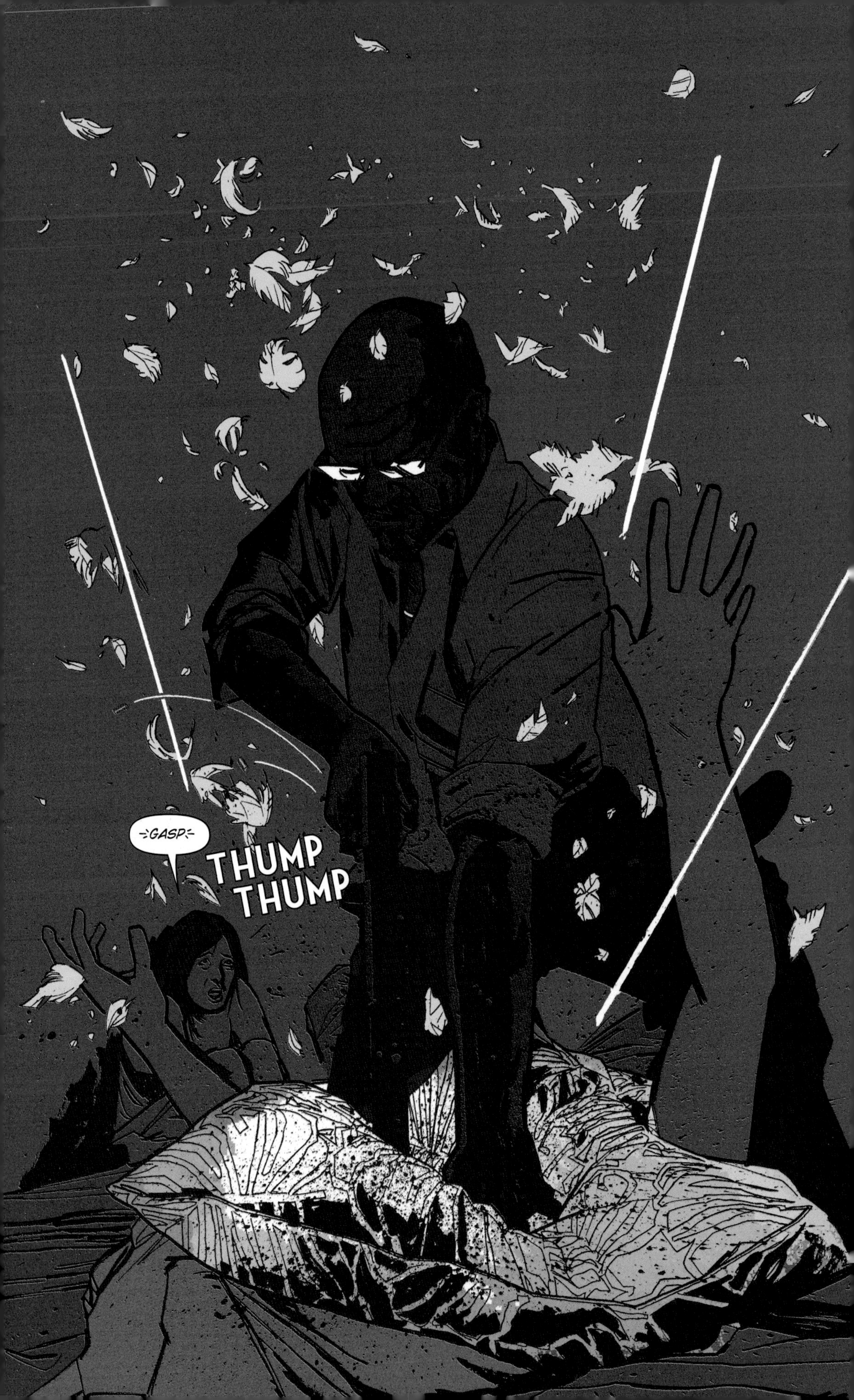
-GASP-
THUMP THUMP

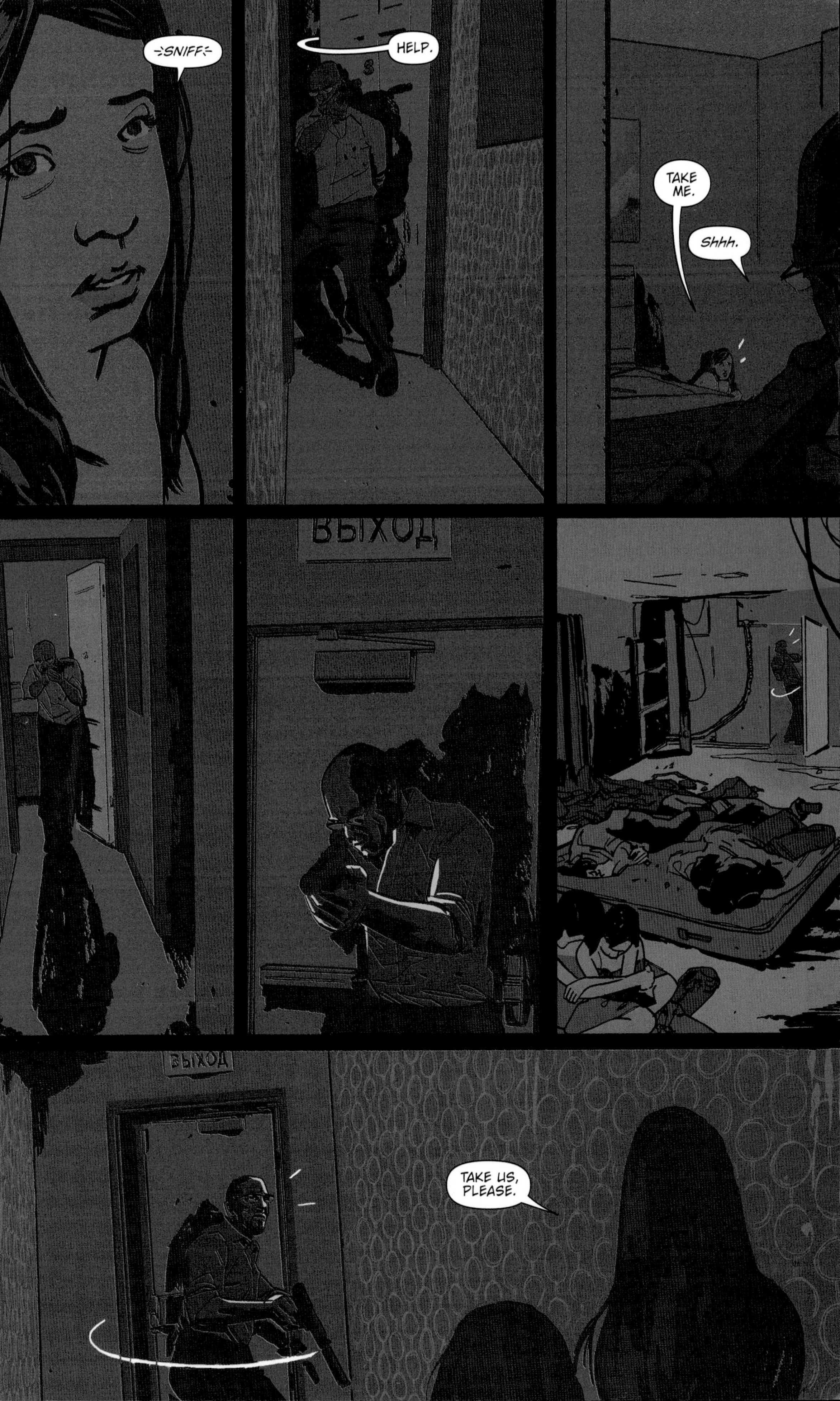

SNIFF
HELP.
TAKE ME.
Shhh.
ВЫХОД
ВЫХОД
TAKE US, PLEASE.

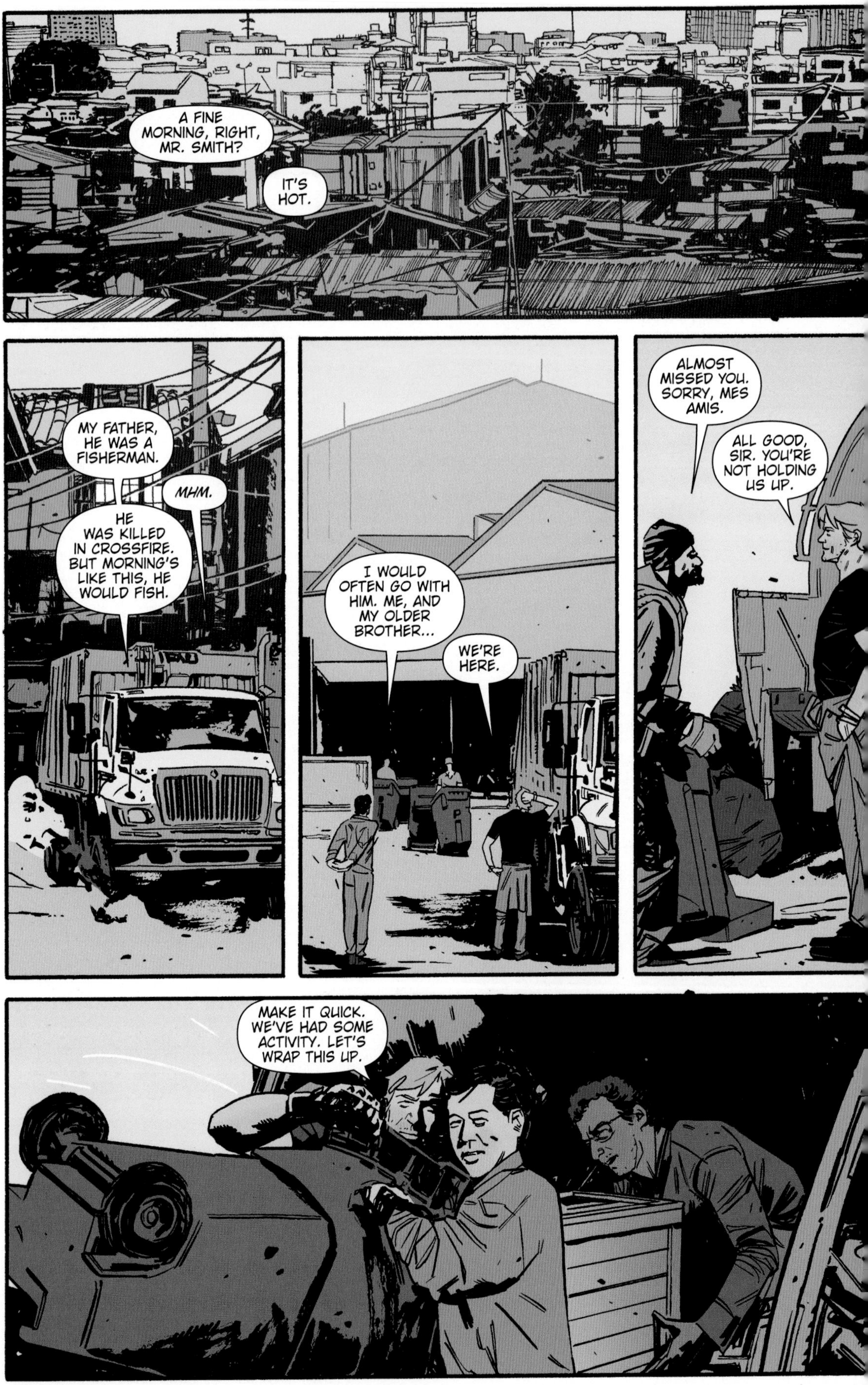

A FINE MORNING, RIGHT, MR. SMITH?
IT'S HOT.
MY FATHER, HE WAS A FISHERMAN.
MHM.
HE WAS KILLED IN CROSSFIRE. BUT MORNING'S LIKE THIS, HE WOULD FISH.
I WOULD OFTEN GO WITH HIM. ME, AND MY OLDER BROTHER...
WE'RE HERE.
ALMOST MISSED YOU. SORRY, MES AMIS.
ALL GOOD, SIR. YOU'RE NOT HOLDING US UP.
MAKE IT QUICK. WE'VE HAD SOME ACTIVITY. LET'S WRAP THIS UP.

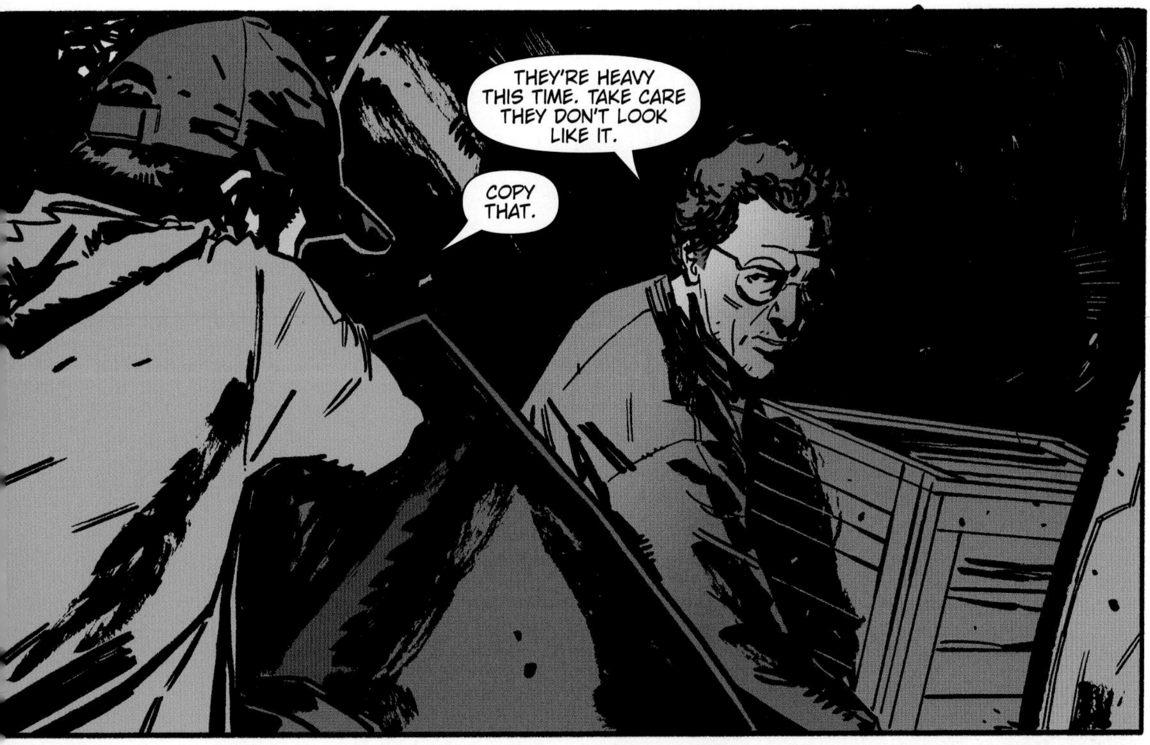
THEY'RE HEAVY THIS TIME. TAKE CARE THEY DON'T LOOK LIKE IT.
COPY THAT.

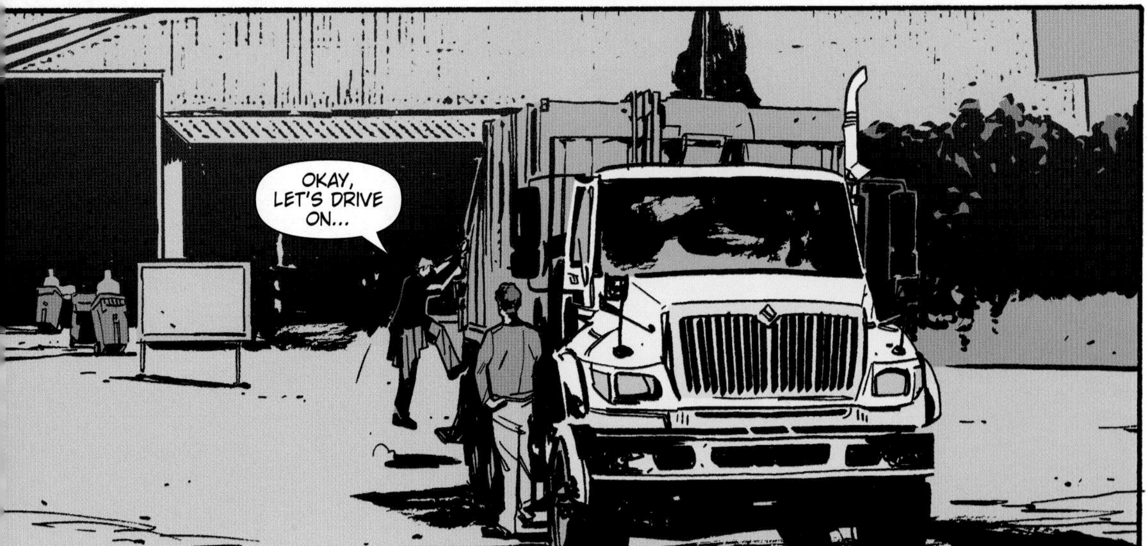
OKAY, LET'S DRIVE ON...

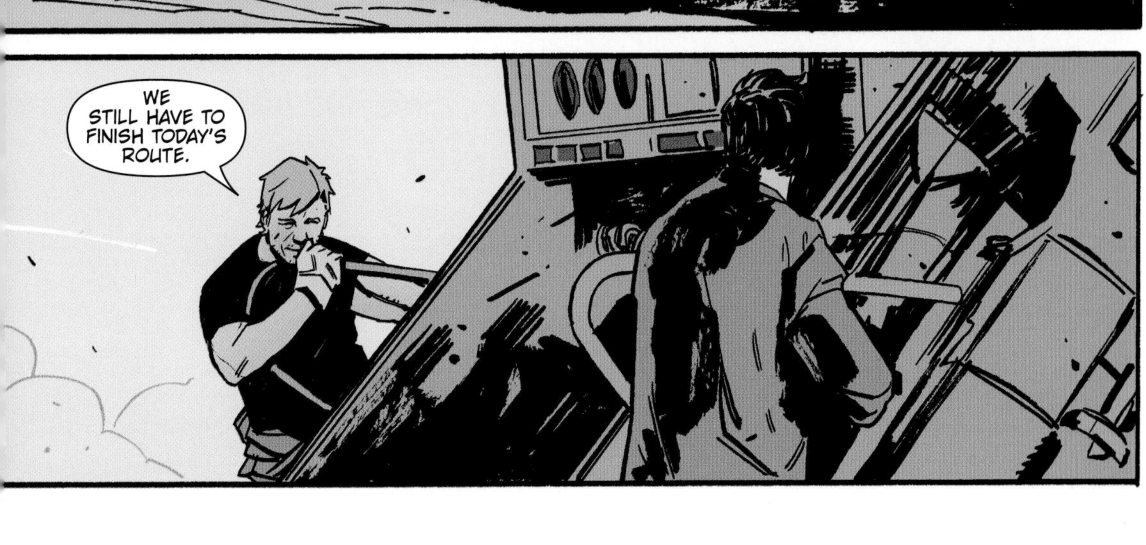
WE STILL HAVE TO FINISH TODAY'S ROUTE.

WE HAVE A PROBLEM.

JEFFREY AND HIS CREW JUST CAME BACK IN. THEY WERE ATTACKED.

ATTACKED?

SAME AS LAST NIGHT, BUSUANGA WASTE. OUR FORMER WASTE DISPOSAL COMPETITION. SEEMS WE TOOK THE BONE AWAY FROM THE DOG.

TRUCK IS DAMAGED. JEFFREY AND HIS CREW ARE OKAY. BUT...

BUT...

GO AHEAD AND CHANGE OVER TO A NEW TRUCK, JEFFREY.

LISTEN. WE HAVE A BIGGER PROBLEM. THE WAY THESE GUYS DEAL WITH BUSINESS DISPUTES...

THEY HOLD GRUDGES. WE'VE HIRED THESE LOCALS, ALMOST LIKE SCABS. WE PUT THE COMPETITION OUT OF BUSINESS. WHEN WE LEAVE TOMORROW, WE PLAN TO CLAIM WE WERE CHASED OUT. HELD THE JOB FOR A MONTH, BUT COULDN'T HANDLE IT.

GOOD FOR US, BUT THEY WON'T FORGIVE JEFFREY, JOSEPH OR THE OTHERS. YOU KNOW WHAT THEY'LL DO.

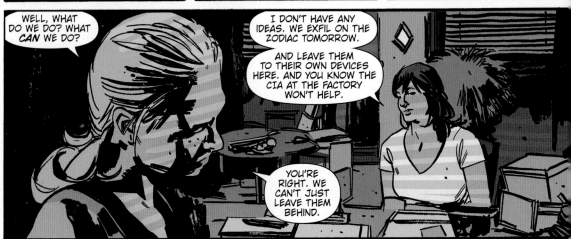

WELL, WHAT DO WE DO? WHAT *CAN* WE DO?

I DON'T HAVE ANY IDEAS. WE EXFIL ON THE ZODIAC TOMORROW.

AND LEAVE THEM TO THEIR OWN DEVICES HERE. AND YOU KNOW THE CIA AT THE FACTORY WON'T HELP.

YOU'RE RIGHT. WE CAN'T JUST LEAVE THEM BEHIND.

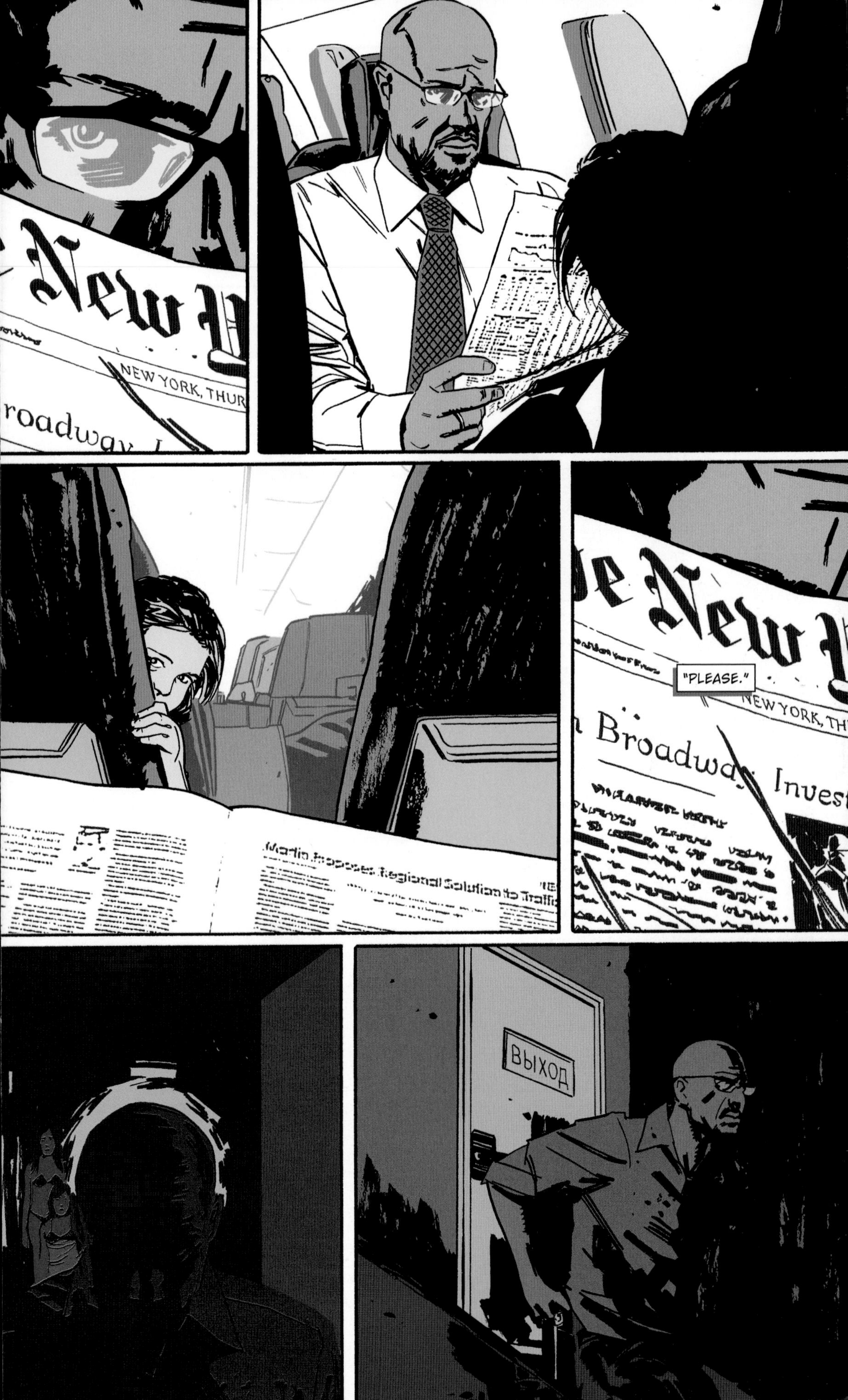
"PLEASE."
ВЫХОД

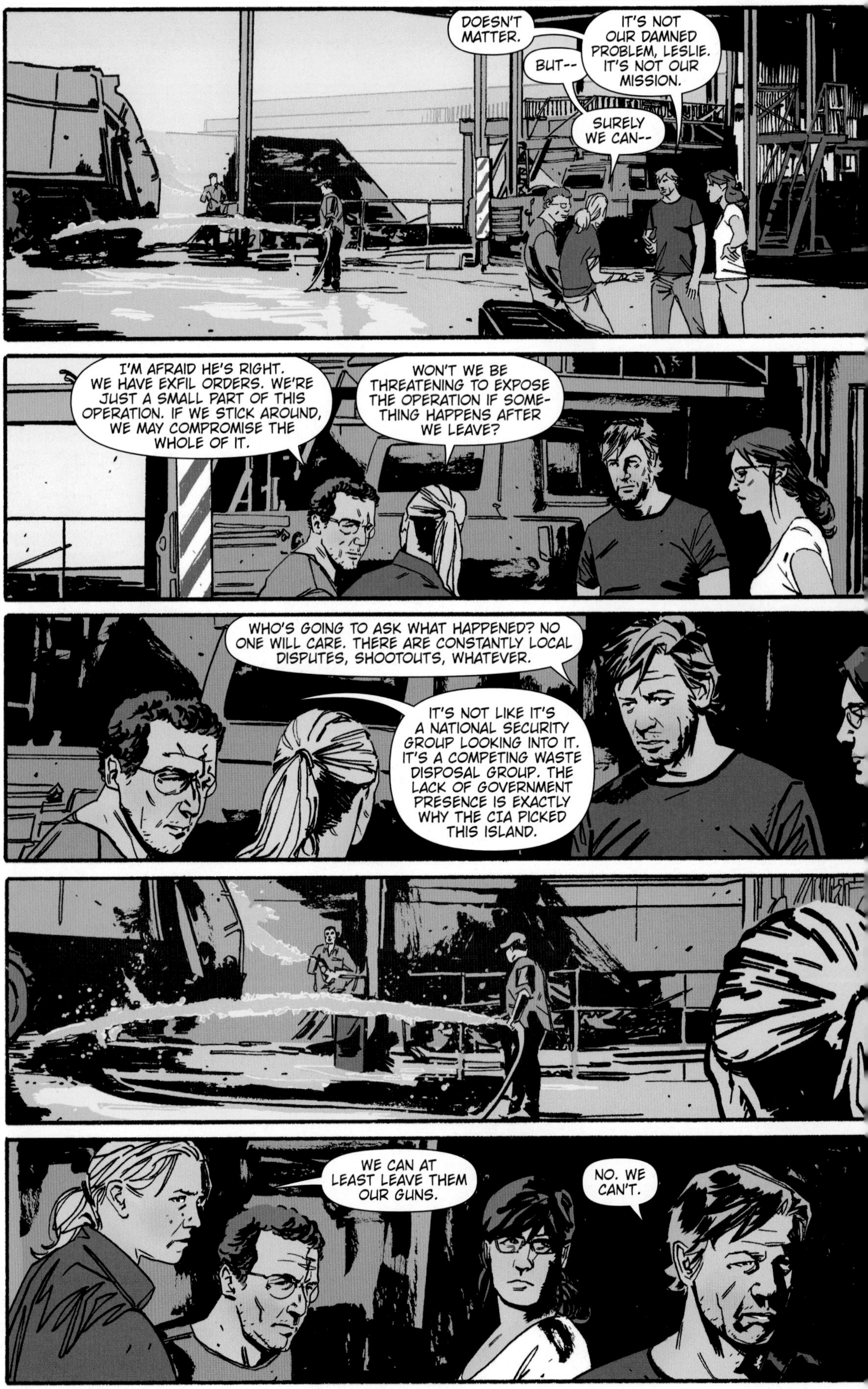
DOESN'T MATTER.
IT'S NOT OUR DAMNED PROBLEM, LESLIE. IT'S NOT OUR MISSION.
BUT--
SURELY WE CAN--
I'M AFRAID HE'S RIGHT. WE HAVE EXFIL ORDERS. WE'RE JUST A SMALL PART OF THIS OPERATION. IF WE STICK AROUND, WE MAY COMPROMISE THE WHOLE OF IT.
WON'T WE BE THREATENING TO EXPOSE THE OPERATION IF SOMETHING HAPPENS AFTER WE LEAVE?
WHO'S GOING TO ASK WHAT HAPPENED? NO ONE WILL CARE. THERE ARE CONSTANTLY LOCAL DISPUTES, SHOOTOUTS, WHATEVER.
IT'S NOT LIKE IT'S A NATIONAL SECURITY GROUP LOOKING INTO IT. IT'S A COMPETING WASTE DISPOSAL GROUP. THE LACK OF GOVERNMENT PRESENCE IS EXACTLY WHY THE CIA PICKED THIS ISLAND.
WE CAN AT LEAST LEAVE THEM OUR GUNS.
NO. WE CAN'T.

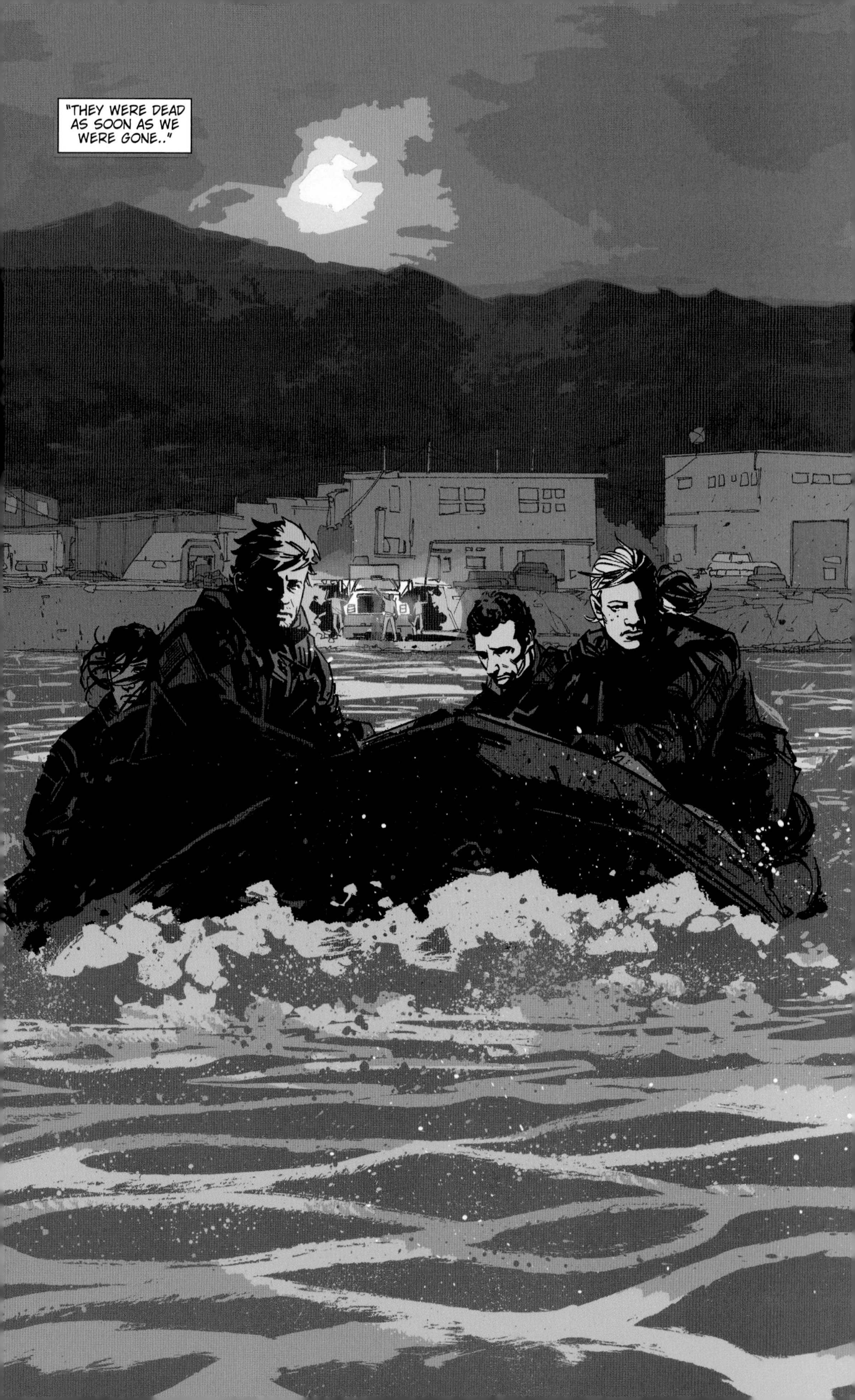
"THEY WERE DEAD AS SOON AS WE WERE GONE.."

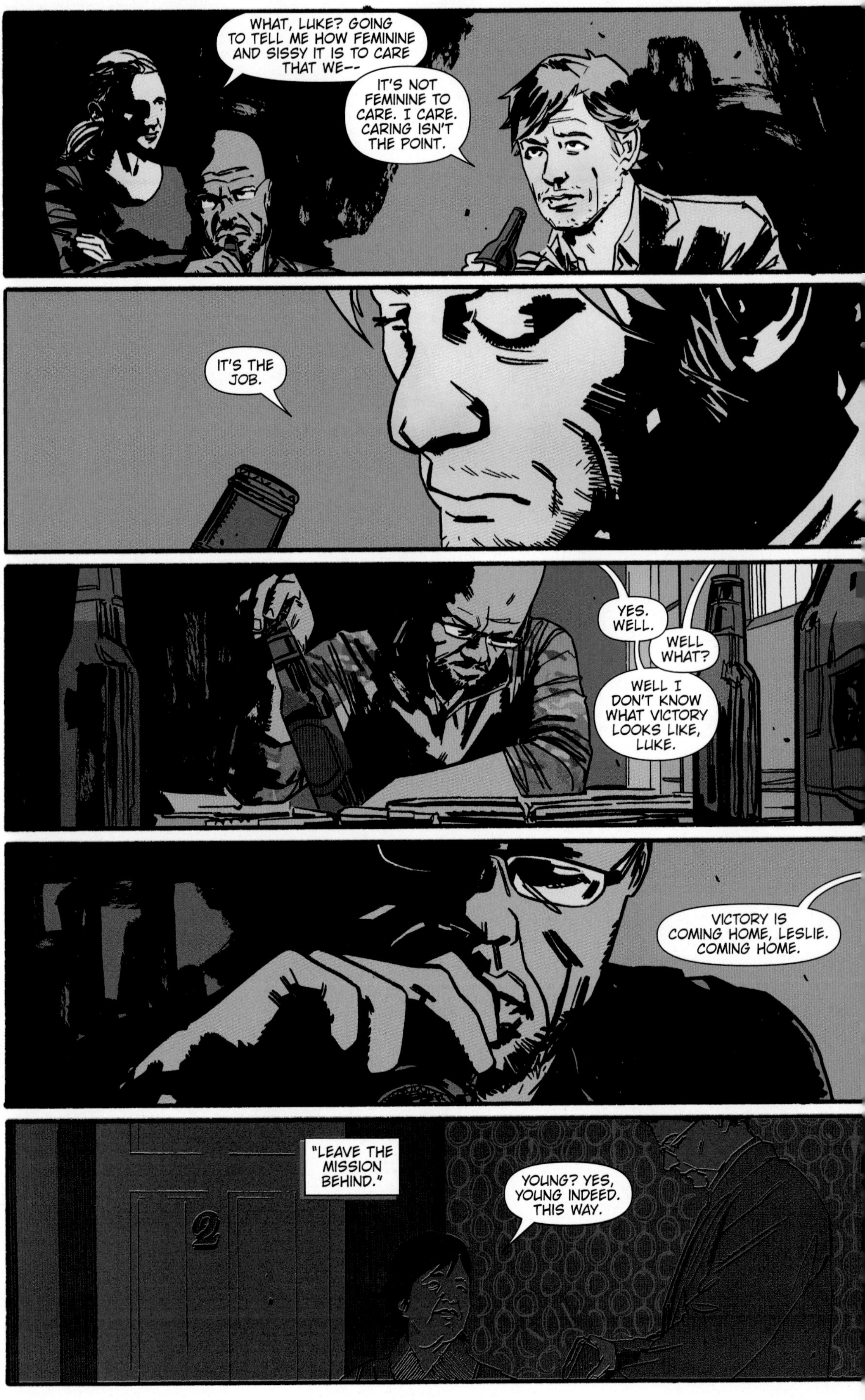
WHAT, LUKE? GOING TO TELL ME HOW FEMININE AND SISSY IT IS TO CARE THAT WE--
IT'S NOT FEMININE TO CARE. I CARE. CARING ISN'T THE POINT.
IT'S THE JOB.
YES. WELL.
WELL WHAT?
WELL I DON'T KNOW WHAT VICTORY LOOKS LIKE, LUKE.
VICTORY IS COMING HOME, LESLIE. COMING HOME.
"LEAVE THE MISSION BEHIND."
YOUNG? YES, YOUNG INDEED. THIS WAY.

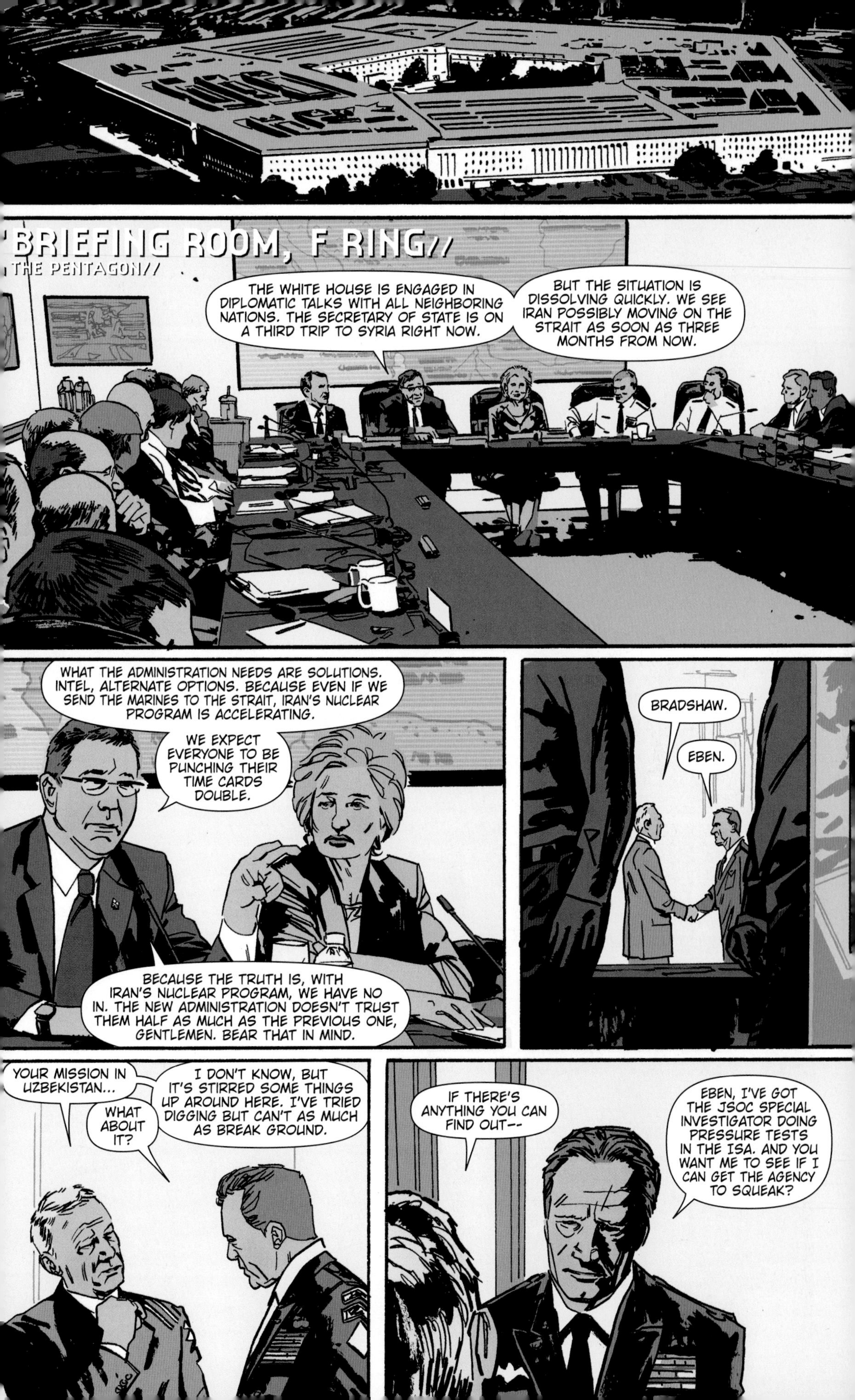
BRIEFING ROOM, F RING//
THE PENTAGON//
THE WHITE HOUSE IS ENGAGED IN DIPLOMATIC TALKS WITH ALL NEIGHBORING NATIONS. THE SECRETARY OF STATE IS ON A THIRD TRIP TO SYRIA RIGHT NOW.
BUT THE SITUATION IS DISSOLVING QUICKLY. WE SEE IRAN POSSIBLY MOVING ON THE STRAIT AS SOON AS THREE MONTHS FROM NOW.
WHAT THE ADMINISTRATION NEEDS ARE SOLUTIONS. INTEL, ALTERNATE OPTIONS. BECAUSE EVEN IF WE SEND THE MARINES TO THE STRAIT, IRAN'S NUCLEAR PROGRAM IS ACCELERATING.
WE EXPECT EVERYONE TO BE PUNCHING THEIR TIME CARDS DOUBLE.
BECAUSE THE TRUTH IS, WITH IRAN'S NUCLEAR PROGRAM, WE HAVE NO IN. THE NEW ADMINISTRATION DOESN'T TRUST THEM HALF AS MUCH AS THE PREVIOUS ONE, GENTLEMEN. BEAR THAT IN MIND.
BRADSHAW.
EBEN.
YOUR MISSION IN UZBEKISTAN...
WHAT ABOUT IT?
I DON'T KNOW, BUT IT'S STIRRED SOME THINGS UP AROUND HERE. I'VE TRIED DIGGING BUT CAN'T AS MUCH AS BREAK GROUND.
IF THERE'S ANYTHING YOU CAN FIND OUT--
EBEN, I'VE GOT THE JSOC SPECIAL INVESTIGATOR DOING PRESSURE TESTS IN THE ISA. AND YOU WANT ME TO SEE IF I CAN GET THE AGENCY TO SQUEAK?

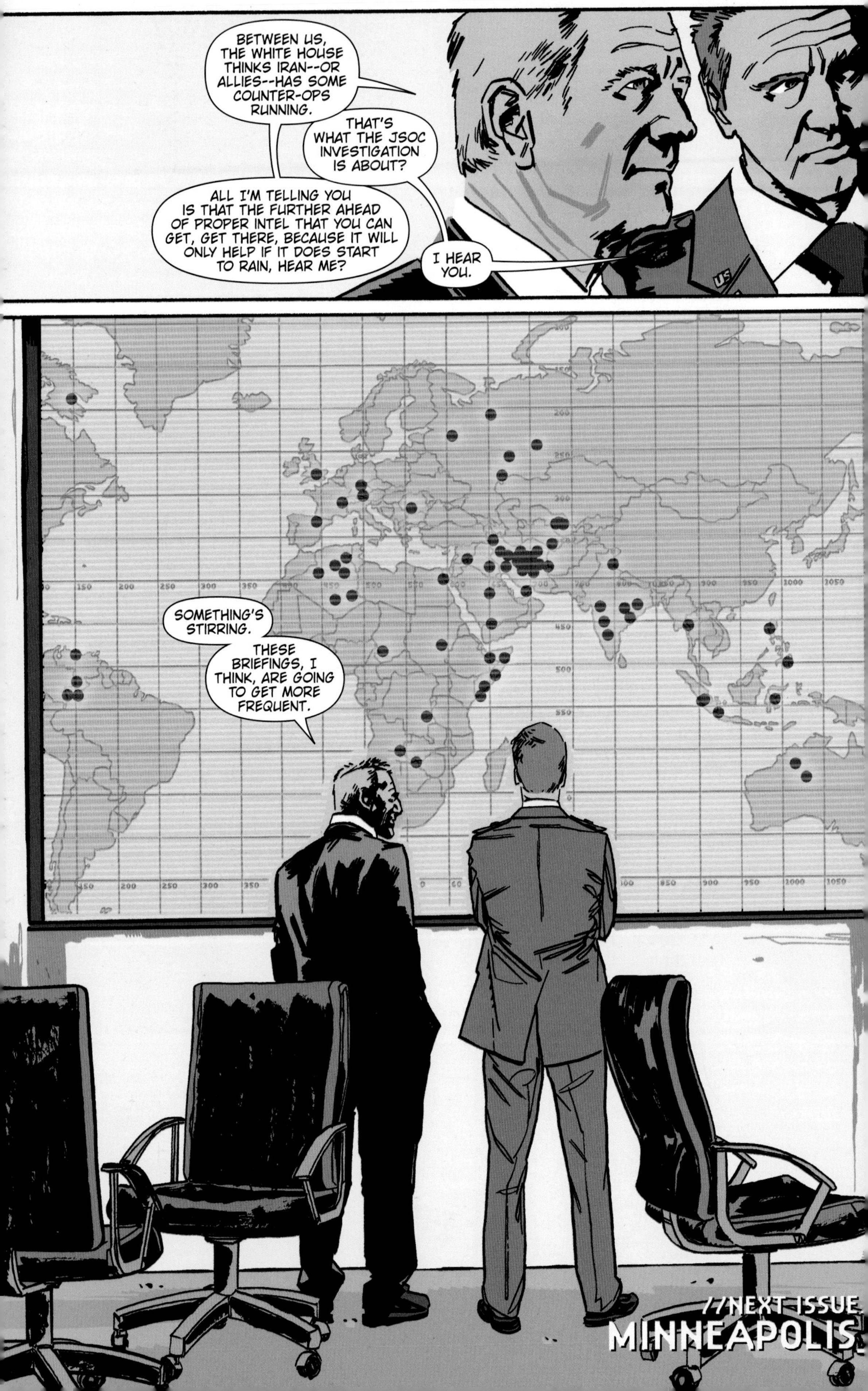
BETWEEN US, THE WHITE HOUSE THINKS IRAN--OR ALLIES--HAS SOME COUNTER-OPS RUNNING.
THAT'S WHAT THE JSOC INVESTIGATION IS ABOUT?
ALL I'M TELLING YOU IS THAT THE FURTHER AHEAD OF PROPER INTEL THAT YOU CAN GET, GET THERE, BECAUSE IT WILL ONLY HELP IF IT DOES START TO RAIN, HEAR ME?
I HEAR YOU.
SOMETHING'S STIRRING.
THESE BRIEFINGS, I THINK, ARE GOING TO GET MORE FREQUENT.
//NEXT ISSUE
MINNEAPOLIS

//_MISSION_DESIGNATE:...
DESTINATION///
//MINNEAPOLIS/MINNESOTA/USA_.

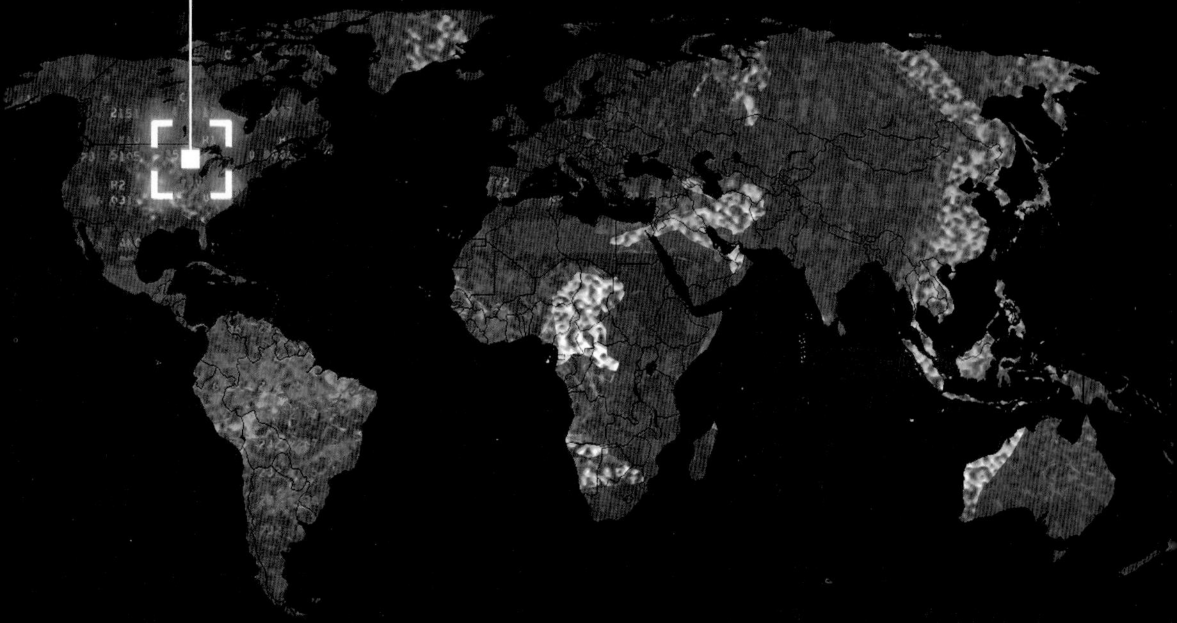

//MISSION_REPORT_
//INITIALIZING____

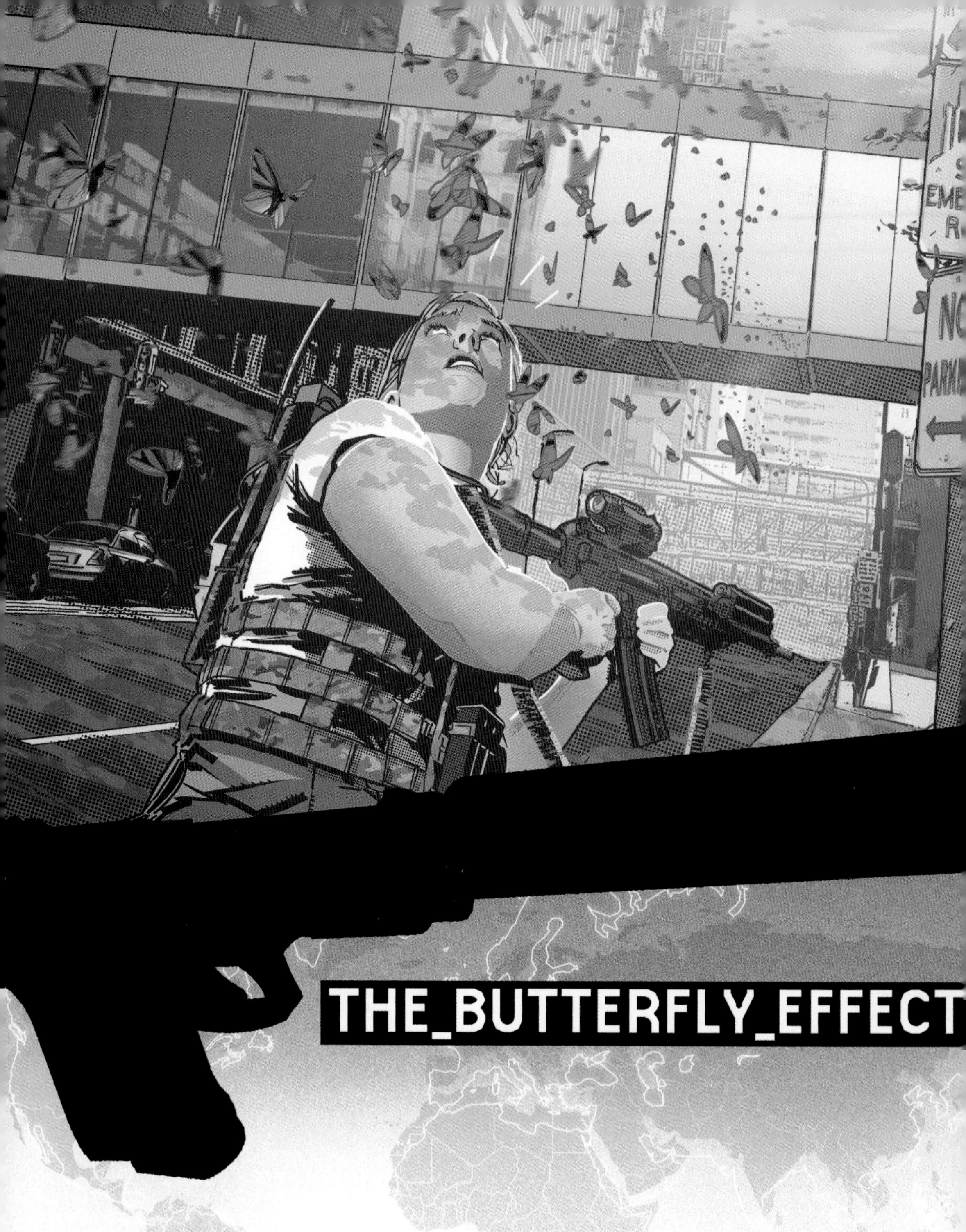
THE_BUTTERFLY_EFFECT

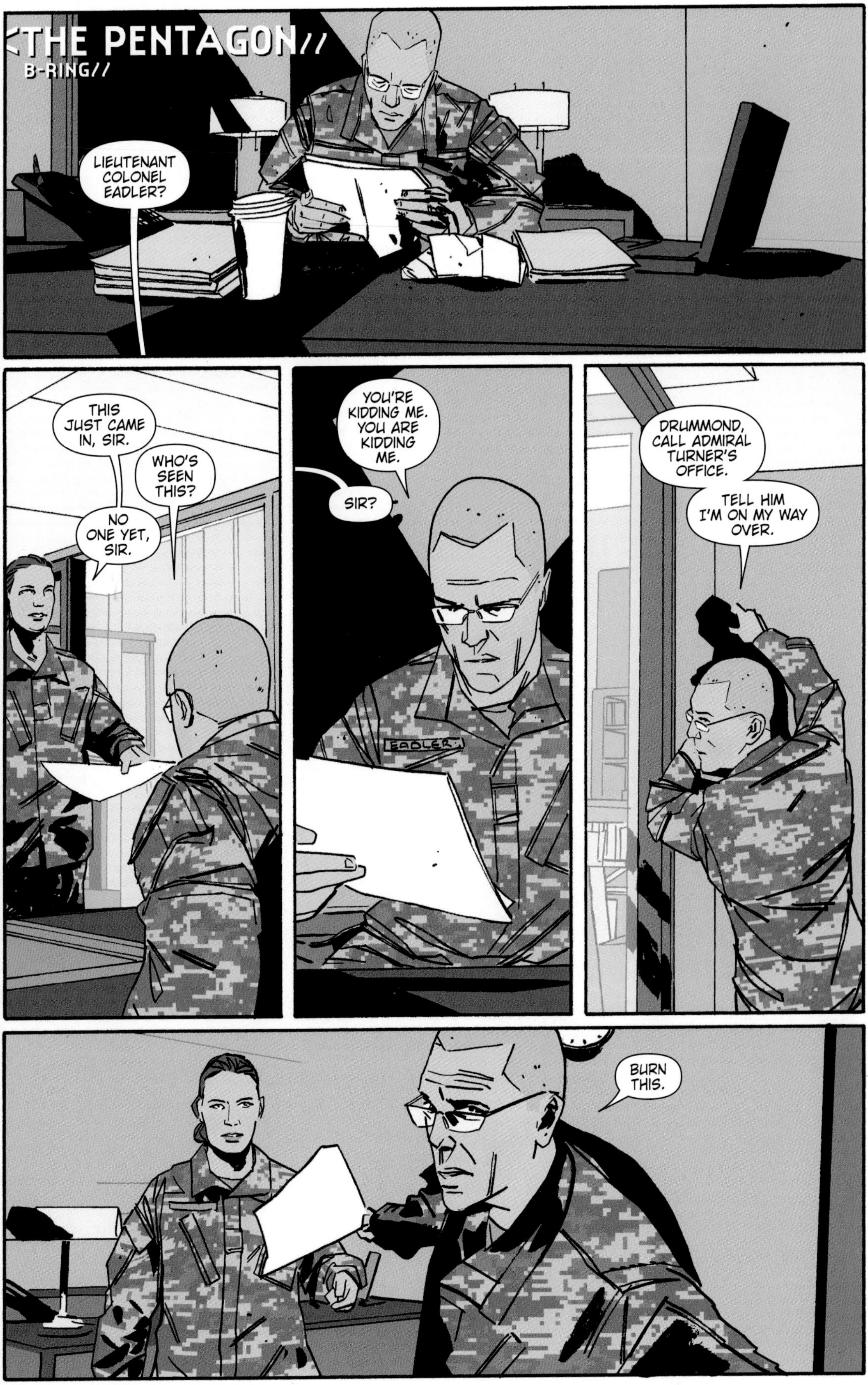
THE PENTAGON//
B-RING//
LIEUTENANT COLONEL EADLER?
THIS JUST CAME IN, SIR.
WHO'S SEEN THIS?
NO ONE YET, SIR.
YOU'RE KIDDING ME. YOU ARE KIDDING ME.
SIR?
EADLER
DRUMMOND, CALL ADMIRAL TURNER'S OFFICE.
TELL HIM I'M ON MY WAY OVER.
BURN THIS.

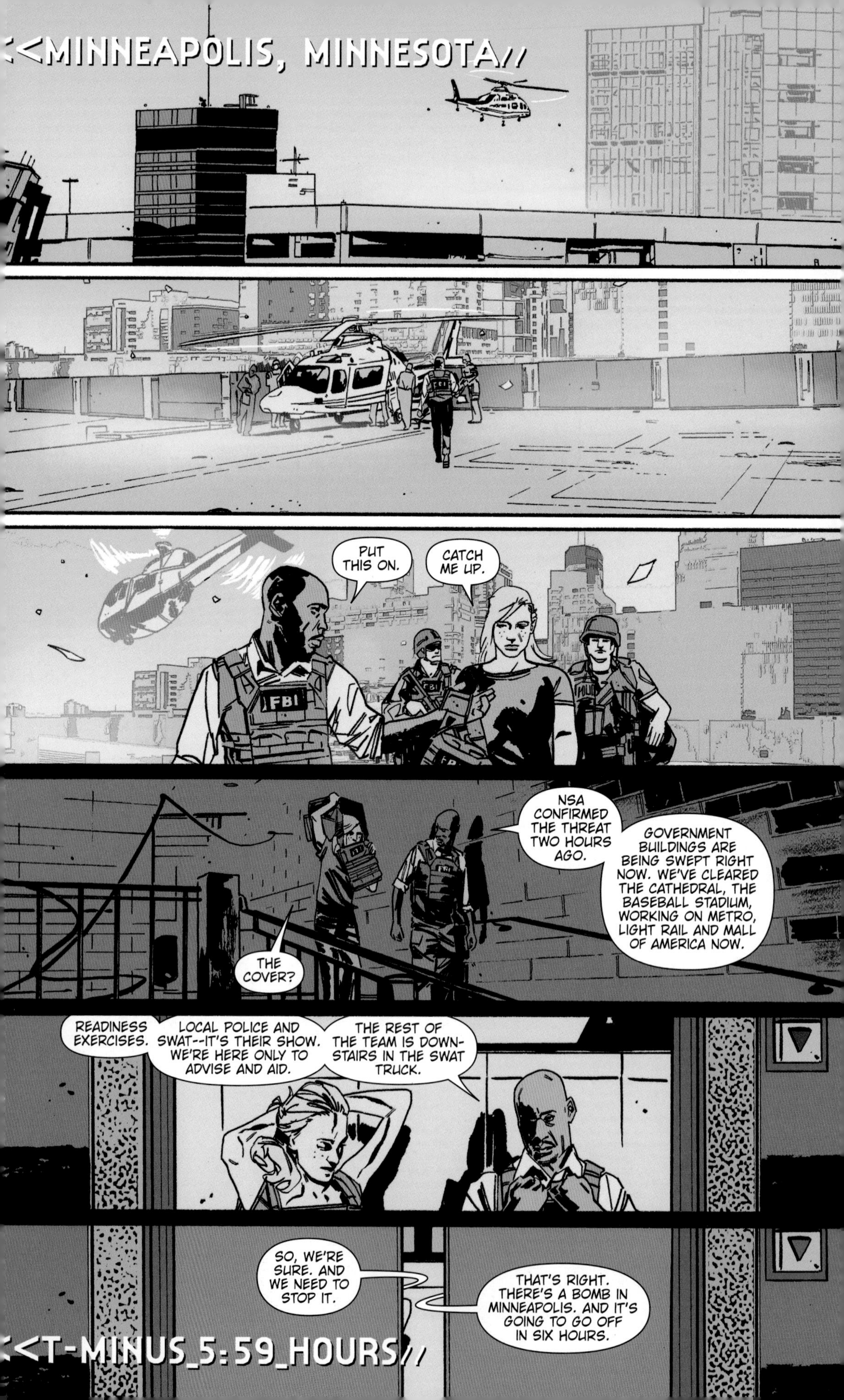
<<MINNEAPOLIS, MINNESOTA//
PUT THIS ON.
CATCH ME UP.
NSA CONFIRMED THE THREAT TWO HOURS AGO.
GOVERNMENT BUILDINGS ARE BEING SWEPT RIGHT NOW. WE'VE CLEARED THE CATHEDRAL, THE BASEBALL STADIUM, WORKING ON METRO, LIGHT RAIL AND MALL OF AMERICA NOW.
THE COVER?
READINESS EXERCISES.
LOCAL POLICE AND SWAT--IT'S THEIR SHOW. WE'RE HERE ONLY TO ADVISE AND AID.
THE REST OF THE TEAM IS DOWN-STAIRS IN THE SWAT TRUCK.
SO, WE'RE SURE. AND WE NEED TO STOP IT.
THAT'S RIGHT. THERE'S A BOMB IN MINNEAPOLIS. AND IT'S GOING TO GO OFF IN SIX HOURS.
<<T-MINUS_5:59_HOURS//

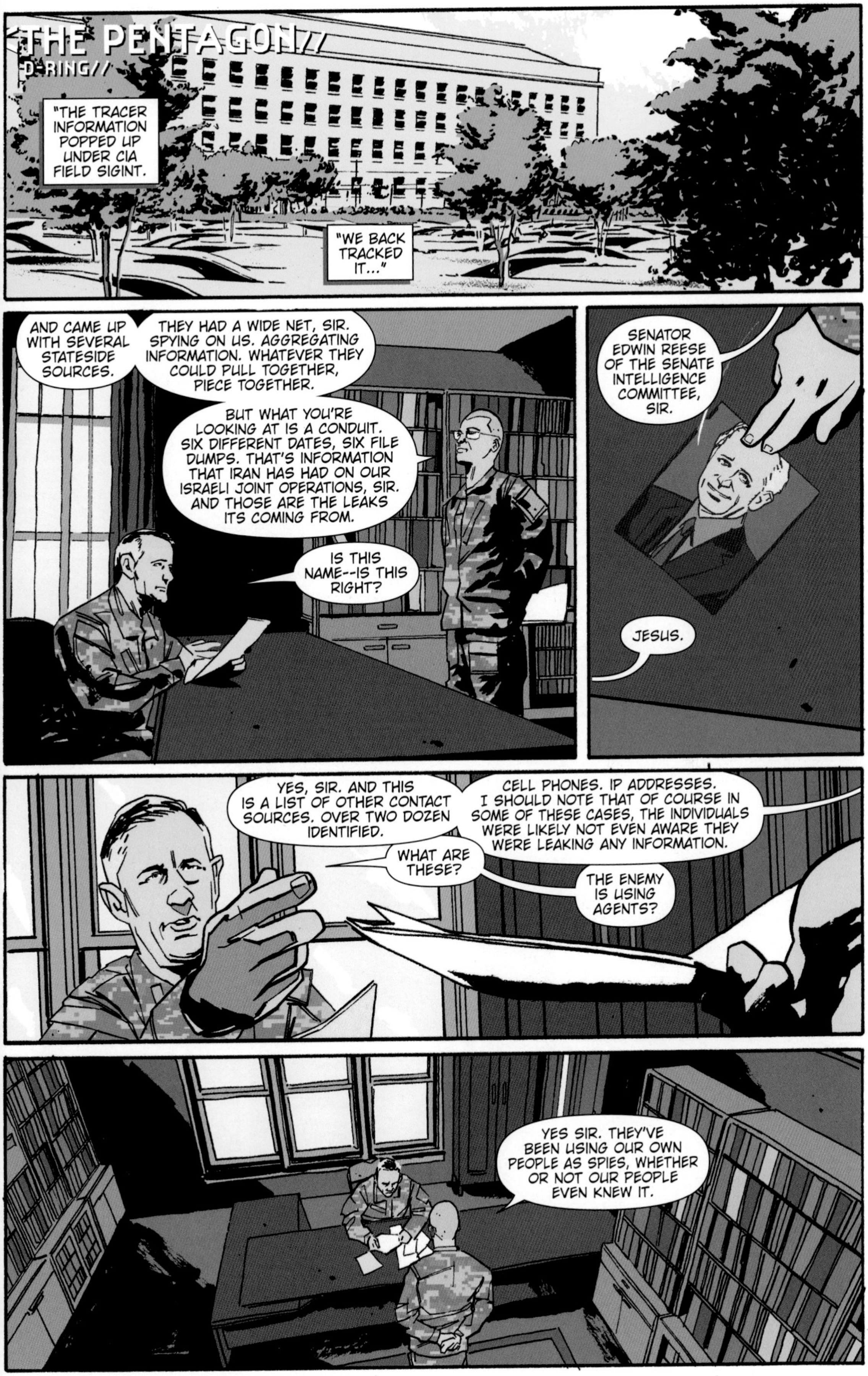
THE PENTAGON//
D-RING//
"THE TRACER INFORMATION POPPED UP UNDER CIA FIELD SIGINT.
"WE BACK TRACKED IT..."
AND CAME UP WITH SEVERAL STATESIDE SOURCES.
THEY HAD A WIDE NET, SIR. SPYING ON US. AGGREGATING INFORMATION. WHATEVER THEY COULD PULL TOGETHER, PIECE TOGETHER.
BUT WHAT YOU'RE LOOKING AT IS A CONDUIT. SIX DIFFERENT DATES, SIX FILE DUMPS. THAT'S INFORMATION THAT IRAN HAS HAD ON OUR ISRAELI JOINT OPERATIONS, SIR. AND THOSE ARE THE LEAKS ITS COMING FROM.
IS THIS NAME--IS THIS RIGHT?
SENATOR EDWIN REESE OF THE SENATE INTELLIGENCE COMMITTEE, SIR.
JESUS.
YES, SIR. AND THIS IS A LIST OF OTHER CONTACT SOURCES. OVER TWO DOZEN IDENTIFIED.
WHAT ARE THESE?
CELL PHONES. IP ADDRESSES. I SHOULD NOTE THAT OF COURSE IN SOME OF THESE CASES, THE INDIVIDUALS WERE LIKELY NOT EVEN AWARE THEY WERE LEAKING ANY INFORMATION.
THE ENEMY IS USING AGENTS?
YES SIR. THEY'VE BEEN USING OUR OWN PEOPLE AS SPIES, WHETHER OR NOT OUR PEOPLE EVEN KNEW IT.

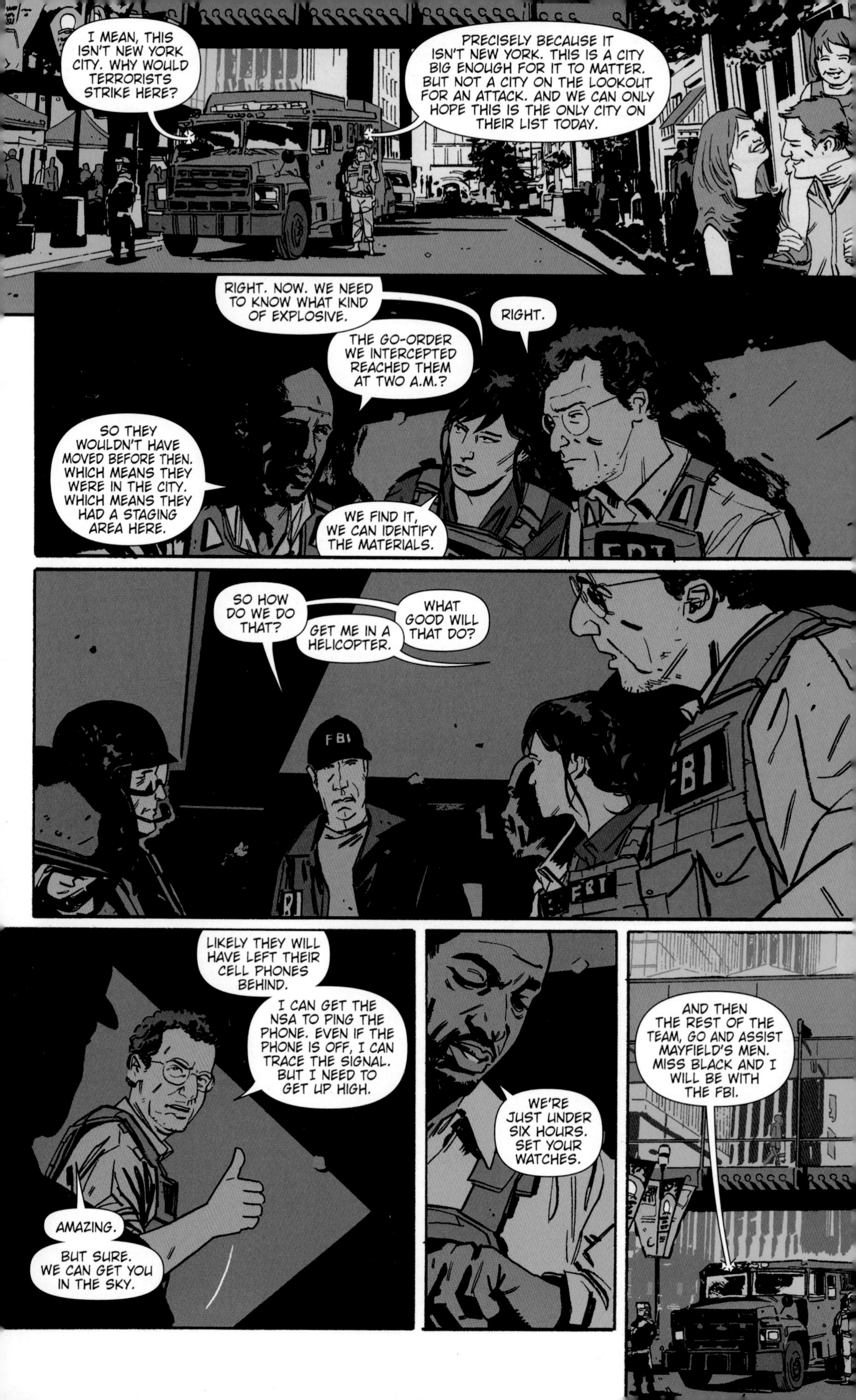
I MEAN, THIS ISN'T NEW YORK CITY. WHY WOULD TERRORISTS STRIKE HERE?
PRECISELY BECAUSE IT ISN'T NEW YORK. THIS IS A CITY BIG ENOUGH FOR IT TO MATTER. BUT NOT A CITY ON THE LOOKOUT FOR AN ATTACK. AND WE CAN ONLY HOPE THIS IS THE ONLY CITY ON THEIR LIST TODAY.
RIGHT. NOW. WE NEED TO KNOW WHAT KIND OF EXPLOSIVE.
RIGHT.
THE GO-ORDER WE INTERCEPTED REACHED THEM AT TWO A.M.?
SO THEY WOULDN'T HAVE MOVED BEFORE THEN. WHICH MEANS THEY WERE IN THE CITY. WHICH MEANS THEY HAD A STAGING AREA HERE.
WE FIND IT, WE CAN IDENTIFY THE MATERIALS.
SO HOW DO WE DO THAT?
GET ME IN A HELICOPTER.
WHAT GOOD WILL THAT DO?
FBI
FBI
LIKELY THEY WILL HAVE LEFT THEIR CELL PHONES BEHIND.
I CAN GET THE NSA TO PING THE PHONE. EVEN IF THE PHONE IS OFF, I CAN TRACE THE SIGNAL. BUT I NEED TO GET UP HIGH.
AMAZING.
BUT SURE. WE CAN GET YOU IN THE SKY.
WE'RE JUST UNDER SIX HOURS. SET YOUR WATCHES.
AND THEN THE REST OF THE TEAM, GO AND ASSIST MAYFIELD'S MEN. MISS BLACK AND I WILL BE WITH THE FBI.

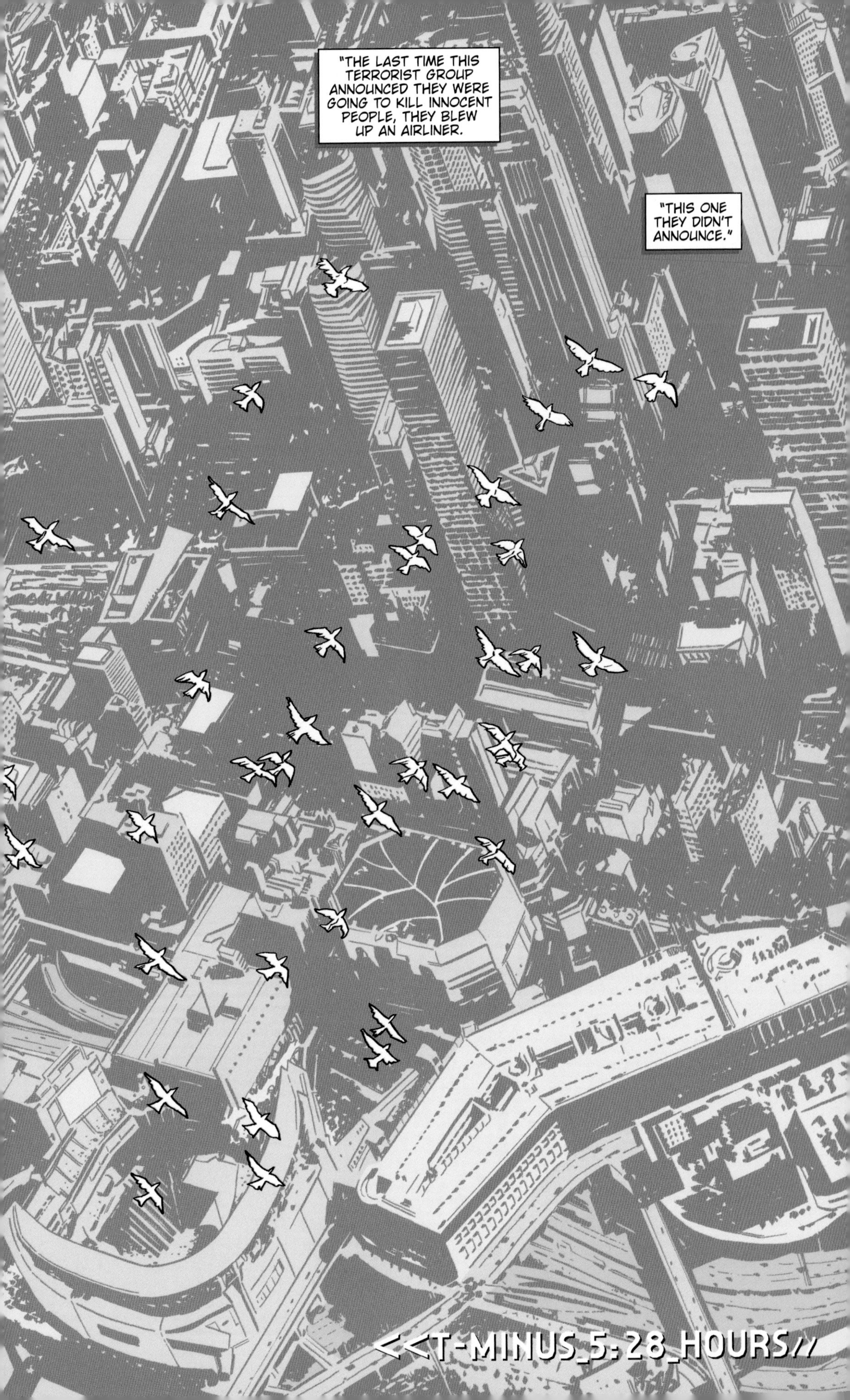
"THE LAST TIME THIS TERRORIST GROUP ANNOUNCED THEY WERE GOING TO KILL INNOCENT PEOPLE, THEY BLEW UP AN AIRLINER.
"THIS ONE THEY DIDN'T ANNOUNCE."
<<T-MINUS_5:28_HOURS//

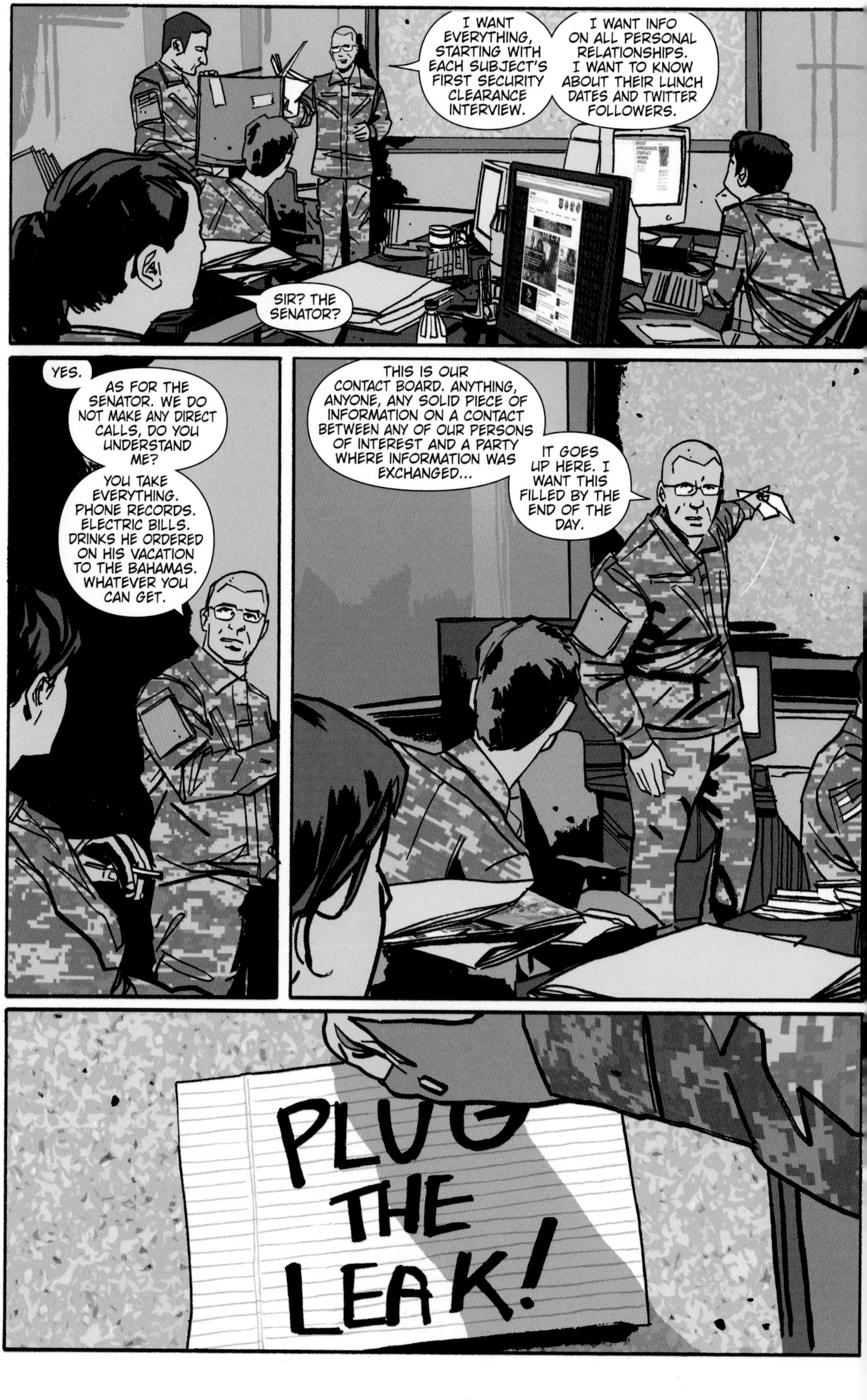
I WANT EVERYTHING, STARTING WITH EACH SUBJECT'S FIRST SECURITY CLEARANCE INTERVIEW.
I WANT INFO ON ALL PERSONAL RELATIONSHIPS. I WANT TO KNOW ABOUT THEIR LUNCH DATES AND TWITTER FOLLOWERS.
SIR? THE SENATOR?
YES.
AS FOR THE SENATOR. WE DO NOT MAKE ANY DIRECT CALLS, DO YOU UNDERSTAND ME?
YOU TAKE EVERYTHING. PHONE RECORDS. ELECTRIC BILLS. DRINKS HE ORDERED ON HIS VACATION TO THE BAHAMAS. WHATEVER YOU CAN GET.
THIS IS OUR CONTACT BOARD. ANYTHING, ANYONE, ANY SOLID PIECE OF INFORMATION ON A CONTACT BETWEEN ANY OF OUR PERSONS OF INTEREST AND A PARTY WHERE INFORMATION WAS EXCHANGED...
IT GOES UP HERE. I WANT THIS FILLED BY THE END OF THE DAY.
PLUG THE LEAK!

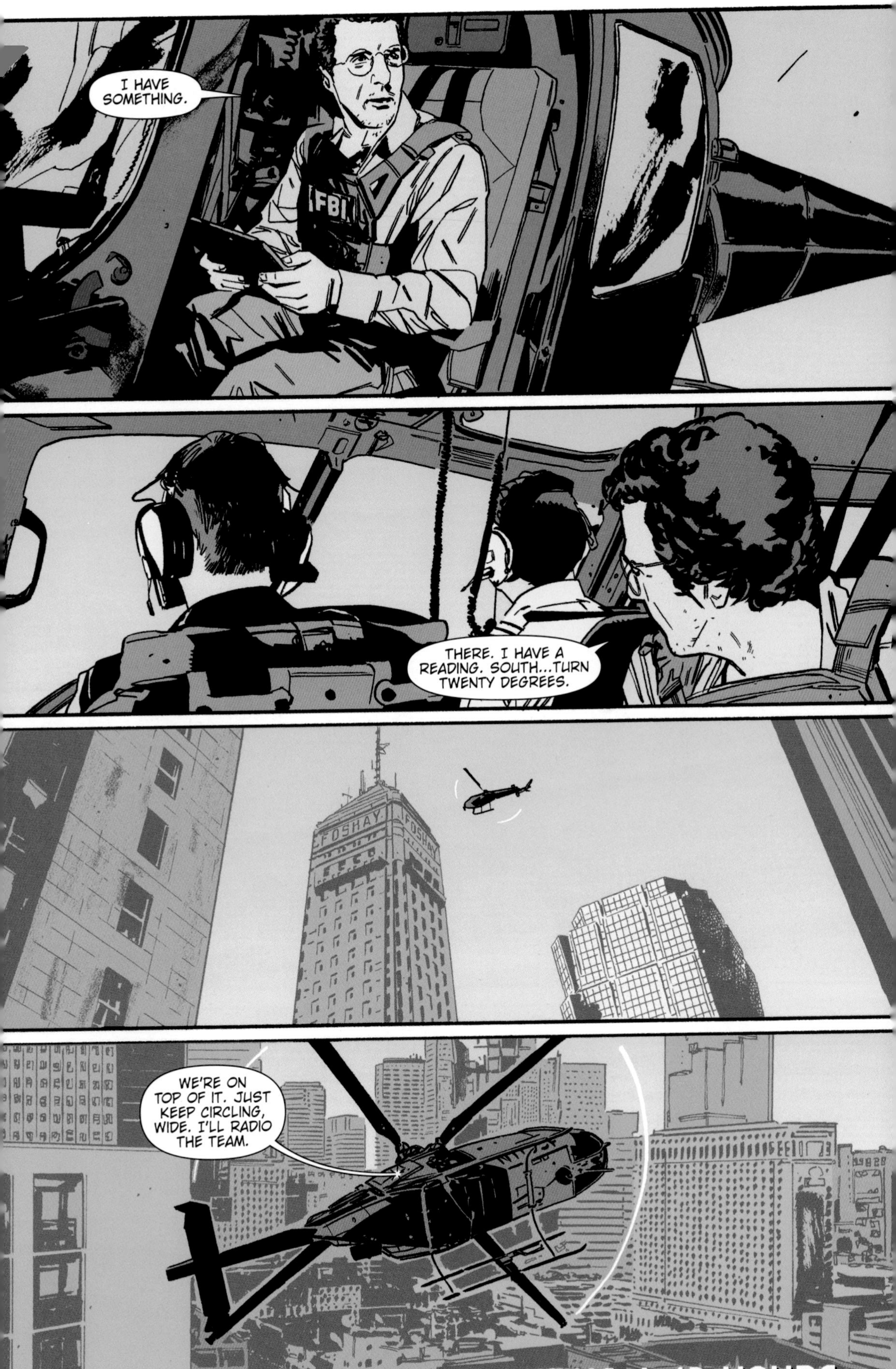
I HAVE SOMETHING.
THERE. I HAVE A READING. SOUTH...TURN TWENTY DEGREES.
FOSHAY
WE'RE ON TOP OF IT. JUST KEEP CIRCLING, WIDE. I'LL RADIO THE TEAM.
<<T-MINUS_4:13_HOURS//

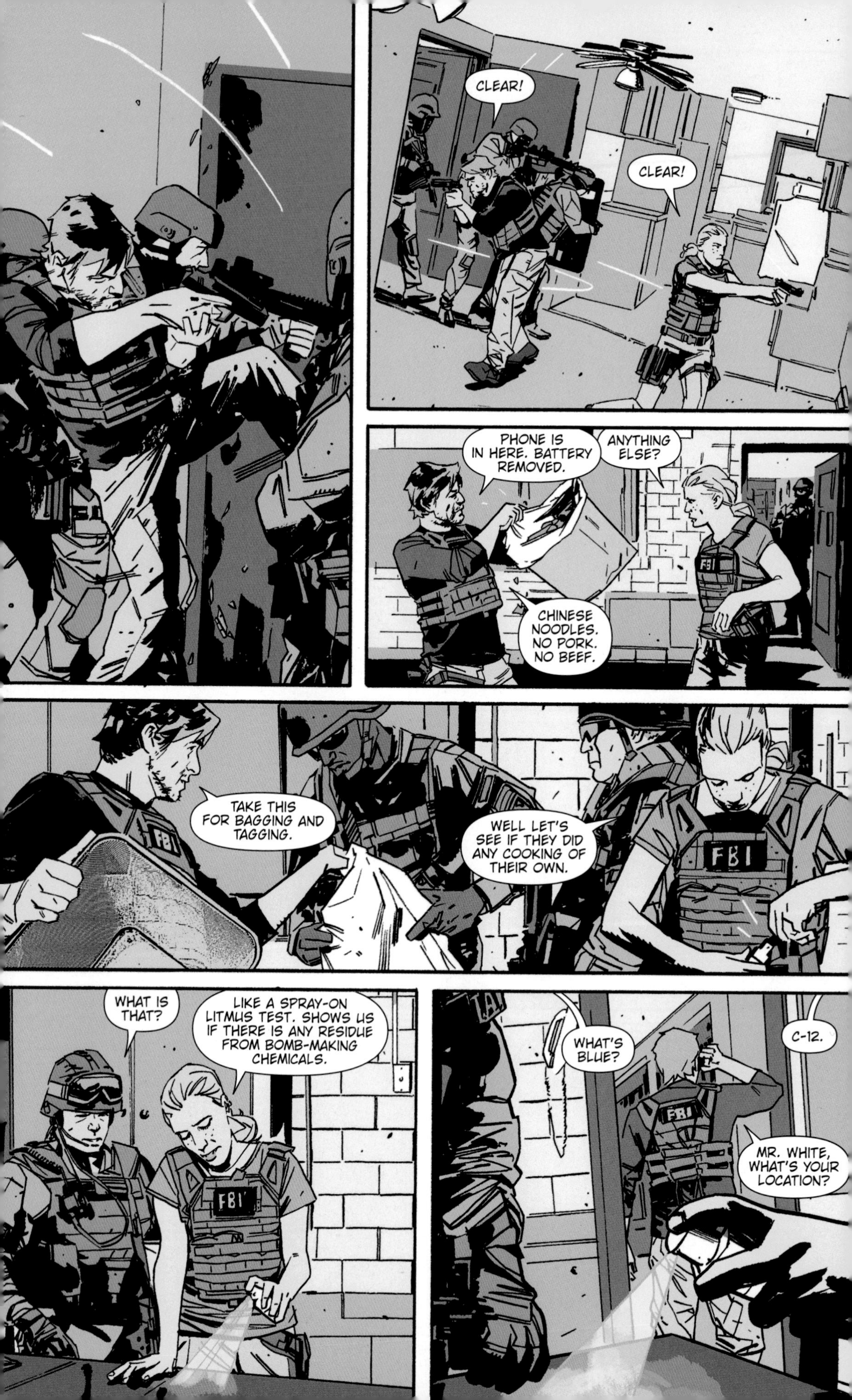
CLEAR!
CLEAR!
PHONE IS IN HERE. BATTERY REMOVED.
ANYTHING ELSE?
CHINESE NOODLES. NO PORK. NO BEEF.
TAKE THIS FOR BAGGING AND TAGGING.
WELL LET'S SEE IF THEY DID ANY COOKING OF THEIR OWN.
WHAT IS THAT?
LIKE A SPRAY-ON LITMUS TEST. SHOWS US IF THERE IS ANY RESIDUE FROM BOMB-MAKING CHEMICALS.
WHAT'S BLUE?
C-12.
MR. WHITE, WHAT'S YOUR LOCATION?

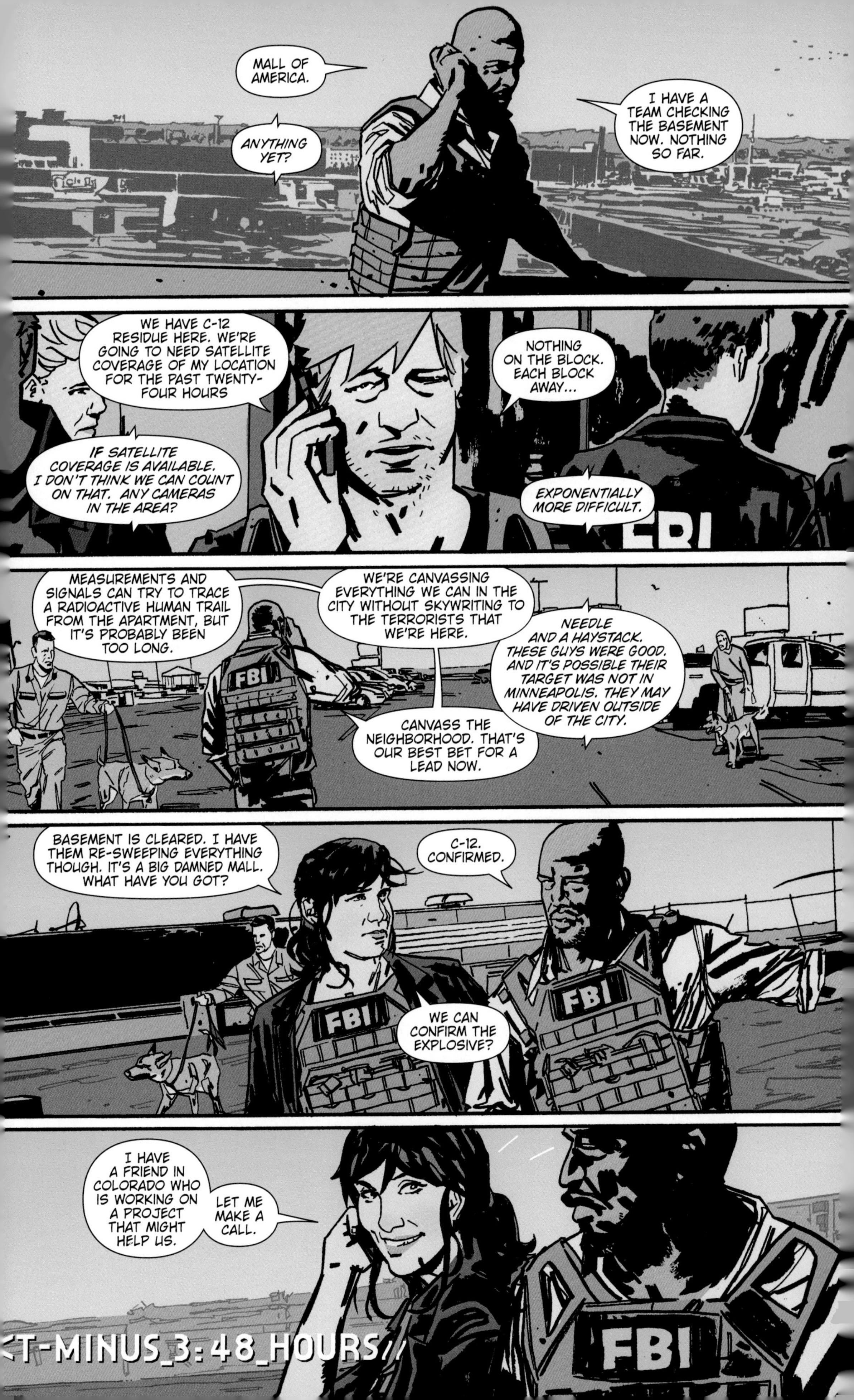
MALL OF AMERICA.
ANYTHING YET?
I HAVE A TEAM CHECKING THE BASEMENT NOW. NOTHING SO FAR.
WE HAVE C-12 RESIDUE HERE. WE'RE GOING TO NEED SATELLITE COVERAGE OF MY LOCATION FOR THE PAST TWENTY-FOUR HOURS
IF SATELLITE COVERAGE IS AVAILABLE. I DON'T THINK WE CAN COUNT ON THAT. ANY CAMERAS IN THE AREA?
NOTHING ON THE BLOCK. EACH BLOCK AWAY...
EXPONENTIALLY MORE DIFFICULT.
FBI
MEASUREMENTS AND SIGNALS CAN TRY TO TRACE A RADIOACTIVE HUMAN TRAIL FROM THE APARTMENT, BUT IT'S PROBABLY BEEN TOO LONG.
WE'RE CANVASSING EVERYTHING WE CAN IN THE CITY WITHOUT SKYWRITING TO THE TERRORISTS THAT WE'RE HERE.
CANVASS THE NEIGHBORHOOD. THAT'S OUR BEST BET FOR A LEAD NOW.
NEEDLE AND A HAYSTACK. THESE GUYS WERE GOOD. AND IT'S POSSIBLE THEIR TARGET WAS NOT IN MINNEAPOLIS. THEY MAY HAVE DRIVEN OUTSIDE OF THE CITY.
FBI
BASEMENT IS CLEARED. I HAVE THEM RE-SWEEPING EVERYTHING THOUGH. IT'S A BIG DAMNED MALL. WHAT HAVE YOU GOT?
C-12. CONFIRMED.
FBI
WE CAN CONFIRM THE EXPLOSIVE?
FBI
I HAVE A FRIEND IN COLORADO WHO IS WORKING ON A PROJECT THAT MIGHT HELP US.
LET ME MAKE A CALL.
FBI
T-MINUS_3:48_HOURS//

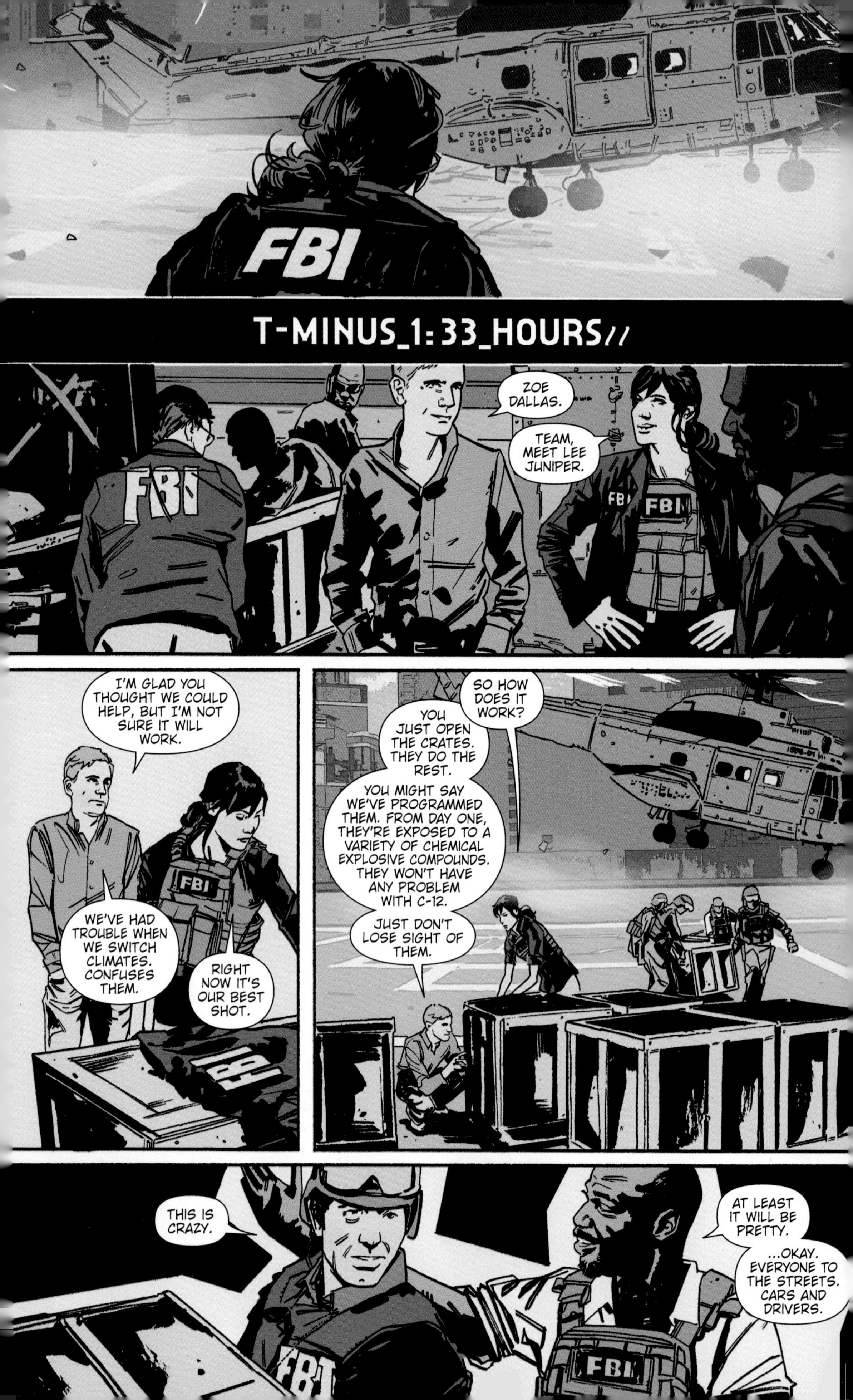
FBI
T-MINUS_1:33_HOURS//
ZOE DALLAS.
TEAM, MEET LEE JUNIPER.
FBI
FBI
FBI
I'M GLAD YOU THOUGHT WE COULD HELP, BUT I'M NOT SURE IT WILL WORK.
WE'VE HAD TROUBLE WHEN WE SWITCH CLIMATES. CONFUSES THEM.
RIGHT NOW IT'S OUR BEST SHOT.
SO HOW DOES IT WORK?
YOU JUST OPEN THE CRATES. THEY DO THE REST.
YOU MIGHT SAY WE'VE PROGRAMMED THEM. FROM DAY ONE, THEY'RE EXPOSED TO A VARIETY OF CHEMICAL EXPLOSIVE COMPOUNDS. THEY WON'T HAVE ANY PROBLEM WITH C-12.
JUST DON'T LOSE SIGHT OF THEM.
THIS IS CRAZY.
AT LEAST IT WILL BE PRETTY.
...OKAY. EVERYONE TO THE STREETS. CARS AND DRIVERS.

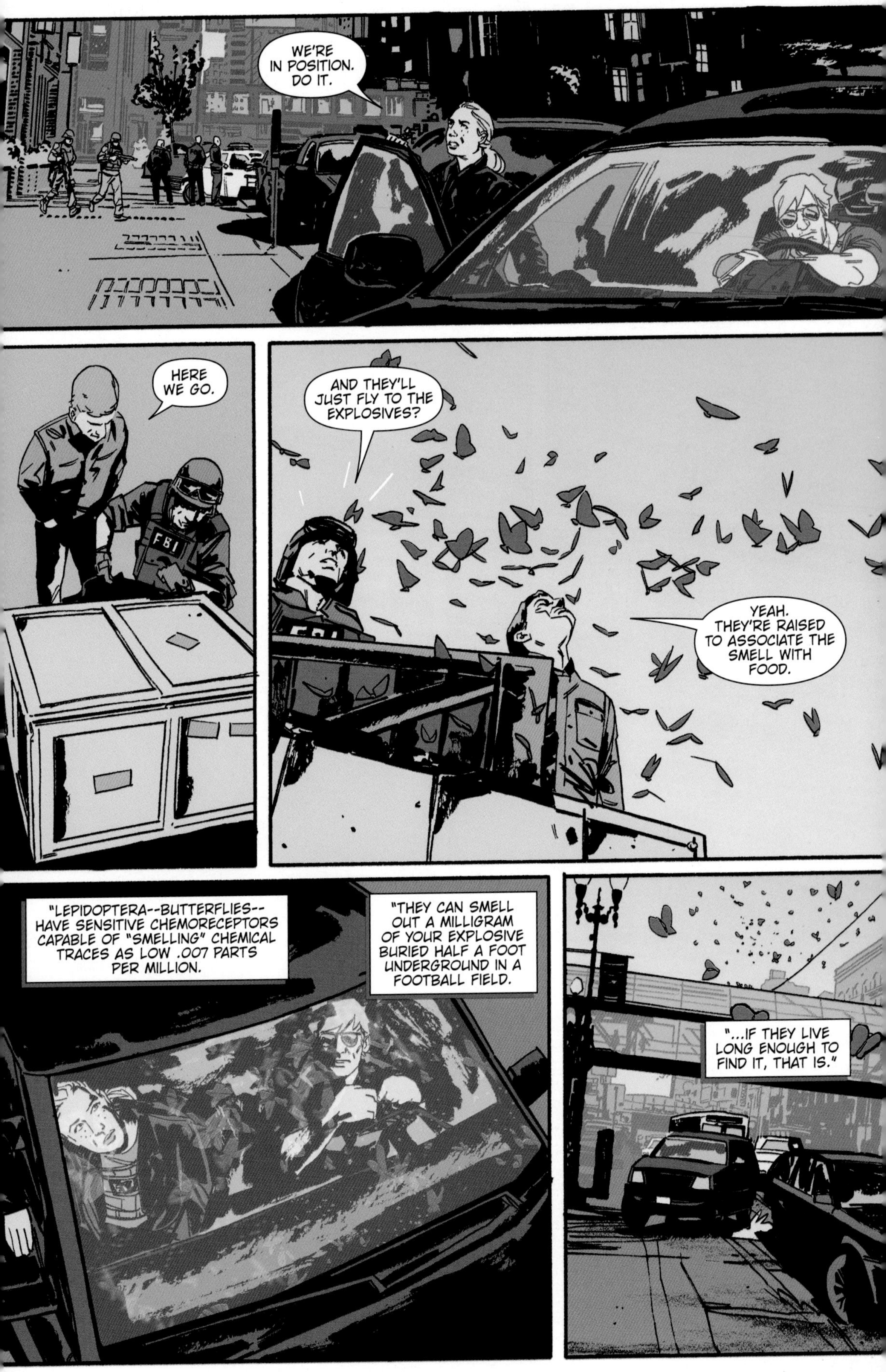
WE'RE IN POSITION. DO IT.
HERE WE GO.
AND THEY'LL JUST FLY TO THE EXPLOSIVES?
YEAH. THEY'RE RAISED TO ASSOCIATE THE SMELL WITH FOOD.
"LEPIDOPTERA--BUTTERFLIES--HAVE SENSITIVE CHEMORECEPTORS CAPABLE OF "SMELLING" CHEMICAL TRACES AS LOW .007 PARTS PER MILLION.
"THEY CAN SMELL OUT A MILLIGRAM OF YOUR EXPLOSIVE BURIED HALF A FOOT UNDERGROUND IN A FOOTBALL FIELD.
"...IF THEY LIVE LONG ENOUGH TO FIND IT, THAT IS."

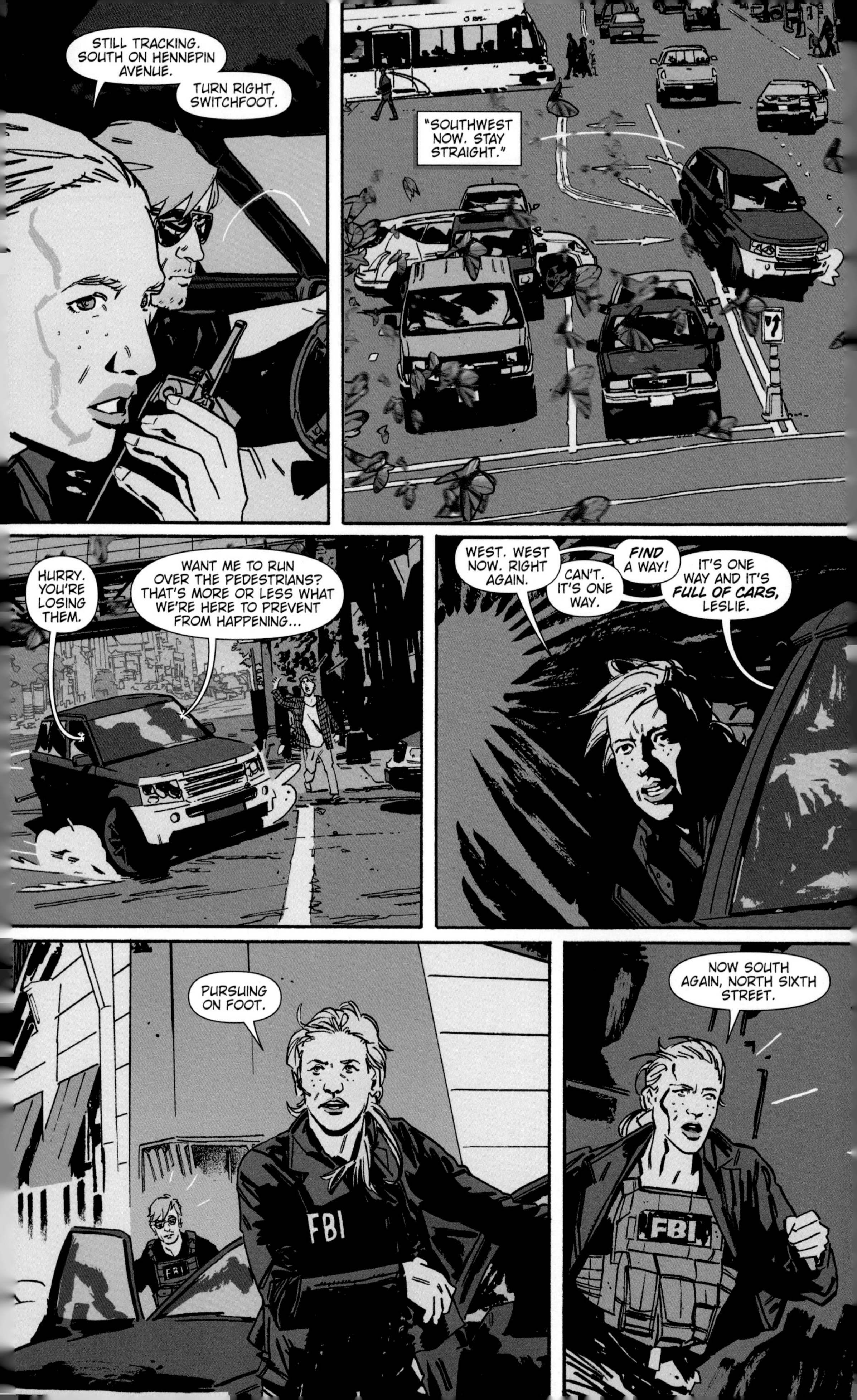
STILL TRACKING. SOUTH ON HENNEPIN AVENUE.
TURN RIGHT, SWITCHFOOT.
"SOUTHWEST NOW. STAY STRAIGHT."
HURRY. YOU'RE LOSING THEM.
WANT ME TO RUN OVER THE PEDESTRIANS? THAT'S MORE OR LESS WHAT WE'RE HERE TO PREVENT FROM HAPPENING...
WEST. WEST NOW. RIGHT AGAIN.
CAN'T. IT'S ONE WAY.
FIND A WAY!
IT'S ONE WAY AND IT'S FULL OF CARS, LESLIE.
PURSUING ON FOOT.
FBI
FBI
NOW SOUTH AGAIN, NORTH SIXTH STREET.
FBI

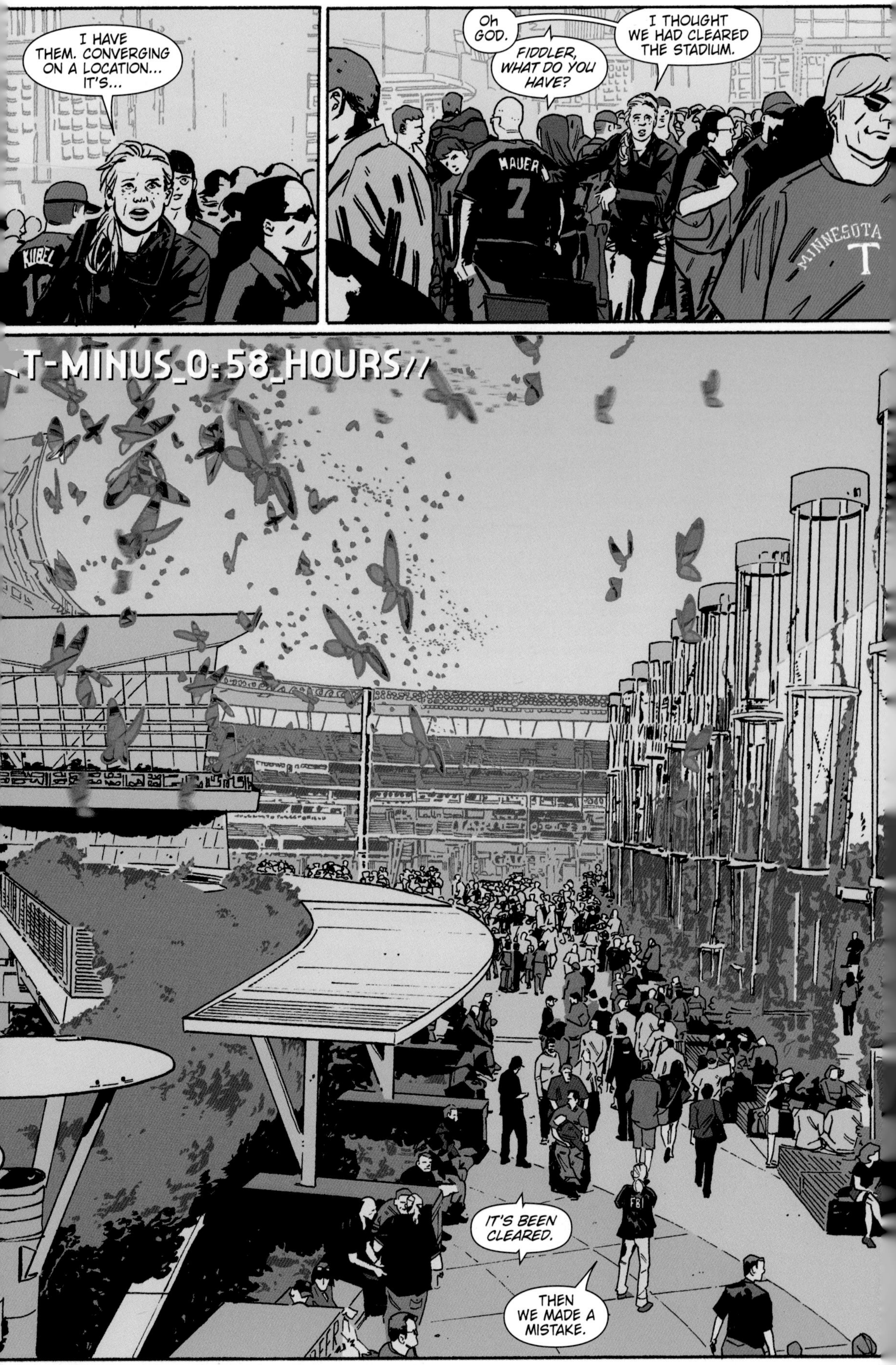
I HAVE THEM. CONVERGING ON A LOCATION... IT'S...
KUBEL
Oh GOD.
I THOUGHT WE HAD CLEARED THE STADIUM.
FIDDLER, WHAT DO YOU HAVE?
MAUER
7
MINNESOTA
T
T-MINUS_0:58_HOURS//
FBI
IT'S BEEN CLEARED.
THEN WE MADE A MISTAKE.

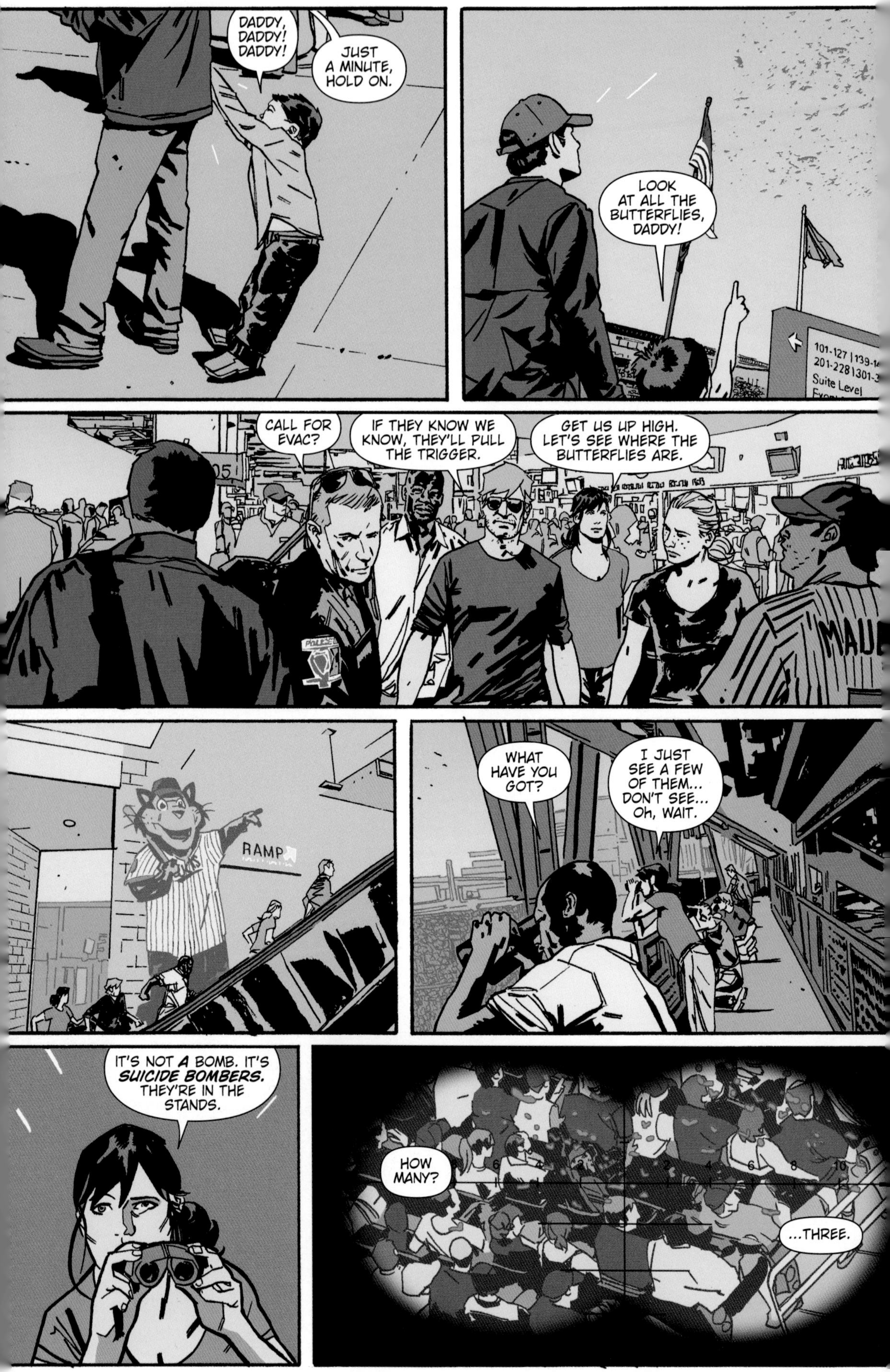
DADDY, DADDY! DADDY!
JUST A MINUTE, HOLD ON.
LOOK AT ALL THE BUTTERFLIES, DADDY!
101-127 | 139-1
201-228 | 301-3
Suite Level
CALL FOR EVAC?
IF THEY KNOW WE KNOW, THEY'LL PULL THE TRIGGER.
GET US UP HIGH. LET'S SEE WHERE THE BUTTERFLIES ARE.
RAMP
WHAT HAVE YOU GOT?
I JUST SEE A FEW OF THEM... DON'T SEE... Oh, WAIT.
IT'S NOT *A* BOMB. IT'S ***SUICIDE BOMBERS.*** THEY'RE IN THE STANDS.
HOW MANY?
...THREE.

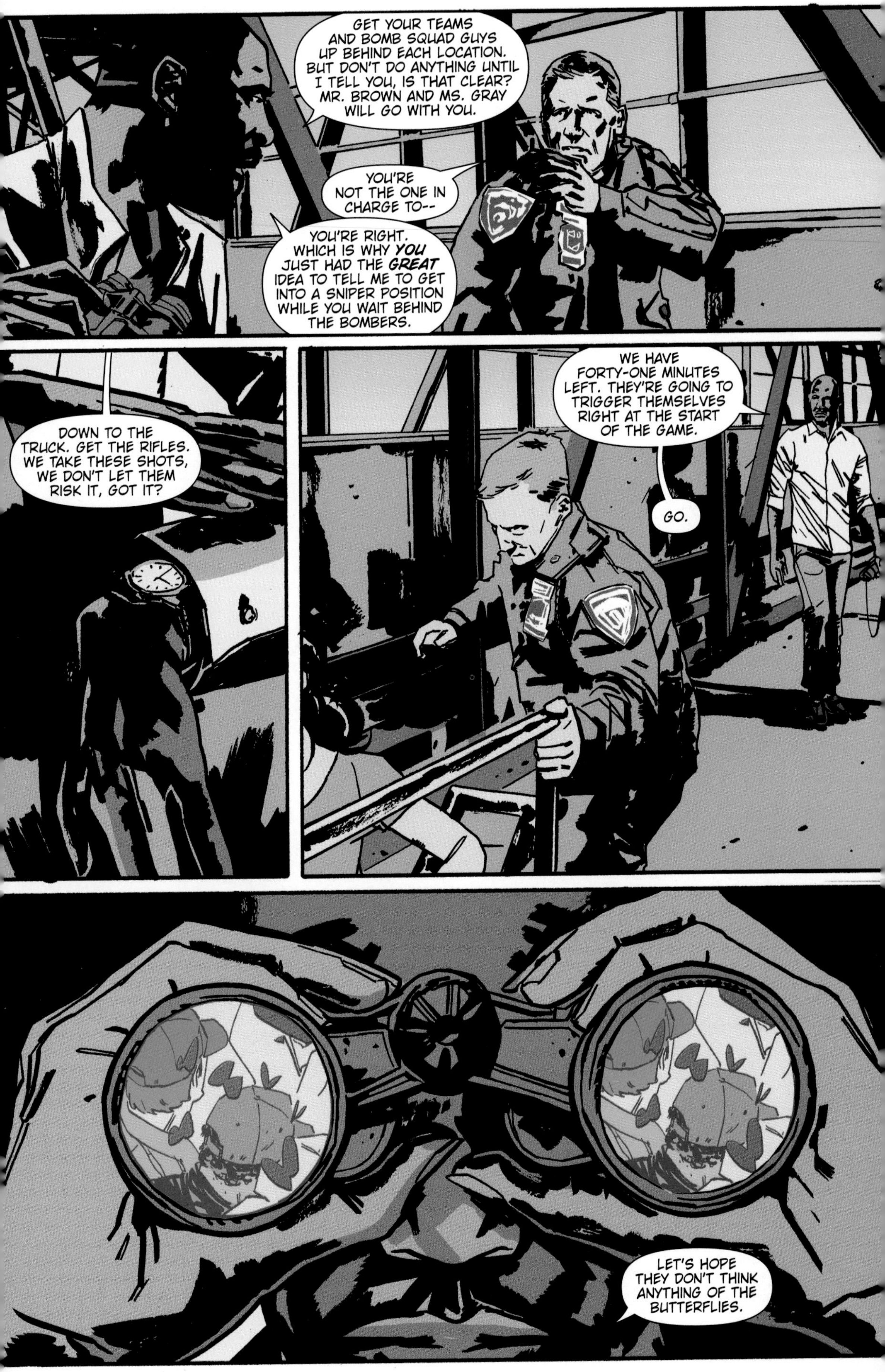
GET YOUR TEAMS AND BOMB SQUAD GUYS UP BEHIND EACH LOCATION. BUT DON'T DO ANYTHING UNTIL I TELL YOU, IS THAT CLEAR? MR. BROWN AND MS. GRAY WILL GO WITH YOU.
YOU'RE NOT THE ONE IN CHARGE TO--
YOU'RE RIGHT. WHICH IS WHY ***YOU*** JUST HAD THE ***GREAT*** IDEA TO TELL ME TO GET INTO A SNIPER POSITION WHILE YOU WAIT BEHIND THE BOMBERS.
DOWN TO THE TRUCK. GET THE RIFLES. WE TAKE THESE SHOTS, WE DON'T LET THEM RISK IT, GOT IT?
WE HAVE FORTY-ONE MINUTES LEFT. THEY'RE GOING TO TRIGGER THEMSELVES RIGHT AT THE START OF THE GAME.
GO.
LET'S HOPE THEY DON'T THINK ANYTHING OF THE BUTTERFLIES.

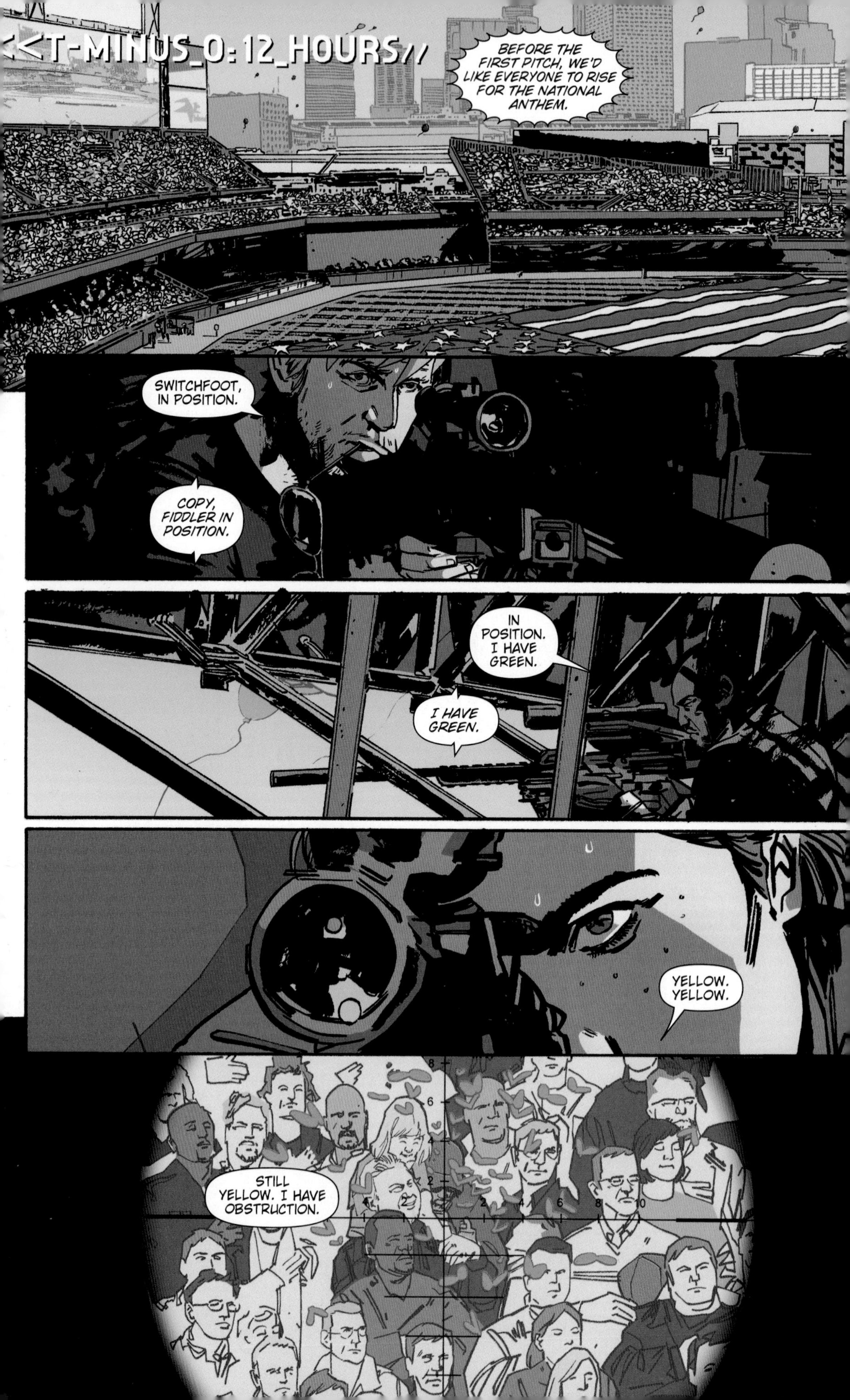
<<T-MINUS_0:12_HOURS//
BEFORE THE FIRST PITCH, WE'D LIKE EVERYONE TO RISE FOR THE NATIONAL ANTHEM.
SWITCHFOOT, IN POSITION.
COPY, FIDDLER IN POSITION.
IN POSITION. I HAVE GREEN.
I HAVE GREEN.
YELLOW. YELLOW.
STILL YELLOW. I HAVE OBSTRUCTION.

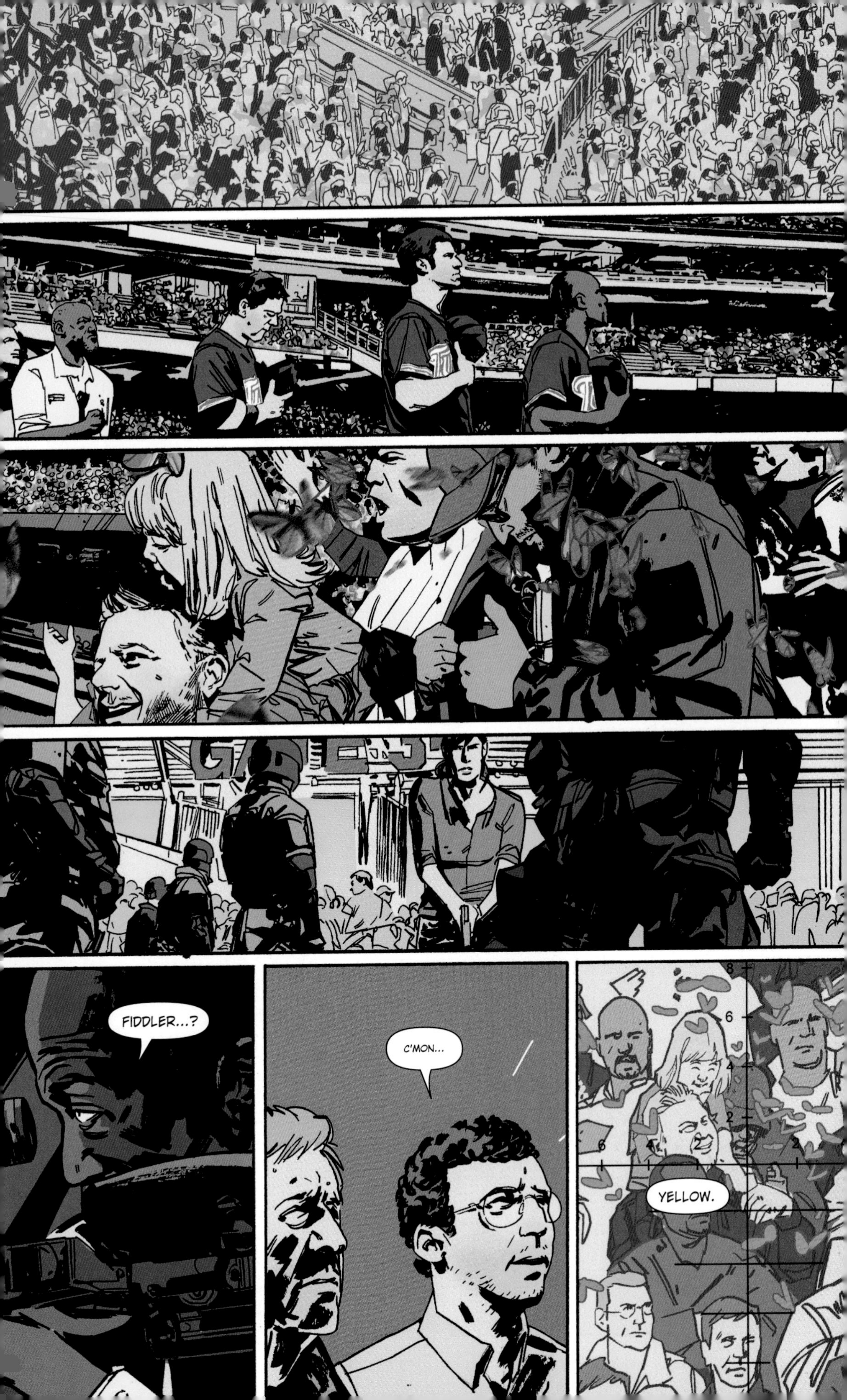
FIDDLER...?
C'MON...
YELLOW.

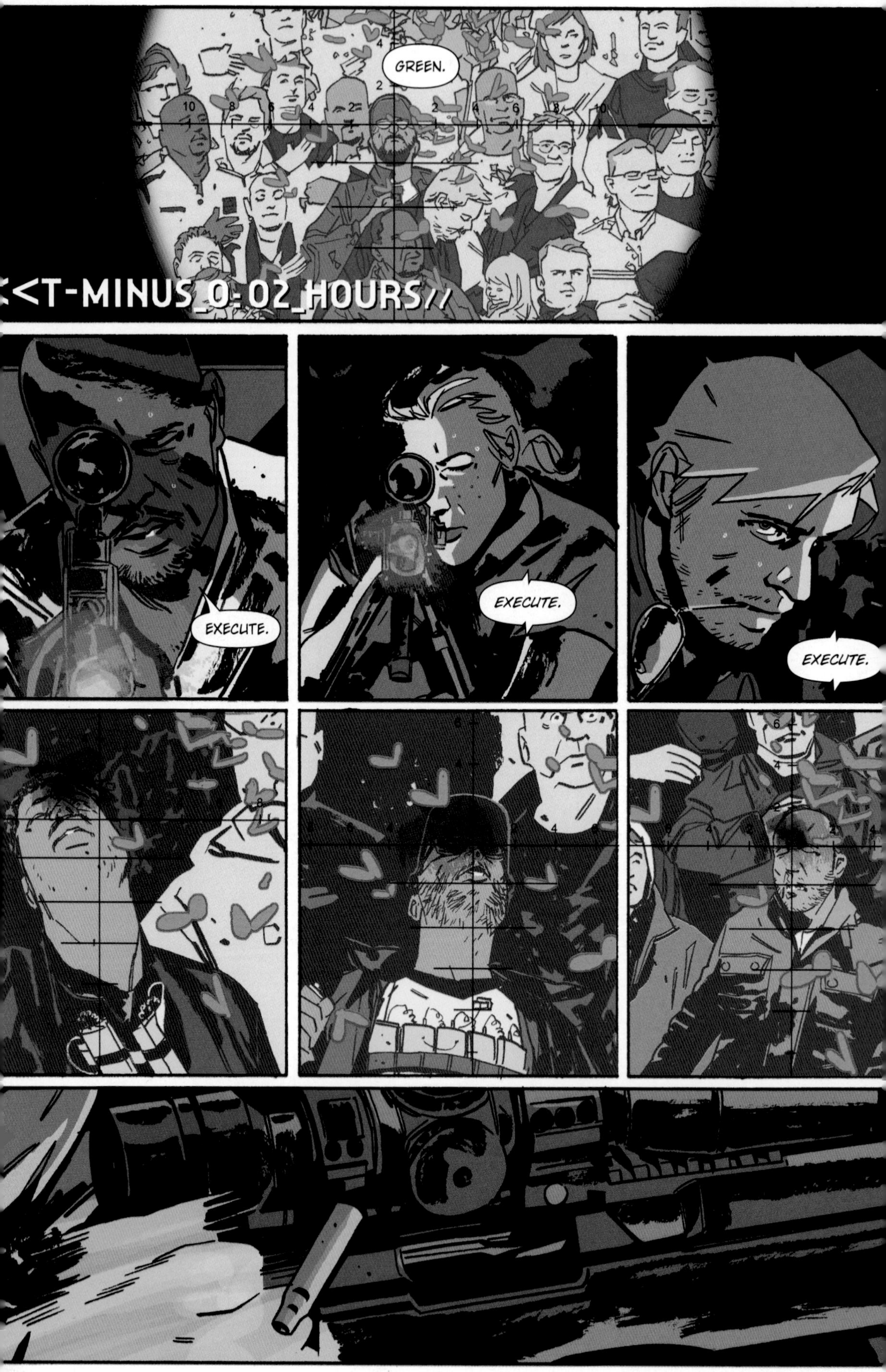
GREEN.
<<T-MINUS_0:02_HOURS//
EXECUTE.
EXECUTE.
EXECUTE.

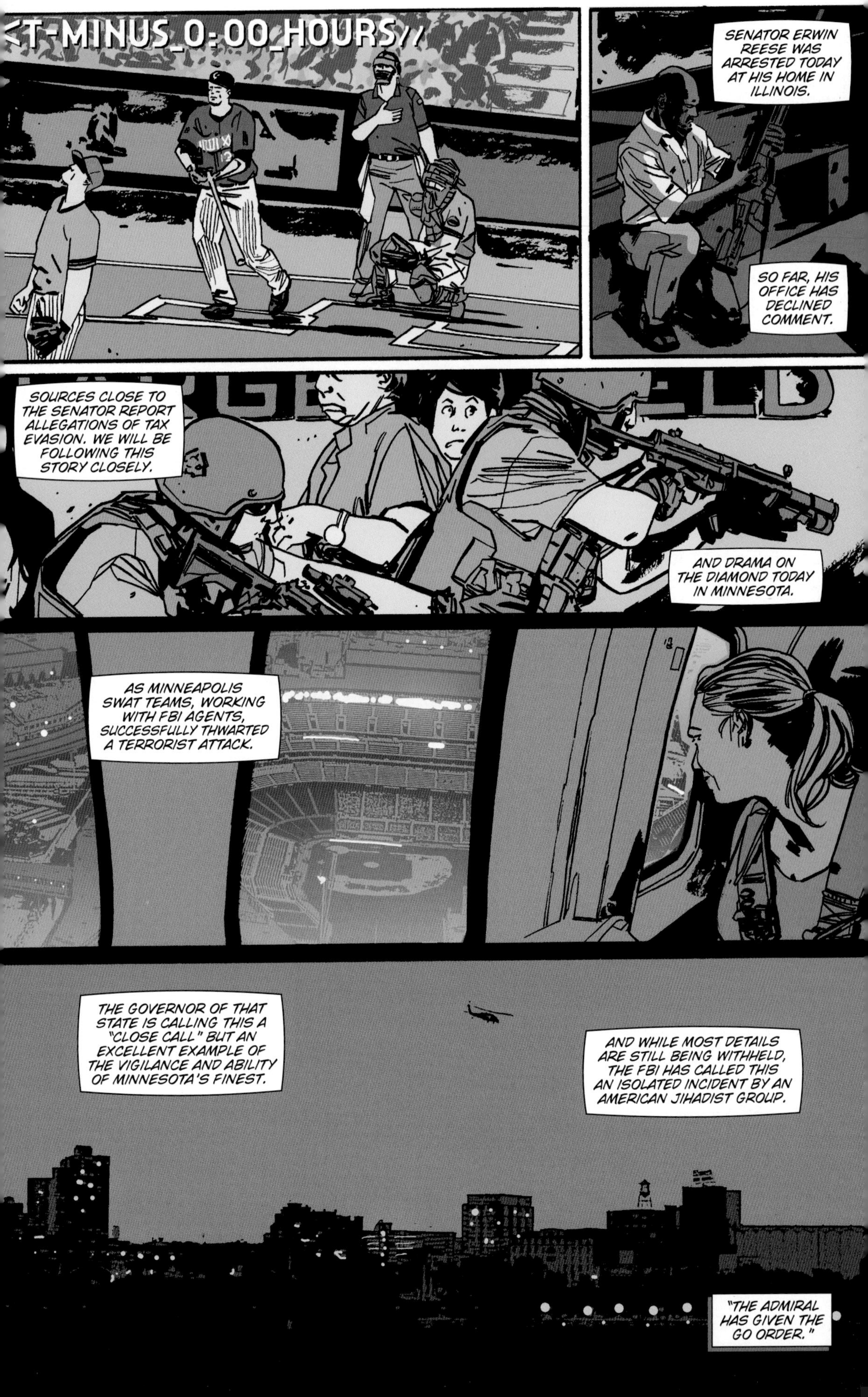
<T-MINUS_0:00_HOURS//
SENATOR ERWIN REESE WAS ARRESTED TODAY AT HIS HOME IN ILLINOIS.
SO FAR, HIS OFFICE HAS DECLINED COMMENT.
SOURCES CLOSE TO THE SENATOR REPORT ALLEGATIONS OF TAX EVASION. WE WILL BE FOLLOWING THIS STORY CLOSELY.
AND DRAMA ON THE DIAMOND TODAY IN MINNESOTA.
AS MINNEAPOLIS SWAT TEAMS, WORKING WITH FBI AGENTS, SUCCESSFULLY THWARTED A TERRORIST ATTACK.
THE GOVERNOR OF THAT STATE IS CALLING THIS A "CLOSE CALL" BUT AN EXCELLENT EXAMPLE OF THE VIGILANCE AND ABILITY OF MINNESOTA'S FINEST.
AND WHILE MOST DETAILS ARE STILL BEING WITHHELD, THE FBI HAS CALLED THIS AN ISOLATED INCIDENT BY AN AMERICAN JIHADIST GROUP.
"THE ADMIRAL HAS GIVEN THE GO ORDER."

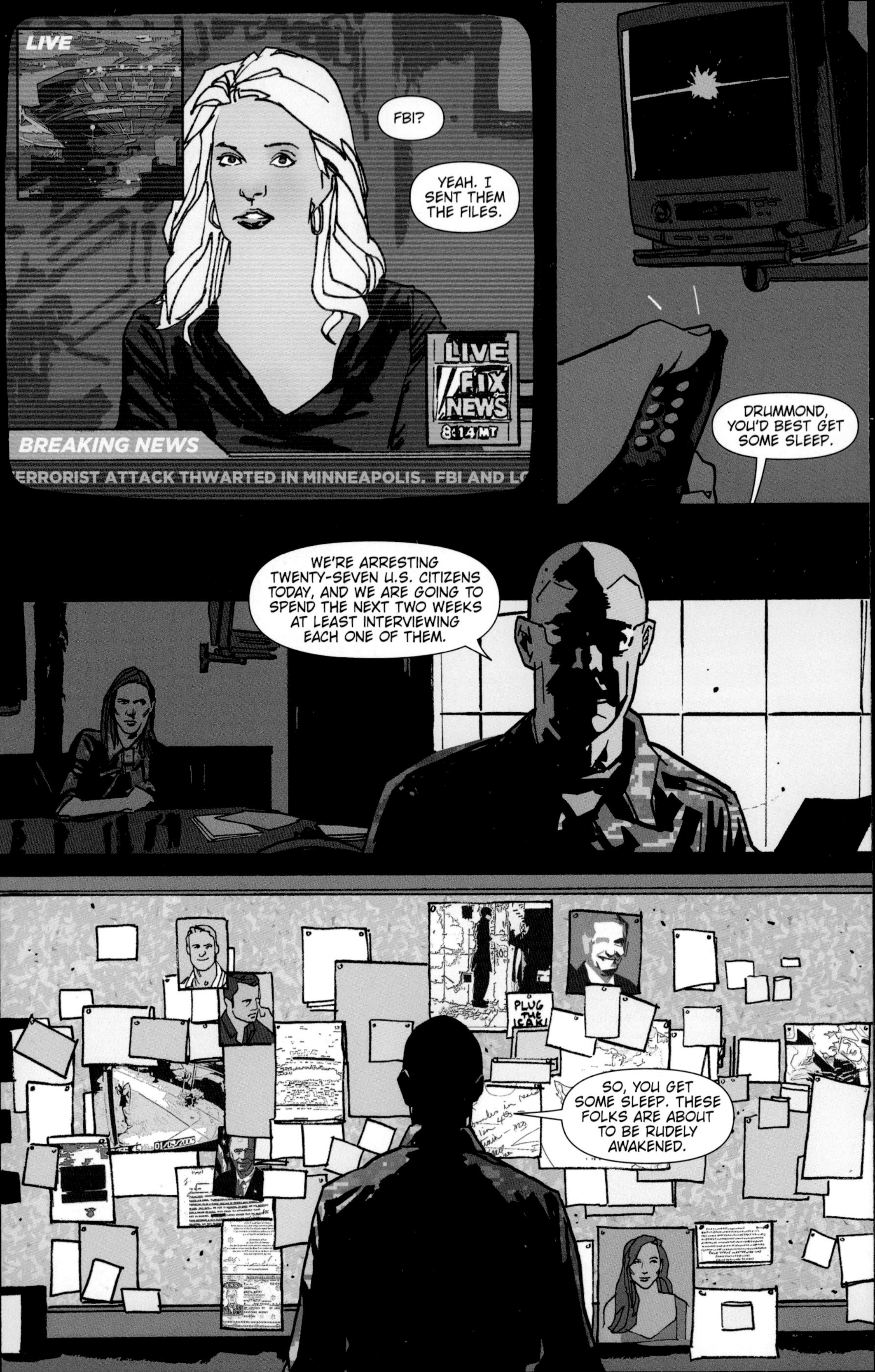
LIVE
FBI?
YEAH. I SENT THEM THE FILES.
LIVE
FIX NEWS
8:14 MT
BREAKING NEWS
ERRORIST ATTACK THWARTED IN MINNEAPOLIS. FBI AND LO
DRUMMOND, YOU'D BEST GET SOME SLEEP.
WE'RE ARRESTING TWENTY-SEVEN U.S. CITIZENS TODAY, AND WE ARE GOING TO SPEND THE NEXT TWO WEEKS AT LEAST INTERVIEWING EACH ONE OF THEM.
PLUG THE LEAK!
SO, YOU GET SOME SLEEP. THESE FOLKS ARE ABOUT TO BE RUDELY AWAKENED.

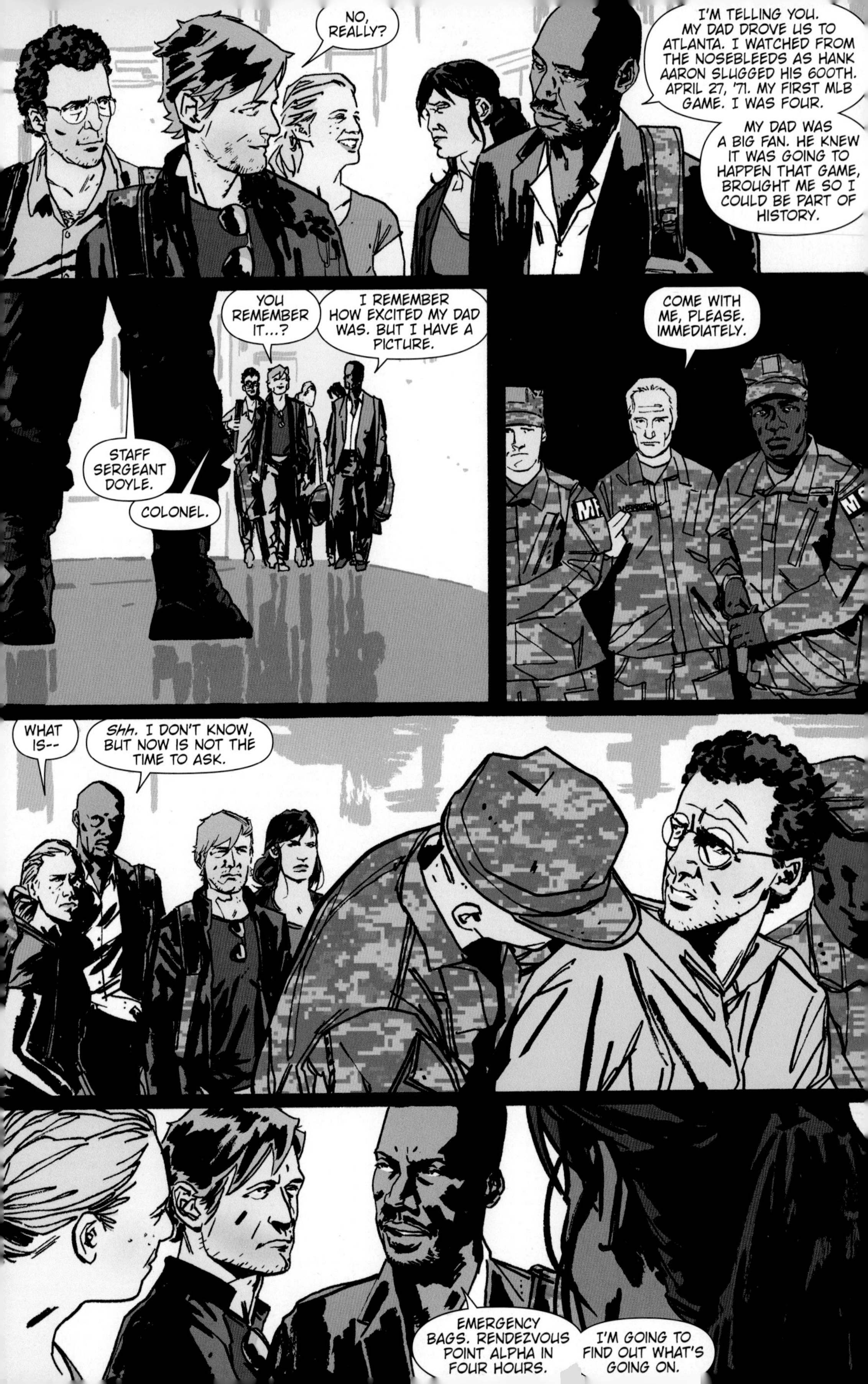
NO, REALLY?
I'M TELLING YOU. MY DAD DROVE US TO ATLANTA. I WATCHED FROM THE NOSEBLEEDS AS HANK AARON SLUGGED HIS 600TH. APRIL 27, '71. MY FIRST MLB GAME. I WAS FOUR.
MY DAD WAS A BIG FAN. HE KNEW IT WAS GOING TO HAPPEN THAT GAME, BROUGHT ME SO I COULD BE PART OF HISTORY.
YOU REMEMBER IT...?
I REMEMBER HOW EXCITED MY DAD WAS. BUT I HAVE A PICTURE.
STAFF SERGEANT DOYLE.
COLONEL.
COME WITH ME, PLEASE. IMMEDIATELY.
WHAT IS--
Shh. I DON'T KNOW, BUT NOW IS NOT THE TIME TO ASK.
EMERGENCY BAGS. RENDEZVOUS POINT ALPHA IN FOUR HOURS.
I'M GOING TO FIND OUT WHAT'S GOING ON.

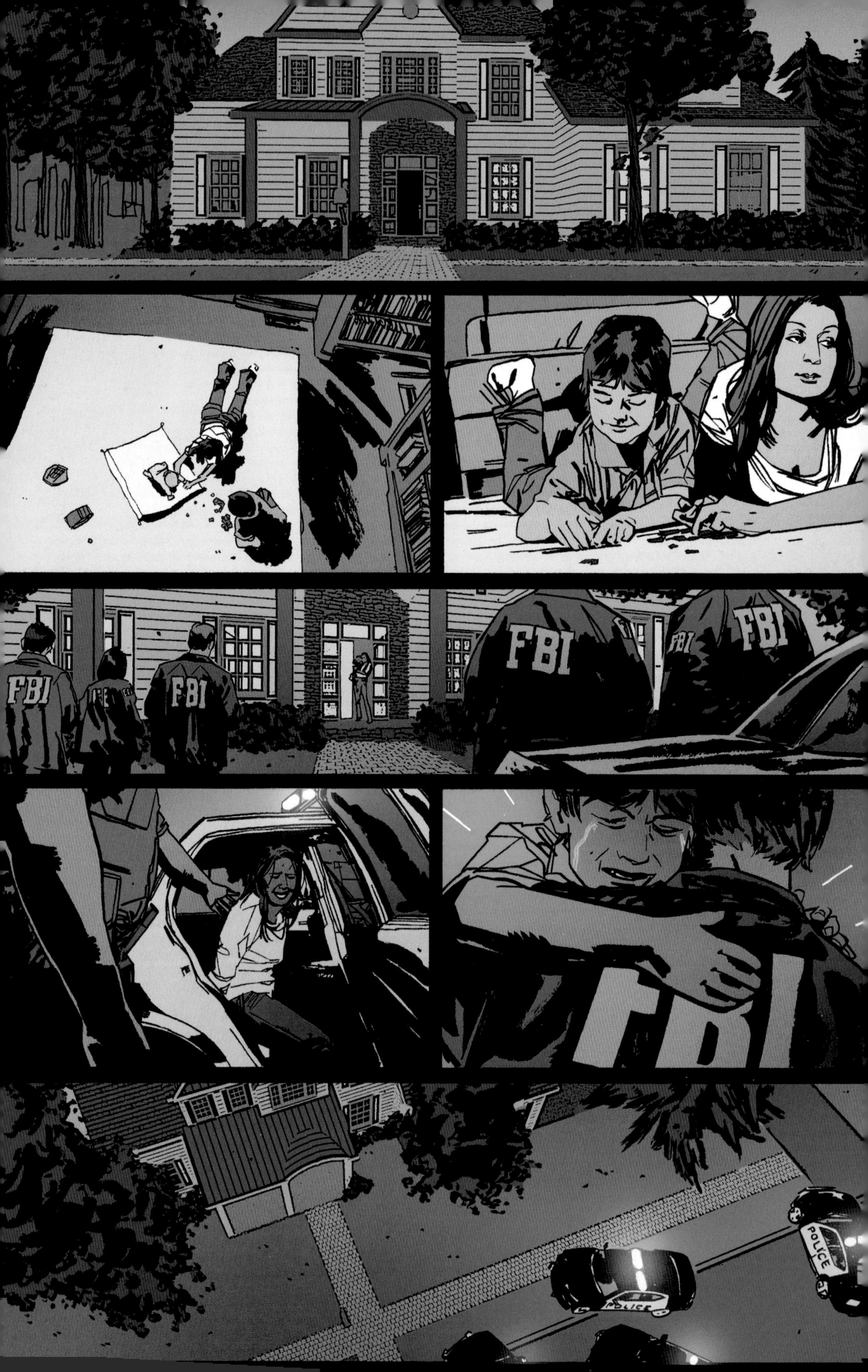
FBI
FBI
FBI
FBI
FBI
POLICE
POLICE

//ADVANCE_MISSION_BRIEFING__
((_TEAM OMAHA FUTURE DEPLOYMENTS_

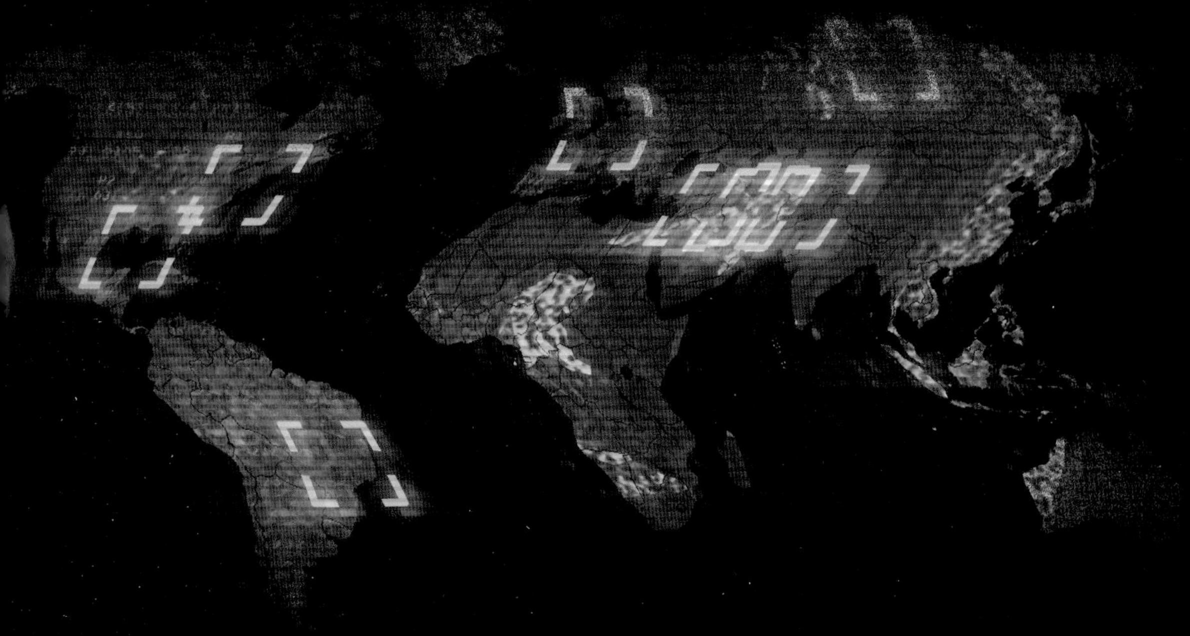

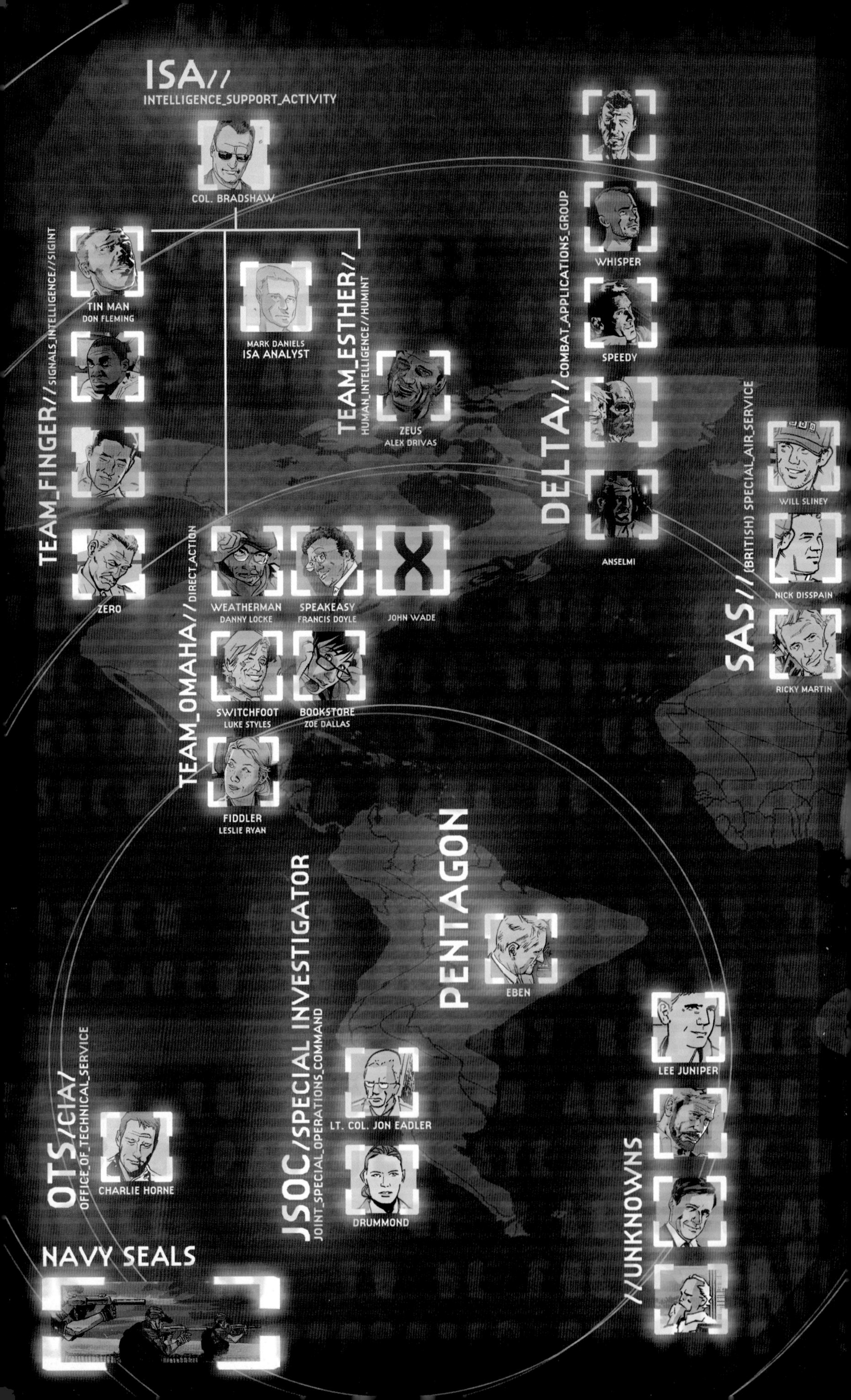
ISA//
INTELLIGENCE_SUPPORT_ACTIVITY
COL. BRADSHAW
TEAM_FINGER//
SIGNALS_INTELLIGENCE//SIGINT
TIN MAN
DON FLEMING
ZERO
MARK DANIELS
ISA ANALYST
TEAM_ESTHER//
HUMAN_INTELLIGENCE//HUMINT
ZEUS
ALEX DRIVAS
TEAM_OMAHA//
DIRECT_ACTION
WEATHERMAN
DANNY LOCKE
SPEAKEASY
FRANCIS DOYLE
X
JOHN WADE
SWITCHFOOT
LUKE STYLES
BOOKSTORE
ZOE DALLAS
FIDDLER
LESLIE RYAN
DELTA//
COMBAT_APPLICATIONS_GROUP
WHISPER
SPEEDY
ANSELMI
SAS//
(BRITISH) SPECIAL_AIR_SERVICE
WILL SLINEY
NICK DISSPAIN
RICKY MARTIN
PENTAGON
EBEN
JSOC/SPECIAL INVESTIGATOR
JOINT_SPECIAL_OPERATIONS_COMMAND
LT. COL. JON EADLER
DRUMMOND
OTS/CIA/
OFFICE_OF_TECHNICAL_SERVICE
CHARLIE HORNE
//UNKNOWNS
LEE JUNIPER
NAVY SEALS

ARTICLE FIFTEEN - A nonjudicial punishment for a minor offense.

AWACS - Airborne Warning and Control System. Typically a Boeing E-3 Sentry, an aircraft that aids in battlefield coordination.

CAG - Combat Applications Group. The 1st Special Forces Operational Detachment-Delta (1st SFOD-D). More commonly called "Delta Force" or "The Unit" and more recently "Army Compartmented Elements." The Army's most elite tier-one direct action counterterrorism unit.

"CALL THE BALL" - A sniper spotter visually designating the target.

CIVIL AFFAIRS - A special operations unit that acts as a liaison between the civil inhabitants of war zones and military forces operating there.

CRYE PRECISION™ - Tactical outfitter specializing in Tier 1 combat apparel and gear.

FLIR - Forward Looking Infrared. Usually mounted on aircraft, a camera that visualizes infrared radiation.

HONEYPOT - In spycraft, using an attractive female to distract and/or bait the target.

KIT - An operator's combination of outfit, gear, and weaponry.

MUTT JEEP - A Vietnam War-era jeep manufactured by Ford, Kaiser, and AM General.

NAVY LNO - Liaison Officer

NINE-LINE - A simplified medical condition report.

"PAINT THE TARGET/SPARKLE TARGET" - Using an IR laser to designate a target for laser-guided munitions.

PRIZE CREW - A team that gathers physical evidence from a mission location.

PRO WORDS - In special operations, operators use single words to indicate mission progress.

PSYOP - Psychological Operations. Warfare designed to mentally distract, demoralize, or confuse the enemy.

SAS - Special Air Service. British Army Special Forces.

SITREP - Situation report

SOCCENT - Special Operations Command Central

TECHNICALS - Small to medium civilian vehicles outfitted by militia for combat.

TIER ONE - The most elite of special operators.

TOC - Tactical Operations Center

TOMAHAWK - A medium- to long-range cruise missile.

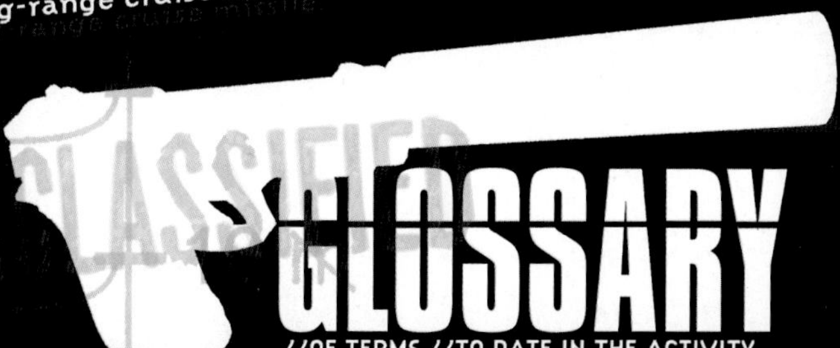

CLASSIFIED

GLOSSARY

//OF_TERMS_//TO DATE_IN_THE_ACTIVITY_

RECOMMENDED READING

THE FOLLOWING BOOKS AND WEBSITES HAVE BEEN AN INVALUABLE
RESOURCE IN CONSTRUCTING THE WORLD OF THE ACTIVITY.

NO EASY DAY: The Firsthand Account of the Mission That Killed Osama Bin Laden
/ Mark Owen with Kevin Maurer

KILLER ELITE / Michael Smith

SPYCRAFT / Robert Wallace & H. Keith Melton

GENTLEMEN BASTARDS / Kevin Maurer

NOT A GOOD DAY TO DIE / Sean Naylor

KILLING PABLO / Mark Bowden

SAS: The Elite Special Forces in their Own Words

LIONS OF KANDAHAR / Major Rusty Bradley with Kevin Maurer

THE COMMAND: Deep Inside the Presidents Secret Army / Marc Ambinder & D.B. Grady

NO WAY OUT / Mitch Weiss and Kevin Maurer

INSIDE DELTA FORCE / Eric L. Haney

NEVER SURRENDER / LTG William G. Boykin

www.SOFREP.com

www.soldiersystems.net

www.shadowspear.com

www.defensetech.org

THE CREATORS OF THE ACTIVITY WISH TO THANK THE FOLLOWING INDIVIDUALS FOR THEIR INPUT AND ENCOURAGEMENT IN THE CONTINUING RESEARCH AND PRODUCTION OF THIS BOOK˟:

˟Some names changed or withheld due to Operational Security.

Kevin Maurer

Major Rusty Bradley / US Special Forces

Lt. Col. Jerry Herbel / USAFR / Retired

CPT Juan Nieves / DHS / DIA / Retired

Undisclosed members of the U.S. Navy SEALS

Kate

Lt. Col. John Clearwater / United States Army OCPA

SSG Shlomo Roman / IDF / Israeli Military Intelligence

Mr. Aleph, 1ST SGT / IDF / Retired

Lt. Col. Matt Yocum / USAF / SOCOM

Jack Murphy

Lt. Lawrence J. Yatch / US NAVY SEALS / Retired

SEALED MINDSET

Uri Fridman

Brad

David Brown

R.

Caleb Crye

Jeff

//_ADDITIONALLY_FOR_THEIR_SUPPORT_

Ford Gilmore

Harris Miller

Image Comics and the Image Production Team

Jacob Berendes

The City of Minneapolis

Brent and Josie Schoonover

Seth White

Lauren Mayfield

Ken Mayfield

Nick Hoople

David Ratz

_and Gretchen and Lauren for their continued support while we're deployed to our desks for so many hours out of the day.

FOLLOW US ON TWITTER:

@NHEdmondson   @MitchGerads   @TheACTIVITY

DIG DEEPER INTO THE ACTIVITY
HTTP://WWW.WARFAREWITHOUTWARNING.COM

//_PERSONNEL_DESIGNATE:

//WRITER/ NATHAN_EDMONDSON.

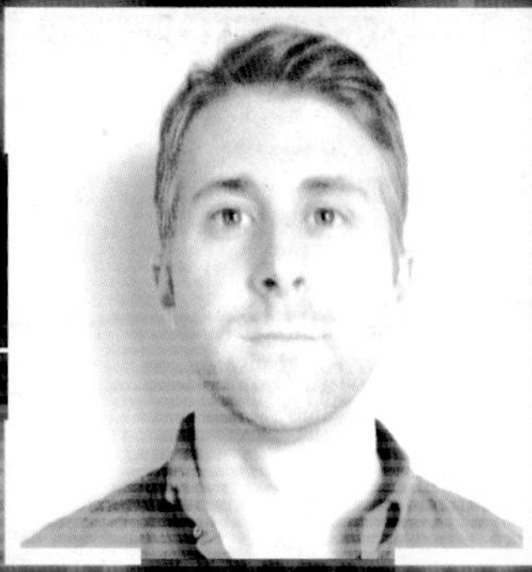

NATHAN EDMONDSON IS THE WRITER AND CO-CREATOR OF /OLYMPUS//THE_LIGHT//DANCER//WHERE_IS_JAKE_ELLIS?/ AND THE EISNER NOMINATED /WHO _IS_JAKE_ELLIS?/. HE HAS ALSO PENNED /ULTIMATE_IRON_MAN//PUNISHER: MAX/ AND /GRIFTER/. HE LIVES IN GEORGIA WITH HIS WIFE AND DAUGHTER.

FIND OUT MORE AT WWW.NATHAN-E.COM

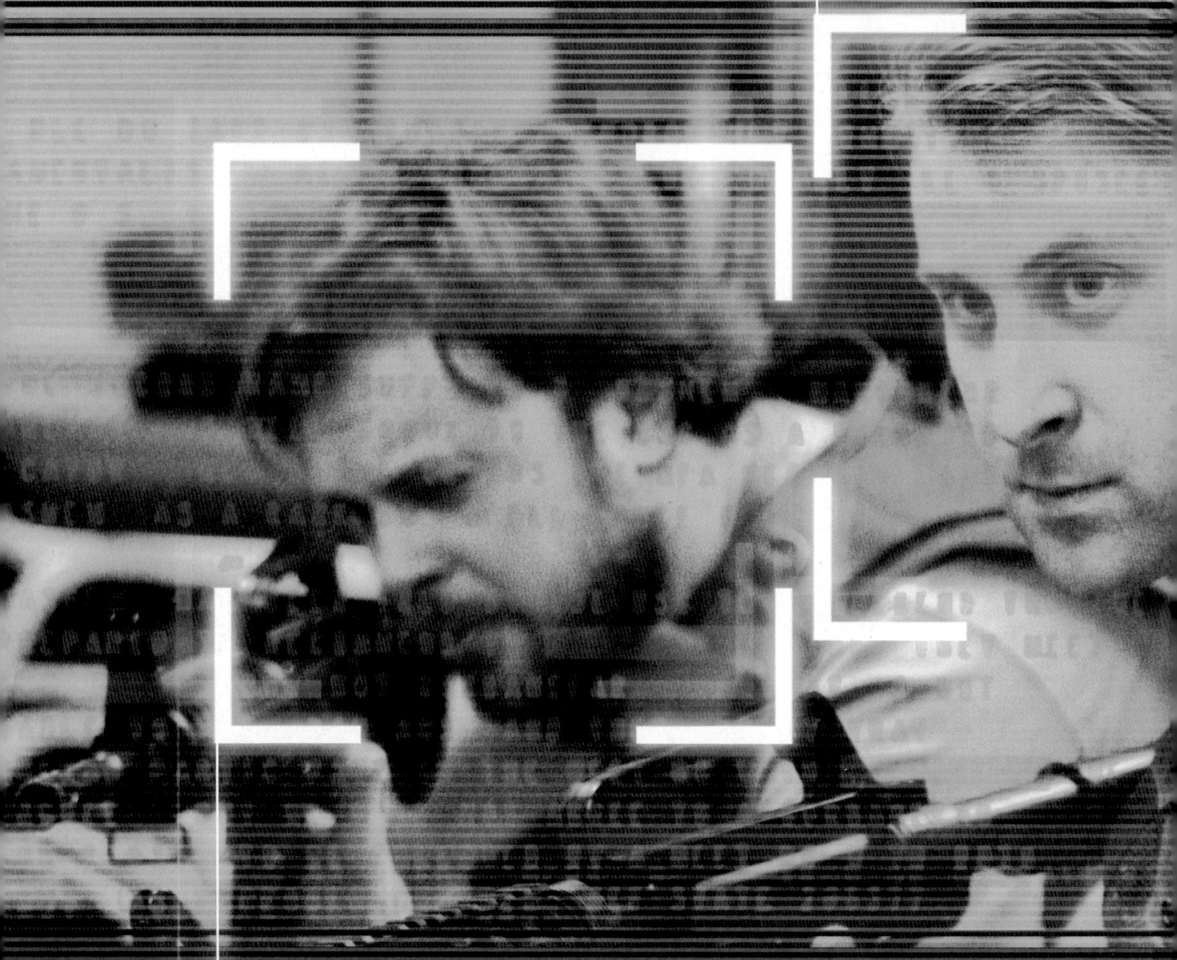

PHOTOGRAPHY BY ED PETERSO

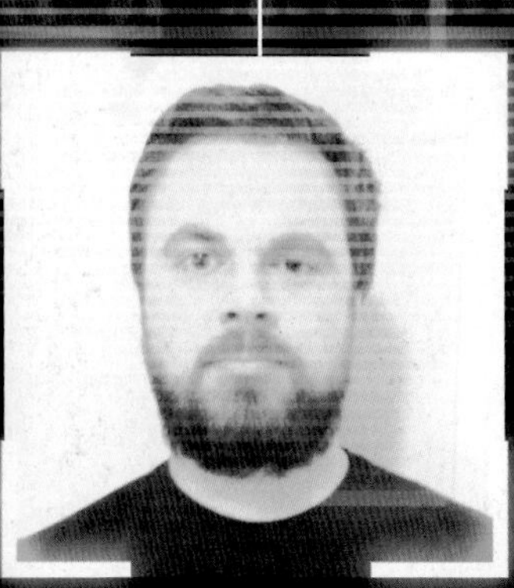

//_PERSONNEL_DESIGNATE:

//ILLUSTRATOR/ MITCH_GERADS.

MITCH GERADS IS THE CO-CREATOR OF /JOHNNY_RECON/ AND AN ILLUSTRATOR IN BOTH COMICS AND THE COMMERCIAL ART FIELDS. INCLUDING WORK ON SUCH TITLES AS /DOCTOR_WHO/ /PLANET_OF_THE_APES/ AND /STAN_LEE'S_STARBORN/. HE LIVES IN MINNEAPOLIS/MN/ WITH HIS FIANCÉE /LAUREN/ AND HIS CAT /NUMCHUCKS/.

FIND OUT MORE AT WWW.MITCHGERADS.COM

ENJOY THESE OTHER GREAT BOOKS BY NATHAN EDMONDSON & MITCH GERADS

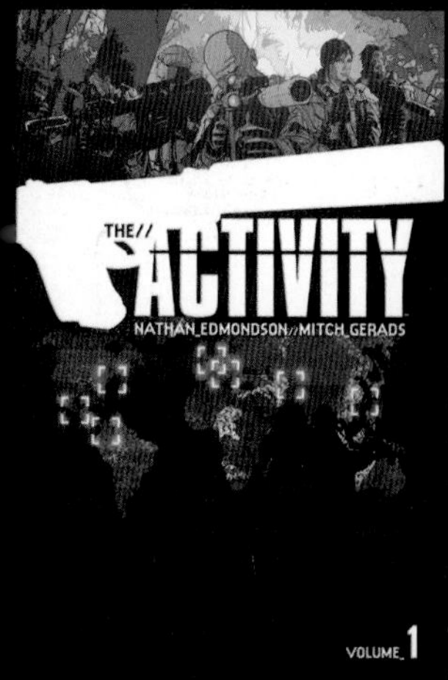
THE// ACTIVITY
NATHAN EDMONDSON//MITCH GERADS
VOLUME_1

THE ACTIVITY

The evolution of global conflict necessitates the evolution of warfare to rise and meet the call. The United States' latest, most advanced, and most secret special operations group is hidden inside the INTELLIGENCE SUPPORT ACTIVITY. They are tasked with fixing botched operations, wielding bleeding-edge tech, and planning and executing lethal action in the utmost secrecy.

ISBN-10: 1607065614
ISBN-13: 978-1607065616

$12.99

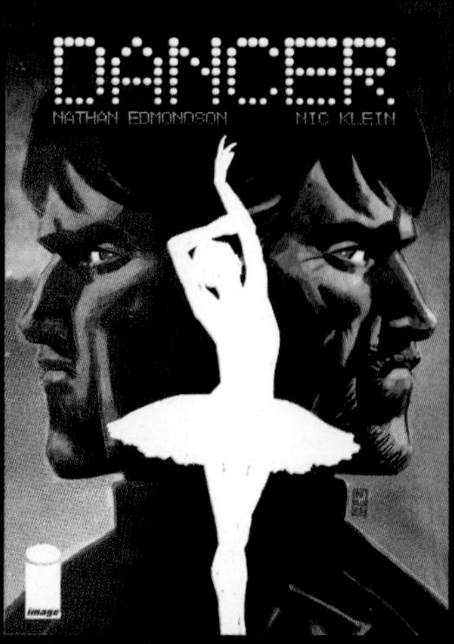
DANCER
NATHAN EDMONDSON
NIC KLEIN

DANCER

The multiple sell-out mini-series from the writer of Who Is Jake Ellis? and the artist of Viking, Dancer is the story of a retired assassin who must protect his ballerina love from a sniper stalking them both through the back alleys of a wintry Europe.

ISBN-10: 1607066270
ISBN-13: 978-1607066279

$16.99

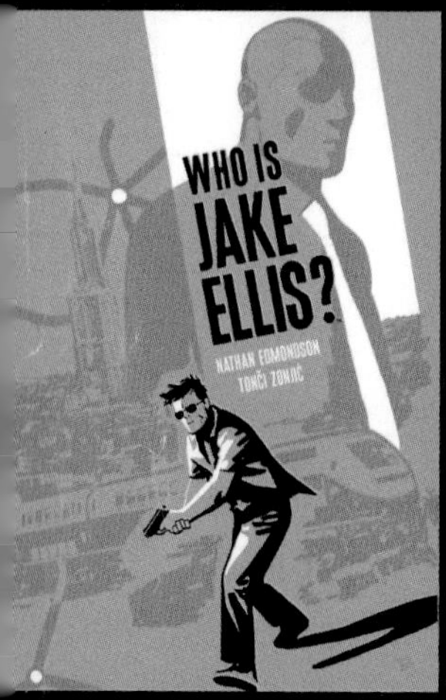
WHO IS JAKE ELLIS?
NATHAN EDMONDSON
TONČI ZONJIĆ

WHO IS JAKE ELLIS?

The Eisner-nominated multiple-sellout mini-series Newsarama calls "a modern noir package that is not to be missed" and MTV "couldn"t put down!" Jon Moore is a mercenary spy on the run across Europe, protected only by Jake Ellis, a man invisible to everyone except Jon.

ISBN-10: 1607064596
ISBN-13: 978-1607064596

$16.99

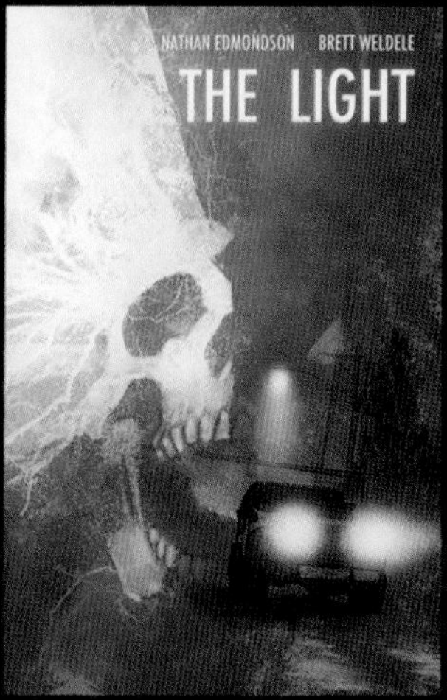
NATHAN EDMONDSON
BRETT WELDELE
THE LIGHT

THE LIGHT

It is as sudden as it is deadly. Its origins are unknown. When it strikes, a father must risk all to protect his daughter and escape across the Oregon countryside - before they are infected by THE LIGHT! Prepare yourself for the wildly acclaimed horror-thriller from writer Nathan Edmondson and artist Brett Weldele. Learn to love the darkness; learn to fear THE LIGHT

ISBN-10: 160706345X
ISBN-13: 978-1607063452

$16.99

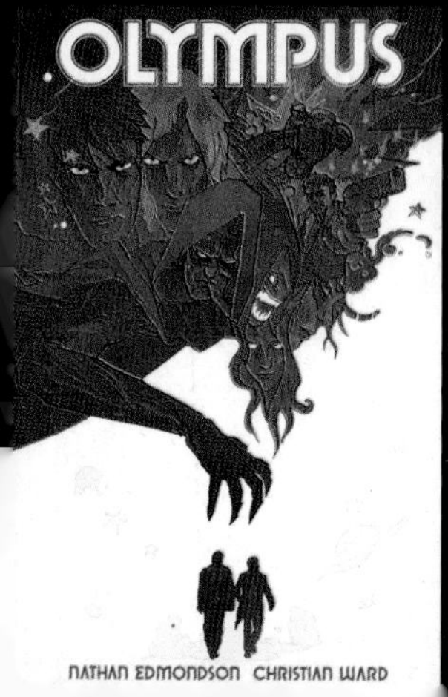
.OLYMPUS
NATHAN EDMONDSON CHRISTIAN WARD

OLYMPUS

Sent to capture a messenger fallen from Olympus, the immortal Gemini brothers accidentally release one of the fiercest prisoners of Hades. Now Castor and Pollux must track and capture this being before his rampant rage yields irreversible damage to the balance between Olympus and the Earth.

ISBN-10: 1607061783
ISBN-13: 978-1607061786

$14.99

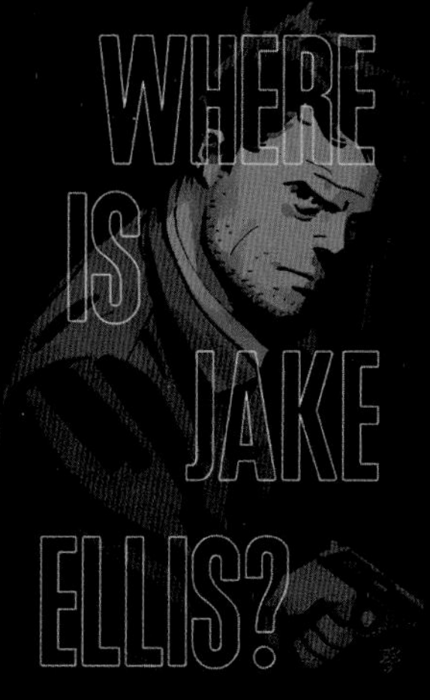
WHERE IS JAKE ELLIS?

WHERE IS JAKE ELLIS?

Out now from IMAGE Comics.

Collection coming SUMMER 2013

WARFAREWITHOUTWARNING.COM

... comply with the ... ... regulations
... ... and procurement ...
... ... vices at BARCOM and ... ...
... regulations

USAISA will develop an Authorized ... ... for approval by ...
non expendable property will ... ... based on the Intelligence
... and accountability in accordance with ... ... 143. Property ...
... for any ... property will be maintained in accordance with AR ...

... ISA will forward to DACSI for coordination as appropriate
... requirements for additional operational capabilities, logistical
... requirement which are for standard or in support of quick reaction
... ... is ... or ... of property from other government ...
... ... approved by the ACSI. Equipment purchased or ...
such purpose will ... ... Book and
... accordance with AR 30 45

... Self ... ... services will be purchased in
... the unit cover. Use of commercial supplies and services is
... required. The LDR USAISA may approve expenditures less than
... expenditure over $10,000 will be approved by the ACSI

... Equipment maintenance support may be requested from BARCOM
... ... of Intelligence property will ... ... with

... Medical Supply Support will be coordinated through USAMMA

... USAISA may establish maintenance, fabrication, repair and armory
... The establishment and operation of such facilities will be
... the ACSI

SECRET ... TALENT